MENSA GUIDE TO
CASINO GAMBLING
WINNING WAYS

**Official Mensa
Game Book**

Andrew Brisman

STERLING PUBLISHING CO., INC.
NEW YORK

To Laurie,
If they asked me, I could write a book …

ACKNOWLEDGMENTS

You can bet that a book of this scope doesn't make it to the shelves without the assistance of many people. Much thanks to them all: Jeanne Chioradio, Michael Kostrub, and Jim Byrnes from Harrah's; Joe Harrington and Mark Keenan at Foxwoods; Patricia Marvell of Shuffle Master; Barbara Hogan from IGWB; Rick Sorensen at IGT; Jason Ader of Bear Stearns; Chuck Weinstock of ConJelCo; Jeffrey Compton; and all the on-line gambling gurus who freely share their wisdom. Thanks also to my editor Peter Gordon for suggesting this project and for his sharp mathematical mind; Phil Jewett for the illustrations; and Angela Vance for all her good counsel.

I must thank my friends for their patience: It's always a long shot that I'll return your calls in a timely fashion, but, believe me, the odds are significantly better now that this book is finished.

I'd also like to thank my parents and siblings for their constant support. Special thanks go to Mom for her devotion and extraordinarily careful reading, and to Deborah for her insightful comments, endless encouragement, and the best chocolate chip cookies. And to my adorable nephew and nieces Abraham, Anna, Sarah, and Hannah: I'm back. What do you want to play?

As for my amazing Laurie, a dedication does not suffice—neither do words. Your perceptive reading and editing made this book infinitely better. Your love and friendship make everything better. Even after all the study of odds and probabilities, I have absolutely no idea how I got so lucky.

Illustrations by Philip Malcom Jewett

Mensa and the distinctive table logo are trademarks of American Mensa, Ltd. (in the U.S.), British Mensa, Ltd. (in the U.K.), and Mensa International Limited (in other countries) and are used by permission.

Mensa as an organization does not express an opinion as being that of Mensa or have any ideological, philosophical, political or religious affiliations. Mensa specifically disclaims any responsibility for any liability, loss or risk, personal or otherwise, which is incurred as a consequence, directly or indirectly, of the use and application of any of the contents of this book.

Library of Congress Cataloging-in-Publication Data

Brisman, Andrew.
   Mensa guide to casino gambling : winning ways / Andrew Brisman.
     p. cm.
   Rev. ed. of: American Mensa guide to casino gambling. c1999.
   "Official Mensa Game Book."
   Includes bibliographical references and index.
   ISBN 1-4027-1300-2
  1. Gambling. I. Brisman, Andrew. American Mensa guide to casino gambling. II. Mensa. III. Title.
GV1301.B75 2004
795—dc22

                          2004003053

10 9 8 7 6 5 4 3

Published by Sterling Publishing Co., Inc.
387 Park Avenue South, New York, NY 10016
© 1999, 2004 by Andrew Brisman
Distributed in Canada by Sterling Publishing
% Canadian Manda Group, 165 Dufferin Street
Toronto, Ontario, Canada M6K 3H6
Distributed in Great Britain by Chrysalis Books Group PLC
The Chrysalis Building, Bramley Road, London, W10 6SP, England
Distributed in Australia by Capricorn Link (Australia) Pty. Ltd.
P.O. Box 704, Windsor, NSW 2756, Australia

Sterling ISBN 1-4027-1300-2

For information about custom editions, special sales, premium and corporate purchases, please contact Sterling Special Sales Department at 800-805-5489 or specialsales@sterlingpub.com.

CONTENTS

INTRODUCTION

You don't have to be a genius to win at the casino. In fact, no matter how much of a "genius" you are, you're more likely to lose than win when gambling. Unfortunately for us, that's the way the casinos design their games—it's what keeps them in business. But that's not to say you can't apply intelligence to make your gambling more successful. Applying intelligence doesn't mean you have to invest in a slide rule or concoct computer algorithms. It simply means you are willing to acquire and use knowledge—the knowledge that is set forth for you in this book.

The truth is this: Being smart in a casino is often merely the absence of being stupid. As glib as that sounds, it's not far off the mark. The casino is specifically designed to make you feel excited, lucky, and reckless, but it's not designed to make you feel competent and in control of your choices. It can be a very intimidating and overwhelming place. You walk onto the casino floor … lights are flashing … people are murmuring … action is all around. You're eager, you're dazed … you're confused. There's that initial rush of adrenaline—Look at the excitement! Look at the winnings!—and then, before you even have your bearings, you're hit by the depressing reality of losing too much money too fast. Your big adventure deteriorates into a bout of self-loathing and regret about "throwing your money away." (Trust me, this syndrome isn't unique to newcomers. Many veteran casino-goers succumb to it over and over again.)

That's where this guide comes in. It will let you make order out of the casino's seeming chaos. Once you know the facts, you can make an informed decision on what appeals to you and what doesn't. You can enjoy your time in the casino. You can revel in the knowledge that you are light-years ahead of the typically flummoxed, frustrated, and frivolous casino crowd.

And what about winning? If effortless winning at the casino could ever be sandwiched within a book's covers, you could guess what would happen next: bye-bye casinos. Casinos rely on their unassailable mathematical advantages to keep their money flowing and their glitz growing. That's why any author who claims to have an easy, no-sweat, surefire approach to winning is either a fraud, uninformed, or delusional. There are games in which you can gain an advantage over the house—blackjack, video poker, table poker, and sports betting—but those advantages come at no small amount of effort and risk. All other games are set up so that the house, to varying degrees, always gets its share of your money.

But that doesn't mean you can't win. On any given day, many people walk away from the casino as winners. (If that didn't happen, the casinos couldn't stay in business.) This book will give you the best opportunity to have those winning days. You'll surely win more than the gambler who doesn't know—or, worse yet, only thinks he knows—the information included here. You will get more value for your recreational dollar, minimize your losses, and improve your chances of winning. Now we have arrived at a working definition of "winning ways": it's an approach that allows you to make informed choices, prolong your fun, and maximize your chances of walking away with the casino's cash. Even if you can't beat the house, you can make sure you don't beat yourself with bad bets and half-baked strategies.

The first two chapters of this book will help you feel more comfortable being in a casino environment. You'll learn the whos, whats, and wheres of casinos. And then, with a short introduction to probability, you'll learn the whys.

In the individual game chapters, you'll learn the details and strategies for nearly every game you can encounter in a casino. You'll know, like a seasoned pro, which games and which bets give the player the best advantage. There's a lot of information in these chapters and I don't spare you the details (at least not the ones I find interesting). If you just want to cut to the chase, read the "How to Play" section followed by the "Essentials" at the end of each chapter. Although I emphasize what's best for the wallet since that tends to tie into a gambler's pleasure, my intent is not to browbeat readers into only playing "good" games and avoiding "sucker" bets. (I hope you'll come around to that on your own.) I also acknowledge factors that may make a game appealing—simplicity, big jackpots, atmosphere—even when it's not a "smart" bet.

In Chapter 16 you'll learn how to make the most of your gambling experience. We'll discuss money management techniques and casino perks.

[Note: Throughout the text, I use both "he" and "she" as third person pronouns. I do this because a) it reflects gender reality (particularly for casino dealers and players) and b) the English language has yet to come up with an elegant (and nonsexist) solution to the pronoun dilemma. Most of my choices are arbitrary and merely reflect how the mood struck me at the time. Another textual note: Whenever a casino term is introduced, it is italicized. Definitions of all such words can be found in the glossary.]

So read (or at least browse through) this guide *before* you play—don't let it sit on the shelf while you're shelling out your bucks. Yes, sometimes it's fun to dive headfirst into an experience without fully knowing the details, but such an adventurous nature will cost you cold cash in the casino. Why not spare yourself the growing pains and learn through someone else's experience?

I hope that this book helps you make informed and intelligent choices; in that way, I'm sure it will help you make your own luck. Here's to winning ways and many, many winning days.

WELCOME TO THE CASINO

In this chapter, we'll get acquainted with the procedures and atmosphere of the typical casino, cover the vast scope of the gambling industry, and tackle some common questions you might have. So let's find out about the world of the casino and get our bearings. It's time to get acclimated.

INSIDE THE CASINO

You enter the casino and are greeted by plenty of stimulation. It's a 24-hour-a-day wonderland that never stops or pauses to catch its breath. The banks of slot machines cling, clatter, and flash; the table game players hoot and holler; waitresses circulate asking if anyone wants drinks. You may feel a bit lost or disoriented. There's plenty of action, but you have little idea what's going on.

CASINO ANATOMY

Most casinos have a similar layout. Much of the space is devoted to *one-armed bandits*—row upon row of slot machines. Toward the center of the casino are the table games, with the largest share of tables devoted to blackjack. Next in number will be craps. Then you will probably find roulette, mini-baccarat, Let It Ride, and Caribbean Stud Poker. A private or semi-private area is usually set aside to cater to baccarat players and others at high stakes tables. Sometimes you need to be a *high roller* to get into these exclusive areas; most often you don't. The keno parlor can be found tucked in a corner somewhere. Poker is also relegated to an area that probably won't immediately strike your eye. Off the casino floor are areas to eat—

perhaps a coffee shop or a large buffet area. In Nevada, you'll also find the sports and racing book off the main floor.

No doubt, you'll also have easy access to ATMs for quick withdrawals from your bank account or cash advances on your credit cards.

Casinos are designed with one mission in mind—to make you play. To get to your hotel room, you will pass the casino. To get to eat, you will pass the casino.

THE CHIPS

In order to play table games, you'll need *chips* (also called *checks*)—colorful "clay" pieces exchanged for cash. They make the play faster and neater, and, much to the casino's pleasure, they also help you lose your understanding of the value of money.

When you buy chips from a dealer, you must wait until the current hand or round is finished. Always make sure that you receive the right value of chips for your money. If you're confused or unsure, ask the dealer.

When you're finished playing and want to cash out, you must take your chips to the *cage* (cashier) to exchange them for cash. Dealers will not change chips back into cash. What dealers will do is "color up" your chips. Coloring up simply means exchanging larger groups of small-denomination chips for smaller groups of large-denomination chips. For instance, you can color up your stack of ten $5 chips into two $25 chips. If you want to color up (often the dealer will suggest it to you), you merely have to push the chips you want to exchange in front of you at the end of a hand. You can say, "Color me up" to get your point across. You can then keep on playing with your smaller stack of chips, go to another table, or go to the cashier.

Across the United States, chip colors are almost universally standardized: red for $5 chips, green for $25, and black for $100. In Atlantic City, the chip colors are a matter of regulation. They are as follows:

White	$1
Pink	$2.50
Red	$5
Yellow	$20
Green	$25
Black	$100
Purple	$500
Orange	$1,000
Gray	$5,000

Gambling chips in Las Vegas used to be an unofficial currency, but that is no longer the case. Nor is it so at other gambling locations. It's a good idea to cash out your chips before you leave a casino—you can always purchase new ones at your next stop.

Slot machines do not use chips. For slot machines (the term includes video poker, video blackjack, and all other machines), you need to put in either coins, tokens, or bills. Most every machine now has a bill acceptor so you can slide in your cash. If a machine doesn't accept bills or you prefer using coins, you can purchase rolls of coins at the cage. Also, casino change people travel throughout the slot area with wheeled carts selling coins.

THE CAGE

The cage is the main cashier area where you can redeem your chips, coins, and tokens for cash. You can also purchase coins or tokens for slot machine play. They won't sell you chips, however; you must *buy in* for chips at the tables. Aside from the cage, there may be smaller cashier areas or change booths where you can also purchase and redeem coins and tokens.

AT THE TABLES

You cruise on over to a table game. The first thing you want to know is what game is being played. This isn't as ridiculous as it may seem. Particularly in games involving blackjack and poker variations, novice or inattentive players sometimes plop down and get very perplexed as the hands play out. So let's assume we'll all take a moment and see precisely what is being played.

Next, you want to know the table limits. The table limits are the restrictions set by the casino to establish both the minimum and maximum amount of money you can wager on one bet. For instance, if the minimum is $5 and the maximum is $500, you cannot make a single bet that is less than $5 or more than $500.

The table limit can usually be found on a small colored placard on the table that will name the game, the betting limits, and, in many places, let you know if the table is for nonsmokers only. These signs are often color-coded to match the denominations of the chips. You'll know a red one indicates a $5 minimum, a green one a $25 minimum, and a black one a $100 minimum. This isn't always the case, so check before you sit. Yes, it is a little embarrassing when you proudly plunk down your $5 bet and the dealer eyes you for a bit before pointing out the table minimum of $25.

Be aware that betting limits vary all the time: from casino to casino and from table to table. The table limit can even be changed at a table you're sitting at because of a shift change or a larger crowd. Some casinos will grandfather you in and let you play at the former minimum; others will not be so generous.

As a rule of thumb, table limits are higher during busy periods such as weekends. As long as the tables are full, many casinos will keep the stakes as high as possible. That's why it can be hard to find $5 tables at a popular mega-resort. Las Vegas, which generally has more of everything, offers plenty of lower-limit gambling in the $2 range. Atlantic City casinos will likely start their table minimums at $5 or $10 but might increase them to $25 or higher as more players come in.

Buying In

Okay, you know the table limit. Now sit down at the table and purchase some chips. Wait for a break in the action to place your cash out in front of you on the table. Don't put it in a betting circle or it may be considered a bet. Don't try to hand your cash directly to the dealer—

that's a big no-no. For security reasons, dealers aren't allowed to take anything from your hands, so let the dealer pick your cash up off the table. The dealer will take an equal value of chips from the large, inset tray of chips in front of him and will push the chips across the table to you. He'll then drop the cash into a slot in the tabletop known as the *drop box*. Don't ask for change—you can't put down a $50 bill and say, "I'll take eight $5 chips and a $10 bill."

Normally, you can take a short break from a specific table if you like. Just tell the dealer that you'll be gone for a little bit and he will save your spot.

The Pit Personnel

A *pit* consists of a group of gaming tables arranged in an oval configuration with personnel working "inside" and players on the "outside." Pits are often based around one game; for example, four craps tables or eight blackjack tables could make up a pit. Within a casino, depending on its size, there may be several pits for each game. The area behind the dealers— the middle of the oval—is officially considered the pit. The personnel within the pit are often referred to, by those in the know, as "pit critters."

Dealer: We've already been introduced to the front-line personnel: the dealers. Ideally, dealers should only enhance your entertainment experience. In most cases, this ideal can be realized. Before you sit down, observe the tables and note the interaction between the dealers and the players. Whether you like a chatty, friendly dealer, or a quiet but efficient one, you should have no problem finding a dealer whose demeanor suits you. Unfortunately, you'll occasionally come across dealers who radiate hostility or are downright rude. This can be explained in two ways: dealers don't make a lot of money (minimum wage plus tips) and some people just have bad personalities. You don't have to tolerate a dealer who is nasty or intimidating; pick up your chips after a hand and go to another table. If the casino you're in seems to have a preponderance of unpleasant dealers, go to another casino.

Dealers not only have to put a good face on for the casino, they also have to know the games they deal and they have to protect the casino's money. This doesn't mean that they root against the player—most seem to be on the player's side. But they will try to detect any attempts at cheating and they'll make sure that all money and chip transactions are done according to protocol and with care. That's why you don't have money directly exchanging hands. And that's why dealers clap their hands as they leave the table—so observers (and the *eye in the sky* surveillance system) know that they're not walking away with any of the casino's money.

Floorperson: Within the table game pit, the casino employee who supervises several tables is known as the floorperson. Each floorperson is usually responsible for only a few tables and has the most contact with employees at those tables. She is supposed to be friendly and courteous to the gamblers. She also watches her assigned tables to make sure no cheating is going on by the dealers or players and she may be on the lookout for *card-counters*.

The floorperson is the person you may see schmoozing with a high roller. This is also the person who would *rate* you and whom you would ask for a complimentary meal. Again, they vary according to personality and casino personality—some will be very friendly, give attention to low rollers, and volunteer a free meal. Others will seem hostile, overly protective of the casino's bankroll, or just plain invisible.

Pit boss: This employee is responsible for all that goes on within a single pit. A pit boss supervises all the floorpersons and their tables. The pit boss can be pleasant, but often he will look a bit tense, suspicious, as if on hyperalert. There is some justification for this; if anything is amiss within a pit—insufficient earnings, lost money—the blame often falls squarely on the shoulders of the pit boss. Players always say how the "pit boss" came over and gave them a complimentary meal or noticed their winnings. More often, it's probably a floorperson and not the actual pit boss who has contact with the players. Still, high rollers or heated disputes will draw the attention of the actual pit boss.

Shift manager: The shift manager doesn't dwell in the pits. This employee is responsible for all the action going on in her area of the casino during a shift. Most casinos run 24 hours a day, and the day is divided into three eight-hour shifts: the day shift (8 A.M. to 4 P.M.), the swing shift (4 P.M. to 12 A.M.), and the graveyard shift (12 A.M. to 8 A.M.). Shift managers are often responsible for a particular game, and the pit bosses for that particular game report to the shift manager.

Casino manager: Shift managers answer to this big kahuna. This executive runs the casino during a particular shift, but is someone you're highly unlikely to encounter.

New players (and even some veterans) often feel that they shouldn't expect any special treatment from casino personnel. Perhaps they feel that in the "rough-and-tumble" world of gambling, a kind word and a smile are not part of the ambiance. Nothing could be further from the truth, which you will happily discover at any quality casino. Casino gambling is a service industry and any decent casino will want to make you happy. This makes perfect sense. If you're happy, you'll play more. And if you play more, they'll win more of your money. The casino is, of course, run by human beings with different personalities and you might very well encounter some surly folks. But make sure that whether you are playing at the tables, at the slot machines, in the keno lounge, or wherever, they keep you as happy as possible.

CASINO SECURITY

If you ask casino employees about casino security, their first thoughts won't turn to the safety of their patrons, but to the protection of the *house*'s money. In the casino, money is ubiquitous, flowing back and forth—the only merchandise they have. As such, casinos keep a very close watch on their inventory.

And it's not just customer cheating that they're worried about. Everyone in the food chain of the personnel is being watched. The casino manager watches the shift managers, who watch the pit bosses, who watch the floorpersons, who watch the dealers. And overhead, hidden within the ceiling, are the video cameras capturing and recording nearly every action in the casino. This surveillance system is referred to as the eye in the sky. And the eye is keen and always watching.

Once you know the eye in the sky exists, much of the protocol and ritual of the casino begins to make more sense. No money exchanged directly into a dealer's hand—something improper could be hidden from the camera. Cards spread out carefully on the table after a hand—the video recording will be able to resolve any dispute.

All vulnerable areas of the casino—table games, slot machines, change booths, cashier cages—are monitored by cameras and two-way mirrors. You don't have only electronic eyes above you, but also human observers who can view individual tables, dealers, or players to detect any sort of foul play. Big Brother is watching, but only to follow the money. All this surveillance could actually work to your advantage in settling a dispute.

PERSONAL SAFETY

Casinos generally place great emphasis on ensuring the safety and well-being of their guests. You may want to inquire about the security measures used by the casino you're visiting and/or staying at. Do they have cameras and security in their parking garage and on the perimeter of the property? What kind of key system is used for the hotel rooms? Are corridors monitored?

Within the casino, trained security officers are available to respond to reports of theft or any sort of alarm. This discussion is not intended to make casinos seem like frightening places. They aren't and it's very rare to run into trouble. Nevertheless, smart casino visitors—or any smart traveler for that matter—should keep the following tips in mind:

- Always be aware of where your belongings are. Chips are among your belongings! You don't have to clutch them in fear, but keep them well within your personal space.
- If a casino patron is making you uncomfortable or seems to hover too near your belongings, trust your instincts and move away.
- Don't hesitate to contact security if anyone harasses you or touches your belongings.
- If you are gambling by yourself, there's no need to broadcast it.
- Don't flash large amounts of cash around. Break your gambling stake into small bills instead of cashing in $100 bills for chips in front of a crowd.

- If you hit a jackpot, get a check for your winnings rather than cash.
- Women should try to leave their handbags in their hotel rooms. Use fanny packs, bags that you can keep comfortably across your shoulder to your hip, or keep your wallet and other necessities in your pocket.
- The more drunk and disoriented you are, the more vulnerable you are (not only to theft, but to poor playing as well).
- If you must travel with large amounts of cash, you can request to have a security guard escort you to your room, your car, or even another hotel.
- Use a hotel safe-deposit box or an in-room safe for your valuables.

OTHER INDULGENCES: EATING, DRINKING, AND SMOKING

You won't go hungry in a casino. Larger casinos offer restaurants, coffee shops, and, of course, buffets. In the spirit of hedonistic indulgence, buffets have become inextricably linked to casino culture. They often have different ethnic cuisines—Chinese, Japanese, Italian, Mexican—and they can cover the distance of half a football field. Since most buffets cost only five to fifteen dollars, the typical thought for the ravenous gambler is, "What could be bad?" (Also, a buffet ticket is often given free as a *comp*, which is discussed in Chapter 16.) I won't go into a culinary critique—suffice it to say the quality varies from inedible to surprisingly good. Be aware that as legendary as buffets are, so are the lines associated with them. For the popular buffets, you should avoid the peak meal hours.

Drinks at table games and slot machines are usually free for players. Tip the waitress who brings you a drink and don't overindulge in alcohol if you have an attachment to your money.

If you're a smoker, you will be surrounded by fellow nicotine junkies. It seems most gamblers like to puff away. Casinos vary greatly in their ability or their efforts to have fresh air circulating throughout the floor—some casinos perpetually smell like ashtrays, others remain quite breathable. If you hate smoke, see if your casino has a nonsmoking area. Some have nonsmoking slot machine areas. At the very least, there should be a few nonsmoking table games.

GETTING COMFORTABLE

If you're new to gambling or even new to a particular casino, here's some good advice: Observe, observe, and observe. Yes, I know the pulsating rhythm of the casino is hard to resist and you are caught between wanting to jump into the action and feeling hesitant. But just relax and take a walking tour of the casino. Find out where the food stops and the bathrooms are. See all there is to see. (Oh yeah, you can consult the tome in your hands to help calm the jitters as well.) You want to feel that you are in control of your environment, not that the environment is controlling you.

Obviously, we're going to discuss all the games in great depth later. But since we're wandering around the casino right now, let me make a quick observation about the offerings. Whether you're a beginner or a regular, you may naturally gravitate to the slot machines. Most people do—that's why they account for over two-thirds of casino revenue and up to 70 percent of floor space. Sure, slots can be fun, but you shouldn't feel compelled to play them just because they are simple and non-intimidating. Table games may take a little more effort to learn, but they can be very enjoyable and a lot less trouble to your *bankroll*.

If you are intimidated by the table games (hopefully you'll be cured of that in later chapters), one way to get over your fear is to act as a spectator and see what's going on. If you're new to a game, you may not want to join a crowded table. Beginners who slow down games may incur the wrath of fellow gamblers and even dealers. Look for a quiet, perhaps empty, table with a friendly dealer. But, if a lone dealer seems content to have an empty table and gives a sense of reluctance about opening up his table for one player, it's probably best to look elsewhere. You don't need the resentment or the hassle.

Some casinos offer free gaming lessons on table games such as craps, blackjack, and roulette. These informal "classes" are generally held in the mornings or afternoons when the casinos are less crowded. These lessons can be an excellent tool to reinforce what you read here and a chance to see the action live and in color. You don't have to sign up for these lessons; you can just show up at the table where they're given. The instructors are usually personable and often entertaining.

The one caveat is that the instructors will rarely tell you about the good bets or the proper strategy. (Management may frown on such advice!) So the lessons are good for seeing game mechanics in action, but not for increasing your knowledge. Through this book and practicing the games during the casino lessons, you'll see that table games are not incredibly difficult to learn—if they were, casinos would drop them.

THE CASINO EMPIRE

Gambling has gone mainstream. Once the sole province of a handful of Nevada casinos, gambling has spread across the American landscape, from Atlantic City to the riverboats along the Mississippi to the multitude of casinos run by Indian tribes. Gambling can't just be dismissed as an aberration unique to the "Sodom" of Las Vegas or the "Gomorrah" of Atlantic City. Despite America's puritanical origins, state legislatures have become very receptive to gambling as a means of generating revenue. Casinos produce enormous tax revenues and that has made the powers-that-be in nearly 30 states open their doors to them.

Right now, you are probably only a few hours' drive from some sort of casino-style gambling. It has been estimated that 90 percent of the U.S. population is within 200 miles of a casino. Whether there will be a backlash to this expansion remains to be seen, but it is highly unlikely that gambling is going away anytime soon.

Casino gambling was one of the highest growth industries in the late 1980s and early 1990s. The growth has slowed, but the revenue generated is still astonishing: $42 billion in 2002. That's roughly equivalent to the gross domestic product of Ecuador. The amount wagered on all forms of legal gambling is about $850 billion. That's roughly $3,000 for every man, woman, and child in the United States.

The industry is highly regulated and is no longer the domain of mobsters and con men. Characters with names like Bugsy and Lucky have been replaced by familiar corporations whose stocks trade regularly on the market. (Is that less frightening?)

Gambling vacations are now intended to be family-oriented, with luxurious casinos offering fine restaurants, diverse entertainment, and resort-worthy accommodations. The vice-like cloud hanging around gambling has been dispersed (or at least repackaged) and now this form of recreation has a sparkle to it.

Casino gaming earnings have leveled off since the '80s, but that was bound to happen. Market saturation and increased competition may lead to the demise of some casinos, but it should also lead to greater values and better conditions for gamblers. Generally, the greater the casino competition, the greater the gambling opportunities for players.

With casinos everywhere present, perhaps popping up at your back door, gambling has become a more acceptable recreation choice. So let's look at where the gambling is, whether you're an old pro surveying the scene or a newcomer preparing for your first experience.

THE PLACES TO PLAY

Travel books and some of the resources in Appendix D will help you determine your gambling destination of choice. (Of particular use is Steve Bourie's *American Casino Guide 2004*.) I'll just provide a quick rundown of some of the major gambling options to be found across the country.

Las Vegas

Gambler's Mecca. The casino capital of the world. Just say Las Vegas and images of glitz, excess, and kitsch pour into one's head. Born a gambler's paradise in the 1950s, the land of neon and spectacle has transformed itself into a family vacation spot. In fact, it's now second only to Walt Disney World as the top vacation destination in the United States.

On the famous Las Vegas Strip, you have all the gigantic theme casinos working hard to entertain you while taking your money. There are elaborate shows (from Broadway-style productions to the iconic Wayne Newton, who is known as "Mr. Las Vegas"), thrill rides high in the air, theme parks, laser shows, and arcades for kids. There are upscale malls and shopping centers. And through it all are the themes that define each hotel and turn Vegas into one big ball of surrealistic kitsch: Egyptian, Roman,

South Seas, pirates, New York, circuses, South America.

In the late 1990s, a new wave of mega-resorts hit town. First and foremost is Bellagio, Steve Wynn's $1.6 billion dream child. It has 3,001 rooms and boasts a $300 million collection of fine art, featuring the works of van Gogh, Monet, Renoir, and Picasso. To complement this highbrow stimulation, there are 2,600 slot machines standing by for tired art appreciators, some of them high-limit slots, including $1,000 machines.

Then comes Mandalay Bay (cost: $900 million, 3,700 rooms); the Venetian ($1.2 billion, 3,036 rooms) with a second phase that brought the cost up to $2.5 billion; Paris ($760 million, 2,900 rooms); the Aladdin ($1 billion, 2,600 rooms). All of these big spenders—Bellagio, Mandalay Bay, the Venetian, Paris-Las Vegas, and the Aladdin—have major upscale shopping facilities. By 2006, the grand total of Las Vegas hotel rooms will reach 140,000. Does excess lead to excess? You tell me. The Bellagio alone generated nearly $1 billion in revenue in 2003—55% from gambling.

When you marvel at all the chrome, observe the free outdoor shows, and chow down at a $5 all-you-can-eat buffet, you know the casinos must be doing a good job at what they need to do—taking visitors' money away. Yes, all the pretty palaces come out of our pockets. Gaming is and always will be the lifeblood of Las Vegas. According to the Las Vegas Convention and Visitors Authority, almost 90% of 2003 visitors to the city gambled, spending an average of four hours each day and a $480 gambling budget in their pursuit of the big win.

Downtown Las Vegas, which is a few miles north of the Strip, offers less glitzy casinos that cater to local clientele. These casinos are not known as mega-resorts, but as places to find more favorable playing conditions. Reno, in northern Nevada near the California border, is a small, scenic city that has also made gambling its reason for existence. The bottom line: You won't find another place on Earth that has the quality and quantity of casinos that Las Vegas—and all of Nevada—has. It will embrace the highest and lowest rollers; competition is the key.

Atlantic City

On May 28, 1978, Resorts International in Atlantic City became the first casino to be found outside of Nevada. Atlantic City (or A.C. as it is affectionately called) has made New Jersey the second powerhouse state in terms of casino revenue. In 2003, the 12 casinos pulled in $4.5 billion (as compared to the almost 400 casinos in Nevada, which made $9.6 billion). The casinos don't have quite the glitz and glamour of the Vegas strip (except for the new Vegas-style Borgata), but they do provide plenty of entertainment for day-trippers, slot lovers, and others. The prevailing gambling conditions aren't awful, but you won't find as many opportunities as in Nevada—of course, this statement would be true for any gambling venue that's not in Nevada. For a long time, A.C. had the East Coast monopoly on gaming.

Riverboat Gambling

When Mississippi passed legislation in 1990 to allow riverboat gambling, the floodgates (so to speak) were opened. States all along the Mississippi and Missouri now have gambling cruises. These boats aren't necessarily throwbacks to the glorious and mythical days of vest-wearing cardsharps with derringers in their sleeves; many offer enough space for 1,500 passengers and very modern, luxurious surroundings. (Interestingly, Louisiana does require their riverboats to look like genuine 19th century riverboats.)

The first Mississippi casino opened up in 1992 and since then the state has skyrocketed into third place among gambling destinations. One of the poorest states in the country is now entertaining over 65 million patrons and obtaining gaming revenues of almost $3 billion per year. Major companies—Mirage Resorts, Harrah's, Circus Circus—have opened swanky riverboat casinos with spacious hotels. To put this boom in perspective, consider this: in 1992, Tunica County in Mississippi had 16 hotel rooms and today it has over 6,000.

Each riverboat may float by different rules, so always find out the details before heading aboard. Some charge admission and some don't. Some cruise and some don't. (In Mississippi, the riverboats are forbidden to cruise by law.) Some put a time limit on how long you can play and some don't.

Cruise Ships

Often called "cruises to nowhere," these jaunts head out to unregulated international waters. The cruise ship companies can apply whatever rules and payouts they choose; they have a captive audience and no state or federal gaming commission looking over their shoulders. That doesn't mean you can't find good deals and favorable rules. Just check it out before you decide to set sail.

Indian Casinos

In 1988, the federal government officially authorized gambling on Native American lands. This was a great boon for many tribes, none more so than the Mashantucket Pequot Tribe in Ledyard, Connecticut. They opened the Foxwoods casino in 1992 and it is now the largest and the most profitable casino in the world. The 6,500 slot machines alone bring in over $2 million a day in earnings! The property has over 300,000 square feet of gaming space and over 11,000 employees.

Foxwoods may be the superstar among Indian casinos but there are nearly 300 others across the country. (There were only 70 in 1988.) In order to have gambling, almost all Indian casinos have worked out a compact with the government of the state in which they are located. (California in particular is embroiled in various legal and political wrangles with its tribes.) These compacts often lead to idiosyncratic and limited forms of gambling within each state. Some Indian casinos are allowed only slot machines while others can offer only card games; many are restricted from having dice or roulette wheels; some must have the "player" bank all the games (which usually means the game is played normally but with a commission taken out of your bet—not a good deal for a smart gambler); some allow video slot machines, but not ones with actual reels. Some Native American casinos will have all the offerings and polish of a decent Vegas casino; others will seem like glorified, smoky card rooms.

It always pays to make a phone call or read a travel book before you assume any casino (including riverboats, cruise ships, and mainstream destinations) has what you're seeking. But you may be pleasantly surprised to find an Indian casino not far from you that has the action you seek.

REGULATION

The casino industry is highly regulated. After all, the states are looking out for their own interest; they don't want to have a hand in cheating voters and they don't want a cent of their taxable casino revenue to be unaccounted for. If you head to any of the major locales, you should feel comfortable that safeguards are in place to ensure you're playing a fair and honest game. If you have any doubts, contact the casino control commission in the state where you plan to gamble. Any casino will give you the number to call.

Call me an optimist, but I feel that even the most out-of-the-way, run-down riverboat or Indian casino is *probably* on the up-and-up. I say probably because 1) you should follow your instincts and not play in a place that seems seedy, sloppily managed, or generally unpleasant (forget about cheating, why would you want to give your patronage to such a place!) and 2) some state gaming commissions aren't as forthcoming with statistics and information as others. For instance, Kansas doesn't release the minimum payback amounts required of their Indian casinos. I wouldn't want to play there. I wouldn't assume that the lack of information means you're getting ripped off, but I wouldn't assume it doesn't mean that. The more information available, the more comfortable the smart gambler feels.

AREN'T ALL CASINOS THE SAME?

On casual observation, one might wonder what distinguishes one casino from another. After all, isn't it just a matter of setting out the same familiar games, leaving the players to their own devices, and raking in the money? For those who cluck their tongues and see gambling as a fool's vice, this would seem to be the whole picture. But like any vice—liquor, cigars, sex—it comes in endless varieties and flavors.

Actually, no casino is quite like another. Each has a unique personality that's comprised of many elements—ambiance, staff, game rules, table limits, service, comps, slot club, food, etc. Within Las Vegas, you have the stereotypical (but not inaccurate) trade-off between the

TIPS ON TIPPING

Although you are waging a war to keep every dollar out of the casino's hands, you're still dealing with a service industry. That means your lower-level service providers rely on tips. Just as you tip waiters and waitresses in a restaurant, you are expected to tip casino employees who provide you direct service. As with any tipping, you're not obligated to do so (particularly for bad service), but it's considered bad form to stiff the help. Below are some guidelines for tipping various casino employees. In the casino world, tips are called *tokes*, and you should feel free to do your toking with chips.

Dealers: This is where the greatest contemplation takes place. Some patrons, unable to dissociate dealers from the money-siphoning house, are very reluctant to tip dealers. But the dealers do rely on tokes. They don't expect to be tipped while you're losing and shouldn't be resentful in that instance. However, if you're winning and the dealer is pleasant, helpful, and friendly, it's proper to tip.

You can do this directly by simply pushing a chip forward and saying, "This is for you." Or you can place a bet for the dealer. For instance, in blackjack, this is done by placing the dealer's bet in front of yours on the betting circle. If you win the hand, the dealer gets the bet and its payout; if you lose, the house—not the dealer—takes your intended tip. You can use either the direct approach or the betting method for any game.

Keep in mind that you don't want to tip so much that you're giving away profits that are tough to come by. If you're winning consistently, you should tip a couple of times an hour at less than your average wager. A $1 tip is appropriate for a $5–$10 bettor. Also, don't expect your tips to somehow increase your chances of winning. The dealer will be appreciative, but is not going to jeopardize her job for your tokes. But a warm smile and a good rapport go a long way toward making your gambling more enjoyable—especially when you're winning. It's psychologically satisfying to feel that the dealer is rooting for you. The dealer may also be more inclined to help you out if she sees you're making an obvious error.

Many players tip when they leave the table. There is nothing wrong with that, but the dealer doesn't know that that's the player's plan. Being human, a dealer might feel less kindly disposed to a player who sits for hours and doesn't tip. While this shouldn't manifest itself in any way, it seems sensible to tip along the way and maintain goodwill if that's your intention anyway.

Change persons: If you hit a large jackpot on the slot machines and the service has been good, a tip is appropriate. Some people say to give 10%. Fifty bucks on a $500 jackpot? That sounds overly generous to me. Ten or twenty dollars seems quite nice unless you hit an astronomical jackpot. (What if they pointed you to the machine? We'll address that dubious bit of assistance in the slots chapter. But do what your heart tells you.)

Poker dealers: In a low-stakes game, a winning pot should bring the dealer 50¢ to $1 or more.

Keno runners: A dollar or so for each run and something more substantial if you get a decent win.

Cocktail waitresses: A buck or two is reasonable. Hey, the drinks are free.

Waiters and waitresses: Keep in mind that they should be tipped even when the meal is comped. (That means a freebie, as is covered in Chapter 16.)

Buffet servers: Since they get your drinks, one dollar per person in your party is about right.

glamorous, finely appointed casinos on the Strip and the more run-down, homey downtown casinos. The mega-casinos are known for their food, service, and opulence while the downtown joints are known to offer more liberal rules. But there are many gradations between these two choices. One lavish Strip casino may have quality food and a generous slot club while another offers up a friendly, efficient staff and a number of tables for low rollers. One downtown casino may have great video poker machines but awful accommodations while another has great blackjack rules and an ornery staff. Another joint has barely any creature comforts and no air conditioning, but provides 25¢ craps and plenty of nickel slot machines.

Of course, it's not always a matter of balancing the good with the bad. Many casinos are very good in almost all respects, but even then the theme, or the particular machines, or the amount of cocktail waitress cleavage may make the difference to your particular tastes.

CASINO CONQUEST

So it's pretty apparent there are lots of places to throw your money around these days. And more keep popping up. Detroit now supports three casinos. New Orleans may reestablish some land-based casinos, although a few failed some years ago.

The pumped-up industry can't wait to squeeze you and your wallet in its massive arms. The casino philosophy was pithily summarized by Bob Stupak, a legendary Las Vegas casino operator, in *U.S. News & World Report*: "It's our duty to extract as much money from the customer as we can and send them home with a smile on their face." Fair enough. Now it's our duty to extract as much knowledge as we can about the casinos, their games, and our best chance of enjoying ourselves. If we can give ourselves the advantage of knowledge, then our departing smiles (even if after a losing session) won't be as forced or vacuous.

COMMON AND NOT-SO-COMMON QUESTIONS

How many people visit casinos in a year?
It has been estimated that 51 million Americans visited casinos in 2002.

What if I think the casino has made a mistake?
Let them know. If you have any problem with a payoff or the play of the hand at a table game, tell the dealer. Most likely a floorperson (perhaps a pit boss) will come over and look into the matter. Smart casinos believe in customer service and will take the player's side unless the mistake is clearly nonexistent or the player's fault. If you have a problem with a slot machine, don't leave your machine. Flag down a host or attendant for service and ask to see a slot manager.

But what if the casino makes a mistake in my favor?
A fine ethical dilemma. After much soul-searching, I must say: Don't tell. It may not be a shining moment for your conscience, but I think it's the right move. The casino doesn't give you back money when you make mistakes. Also, many dealers won't want to know about an error. The more attention it draws, the bigger headache it is. Still, if it feels bad to you, say something. Guilt can be more taxing than the house edge. However you are not under any obligation to speak up. (And if your Jiminy Cricket act affects other players' bets, prepare for the consequences.)

Can I view the videotape from the eye in the sky if I have a dispute with the casino?
No. If you are not satisfied with the result of casino management reviewing your complaint, you can't see the goods yourself. You can go to the state's gaming commission and it will review the tape and reach a decision. The purported reason that a player can't see the tape is that it would allow cheaters access to casino surveillance techniques.

Do casinos cheat?
Despite the rantings of losing players and conspiracy theorists, the answer is almost definitively no. The casino industry is highly regulated, and most casinos are publicly traded corporations that wouldn't toy with such a public relations disaster. Furthermore, the casinos don't need to cheat; as we'll discuss in detail, the games have a built-in mathematical advantage that provides plenty of revenue. Does that mean that there are no crooked dealers or pit bosses? No, but the many safeguards in the

INTERNET GAMBLING

Take the Internet—the world's hottest and fastest-growing medium, and one that promises instant gratification. Take gambling—a recreation and form of excitement that plenty of people would love to have instant access to. Seems like a match made in heaven, yes? Personally, I don't think so. But let's look at both sides of the issue.

First, let's delve into the obvious appeal of cyber-gambling. Can't make it to the casino? No problem—a virtual casino will come to you. Just log on and go to one of over a hundred casino sites, download some software, and the cards, slots, wheels, and dice will follow. Not only that, but it's completely private, self-directed, and non-intimidating. You can play at your own pace, with your favorite food at your fingertips, and—best of all—in your underwear. It's a decadent delight. Plus you don't have to deal with noise, smoke, drunken patrons, or surly dealers. Ah, the wonders that a computer and a phone line can bring.

Here's catch number one: It's illegal. The Federal Interstate Wire Act forbids the use of U.S. telephone lines to conduct a betting or wagering business whether in the United States or overseas. Many states have been very active in prosecuting on-line operators who offer sports wagering or casino gambling. The United States government believes all Internet casinos are unlawful, which is why the casinos have their host computers on foreign soil, typically in the Caribbean. Right now, it's not a crime for you to bet at an on-line casino, but some elected officials are pushing legislation that would turn on-line bettors into criminals.

Whether the states and the federal government are really concerned about unprotected consumers or whether they don't want to lose the tax revenue can be debated. Still, Internet gambling critics rightly point out that regulation may be lax or absent for on-line casinos. Which brings up problem number two (one that's even more troubling to me): whether or not you get an honest game. Casino-on-demand sounds less attractive when you're giving out your credit card number or bank account information to casinos that are faceless, off-shore, unregulated entities. You can't be certain that they will offer a fair game or pay up when you win.

The Internet casinos don't think of themselves as outlaws. As far as they're concerned, they're merely conducting business using a global medium. Many on-line casinos have gained good reputations and the trust is reinforced by the repeated play of satisfied customers. In this growing industry, quality on-line casinos want to be known as trustworthy and respectable in order to keep their competitive edge. The well-run casinos have numbers and e-mail addresses for concerns and complaints. And many supporters claim that since the Internet thrives on communication among its many savvy users, any casino that has a tinge of crookedness will soon be exposed and abandoned.

Nonetheless, there have been many incidents of ripoffs and frauds. And if you get scammed, you don't have much recourse. As a general rule, gambling debts are non-recoverable, and how are you going to chase down a company thousands of miles away in the Caribbean? Call me cynical, but I'm reluctant to risk money when I'm not playing in live conditions, don't know the quality of regulation, and know that a computer program can easily be altered to provide any result an on-line casino wants. Yes, word will spread fast if a casino doesn't pay winners. But it would be very difficult to detect if the casino is shortchanging players with non-random events—in other words, stacking the deck. This would require more analysis and worry than I care to deal with.

Internet gambling's greatest danger is often touted as its greatest virtue—easy accessibility. Perhaps it is wise to have people exert some effort and deliberate thought in pursuing this brand of entertainment. Gambling can turn into compulsion. I'm not saying the Internet will turn everyone into jewelry-pawning desperados, but some temptations don't need to be that convenient—just like it's easier not to pig out when your home isn't filled with Twinkies and chocolate bars.

Despite my misgivings, I'm sure some of you will want to try your luck in virtual casinos. At the very least, check the recommended Internet sites in Appendix D before risking any real money. These will provide good starting points to inquire about casinos and investigate their reputations. For my money, I think the only bet that should be made—if the taint of illegality doesn't bother you—is sports betting. Only in sports can you have verifiable results and the reassurance that you're playing on a level field. But you still have to be confident that your winnings will be paid and your credit card won't be maxed out.

Perhaps the best use of an on-line casino is for practice, practice, practice. But not with real money. Many of the cyber-casinos allow you to download the software and then play for fun. (In fact, casinos that don't want to raise the ire of the U.S. government have a note saying that Americans should use only this mode.) This is a reasonable way to get familiar with the games and try out the strategies you'll learn in this book.

So we'll keep an eye on what develops. If some sort of regulation and consensus of security is reached, I will reconsider my rather negative stance. Even given the reassurance of an honest game, I do believe the ease of access could spur problem gambling in those who are susceptible. No matter what I believe, the casinos aren't going away. It's estimated that 350 million people worldwide access the Internet on a regular basis and the number is growing. Though no one knows for sure, Internet gambling is currently considered a $10 billion industry. No surprise. Where the people and their purses go, the casinos are sure to follow.

casino would likely weed such a person out. (Plus, the cheat may be more interested in ripping off the casino than the patrons.)

Don't casinos put things in the ventilation system to make you gamble more?
They might try. Casinos have been said to do research on whether certain scents affect mood and make players more likely to gamble. Whether they've come up with anything that has a palpable effect is unknown, but regulators would put a stop to anything harmful or truly mind-altering. However casinos have no qualms about making you primed to gamble—consciously or unconsciously—through sounds, sights, lighting, layout, etc. For more on this, see the Money and Psychology section on page 240. It's often been claimed that casinos pump high doses of oxygen into the casino in order to keep gamblers awake and raring to gamble.

This wouldn't be wise since pure oxygen would create quite a fire hazard, but casinos do try to keep the air cool and fresh so you stay right where they want you.

If I cheat, how much trouble could I get into?
Morality aside, cheating can land you in jail. In Nevada and New Jersey, cheating—no matter how small—is a felony. Would casinos prosecute you rather than just kicking you out? It's not something I would gamble on.

Can I bring a computer into the casino?
That would be nice, wouldn't it? Especially for beatable games like blackjack and video poker. Unfortunately, the casinos aren't PC-friendly. A Nevada statute strictly forbids using any "device" to assist in playing a game. Other states have similar prohibitions against mechanical assistance. Most casinos will even

forbid you from using the old-fashioned paper and pen, especially at blackjack tables. Using one's brain isn't unlawful yet, but card-counters find that it can be prohibited.

Are there really professional gamblers in casinos?
Yes, there are professional players, but they are a rare—and somewhat strange—breed. Professional gambling is certainly not as exciting as you might think. It involves a great deal of boredom and drudgery. People who are earning their livings as gamblers, not just supplementing their paychecks, live a tough, exhausting life filled with mathematical analysis and endless hours in the casino. Very, very few people have the funds, temperament, endurance, and skill to even eke out a living as a gambler. But many, many people have little inhibition or shame about calling themselves pros. Hey, it sure sounds romantic.

Only a few games allow a highly skilled player to gain a mathematical advantage—blackjack, video poker, live poker, and sports betting. In any other casino game—aside from rare promotions, casino errors, and occasional progressive jackpots—it's impossible to win in the long term. Ergo, it's impossible to be a pro.

Can you take photos inside a casino?
That depends on the casino. Just ask a security person if it's allowed, or snap away and hope no one tells you to stop. The reason for the prohibition would be concern about casino security—I suppose to discourage photographic reference for your grand cheating scam. You can always get your picture taken with the display of $1 million in cash at Binion's Horseshoe in Las Vegas.

Can I sit at the gaming tables and not play?
The house always prefers a player to a kibitzer. But if the casino isn't crowded, it shouldn't be a problem. But if the dealer tells you to play or leave, try not to be insulted—just play or leave.

Just what is the difference between gambling and gaming?
Just a "b," an "l," and a silly euphemistic attempt at respectability. Apparently those in the gambling—I mean gaming—industry thought "gaming" carried less of a negative connotation. Gambling is a vice associated with reprobates, the stuff of fire-and-brimstone sermons. Gaming is a service provided by the casino industry and regulated by responsible state agencies; it's an entertainment. Well, by any other name, the profits still smell as sweet.

What's the average life span of a deck of cards in a casino?
Although casinos use the most durable and high-quality cards, they hold up for only about one shift (eight hours).

What about dice?
Dice can take a lot of wear and tear, but they'll usually be disposed of after a shift or at the end of the day.

What is the most popular number in the casino—particularly in roulette?
Seventeen is quite popular because it is the number that James Bond bets in his films. (You'd think it would be 00 or 7.) Another hot number, at least on the silver screen, is 22, which shows up in *Casablanca*, *The Sting*, and *Lost in America*.

THE ESSENTIALS FOR FEELING LIKE A GENIUS IN ANY CASINO

The casino is its own world with its own rules of order and etiquette. Every player has been new to it at one time and every player has made many a faux pas. At best, you get some flushed cheeks; at worst, you lose some money. Here are some rules to help you feel comfortable and avoid the most common boo-boos.

- In almost all locations, the minimum gambling age is 21. Aside from not wanting to expose your children to gambling at a vulnerable age, keep this deterrent in mind: If a minor wins a jackpot, the casino will *not* pay it.
- Keep valid identification on you when you're playing. If you win a jackpot of $1,200 or more, the casino will usually ask for two forms of identification while you fill out a W2-G form for the IRS. Carry your driver's license or social security card to make life easier.
- When in doubt about protocol, follow the other players. If you are not sure when to pick up your cards, when to place your bet, etc., observe the other players' actions. Note: This advice does not apply to strategy!
- Know the table limits. Just check the sign on the table. It's humbling to mosey up with $50 to a $100 minimum table.
- Don't play beyond your means just because all the lower-limit tables are filled up. Wait for a table to open up that you're comfortable with.
- Check out games early in the morning before they get crowded. You can get more attention and help from the dealer.
- Let dealers know when you're new to a game. They'll explain things to you and may head you off before you make obvious errors.
- Don't try to hand money directly to a dealer. Just put it down on the table and let the dealer do the rest.
- Don't expect the dealer to give you cash for your chips. That's what the cage is for.
- Don't touch your wager until you get paid. Once your bet is down and the action starts, don't fiddle with it. Just wait until your bet gets paid or until it loses. Casinos worry that players might try to *pinch* (remove chips from) or *cap* (add chips to) their wagers.
- Don't take offense when dealers make you follow proper etiquette. They're not singling you out. They are merely adhering to the rigid casino security policies and protecting their own jobs.
- Never think you deserve any rude or obnoxious treatment from dealers (or players). No matter how unsure you feel about a game, you never should be hassled. Either complain to the shift manager or leave the casino.
- An occasional cuss uttered in frustration won't shock the typical casino patron. Still, it's always preferable to have good comportment. And your verbal venom should never be directed at a particular individual.

2
BECOMING A SMART PLAYER—PART I

This chapter will give you an understanding of the lingo that flows so freely throughout the rest of the book: *odds*, *probabilities*, *payback percentages*, *house edge*, *expectation*. It will also clue you in as to why the casinos make so much money and why players usually leave with less money than they came with. The fundamental concepts discussed in this chapter are essential to becoming an informed and savvy gambler. You will be given the ammunition to differentiate a good bet from a bad bet, and you will be in more control of your experience.

I can't tell a lie: In order for the numbers to have meaning, there will be math. Some of you will be insulted that I issued that warning. However, others will have visions of tortures involving razor blades and bamboo shoots. For those math-phobes, I can promise that it won't be so bad. On the contrary, it can be very enlightening. Once you grasp these concepts, you may not always know the specifics on any given bet, but you will be aware of what you *want* to know about that bet. Having a sense of your environment and how to cope with it— that's certainly one way to feel like a "genius."

The intent is to increase your pleasure of the games and increase your ability as a gambler. And it will help you against the enemy—that's a rather dramatic term, but let's be honest, you would love to take the casino for all they're worth and they feel the same way about you (as long as they can get you to come back again). I'll fall back on an old cliché: Knowledge is power. And for the casino, an educated consumer is its toughest customer.

I hear the protests anyway: "Don't bother me with math and lessons. Just tell me how to win."

Well, you can learn the rules of the games and follow the gaming advice in the book by rote, using it as a Baedeker to the best bets and smartest moves in the casino. If it serves that function for you, good enough. That will put you ahead of 90% of the gamblers out there. But if you really want to understand gambling, how casinos work, and why it's so tough to beat the house, you have to come back to this chapter.

UNDERSTANDING ODDS AND PROBABILITY

When we talk about gambling, we inevitably talk about the odds. As you may know, odds are based on the branch of mathematics known as probability. Probability is used in all aspects of our lives: weather, science, genetics, medicine, business, stocks, insurance. Is it likely to rain tomorrow? The average male is expected to live how long? What are the odds that your child will have your blood type? What are my chances, doc? Shocking as it may seem, this essential branch of mathematics was raised on the shoulders of gambling and its analysis.

A QUICK PROBABILITY CLASS
So what is probability? It's the formal study of the laws of chance. Most of us are familiar with its basic concepts—probability measures how often things occur, or, more precisely, can be expected to occur. Some probabilities we can't be sure of, although specialists try to estimate them; for example, the probability of the Earth being hit by an asteroid, or the probability of a certain child growing up to be a millionaire or Olympic athlete.

Other probabilities, including those in gambling games, involve mechanisms in which we know all the possible outcomes and therefore we can make predictions with accuracy. If you have a fair coin and you flip it, you can get either heads or tails. There are two possible outcomes (heads and tails) for the flipping of a coin, and one "event" (let's say heads) that you want. Thus, the probability of getting heads is ½—you have a 1 in 2 chance of getting heads.

So, probability is the likelihood that a specific event (let's call it X) will occur. It measures the number of ways X can happen compared to the total number of possible outcomes (let's call that Y). We can express this probability—written as P(X) and read as "the probability of X occurring"—as a ratio or fraction.

$$P(X) = \frac{\text{number of ways to get outcome X}}{\text{number of all possible outcomes (or Y)}}$$

So, the probability of picking an ace in a standard 52-card deck is:

$$P(\text{picking an ace}) = \frac{\text{number of aces}}{\text{total number of cards}}$$

$$= \frac{4}{52}$$
$$= \frac{1}{13}$$

A CHANCE BY ANY OTHER NAME

There are many ways to express probability. They all say the same thing, but one might be more convenient than another, depending on the circumstances. Let's look at the probability of picking a club from a 52-card deck.

$$P(\text{picking a club}) = \frac{\text{number of clubs}}{\text{total number of cards}}$$

$$= \frac{13}{52}$$
$$= \frac{1}{4}$$

First thing you'll notice is that the fraction $\frac{13}{52}$ is reduced to ¼. It's usually more meaningful and more pleasing to the eye to put things in their most reduced, simplest forms. If you run across a probability in the book that doesn't seem intuitive, consider that it might be reduced.

Let's look at all the ways we can express the probability for plucking out a club. We can express the 1 in 4 chance as a decimal, 0.25, or we can say that there is a 25% chance of getting a club.

When people say a probability is 50-50, they are saying that it has a 1 in 2 chance of occur-

ring, meaning 50% of the time it will happen and 50% of the time it won't. To describe probability, sometimes we use fractions, sometimes decimals, sometimes percentages.

DIFFERENT WAYS TO DESCRIBE THE PROBABILITY OF AN EVENT

Event	Picking a club
Description	$\frac{\text{number of clubs}}{\text{total number of cards}}$
Fraction	$\frac{13}{52} = \frac{1}{4}$
Decimal	0.25
Percentage (decimal × 100)	25%
Will occur	1 in 4 times
Odds	3 to 1

BASIC PROBABILITY RULES

If you can get comfortable with the following rules, the explanations and analyses of most gambling problems will make sense.

1) The probability of an event occurring will always have a value from 0 to 1. When a probability is 0, the event is impossible; for example, the probability of rolling a 7 on a normal six-sided die. It cannot possibly happen. When the probability is 1, the event is certain or 100% likely; for example, the probability of rolling any number from 1 to 6 (but not a particular number) on a normal six-sided die is 1. This must happen. (I'm excluding the possibility that the die can land on an edge!) Probabilities are never negative—0 means something can't happen, less than 0 doesn't mean anything at all.

2) The probability of an event occurring plus the probability of that event not occurring equals 1. Why? Because the total probability of all the possible outcomes can't help but equal 1 (100%)—*something* has to happen, either the event you're looking for or *not* the event you're looking for. For example, the chance of rolling a 2 on a die (⅙) plus the chance of not rolling a 2 (⅚) equals 1 (⅙ + ⅚ = 1). This may seem painfully obvious, but it can be a powerful tool when we have to figure out the chance of an event indirectly. Let's say you wanted to know the probability of picking a club from a standard

A CLASSIC PROBABILITY EXAMPLE

Now that we're comfortable with the basic concepts of probability (we are, aren't we?), let's look at a classic example that shows us where the whole modern theory of probability got started. In the 17th century, a French nobleman and hustler named the Chevalier de Mère was using dice to supplement his income. He would wager even-money odds that on four rolls of a die, at least one 6 would come up. His reasoning was as follows:

$P(6) = \frac{1}{6}$

$P(6)$ in four rolls $= 4 \times \frac{1}{6} = \frac{2}{3}$

He made a pretty profit off this wager. His reasoning was off—we'll soon see why—but he still had the advantage. (Did you already catch his faulty thinking?)

When suckers dried up for this proposition, the Chevalier moved on to another bet. He wagered even money that double-6 would come up at least once in 24 rolls of two dice. His reasoning for this bet was:

$P(6,6) = \frac{1}{36}$

$P(6,6$ in 24 rolls$) = 24 \times \frac{1}{36} = \frac{2}{3}$

To his amazement, he started losing money on this bet. So he put the question of why this was happening to his friend, the mathematician and genius Blaise Pascal. Pascal took enough interest in the Chevalier's game to consult yet another mathematics genius, Pierre de Fermat. Their written correspondence set forth the modern theory of probability. (And we owe it all to a Renaissance hustler!) Let's see how the fruit of their analysis applies to the Chevalier's problem.

In the first instance, we know that the chance of rolling a 6 on any given roll is $\frac{1}{6}$. But, the way to really look at the problem is to see what the chance is of *not* rolling a 6 on any given roll. Naturally, this would be $\frac{5}{6}$. So for the Chevalier to really know what he's up against, he needs to know what the chances are of getting no 6s in four throws. Each roll is independent and, using the formula for independent events discussed on page 25, we see the following:

P(not rolling 6 in four rolls)

$= \frac{5}{6} \times \frac{5}{6} \times \frac{5}{6} \times \frac{5}{6} = 0.482$

That means there is a 48.2% chance of not getting a six, and thus the Chevalier loses the bet. The chance of getting a 6 is now easy to calculate. Remember, some outcome must occur, which is why we subtract 0.482 from a probability of 1.

P(rolling a 6 in four rolls)

$= 1 - P$(not rolling 6 in four rolls)

$= 1 - 0.482$

$= 0.518$

So, the Chevalier had a 51.8% chance of winning his even-money bet. That's why he made money, even though his chances weren't $\frac{2}{3}$ as he thought. Working backward to solve this problem may seem counterintuitive, but it actually makes it easier to solve.

The Chevalier's original reasoning also doesn't hold up when we take it a step further. Using his faulty approach, a dice roller would be *guaranteed* to roll a 6 if given six rolls ($6 \times \frac{1}{6}$). Obviously, this is wrong and shows why it sometimes makes more sense to evaluate the chances of an event *not* happening.

Now let's look at the Chevalier's losing proposition. He wanted to know the probability of getting double-6 in 24 rolls and wrongly assumed it was $\frac{24}{36}$. Again, it's easier to describe the chance of not getting the desired outcome:

P(not rolling a 12 in 24 rolls)
   $= (^{35}\!/_{36})^{24}$
   $= 0.509$
And therefore:
P(rolling a 12 in 24 rolls)
   $= 1 - $ P(not rolling a 12 in 24 rolls)
   $= 1 - 0.509$
   $= 0.491$

Aha! The Chevalier's probability in this second bet was only 0.491, which accounts for his losing money on an even-money bet. The old con man outhustled himself, but he did get lucky that some of the finest minds of his time were there to bail him out.

deck of cards, but you knew nothing about the composition of a deck of cards. You are reliably informed that the chance of *not* picking a club is ¾. That's all you need to know.

P(picking a club) = 1 − P(not picking a club)
   = 1 − ¾
   = ¼

See "A Classic Probability Example" on page 24 for a slightly more sophisticated application of this rule.

3) The probability of the occurrence of a sequence of independent events equals the product of the individual probabilities. Yes, it's a mouthful, but you're probably already familiar with the application of this rule. Let's say you want to calculate the probability of rolling two ones (*snake eyes*) on a pair of dice. The probability of getting a 1 on a single roll of a die is ⅙. (Six total possible outcomes, only one that you want.) The probability of getting two 1s is: ⅙ × ⅙ = ⅟₃₆. Each roll is an "independent event" (one has no bearing on the other) and the probability for the "sequence" (rolling two 1s) is the "product" (meaning we multiply) of the individual probabilities (⅙). By the way, this doesn't have to be done with one die as a sequence. Rolling two dice simultaneously can be construed as a sequence—because the two events are independent.

Another example: You throw a die and a coin at the same time. What is the probability that you'll get a head on the coin *and* a 1 on the die? Since these events don't affect each other, the chance of both is the product of the individual probabilities. The chance of a head on the coin is ½ and the chance of a 1 on the die is ⅙. Therefore, the probability of both these things occurring is ½ × ⅙ = ⅟₁₂.

4) The probability of non-independent events also equals the product of the individual probabilities. However, given that the events have occurred, each sequential probability will be affected by the event that came before. Once again, extremely confusing to read, but sensible in application. Let's say you want to calculate the probability of pulling three straight clubs from a single deck of cards. The probability is ¹³⁄₅₂ (13 clubs and 52 cards total) × ¹²⁄₅₁ (one club—and one card—has already been drawn) × ¹¹⁄₅₀ (two clubs—and two cards—have been drawn) = 0.013 or 1.3%. If you placed the card you drew back into the deck after each draw (making it a whole deck again), then each drawing would be completely independent and the probability of drawing three clubs would be ¹³⁄₅₂ × ¹³⁄₅₂ × ¹³⁄₅₂ = 0.016 or 1.6%.

THE ODDS

Once we've got the probability of an event, the next step is to think about the odds of that event. If probability describes the relationship between a desired event and all possible events, the odds describe the relationship between a desired event and all non-desired events.

For convention's sake, odds are usually considered as the "odds against" something happening. This is probably the first thing you'll be interested in when you approach any game in the casino.

Let's look again at picking a club. We know the probability is ¼. There is one chance in four of success; there are three chances to fail.

Therefore, the true odds against this event (picking the club) occurring are 3 (chances to fail) to 1 (chance to succeed). Here's an instance where you may be frowning for a moment and saying, "But aren't there 52 cards in a deck? What does 3 to 1 really mean?" Okay, 3 to 1 is the same as saying 39 (number of non-clubs) to 13 (number of clubs). The fraction has just been reduced.

You roll a die, hoping to get a 2. The probability of getting that 2 to come up is ⅙. The odds against are 5 to 1; this could also be written as 5–1. Realize that "A–B" is the same as saying "A to B."

The odds may not always conveniently be "something to 1," but any probability can be expressed as odds. A general rule: Take the probability as a fraction, say X/Y. Remember, Y is all the possible outcomes and X is the successful or desired outcomes. So subtracting X from Y will give you all the undesirable outcomes from which we can get the odds. The odds against event X occurring are "Y – X" to "X." Let's say the probability of something occurring is 9/35. Not a pretty number, but we can deal with it. The odds against the event occurring are 26 to 9. Very often, we'll reduce these odds to a more easily understood form even if we don't have a whole number. For example, 26 to 9 can be reduced to 2.89 to 1.

CASINO ODDS

True odds, which are based on the actual probability of a chance event occurring, will rarely be seen in a casino. Otherwise, over the long run, the casino wouldn't make its profit. Casino odds show you what you should expect to get paid for your bet. If the casino's odds are 2–1 and you win, that means for every one unit bet, you will receive two units back along with your original bet. So if you bet $1 on a 2–1 bet and win, you should get back $2 profit plus your original $1 bet, for a total of $3. (Odds can be shown with various notations: "2 to 1," "2–1," and "2:1." Throughout this book I'll typically use "A to B" or "A–B.")

An *even-money* bet refers to odds of 1–1. In this case, you profit by the amount of your wager if you win. A $1 even-money bet will return $2—your original bet plus $1 profit.

Some games may represent their odds as "A

for B" rather than "A *to* B." If this is the case, for every bet of B, a *total* amount of A will be returned to the player, which includes the player's original bet. For instance, if a wager pays 5 for 1 and you bet $1 on it, you will receive $5 back, an amount that includes your original bet. So your profit is only $4. This 5 *for* 1 bet is equivalent to a 4 *to* 1 bet. This is an important distinction. Don't think you're getting a higher payback just because the number is higher—see if it says "for" or "to." Realize that "A for B" is equivalent to "(A – B) to B."

UNDERSTANDING THE CASINO'S ADVANTAGE

I can hear you now: "Thanks for the probability lessons, but I'm ready to go gamble." Not so fast. Don't you want to know how the casino extracts money from you and at what rate it does so? Probability and true odds let you know what to expect in a fair world, but the casino is not a fair world, my friend.

The basic reason money moves from players' pockets to casino coffers is that the casinos don't pay what they should. They don't cheat. They don't rig games. They don't rely on players being unlucky or foolish (though that helps). They rely on math. Let's see how it works.

EXPECTATION

It's time to pull out Gambling 101's favorite learning tool. Yes, you guessed it, the coin. Let's say a friend offers you a game: she'll flip a coin and you call it in the air. If your call is right, you win $1. If it's wrong, you lose $1. Assuming the coin isn't loaded, this is a fair, though incredibly dull, game. Over the long run, half the time you'll win $1 and half the time you'll lose $1. You are being paid the true odds (1–1), and, in the long run, you won't win or lose any money. Your *expectation* for this game is zero.

Don't expect your local casino (or your more conniving friends) to offer you a game like this. The casino version of the game would likely work as follows: If you call the coin result correctly, you win 90¢; if you get the call wrong, you lose $1. Already, you know this is bad. What exactly is your expectation for this game? Expectation, which may also be referred to as "expected value" or "expected outcome" or "expected winnings" or "expected return," tells you how much you can expect to win or lose on your wager over the long run. In order to figure out how much we can expect to win (or lose) on a particular bet, we need to look at the probability of both the winning and losing outcomes and the monetary gain and loss associated with each. This will tell us the expectation (abbreviated as E throughout the book) for a particular bet. Let's look at your expectation for this game:

$$E = [P(\text{winning outcome}) \times (\text{amount won})] +$$
$$[P(\text{losing outcome}) \times (-\text{amount lost})]$$
$$E = [P(\text{correct coin call}) \times (\$0.90)] +$$
$$[P(\text{incorrect coin call}) \times (-\$1)]$$
$$= [(\tfrac{1}{2}) \times (0.90)] + [(\tfrac{1}{2}) \times (-1)]$$
$$= -0.05$$

Therefore, for every $1 bet, you can expect to lose 5¢ ($0.05). If you played this game long enough, the casino would have all your money.

We use a coin because it's simple to understand, but in no way is it an oversimplification; the principle demonstrated applies to almost every casino game. Essentially, casinos make their money by paying off bets at less than the true odds. You may not be able to crunch every number or know the exact statistics for a particular game (that's why I'm here), but now you know that when you're not getting the proper payout in respect to the odds, you're at a disadvantage, just as in the coin example.

You can't get serious gamblers to shut up about expectation. And for good reason—expectation lets you know what you should plan on getting back from playing a game (or making a particular bet) in the long run. You can use expectation as your gold standard of a game's worth or you can easily convert expectation to an even more familiar term—*house edge*.

THE HOUSE EDGE

The house edge, also called the *house advantage* or *casino advantage*, is the most commonly used indicator of the value of a particular game or bet. The higher the house edge, the bigger an advantage the casino has.

Quite simply, house edge is a conversion of expectation into a percentage. How is this done? First it always helps to look at numbers in the simplest form, so you divide the expectation by the total amount bet to obtain your expected outcome per dollar bet. For example, if your expectation was −$0.60 on a $3 bet, the expectation per dollar bet would be $^{-0.6}\!/_3$ or −$0.20. (When possible, we calculate expectation based on a $1 bet and thereby cut out this step since the result is already in terms of expectation per dollar bet.) You then simply drop the minus sign from the expectation and multiply it by a hundred to make it into a percentage. The convention of presenting this value as a "positive" number—from the house's point of view—is a concession to the reality that almost all casino games are in the house's favor.

For the coin tossing game, you would have the following (I show the division by the $1 bet, although this normally wouldn't be necessary):

$$\text{House edge} = {}^{(0.05 \,\times\, 100)}\!/_1 = 5\%$$

The house edge is telling us exactly what the expectation did: 5 cents of every dollar (5% of $1) will go to the casino over the long run. From the player's point of view, it should be seen as negative. What if you have the rare instance where the player's expectation is positive—meaning that you expect to make money on the bet? In that case, the house edge is negative, which is confusing, but consistent if you're looking from the casino's viewpoint.

Throughout the book the house edge will be presented as a positive number, which means it's negative for you. The higher it is, the worse it is. When it is appropriate, we'll talk of

DIFFERENT WAYS OF DESCRIBING A GAME'S EXPECTATION

Roulette	
Player's expectation per dollar bet	−0.0526
House edge	5.26%
Theoretical amount lost per dollar bet	$0.0526
Payback percentage	94.74%
Theoretical amount kept per dollar bet	$0.9474

a *player's* positive expectation. Another way of referring to these same numbers is to talk about *payback percentage.* This is most often used with slot and video poker machines. Instead of talking about the amount that is kept by the house (house edge), payback percentage refers to the amount kept by the player. When something has a 97% payback percentage, that means in the long run it returns 97 cents of every dollar bet and therefore has a house edge of 3%.

Other Ways the House Gets the Edge

The house edge doesn't always come about from the casino paying less than true odds. Other methods include advantages present in the rules (for example, players busting before the dealer plays in blackjack) or commissions on winning bets (as in baccarat).

LET'S PLAY A GAME

Let's apply what we know so far to a very simple game of chance. Your local casino is rather desperate and came up with this boring game. There's a black bowl filled with 13 marbles: 9 blue and 4 red. All the marbles are the same size and weight with no way to differentiate them except by sight. On each round of play, a marble is selected at random (no peeking!). You can bet on blue or red. The casino odds are 7 for 5 on blue and 3 to 1 on red. Should you play this game? What bet, if any, should you make? First, let's express the true probability in all the various ways we can:

MARBLE GAME PROBABILITY

Event	Blue selection
Fraction	$\frac{9}{13}$
Decimal	0.6923
Percentage	69.23%
Odds against	4 to 9
Will occur	1 in 1.44 times

Event	Red selection
Fraction	$\frac{4}{13}$
Decimal	0.3077
Percentage	30.77%
Odds against	9 to 4
Will occur	1 in 3.25 times

Let's see what happens when you bet blue. Since it pays off at odds of 7 *for* 5, it really pays 2 to 5 (look back to page 26 if you're confused). That means you'll profit $2 when you bet $5 and you'll get your $5 bet back (for a total of $7). Compare the casino odds of 2 to 5 to the true odds of 4 to 9. In the casino, you would have to bet $10 to win $4, but the true odds show that you should have to bet only $9 to win $4. Already, we can see the casino getting its edge in its typical style by paying back less then the true odds. Now let's calculate the expectation and house edge. Remember, you are betting $5 on each hand and a blue win gains you only $2:

$$E = [\tfrac{9}{13} \times (+2)] + [\tfrac{4}{13} \times (-5)] = \tfrac{-2}{13} = -0.1538$$
$$E \text{ per dollar bet} = \tfrac{-0.1538}{5} = -0.0308$$
$$\text{House edge} = 3.08\%$$

So we expect to lose about three cents on every dollar bet. That's not horrific, but it's not great. Further down we'll discuss how to evaluate a house edge.

Now let's take a look at a bet on red. The odds say that they pay at 3 *to* 1. Compare those odds to the true odds of 9 to 4. If you bet $4 on red, the casino would pay you $12, plus your original wager. The true odds say you should win only $9. Hmm. Let's calculate the expectation and house edge:

$$E = [\tfrac{9}{13} \times (-4)] + [\tfrac{4}{13} \times (+12)] = \tfrac{12}{13} = 0.9231$$
$$E \text{ per dollar bet} = \tfrac{0.9231}{4} = 0.2308$$
$$\text{House edge (?!)} = -23.08\%$$

Look's like something went very wrong for the casino. The house edge isn't an edge (thus the negative sign); this bet is to the player's extreme advantage. A player betting red would expect to win 23¢ on every dollar bet in the long run. For the casino, this imaginary game would officially be named Unlucky 13.

You may have noticed the discrepancy in the way the odds were stated: 7 *for* 5 as opposed to 3 *to* 1. This was done to further acquaint you with the two ways of stating odds, but I also snuck it in as an "error" that every casino dweller dreams of finding. (Don't get your hopes up. You will rarely—more like never—find such a mistake. Probability very near zero.) A sensible casino would have intended the odds on the red marble to be 3 *for* 1, meaning 2 to 1. This completely changes the bet's expectation and results in a nasty house edge of 7.69%! That's quite a difference. (Do the calculations for yourself—come on, you know you want to.) A little printing error on a game's layout could mean heaven for the shrewd bettor and disaster for the casino. As I said, you will never find anything like it or anything even close. But it did make a tantalizing example and a good—if somewhat extreme—demonstration of why it's worthwhile to know and understand the bets you place.

THINKING ABOUT THE HOUSE EDGE

The number-crunching can give us a concrete sense of how much of an advantage the house has on us. But let's not lose sight of what the edge really tells us—the casino is exercising its advantage not when we lose, but when we win. Yes, you read that right. In most games, the house edge drains you on your winnings, not on your losses. Why? Because you're not receiving a fair payout on your winning wager.

We've seen this already. Go back to the coin tossing example. What really hurts you is not your losses of $1, but the fact that your wins pay you only 90¢. Over the long term, your wins and losses—in terms of guessing heads or tails—will even out. But your money won't even out, because you aren't paid enough on your wins. That's the secret tax of the casinos. Players bang their heads about their losing streaks—and of course those hurt in the short-term—but they should really be worried about how much they're "losing" during their winning streaks. Very few players realize or appreciate that the short payouts on their wins keep them from playing even with the house.

You may be smirking and thinking, "Don't try to dazzle me with a seeming paradox. I'll take winning over losing anytime." I agree. If I knew I would win all the time, then I wouldn't be concerned with getting true odds or good odds. But, sadly, reality and probability insist that we will lose some and win some. Put it in these terms: If you have a casino game that offers only two bets and you bet on both of them, you will end up losing. You won't be even. The reason you won't be even is that the winning bet—which must occur since there are only two bets—doesn't pay what it should. The losing bet is irrelevant.

This is most apparent on the roulette wheel. Cover every number with the same size bet. The wheel spins and lands on one of your numbers, of course. Are you a winner? Of course not. The true odds on single numbers are 37 to 1, but the casino pays only 35 to 1. If you were to cover the board with $1 on every number ($38), you would win back only $35 for the number that won plus your original $1 bet on that number, for a total loss of $2. You don't get your fair share and that's the house edge.

It's important to realize this sly mechanism is at work as you play. Don't think you're fighting the house in a guessing game in which your bad hunches or your bad timing or your rotten luck leave you floundering. You're really fighting them in a numbers game that is designed so that you can't win in the long run.

Take heart—I'll show you the strategies and bets that will give you the best chance of winning. Your goal as an educated casino player is to lessen the casino's concealed charge.

THE HOUSE EDGE AND THE GRIND

Okay, you've accepted the cosmic injustice—and, for casinos, the economic necessity—of the house edge. Now that you've resigned yourself to it, you may be consoling yourself with the following thought, although you may suspect it doesn't ring true: "Fine. So the house has a 5% edge in the game I like. I come to the casino with $100 and I'm expected to lose $5. That doesn't seem so awful for a night's entertainment. Plus, I may end up winning."

I have some more bad news. Obviously, if you've gambled at all, you know that the line of reasoning above doesn't hold water. But it does have a certain specious appeal. The sobering truth, which was shown in our explanation of house edge, is that the 5% is applied to all the money you actually play, your *action*; it's not just in relation to your *bankroll*.

What's the difference? Your bankroll will supply you with more money to be played than just itself. Because you don't lose all the time and you're often rebetting your winnings, a $100 bankroll could result in $1,000 worth of bets. Let's say you're playing blackjack and the house has a 2% advantage (in the blackjack chapter, I'll show you how to make it far less than that). You come to a $5 minimum table with a bankroll of $100. It would be unlikely that you'd lose 20 hands in a row. You may end up betting 50 hands of $5 each during the hour, so your expected loss for the hour would be $5/hand × 50 hands/hour × 0.02 house advantage = $5. Already, that's more than the house edge on a $100 wager, which would be $2.

It's this constant betting and rebetting of money that grinds your bankroll down. After 20 hours of blackjack play, your expected loss would be 20 hours × $5 × 50 × 0.02 = $100. That's your whole bankroll. Gone in a game that has only a 2% house edge.

This phenomenon is known as *churn*, and it keeps the casino's coffers full. Most people recycle their money back into their games. Although churn is at work in all games, its effects are very vivid in the ultimate "recycling" machine—the slot machine. Look at the slots chapter for a further discussion of churn. The more you play, the more the house edge will eat at you.

FROM THEORY TO REALITY

Now you have a firm grasp on evaluating expectation and house edge for bets. But something still may not sit right with you. It all sounds too theoretical. You know from experience or common sense that after making $1,000 in blackjack bets, you would almost never be down exactly $20 (assuming a 2% house edge). In fact, you're sure you would be up or down quite a bit more than that. You know in your bones that wins or losses in normal playing sessions won't come out looking anything like what we predicted mathematically. You know that any bet, no matter how bad the odds, pays off sometimes. You're absolutely right.

As you may have noticed, I often qualify the expectations for betting results with the phrase "in the long run." That's because, in the short run, you can expect your money to go up and down like a roller coaster. Any given person can win money during any given playing session—if this weren't so, the casinos wouldn't draw customers—but over enough sessions, the casi-

no is guaranteed to get its expected due. Given enough sessions, you will lose money in a negative expectation game—in other words, a game with a "positive" house edge.

How long is the long run? This is difficult to answer with complete certainty—it involves some statistical analysis, a determination of what kind of bet is made, and the expectation. When will you encounter the long run? It depends on the number of sessions and trials that you expose yourself to. For a casual player who visits the casino a few times a year, it could be his whole playing career. For the committed recreational player who shows up every weekend, the long run could be a few years. For a professional gambler who is in the casino nearly every day, it could be a few months. For the casino itself, which has a high volume of action every day, the long run isn't so long—it can be a single day or a week.

The significance of the long run and short run is an extension of probability theory. What we're dealing with is really the "law of averages," also called the "law of large numbers," which is very appropriate to our discussion. It is this mathematical law that bridges the gap between our theoretical expectations and our real-life experiences. The law is essentially this: *In repeated, independent trials of the same experiment, the observed fraction of occurrences of an event eventually approaches its theoretical probability*. In plain English, that means the more bets ("trials of the same experiment") you make, the closer you will you get to the expected results ("theoretical probability").

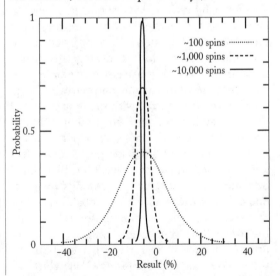

Let's look at the elegant game of roulette. All bets have a −5.26% player expectation. If you were to make an even-money bet (on black, let's say) 100 times, all your results would fall somewhere on the dotted-line curve on page 30. This is the familiar bell curve used for exam scores, mortality rates, research studies, etc. It provides a symmetrical distribution of numbers around the mean or average (in this case, −5.26%). The vertical axis has the probability of the outcomes ranging from 0 to 1. The horizontal axis represents the percentage ahead or behind the player may be. The points on the curve plot the probability of having the particular outcome. As you can see, the most common outcome is the expected one, −5.26%. But there is a wide range of other outcomes.

With only 100 trials, there's a great deal of leeway in what our expected outcome may be. The good news is that you can win in the short term. The bad news is that it won't happen in the long term. The more you play, the tighter this curve gets. It eventually squeezes around −5.26% and the outer possibilities become less likely. In 10,000 spins (the solid-line curve on page 30) the curve is so skinny that it is nearly impossible to be in positive percentage territory.

The inexorable and unyielding quality of the law of large numbers holds true for any bet in the casino. The more trials you attempt, the more you squeeze the curve to its expected outcome. This also holds true for positive expectation games, which is to our advantage.

And don't think that you can fool the long term or circumvent it. Playing shorter sessions, switching between games, taking long breaks, only betting when you feel "lucky" (et cetera and ad nauseum) will not change the long term. If you play 1,000 sessions of one bet each or one session of 1,000 bets, the law of large numbers will be working its same magic. (That's not to say that 1,000 trials guarantee the expected outcome—for most games that number isn't large enough to assure the result.) Every time you make a particular bet, you're making it for a lifetime; it goes toward your grand total of trials.

Standard Deviation

Given a negative expectation, it's hard to see beyond the doom and gloom. So why does it ever work out well for the player? Why do many people come out winners? What's happening in the short term?

As we covered earlier, any given session for a gambler is a short-term event—its outcome can fluctuate wildly from what we expect in the long term. In a day trip to the Mississippi Coast or even a week's vacation to Las Vegas, you're not condemned to the expected outcome. You simply won't produce enough "trials" to get there. That sounds good, doesn't it? It might be. You can win much more than your theoretical expectation. Must I point out that you can lose a lot more as well?

To account for why this happens, we need another tool from the world of probability and statistics known as the *standard deviation*. The standard deviation describes the variation one expects to find in a prediction. Put another way, the amount we stray from the expected outcome is the standard deviation. It gives us guidelines and boundaries for our predicted outcome. It explains the *variability* you may find in your results.

Let's go back to a coin-flipping example. If we were to flip a fair coin 100 times, probability would tell us to expect 50 heads and 50 tails. That may be the expectation, but it's not the reality. In real trials, it would be very unusual to get that exact result; just try it yourself. Mathematicians can calculate the variation from the expectation with great certainty. This

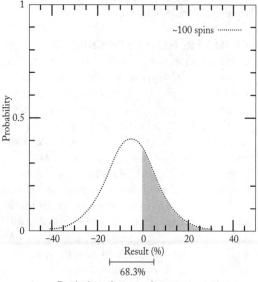

Deviations from roulette expectation

variation is the standard deviation—which is measured from the expected result (50–50). For instance, there is a 68.3% chance of ending up with anywhere from 55 heads and 45 tails to 55 tails and 45 heads. This is plus or minus one standard deviation. There is a 95% chance of ending up with between 40 and 60 heads. This is plus or minus two standard deviations. What does this mean? You "expect" 50 heads, but the reality is that 68.3% of the time you'll get between 45 and 55 heads, and 95% of the time you'll get between 40 and 60 heads.

Let's adapt this concept to the bell curve on page 31, in which we have marked off one standard deviation for 100 spins of a roulette wheel. If we go minus one standard deviation, we'll end up at −15.26%. Conversely, if we go plus one standard deviation, we'll end up at +4.74%. So if we bet one dollar on each spin, 68.3% of the time we can expect to end up in the range of losing $15.26 to winning $4.74.

Looking at the shaded portion of the graph, you see that you can end up in positive territory a significant percentage of the time. That's why you sometimes walk away a winner, even at a game with a steep house edge. As mentioned before, though, the more trials you perform, the less "spread" your curve will have. Look back at the curves on page 30. After 1,000 trials, you can expect to have a positive expectation (above 0%) less than 5% of the time. After 10,000 trials, even three standard deviations (covering 99% of the curve) won't bring you into positive territory.

FROM THE HOUSE'S POINT OF VIEW

If this all sounds like very good news for the casino, it is. It's always wise to have the numbers on your side. Remember, a game that has a negative expectation for the player has a positive expectation for the house. It's not a far trip to the "long run" for casinos. A casino may average 30,000 customers a day. Any given customer, from his point of view, is experiencing short-term outcomes on his bets of choice. But the casino benefits from the total volume of all these individual bettors; collectively, all the customers create enough trials that the casino is virtually assured of having its theoretical advantage become a reality. Look at that bell curve; it doesn't take

long for the casino to accumulate enough bets to have it collapse right around the expected outcome.

In his book *Smart Casino Gambling*, Olaf Vancura tells us that a casino that has 100,000 roulette spins in a three-month period has a 99.99% chance of making between 4% and 6.5% of the amount wagered. The chance that the casino would lose money? Less than 1 in 10,000,000,000,000,000,000,000,000,000,000, 000,000,000,000,000,000,000,000,000,000!

The casino is not worried that you're going to get "lucky." On the contrary, if you do win some money, assuming you're not doing anything that would give you an edge in the long term (like counting cards), the casino couldn't care less. In fact, they hope you will spread word of your win: tales of your conquest will surely bring in more customers. More customers feed into the law of large numbers and guarantee the casino's constant win. As for your little fortune? If you return to the casino enough, they'll take back that money also. The more you try to "take them" for, the more certain it is that they'll come out ahead.

Not only do casino's have a built-in, mathematical edge, but they also have another huge advantage—lots and lots of money. Their "bankroll" is much larger than any individual player's and they can stay in the game a lot longer than any player. The casino doesn't have to worry about the standard deviation swings that give some customers big, medium, and small wins; the casino has the money to handle these winners and still siphon off the many, many losers.

The bank's infinite supply of money (at least in relation to Joe Gambler) takes us to the harsh but inescapable concept of *gambler's ruin*. Basically, gambler's ruin is a dramatic way of saying "going broke." It is most often analyzed by gambler/mathematicians who want to figure out the chances of losing a specific bankroll (say $500) before achieving a certain goal (say doubling or tripling your starting amount).

Such analysis inevitably leads to the conclusion that the longer you play a negative expectation game, the more likely you are to suffer gambler's ruin. (Of course, a game with lower house edge will normally increase your longevity.) In fact, losing your whole stake is inevitable if you play a negative game long enough. Why? Because no matter how many positive fluctuations you experience, the house will stick with you and stick with you—they're not going to quit and take their games home with them. And, in the long run (our favorite phrase), you will lose everything. The casino can always outlast you.

BET WITHIN YOUR BANKROLL

Keep in mind another sobering fact: Even if you're playing a game where you're even with the house or you have an advantage, you have a good chance of being "ruined." This *isn't* inevitable, but it's very likely to occur if you're betting at a level that you can't maintain over thousands and thousands of bets.

For instance, let's say you gleefully rush over to the mythical casino game of "coin toss." A fair game—no house edge, with a maximum bet of $1,000. You have a hefty bankroll of $5,000 burning a hole in your trousers and you think to yourself that this is a dream come true. You're going to bet the $1,000 max on every flip—heck, at worst, you're even and maybe those "standard deviations" will kick in and you'll win an obscene amount of money. You won't. You'll go broke. Your bet is much, much too big for your bankroll. The standard deviation will almost certainly take you on a losing streak at some point and you'll lose all your dough. Even if you get off to a hot start, the house will be able to ride out your winnings (remember, they have the nearly unlimited funds). The house will rightly expect that you'll take a downturn and lose the whole kit and caboodle.

However, if you made $1 bets, your $5,000 stake will almost surely last you forever. It may seem counterintuitive, but if you have the advantage (or are even), the wisest thing to do is to make bets that you can sustain when the pendulum swings against you, bets that allow you to stick around for the long run.

FIGHTING THE EDGE

The fluctuations add excitement to casino gambling and provide the illusion that you can conquer negative expectation games. Knowing this, your best bet is to walk away from the table when you find yourself in the plus column. Simply put, the longer you play, the more chance you have of getting closer to the expectation, which will most often be negative. As rational as this line of reasoning is, it can cut down on your playing time, and that might not suit your entertainment objective. Similarly, if you don't have an advantage, the smartest thing to do with your bankroll is place it on a single bet. Go ahead and risk that $50, $500, or whatever it is you're willing to lose in one lump sum. This will reduce your bankroll's exposure to the negative expectation—the fewer bets you make, the less chance that you'll meet the long-term expectation. But this approach would also make for a very short trip to the casino, and an all-or-nothing outcome for your bankroll. We'll cover considerations such as these and what you want to get out of your gambling in Chapter 16.

Also, be aware that some games have more variability, also known as *volatility*, than others. These games may move very fast with a lot of money potentially being bet (craps) or they may rely on rare big payouts to reduce the negative expectation (video poker). Such games can be fine, but they must suit your temperament. If you have the time and money to stick with them, and don't mind their streakiness, then they can offer some good bets. In any case, pursue those games that are in your favor or have a minimal negative expectation. They're your wisest choices.

DOESN'T ANYTHING MAKE THE CASINOS SWEAT?

Well, casinos can encounter unlikely fluctuations and stray a bit from their theoretical advantage—but this is unusual and doesn't last very long. The bigger threat to the casino (especially depending on the casino's size) is the big bet. I'm talking really big bets, perhaps starting at $10,000 and moving well on up. Why should these bets be adrenaline-producing for casino managers? Because of the short-term possibilities. If a *whale* (a super high roller) gets on a lucky streak, he may make a serious dent in the casino's bottom line. Casinos aren't always comfortable "outlasting" these players, because the short-term wins could climb into the millions. That starts to make some casinos' "infinite" bankrolls seem more finite.

A casino would much rather see 100,000 $1 bets made on a roulette wheel than a single $100,000 bet. In the long run of 100,000 bets, they're guaranteed their take. In the short term of a single bet, they can't be so certain. And there aren't enough customers betting at the level of these whales to guarantee that the law of large numbers will kick in. That's why casinos protect themselves with table limits. Even so, many casinos accommodate and competitively woo the whales. That's because most super high rollers provide a lot of action; they don't just make a couple of bets and walk away. Casinos figure, most often correctly, that when these whales play enough, the house edge will show itself. And then the casino will show a huge profit.

A story has circulated about a Japanese gambler who won over $6 million in two days at an Atlantic City casino. He was betting $200,000 a hand at baccarat. The casino considered cutting its losses and stopping the game, but a statistician let them know that if the man continued to play, he would eventually lose. (Baccarat has a slightly negative expectation for the player.) The high roller apparently didn't plan to quit and so his play continued. A few days later, he owed the casino nearly $2 million. They welcomed him back on another occasion and he lost $10 million. Dealing with the mind-boggling wagers of whales is a risk that well-capitalized casinos are willing to take.

What else do the casinos fear? They don't want to give the player a positive expectation game. That's why it's so hard to find one in the casino. Card-counters in blackjack, who play with a positive expectation, are either barred by casinos or daunted by unfavorable rules intended to offset their advantage. Video poker machines that offer a positive expectation with perfect play often disappear when only those "in the know" play them. Casinos can't afford—in both practical and greedy terms—to give up their pipeline to your wallet through the house edge. And, as you'll see later in the book, they don't take chances with many games—some have quite larcenous house edges. If you follow the advice in this book by making the best bets with the best strategy, you can cut down the casino edge significantly. Even when your expectation is negative, it can be quite small. If every player played that way, the casinos might not go bankrupt, but they would certainly sweat.

WHAT IF THE PLAYER HAS THE EDGE?

So it seems the answer to all this doom and gloom should be playing the few positive expectation games available: video poker (certain machines while using optimum strategy), blackjack (with card-counting), sports betting (if you're a great handicapper), and poker (with great skill). But these games still require an ability to roll with the punches. We've shown through standard deviation how you can win money from the casino even when you have a negative expectation—the reality of what *can* happen in the short term. Conversely, you can lose plenty of money even when you have the advantage. You would need to be in it for the long haul to come out ahead even with a positive expectation. Most players don't have the bankroll or the time—the sheer nonstop volume of play—to guarantee winnings at the end of a day or a week. Sometimes a positive can be a negative.

A PEEK OVER THE EDGE

Hopefully, the preceding information didn't strike you as too abstract or academic. Because if you absorbed what was just covered, you are well on your way to enjoying what a casino has to offer—both financially and emotionally.

As I have mentioned ad nauseum, almost all casino games carry a house edge. Within each game, the house edge may vary based on the different bets and the player's skill. The chapters on the individual games will give more insight on how the house edge is calculated and the variations on the house edge within each game. Also, in Appendix A you will find a master chart of almost every bet available in the casino, with each bet ranked according to its house edge. It's clear from a quick look at that chart that the house will win its money. It's also clear that you can reduce its ability to do so.

In general, games that have big payouts and rely purely on chance have large house edges.

Whenever you can supposedly win a lot of money for a small investment, watch out. Also, new games, variations, and side bets are often unfavorable. Games that require skill and some thought have smaller house edges. Look at the games discussed in the book and see what suits your taste. Try them in the casino. Don't be put off by the games that require preparation; for many gamblers, they deliver more satisfaction—and more money—than games that just rely on luck.

AVOIDING PITFALLS

While probability and math are certainly useful in understanding life in the casino, the misapplication of these principles can be a very dangerous thing. For instance, a hazy understanding of the "law of averages" is the most common path to self-destruction for many gamblers. In fact, I was hesitant to refer to this "law" earlier because it is so misused and abused.

The misunderstanding of the law of averages typically occurs in the following manner. A coin is flipped ten times and ends up with eight heads and two tails. Many gamblers, veteran and newcomer alike, would expect more tails to show up in subsequent flips in order to "even out" things. This common pitfall is called the *gambler's fallacy*. The assumption is that events in the short term will behave in a way to mimic the long-term expectations. The misguided observer says, "I know a coin flip is a 50–50 deal. If heads are in abundance, then a lot of tails are coming because they're lagging behind." That sounds reasonable, but to appreciate the flaw, we have to focus on our friend "the long term."

Yes, the more we flip a coin, the closer it will eventually come to its expected outcome. But this can involve thousands of trials (flips), and, more important, is about percentages, not short-term sequences of results. In our example, the first 10 flips created a difference of 6 between heads and tails and an 80% showing for heads. If we flipped the coin a thousand times, the difference will most likely *grow* in absolute terms. It's not the absolute numbers that conform to our expectations in the long run, but the percentages. We may have 510

heads and 490 tails (or 490 heads and 510 tails). That's a difference of 20, but the percentages are pretty close to what we expect—51% heads and 49% tails. Do you think the next 20 flips will all be tails to completely even things out? Of course not. The percentages will fall in line over the long haul, but we have no way of predicting any short-term sequences. The deviations that we see aren't "corrected" as time goes on, but they are diluted.

Each coin toss is independent; the coin has no memory of previous tosses nor does it know that it has an "obligation" to even out heads and tails in the long run. A further lesson about independent trials and probability: Any particular sequence is as likely to occur as any other specific sequence. A coin-flipping sequence of HHHHHHHHHH is just as likely to occur as a flipping sequence of THHTHTTHTT or of HTHTHTHTHT. Just because we recognize a pattern doesn't mean it isn't random. A poker hand of 10♦ J♦ Q♦ K♦ A♦ is just as likely as a specific hand of 4♣ 7♦ 9♠ 10♥ J♥. But we assign value to one and not the other, so it *appears* more rare when it shows up.

The take-home lesson: If you're playing roulette and the color red shows up seven times in a row, don't assume that black is "due." Each spin is an independent event. A string of seven on the same color is slightly unusual (about a one in 190 chance), but that's only before it occurs. Once it's happening, every individual spin still has the same chance it always does. The ball and the wheel don't know that black has to play catch-up with red. (Or continue the streak, which is another fallacy.) Things will work themselves out over many, many spins—not under the gambler's watchful eye.

Let me play devil's advocate for a moment and use the flawed logic of the gambler's fallacy to argue against its worth. Back to the roulette table. You see black coming up almost all the time and are convinced that red must soon get hot. But what if black is "making up" for its lackluster performance from yesterday? Maybe black has a lot more work to do because it "lagged" so far behind red before you arrived. And there you are, poor soul, thinking that red has fallen behind black and will soon start appearing with greater frequency.

You can see how futile and rather silly this

approach is. From now on, when the phrase "law of averages" pops into your head, replace it with the synonymous "law of large numbers." And then, to be safe, remind yourself that you are a small number. You rely on the law of large numbers to dictate your play (by knowing expectations and proper strategy), but you can't rely on it to help you predict short-term decisions and results.

The gambler's fallacy and its nearsighted view of the law of averages wouldn't be so dangerous if it just flustered our efforts to be psychic. Particularly in a pure game of chance, it doesn't really matter what reasons we use to select an outcome, as long as we're making sensible bets. The danger comes when players are convinced that their "luck" has to turn around when they're losing. They convince themselves that the law of averages will kick in and start offsetting their losses with wins, that every bad streak must be balanced by a good streak. This kind of thinking can be devastating—to both your wallet and your psyche. Remember, casino games come with a negative expectation; if you're behind, there's no reason to think you won't stay behind. Never, never risk money you're not comfortable risking because you're sure that you're "due."

It's a well-intentioned—perhaps desperate—instance of a "little knowledge is a dangerous thing." You can't allow your knowledge of the long term to affect your strategy in the short term. If a coin lands heads up 10 times in a row, the odds on the next toss are … the same as they always are! Exactly even. Don't bet on tails to even things up. If anything, you may want to take heads just in case the coin is loaded.

LUCK

Perhaps you're asking yourself, after all this mathematical analysis: "What about luck?" Isn't gambling about the rush of adrenaline and the hope that good fortune will smile on you? Well, that depends on the individual. For the average gambler, gambling boils down to the following: getting the most entertainment value for your dollar. If you want to play blackjack blindfolded and make your decisions according to divine inspiration, go right ahead. Just make sure you have a bankroll (and loved ones) that can tolerate this sort of indulgence.

I believe in luck to this extent: You experience good streaks and you experience bad streaks. When every card, roll, or spin goes your way, you feel lucky; when the opposite happens, you don't. Even with this rational approach, I can't resist the temptation to believe that higher forces are on my side when every card in blackjack works to my favor or I keep making points in craps. But the rational part of my mind knows that I'm caught up in a very typical statistical streak. No combination of rabbit's feet, prayers, lucky socks, or hairstyles will affect what happens.

This is not to preach a defeatist attitude—one should feel upbeat and assume the best. But attitude has little to do with gambling. The fact is the smarter you play, the better chance you'll have of getting lucky. The greater the house advantage, the more "unlucky" you will be in general. In the long run, you're going to end up with no money left when you play a negative expectation game.

What makes gambling tantalizing is that no one can tell what the short run will bring. No one is more lucky than another person.

THE ESSENTIALS FOR UNDERSTANDING WHAT YOU'RE UP AGAINST

- Probability is the likelihood that a specific event will occur. Odds are one way to express probability.
- Casino odds describe the amount you'll be paid for a winning bet. This will rarely be the same as the true odds for that bet.
- Expectation tells us how much we can expect to win or lose on a particular bet.
- The house edge indicates the percentage of a bet that, on average, will go to the casino.
- In general, the lower the edge, the greater your chance of winning.
- Most casino games are set up in the house's favor—they have a negative player expectation.
- The longer you play a negative expectation game, the more certain it is that you will lose.
- You can win money playing a negative expectation game in the short term.
- Positive expectation games are rare. Such games will make you money in the long run—if you can stick around for the long run.
- Lucky or unlucky streaks only refer to what happened in the past. Future events are subject to the same probability rules no matter what happened in the past. These events are random and unknown—unless you believe in tea leaves, oracles, or fortune cookies.
- Understand the value you get from gambling. Put a price tag on it.
- Enjoy yourself!

3

BLACKJACK

With all due respect to the other casino offerings, none has quite the aura and appeal of blackjack. It has a certain cachet that other games lack.

Blackjack (also known as "*21*") attracts both casual and discriminating players. It is the most popular table game in the casino, bringing in the most revenue and taking up the most floor space. (Notice the emphasis on table game—slot machines are far and away the biggest earners and space consumers for today's casinos.) It steadily earns 50% of the table game revenue and 15% of the overall casino revenue. A single blackjack table can bring in a handsome $500,000 per year for the casino management.

Why is blackjack so popular? One factor is its simple play. The object of the game is to beat the dealer. You achieve this by having a hand of higher value than the dealer's without going over 21.

Blackjack thus embodies the quintessential "us against them" casino game. The enemy is clearly defined—it's the house, which is personified by the dealer. When the dealer fails, everyone succeeds. This creates an air of high drama and table camaraderie—who doesn't love to root against the dealer? (Just remember that we're talking about playful antagonism, not pathological hostility.)

Moreover, players get to guide their own destiny by using skill. Few other casino games allow the player to make meaningful decisions during play that actually affect the outcome of their wagers.

Perhaps the biggest ingredient in blackjack's success is that everyone knows—or thinks—the game is beatable. Thanks for that go to Edward Thorp and his 1962 bestseller *Beat the Dealer*, which detailed the proper strategies for playing blackjack and introduced the world to card-counting (we'll learn more about that on page 64). Soon after the book's publication, blackjack overtook craps in the popularity game and it hasn't looked back since.

Ever since Thorp's book, blackjack has been a much-studied, analyzed, and pored-over game. There are more books, articles, video tapes, and computer programs dedicated to blackjack than any other casino offering. Yet for all the information available, it's safe to say that 90 percent (if not more) of blackjack players don't play the game properly. The average blackjack player often possesses one of two contradictory and erroneous perspectives: some think the game is beatable just by virtue of sitting at the table (certainly not true); others think that you can improve your chances of winning *only* by counting cards (also untrue).

What is true is that with proper play—and *without* card-counting—you can shave the house's advantage to almost zero. Unfortunately, few people know how to play properly. That's why the casinos didn't cart away everyone's favorite game a long time ago. Casinos have profited very nicely from the combination of blackjack's player-friendly reputation and the public's ignorant play.

Yet playing well requires only some familiarization with strategy guidelines called *basic strategy*. I mention it here to get you prepared. You'll be hearing a lot more about it. It is the guts of the chapter because it's the average player's best chance for glory. It involves a little

BLACKJACK PAYS 3 TO 2
Dealer must draw to 16 and stand on all 17s
INSURANCE PAYS 2 TO 1

study, but it's neither complex nor daunting. You don't need to have uncanny powers, just a few hours of patience and practice.

HOW BLACKJACK IS PLAYED

Blackjack can offer the most satisfying brand of game-playing in the casino; it involves suspense, decision-making, and skilled play. Better yet, it's usually the best bet in the house. All you have to do is learn the right way to play it. Let's go do that.

THE SCENE
The blackjack table is a semi-circle. Most often it will have a padded edge for up to seven seated players to lean on as they play, although a few tables seat only five or six players. (See above.) The dealer stands opposite the players, at about where the center of the circle would be. On the table in front of him is a large, inset tray of chips with several "columns" of each chip denomination.

Because the blackjack table design is used as a standard for most new casino games, you may accidentally sit down at a blackjack-sized table that isn't actually dealing blackjack. Make sure to carefully take in your surroundings and read the information posted at a table before you sit

down at what you assume is a blackjack game.

One feature that immediately distinguishes blackjack from other games is the simplicity of the table layout. The design will probably include only betting circles for each player and two lines of house rules.

There are two broad categories of blackjack games you'll encounter: *hand-held* and *shoe games*. Hand-held games are played with either one or two standard 52-card decks and are—would you believe—dealt out of the dealer's hands. In these games, the cards are dealt face-down in front of the players, who are then allowed to touch them. (In general, hand-held games have a lower house edge. They can be found throughout Nevada and Mississippi, though you should keep your eyes peeled for them wherever you go.)

Shoe games use four, six, or eight decks. The shuffled cards are dealt from a rectangular wedge-shaped holder (called, you guessed it, a *shoe*) which is placed to one side of the dealer. These multiple-deck games are played face-up and the players cannot touch the cards. One bit of lingo you should be aware of: All the cards in play at a table may be referred to as a *pack*. Throughout this chapter, though, I'll most often use the more common "deck" in discussing the cards in play.

The next thing to look for is the table minimum. Minimum bets range from $2 or $3 to as much as $100. Concomitant bet maximums could be $500 to $5,000. As with any game you want to play, make sure you are aware of the betting limits of the table you choose. The lower-limit blackjack tables tend to be crowded so you might have to wait to get in. Don't play above where you and your bankroll are comfortable just so you can sit down right away.

THE ACTION

Once you do get a spot at the table of your choice, you'll need to buy in for chips. The hand begins once all players place the chips they want to wager in their betting circles on the table.

The action of blackjack centers around the decision-making process as you try to beat the dealer in one of two ways:

1) By getting a higher total than the dealer without exceeding a total of 21; or
2) By having the dealer go over 21 when you don't.

If you succeed in that endeavor, your bet is paid off at 1 to 1.

Card Values

The first thing you'll need to know in blackjack is how to value the cards and thus value your hand:

- Cards 2 through 10 have their face value; that is, a 2 is worth 2, a 10 is worth 10, etc.
- Jacks, queens, and kings (*face cards*) are all valued as 10. Face cards and 10s will be collectively referred to as 10s throughout our discussion.
- Aces can be counted as either 1 or 11, depending on the player's preference.
- Suits have no meaning.

Hand Values

The hand value is determined by simply adding the card values. For example, a jack and queen is a hand of 20. An ace and 4 can be either 5 or 15. A hand of 4, 8, 6 has a value of 18 as does a hand of jack, 3, 3, 2. Now's a good time to get familiar with some of the special nomenclature you'll hear at the blackjack table.

Blackjack: The name of the game refers to the most desirable hand—a total of 21 on your first two cards. To earn this title, and the larger 3 to 2 payoff that goes with it, they must be your *first* two cards. Therefore, blackjack (also called a *natural*) can only be an ace and a 10-value card. A dealer with blackjack beats everyone at the table—even those with three or more cards totaling 21. Only a player with a natural is immune; she will tie with the dealer.

Stiff hands: Stiffs are hands that have a chance of busting with one more card. Hands with a total value of 12 through 16 fall into this category.

Pat hands: Hard hand totals (see below) of 17 through 21 are considered *pat* hands. Players following basic strategy—or even basic instinct—would not draw additional cards to a pat hand.

Soft hands and *hard hands:* Because the ace can be counted as either an 11 or a 1, it gives a hand some flexibility. A *soft hand* contains an ace that can have either value without making the hand bust. Any initial hand of two cards that contains an ace is a soft hand. For instance, if you are dealt an ace and 3, you have a soft hand of 14. If you draw another ace after that, you would have a hand that could be worth either 5 or 15 (ace, ace, 3).

A hand that lacks the flexible, dual-purpose ace—either because the ace can only be counted as a 1, or because it doesn't have an ace at all—is a hard hand. So a hand of 9 and 5 is a hard 14. If you were to draw an ace to this hand, you would have a hard 15.

Let's say you are dealt an ace and then a 6, you have a soft 17. Your next card is a 10. Now you have a hard 17. (The distinctions between hard and soft hands will make more sense when we get to the strategy charts.)

One more little tidbit before we move on: Technically, of course, a blackjack is a soft hand, but you would have to be soft in the head to want to count that hand as an 11. In fact, many casinos won't even give you the option to be so goofy—they pay you your 3 to 2 and don't allow you to play out the hand.

Push: Push is the gambling word for tie. Any hand of equal value to the dealer's hand is a push and no money is exchanged. A push is indicated by the dealer with a knock or pat on the table in front of the player's cards.

Bust: When a hand value exceeds 21, it is *busted*, and it loses. One important way the casino gets an edge in blackjack is that the player can bust (and therefore lose) before the dealer has to play. If the dealer busts, all players who have not busted are automatic winners no matter the value of their hands.

The Deal

In the hand-held and shoe games, dealers perform a specific shuffle procedure as indicated by each casino's regulations. The final step in the shuffle of most shoe games is the cutting of the pack. The player who was dealt the plastic *cut card* on the previous hand has the honor of cutting the cards after the shuffle. The dealer divides the deck at the randomly selected point where the player inserted the cut card, taking the front cards and placing them behind what was the last card.

With the cards now properly arranged in the shoe, the dealer again takes the cut card and slides it between two cards in a roughly predetermined spot in the pack. When the cut card comes up in the course of the deal, the dealer finishes out the current hand, and then reshuffles. The level of *penetration*—how far into the pack the dealer goes before reshuffling—will vary from casino to casino. (Later on, we'll find out why penetration is something card-counters and pit bosses obsess about.) In a shoe game, you'll see the plastic card again after two-thirds to three-quarters of the pack has been played through. In hand-held games, the dealer generally has more flexibility but will shuffle up about halfway through the pack.

The dealer has one last ritual to complete before we really start to play: *burning* or discarding the top card. In hand-held games the burn card is placed at the back of the pack, face-up. In the shoe games, a separate, plastic discard tray positioned to one side of the dealer holds the burn cards. Other discarded cards (taken from players who bust, for instance, and all cards at the end of a hand) will be handled in the same manner.

With the cards shuffled and arranged, and all bets in place, the deal begins. The deal and the play always start at *first base*, the seat directly to the dealer's left, and end at *third base*, the position on the dealer's right. (These names are merely designations. Although wrongheaded players will try to tell you otherwise, seating arrangements have no effect on play.) Using a graceful, sweeping motion, the dealer quickly places one card in front of each player and then himself. The second card is dealt to the table in the same fashion. In both the shoe and the hand-held games, one of the dealer's cards is face-up (cleverly called the *upcard*) and one is dealt face-down (the *hole card*).

HOW THE HAND PLAYS OUT

Part of the pleasure of blackjack is the amount of control players have over the play of their hands. Below are descriptions of the choices you have as a player—*hit, stand, double down, split, surrender*, and taking *insurance*. Most decisions are indicated to the dealer through the use of hand motions, not words. Descriptions of motions used in shoe games are included below; for a complete guide to hand motions and other technicalities for both hand-held and shoe games, see the chart on page 42.

HITTING AND STANDING

Once you have totaled your initial two cards, most often you will be deciding whether to hit (be dealt another card) or stand (stay with your current total). If you want to hit, tap the table with your finger. You can take as many cards as you like until you bust or you indicate you'd like to stand. To stand with your current total, wave your hand with your palm down over your betting circle or cards. If you draw a card that makes you bust, your bet will be collected immediately and added to the dealer's tray of chips; your cards will also be immediately discarded.

DOUBLING DOWN

Doubling down provides you with an opportunity to increase your wager in a potentially advantageous situation. You place an amount up to the value of your original bet next to your first wager, and are given one final card. In the

SIGN LANGUAGE

Whatever decisions are made in blackjack, they must be communicated with unique hand signals; this way all is made universally clear to both the dealer and the eye in the sky. This chart lays out the differences between the hand-held and shoe games so you can look like a veteran no matter which one you play.

	Hand-held game	Shoe game
Pack	One or two decks.	Three or more decks (usually four, six, or eight).
Cards	Face-down.	Face-up.
Card handling	Players can touch their first two cards with one hand only and must hold them over the table.	Players are not allowed to touch their cards.
Hit	Lightly scrape one corner of your first two cards against the felt. (Additional cards are dealt face-up and cannot be touched.)	Tap the table with your fingers.
Stand	Slide the edge of your first two cards under your chips. (Use one hand, don't lift your bet up.)	Wave your hand over your area, palm down.
Split and double down	Lightly toss your first two cards face-up in front of your chips. Place a matching bet next to original bet.	Place a matching bet next to original bet.
Bust	Turn your cards face-up.	No motion necessary. (Look of defeat optional.)
Blackjack	Turn your cards face-up immediately.	No motion necessary. (Look of victory optional.)

shoe game, this card is sometimes placed perpendicular to your original two cards to indicate that it is the last card to be dealt to that hand. (In the hand-held game, the dealer places the double down card under your chips. You are entitled to look at that card right away, but you'll appear so much more suave if you wait until the rest of the hands at the table are resolved.)

Any payouts or losses are now based on your new total wager. The only exception to this is if the dealer has blackjack; in that case, only your original wager is lost.

SPLITTING PAIRS

If your first two cards are a pair, you have the opportunity to play two independent hands. Indicate you want to split your pair by placing an equivalent stack of chips next to your original bet. The dealer will separate your cards,

deal another card to the first hand, resolve the hand with you, and repeat the same procedure with your second card.

With the exception of split aces (a very strong hand where most casinos allow only one more card on each ace) each "hand" is played out as any other would be. For example, many casinos will let you double down after splitting so you might have four bets out, in total. Actually, you could have even more than that. Some casinos allow you to re-split up to four hands; if you double down on each of them … you could end up with eight times your original bet on the table.

One other thing to keep in mind when you split pairs of aces: If you are then dealt a 10-value card to one of them—that is 21, but not blackjack—you will be paid 1 to 1 (if you don't push a dealer's 21 or lose to a dealer's blackjack), not 3 to 2.

In nearly all casinos, all 10-value cards are considered pairs. So you could split a jack and a king. But you don't ever want to split 10s, so forget I mentioned it.

INSURANCE

After everyone has been dealt the initial two cards, if the dealer's upcard is an ace you'll be offered insurance before anything else happens at the table. A side bet that supposedly "protects" against the dealer's potential blackjack, insurance bets are made at half the value of the original wager. This bet is placed in the stripe on the table that says, "Insurance pays 2 to 1" and, true enough, you will get paid 2 to 1 if the dealer has blackjack. Even though this is the procedural section of the chapter, I can't resist slipping in a bit of advice: Never take insurance. It's a bonehead play for anyone who doesn't know how to count cards.

If a player has blackjack, she can request *even money* when the dealer shows an ace. The rationale behind this bet is that the player with blackjack may push with the dealer and not win at all. If the player is willing to accept even money (1 to 1 instead of the usual 3 to 2 blackjack payout), she can get paid before the dealer checks the hole card for blackjack. This is also one of the easiest decisions in blackjack—never do it.

Once these side bets are made, the dealer sometimes peeks at his hole card, either by actually bending up a corner to see it or using a special device. (Some casinos, anxious to speed up the game, have their dealers check the hole card under a 10 even though this is not a situation in which players would be offered insurance.) If the dealer does peek and does have blackjack, players' blackjack hands push, all other hands lose, and insurance bets are paid off. The next hand is then dealt out. If the dealer does not have blackjack, players' naturals are paid immediately, insurance bets are taken away, and the other hands are resolved individually as described above.

SURRENDER

This option is not offered in many casinos, but it is advantageous for the player. (Guess that explains why it's not in many casinos. In fact, it will rarely be included on the table as part of the rules. You'll need to ask if it is in effect when you sit down.) If available, this option allows you to "surrender" half of your bet rather than playing out the hand. It's important to note that surrender is not an option after you have taken other action on your hand, for example, hitting, splitting, or doubling down. Surrender is the only blackjack play made verbally—players wishing to do so say "surrender" before playing their hand out.

Of the few casinos that offer surrender, almost all offer "late surrender," meaning it is only an option after the dealer has determined that his hand is not a blackjack. "Early surrender" is nearly extinct but may occasionally pop up in a promotion. Under this rule players can surrender before the dealer checks for a natural. This is very player-favorable—if you can manage to find it.

DEALER'S PLAY

When the final player has completed making decisions on her hand, it is then the dealer's turn. The dealer, however, has no decisions to make. The casino makes the decisions for the dealer and prints them clearly on the table for all to see. Most use one of two rule variations.

1) "Dealer stands on all 17s": Under this rule, the dealer hits his hand until it totals at least 17. Here a dealer would stand on a hand of ace, 6 as well as 10, 7 and 8, 4, ace, 4. This is the most common rule.

2) "Dealer hits soft 17s": Playing under this rule, the dealer hits his hand until it totals a hard hand of 17 or higher or a soft hand of 18 or higher. So the dealer would hit ace, 6, but would stand on 4, ace, 3. This rule increases the house advantage.

BLACKJACK PROTOCOL AND ETIQUETTE

Blackjack is a social game. Mostly it will be fun and you'll develop a sense of camaraderie with your fellow players. No doubt you'll also encounter grumblers and blowhards. To avoid some awkward moments and minor scolding from dealers, you'll need to know the proper etiquette:

• Use clear, unambiguous hand signals, not words.

• Never touch your bet once the cards are dealt.
• In a face-up game, don't touch your cards.
• In a face-down game, use only one hand to touch your cards, don't bend them, and be sure to keep them over the table.
• Place your chips in one neat stack in the center of your betting circle, with the largest denomination on the bottom of the stack.
• You can tip the dealer by placing a bet for him. Place the tip on the edge of your betting circle closest to him. If your hand wins, the dealer keeps that bet and its winnings.
• Some players, particularly big bettors, like to get into a situation where they are playing the dealer one-on-one. For the sake of diplomacy, ask a lone player if he minds you joining in.
• While you should feel free to keep a basic strategy card with you as you play, you shouldn't refer to it on every hand. Before you sit down to a live game in a casino, practice with a deck of cards or a computer program (see Appendix D). You should have the fundamentals down pat before you venture out to the tables.
• Be prepared to make your play when the dealer gets to you. You can put out your chips for doubling or splitting before the dealer turns to you.
• Let the dealer know if an error was made. Don't let him pass you by if you wanted a card. Do your own totaling—dealers are human and sometimes make mistakes. (You don't have to correct them if the mistake is in your favor.)
• Be sure to ask about your point total if you're confused. Especially in the shoe game, players can ask advice from the dealer about how to play the hand. It's also pretty likely that you'll get advice from other players at these games, whether you want it or not. In that case, just smile and follow the strategy that comes a bit later in this chapter. No doubt, you'll be smiling long after the know-it-all next to you isn't quite as jovial.

BLACKJACK STRATEGY AND SMARTS

Blackjack is a game of skill. Why? Because you can make meaningful decisions about your hand. The right decisions will help you win (or save) money while the wrong decisions will cost money. Ever since the mathematicians, theoreticians, and thinkers tackled the game from the late 1950s on, there has been no doubt that there's a smart way to play blackjack.

The correct rules for decision-making are collectively known as basic strategy. These rules aren't a matter of guesswork or hunches. They have all been worked out to a mathematical certainty. The reward for skillful play? A game that will have a house edge in the vicinity of 0.5%. You can't do much better than that in the casino.

If you want to cut to the chase and find out how to give yourself the best advantage, check out the basic strategy charts on pages 48 and 49. For most beginners, that's a bit overwhelming. So let's start with an understanding of what players are up against.

THE HOUSE ADVANTAGE

It's difficult to say what the house edge is against a "typical" blackjack player. With most other bets in the casino, once the bet is made, the player's work is done. The mathematical edge then has its way with the wager. Because players make decisions on how to play their hands, the picture is fuzzier with blackjack.

Taken to a ridiculous extreme, the world's most self-destructive player could purposely lose every hand by drawing until he busts. The house edge against this demented player would be 100%. (Okay, nitpickers, I grant that a player may be forced to win on a blackjack, since many casinos won't let you hit a natural.) Blackjack is the only game where you can guarantee a loss after placing your bet. By extension, much of the house edge is dependent on the player's decisions.

Estimates are occasionally printed that the house edge against the uninformed player ranges from five to ten percent. These seem to be gross overestimates. Most people—either through common sense, intuition, or mimicry of their fellow players—would not create such a large casino advantage. A weak player is likely to face a house edge in the range of two to three percent. That's not so awful compared to many other casino bets, but one can do much, much better as we'll soon see.

Where does the house get its advantage aside

from incorrect play? The only built-in edge that the house has over the player is this: If both the dealer and the player bust, the dealer wins. It's quite simple and quite effective. By playing out the hand first, the player who goes over 21 has his money swept away. The money doesn't come back if the dealer also busts. It's the one "push" that the house always wins. Considering that even a basic strategy player will bust about 16% of the time, this is a sizable advantage.

There are certain tools in the player's arsenal that counter the house's built-in advantage:

- The player gets paid 3 to 2 for blackjack whereas when the dealer gets blackjack, the player only loses his original bet.
- The player can make his own playing decisions whereas the dealer has to stick to preset rules.
- The player can double down when it's advantageous to do so.
- The player can split when it's advantageous to do so.
- The (card-counting) player can take insurance when it's advantageous to do so.

THE BASIS FOR BASIC STRATEGY

Mark Twain once defined a classic as a book that people praise and don't read. Much the same can be said about basic strategy. Most people who play blackjack regularly claim they know basic strategy. Once *you* know basic strategy, you'll discover that the majority of these players are sadly mistaken about their knowledge.

So just what is basic strategy? Basic strategy is a set of rules that tells you the correct way to play your hand when you have no knowledge of the remaining cards. Basic strategy reveals when to hit, stand, double, split, or surrender by taking into account only two things: your cards and the dealer's upcard.

In the long run, basic strategy will allow you to win more and lose less. The rules of basic strategy will maximize your expectation, bringing you very close to even with the house. It's the best you can do without counting cards—and that's pretty good. "Basic" doesn't mean watered down or simplified; think of basic as meaning essential and integral to your success.

How important is it to play basic strategy? Nothing is more important. It's true that the best way to win is card-counting since that may bring you into positive territory in the battle against the house. But the only way to start is with basic strategy—that's where everyone must begin. And playing by basic strategy is a lot easier than card-counting.

Is it worth it? The answer can best be seen in dollars and cents. Let's assume that you play $10 a hand and 100 hands per hour. If you're a weak player, you're expected to lose about 2.5% of what you wager in the long run. If you're a basic strategy player, you can probably knock that down to 0.5%. Doesn't sound like much of a difference? Those percentages translate to dollars. The average hourly loss for the weak player is $25 (100 hands × $10 × 2.5%). The average hourly loss for the basic strategy player is $5 (100 hands × $10 × 0.5%). That's a $20 difference. Put it this way: The weak player loses five times as much money as the basic strategy sharpie.

Where does basic strategy come from? It's a reflection of statistical truths. For each hand you hold versus each possible dealer upcard, there exists only one correct action with the highest mathematical expectation. The expectation is calculated inside a vacuum; the only considerations are your cards, the dealer's upcard, and the rules of the game. The other cards in play and the other players are of no account; it's as if you always have a freshly shuffled deck of cards and it's just you and the dealer at the table. That's the perfectly sensible way to approach the game. It's the only way—unless you count cards.

As much as I like to provide you with enlightening bits of math, I will not even attempt to explain the derivation of basic strategy. It is beyond the scope of the book (and my brain cells). Suffice it to say that the correct playing decisions were derived and confirmed through calculations using combinatorial analysis and through computer simulations involving the play of millions and millions of hands. (After Edward Thorp, Julian Braun, an IBM programmer, was the next major figure in perfecting basic strategy. Since then, analysts such as Peter Griffin, Stanford Wong, and Don Schlesinger have brought the strategy to a pristine state of reliability and have adapted it to a variety of playing conditions.)

THE BASICS OF BASIC STRATEGY

Proper basic strategy always gives you the best house edge possible—it milks the game for all it's worth. However, no strategy has value if it's not used. That's the reason for the simplified strategy presented below. If you used only these simple rules, you would still be ahead of the vast majority of the people playing the game.

Using this simplified strategy will give the house back somewhere around 0.3% of an advantage as compared to a full-fledged, game-appropriate strategy. That should still leave you at under a 1% house edge for most conditions. That's not a bad place to get started if working with fewer rules makes you more comfortable. Eventually, you should learn the complete blackjack basic strategy. But for starters, this abbreviated basic strategy will hold you in good stead.

Hard hands
• 9 or lower → hit.
• 10 or 11 → double down if your total is more than dealer's upcard; hit otherwise.
• 12 through 16 → hit when dealer's upcard is 7 or higher; stand otherwise.
• 17 or higher → stand.

Soft hands
• 13–18 → double down when dealer's upcard is 5 or 6.
• 17 or lower → hit.
• 18 → hit when dealer's upcard is 9 or more; stand against a dealer's 2, 3, 4, or 7.
• 19 or higher → stand.

Pairs
• Always split a pair of aces or 8s.
• Never split 10s, 4s, or 5s.
• Split all other pairs when dealer's upcard is 6 or less.

Never take insurance.

This is not child's play. If you want to give general advice on what to do with a player's 13 vs. a dealer's upcard of 7, you have to consider 7-6, 8-5, 9-4, 10-3, 2-3-3-5, etc. Oh yes, and then the results of every possible combination of hits to your cards and to the dealer's cards must be taken into account. God bless the pioneers and their wonderful calculating machines.

After all the analysis and simulation, the ultimate message is that one should make the play with the highest expected return. This is the guiding principle of all smart gambling. Each play in the basic strategy is the one that will give you the highest average expected return over the long run. Why do you hit 13 versus a dealer's 7? Because it will return more money to you in the long run as compared to standing. The same reasoning applies to every basic strategy decision.

BASIC STRATEGY CHARTS

Okay, the sidebar above is the spoonful of sugar version of basic strategy. Not so bad, right? Now come the full charts. They add the niceties that the above strategy left out, and they will usually shave the casino edge to 0.5% or lower.

Don't let the charts send you into a sensory overload tailspin. I find them comforting, but many think they are confusing and intimidating. They actually aren't hard to comprehend. Remember that they are just a tool for your benefit—not a test.

You can anchor yourself pretty quickly. All you have to know are your cards and the dealer's upcard. Use the shading of the decisions to give you a sense of how plays cluster. There are no mysteries of the universe involved; the charts just tell you whether to hit, stand, double down, or split. Don't try to swallow everything in one gulp. Glance at the charts and then head over to "Basic Strategy Insights" so you have some understanding of what makes them tick.

How the charts work:

- All the possible values of the dealer's upcard are listed at the top of the chart.
- All the player's possible hands are listed on the left side of the chart.
- To find the correct play decision, simply find the box where your hand (the row) and the dealer's upcard (the column) intersect. You will find one of four decisions: stand, hit, split, or double down.
- The charts are broken down into hard totals, soft totals, and pairs. The pairs section is divided into two parts to account for whether the rules allow you to double down after splitting or not.
- Look at the appropriate section for your hand. When you have ace-2, think "soft 13," not just "13." When you have 7-7, think "pair of 7s," not just "14."
- Realize that the hand totals represent your hand at any given time. They can be made up of more than two cards. After you take a hit, retotal your hand and base your next decision on the new total. Remember, any hand that counts an ace as 11 is a soft hand but soft hands become hard hands once you can't count the ace as an 11 anymore.
- Surrender is not included in the charts, since it is uncommon. It will be covered in its own section.
- Here's an example of how to use the charts: You're playing a multiple-deck game and you're dealt a 4 and 2, and the dealer has a 6 as her upcard. Your total is 6. You look at the chart and see that for any total of 8 or less against a dealer 6 (or any dealer upcard for that matter), you hit. So you hit and get an ace. You now have a soft total of 17 (4 + 2 + ace). You cross-reference that total against the dealer's 6, and you discover you should double. But you

can't, because you've already taken a hit. So you hit instead (if you can't double when it says "double," you hit, unless there's an asterisk after the "double") and get a 7, which gives you a hard total of 14 (4 + 2 + ace + 7). The chart says to stand. You stand, the dealer flips over a 10, and hits a 3, to get 19, and you lose. You did everything right. That's how the chart works—and how the cookie crumbles.

I'll also let you in on a little secret. If you're going to master only one chart, make it the one for multiple decks. First of all, most games you'll encounter will use multiple decks. Second, if you use the multiple-deck strategy for single-deck games, you'll only be sacrificing a few hundredths of a percent in return. So why did I even include the chart for a single-deck game? Because I think many people take pride in knowing the fine points of the activities they pursue and in playing with the utmost precision. If you are of the mind-set (as I hope you will be) to seek out the games with the smallest house edge, you will often play in favorable single-deck games. If you're going to make that effort, you may very well want to squeeze every last cent out of the game by using the perfect strategy.

BASIC STRATEGY INSIGHTS

The indisputable reason for following basic strategy is that the mathematicians and the computers have proven it's the right way to go. However, even if you don't have the computer analysis in front of you, you can find the rhyme and reason in basic strategy. There are patterns and trends that guide our way.

To be honest, the point of all the following chitchat is to help you memorize the basic strategy chart. Something has a much better chance of sticking with you if it makes sense. But you won't be able to reason out every basic strategy move—some things you'll just have to take on mathematical faith. I recommend that you refer to the strategy charts as you read through the next sections.

THE DEALER'S CARD

Basic strategy, as we discussed, is all about getting the highest expected return. Sometimes

Here are the blackjack strategy tables. Across the top of each chart is the dealer's upcard, and along the left side is your hand. At the intersection is the action you should take.

MULTIPLE-DECK BASIC STRATEGY

	2	3	4	5	6	7	8	9	10	Ace
8 or less	Hit	Hit	Hit	Hit	Hit	Hit	Hit	Hit	Hit	Hit
9	Hit	Double	Double	Double	Double	Hit	Hit	Hit	Hit	Hit
10	Double	Double	Double	Double	Double	Double	Double	Double	Hit	Hit
11	Double	Double	Double	Double	Double	Double	Double	Double	Double	Hit
12	Hit	Hit	Stand	Stand	Stand	Hit	Hit	Hit	Hit	Hit
13	Stand	Stand	Stand	Stand	Stand	Hit	Hit	Hit	Hit	Hit
14	Stand	Stand	Stand	Stand	Stand	Hit	Hit	Hit	Hit	Hit
15	Stand	Stand	Stand	Stand	Stand	Hit	Hit	Hit	Hit	Hit
16	Stand	Stand	Stand	Stand	Stand	Hit	Hit	Hit	Hit	Hit
17–21	Stand	Stand	Stand	Stand	Stand	Stand	Stand	Stand	Stand	Stand
Soft 13	Hit	Hit	Hit	Double	Double	Hit	Hit	Hit	Hit	Hit
Soft 14	Hit	Hit	Hit	Double	Double	Hit	Hit	Hit	Hit	Hit
Soft 15	Hit	Hit	Double	Double	Double	Hit	Hit	Hit	Hit	Hit
Soft 16	Hit	Hit	Double	Double	Double	Hit	Hit	Hit	Hit	Hit
Soft 17	Hit	Double	Double	Double	Double	Hit	Hit	Hit	Hit	Hit
Soft 18	Stand	Double*	Double*	Double*	Double*	Stand	Stand	Hit	Hit	Hit
Soft 19–20	Stand	Stand	Stand	Stand	Stand	Stand	Stand	Stand	Stand	Stand

*If unable to double in these circumstances, stand. In all other cases, hit when unable to double.

NO DOUBLE AFTER SPLIT

	2	3	4	5	6	7	8	9	10	Ace
2, 2	Hit	Hit	Split	Split	Split	Split	Hit	Hit	Hit	Hit
3, 3	Hit	Hit	Split	Split	Split	Split	Hit	Hit	Hit	Hit
4, 4	Hit	Hit	Hit	Hit	Hit	Hit	Hit	Hit	Hit	Hit
5, 5	Double	Double	Double	Double	Double	Double	Double	Double	Hit	Hit
6, 6	Hit	Split	Split	Split	Split	Hit	Hit	Hit	Hit	Hit
7, 7	Split	Split	Split	Split	Split	Split	Hit	Hit	Hit	Hit
8, 8	Split	Split	Split	Split	Split	Split	Split	Split	Split	Split
9, 9	Split	Split	Split	Split	Split	Stand	Split	Split	Stand	Stand
10, 10	Stand	Stand	Stand	Stand	Stand	Stand	Stand	Stand	Stand	Stand
Ace, Ace	Split	Split	Split	Split	Split	Split	Split	Split	Split	Split

DOUBLE AFTER SPLIT ALLOWED

	2	3	4	5	6	7	8	9	10	Ace
2, 2	Split	Split	Split	Split	Split	Split	Hit	Hit	Hit	Hit
3, 3	Split	Split	Split	Split	Split	Split	Hit	Hit	Hit	Hit
4, 4	Hit	Hit	Hit	Split	Split	Hit	Hit	Hit	Hit	Hit
5, 5	Double	Double	Double	Double	Double	Double	Double	Double	Hit	Hit
6, 6	Split	Split	Split	Split	Split	Hit	Hit	Hit	Hit	Hit
7, 7	Split	Split	Split	Split	Split	Split	Hit	Hit	Hit	Hit
8, 8	Split	Split	Split	Split	Split	Split	Split	Split	Split	Split
9, 9	Split	Split	Split	Split	Split	Stand	Split	Split	Stand	Stand
10, 10	Stand	Stand	Stand	Stand	Stand	Stand	Stand	Stand	Stand	Stand
Ace, Ace	Split	Split	Split	Split	Split	Split	Split	Split	Split	Split

SINGLE-DECK BASIC STRATEGY

	2	3	4	5	6	7	8	9	10	Ace
7 or less	Hit	Hit	Hit	Hit	Hit	Hit	Hit	Hit	Hit	Hit
8 (6,2)	Hit	Hit	Hit	Hit	Hit	Hit	Hit	Hit	Hit	Hit
8 (5,3)	Hit	Hit	Hit	Double	Double	Hit	Hit	Hit	Hit	Hit
9	Double	Double	Double	Double	Double	Hit	Hit	Hit	Hit	Hit
10	Double	Double	Double	Double	Double	Double	Double	Double	Hit	Hit
11	Double	Double	Double	Double	Double	Double	Double	Double	Double	Double
12	Hit	Hit	Stand	Stand	Stand	Hit	Hit	Hit	Hit	Hit
13	Stand	Stand	Stand	Stand	Stand	Hit	Hit	Hit	Hit	Hit
14	Stand	Stand	Stand	Stand	Stand	Hit	Hit	Hit	Hit	Hit
15	Stand	Stand	Stand	Stand	Stand	Hit	Hit	Hit	Hit	Hit
16	Stand	Stand	Stand	Stand	Stand	Hit	Hit	Hit	Hit	Hit
17–21	Stand	Stand	Stand	Stand	Stand	Stand	Stand	Stand	Stand	Stand
Soft 13	Hit	Hit	Double	Double	Double	Hit	Hit	Hit	Hit	Hit
Soft 14	Hit	Hit	Double	Double	Double	Hit	Hit	Hit	Hit	Hit
Soft 15	Hit	Hit	Double	Double	Double	Hit	Hit	Hit	Hit	Hit
Soft 16	Hit	Hit	Double	Double	Double	Hit	Hit	Hit	Hit	Hit
Soft 17	Double	Double	Double	Double	Double	Hit	Hit	Hit	Hit	Hit
Soft 18	Stand	Double*	Double*	Double*	Double*	Stand	Stand	Hit	Hit	Stand
Soft 19	Stand	Stand	Stand	Stand	Double*	Stand	Stand	Stand	Stand	Stand
Soft 20	Stand	Stand	Stand	Stand	Stand	Stand	Stand	Stand	Stand	Stand

*If unable to double in these circumstances, stand. In all other cases, hit when unable to double.

NO DOUBLE AFTER SPLIT

	2	3	4	5	6	7	8	9	10	Ace
2, 2	Hit	Split	Split	Split	Split	Split	Hit	Hit	Hit	Hit
3, 3	Hit	Hit	Split	Split	Split	Split	Hit	Hit	Hit	Hit
4, 4	Hit	Hit	Hit	Double	Double	Hit	Hit	Hit	Hit	Hit
5, 5	Double	Double	Double	Double	Double	Double	Double	Double	Hit	Hit
6, 6	Split	Split	Split	Split	Split	Hit	Hit	Hit	Hit	Hit
7, 7	Split	Split	Split	Split	Split	Split	Hit	Hit	Stand	Hit
8, 8	Split	Split	Split	Split	Split	Split	Split	Split	Split	Split
9, 9	Split	Split	Split	Split	Split	Stand	Split	Split	Stand	Stand
10, 10	Stand	Stand	Stand	Stand	Stand	Stand	Stand	Stand	Stand	Stand
Ace, Ace	Split	Split	Split	Split	Split	Split	Split	Split	Split	Split

DOUBLE AFTER SPLIT ALLOWED

	2	3	4	5	6	7	8	9	10	Ace
2, 2	Split	Split	Split	Split	Split	Split	Hit	Hit	Hit	Hit
3, 3	Split	Split	Split	Split	Split	Split	Split	Hit	Hit	Hit
4, 4	Hit	Hit	Split	Split	Split	Hit	Hit	Hit	Hit	Hit
5, 5	Double	Double	Double	Double	Double	Double	Double	Double	Hit	Hit
6, 6	Split	Split	Split	Split	Split	Split	Hit	Hit	Hit	Hit
7, 7	Split	Split	Split	Split	Split	Split	Split	Hit	Stand	Hit
8, 8	Split	Split	Split	Split	Split	Split	Split	Split	Split	Split
9, 9	Split	Split	Split	Split	Split	Stand	Split	Split	Stand	Stand
10, 10	Stand	Stand	Stand	Stand	Stand	Stand	Stand	Stand	Stand	Stand
Ace, Ace	Split	Split	Split	Split	Split	Split	Split	Split	Split	Split

that means letting the dealer incur the risk; sometimes it means that we have to take the risk. This section will give you some insight into the dealer's risk and how we respond to it through basic strategy.

Why is the dealer's upcard so crucial? Because it's a gauge of the strength or weakness of the dealer's hand. Look at the chart below, which shows the probability of the dealer achieving certain hands based on his upcard. Many of the trends of basic strategy should make sense once you digest this chart and what it means.

So what does it mean? The chart shows that on upcards of 2 through 6 the dealer has a much higher probability of busting than on cards 7 through ace. Certainly when the dealer has a 2–6 up, he has a much higher chance of having a stiff hand. So cards 2 through 6 "show weakness." The upcards 5 and 6 are particularly weak—note that they have the highest bust percentages. Conversely, when he has a 7 through ace up he has a good chance of having a pat hand. We can say that he is "showing strength" or that he has "strong card" up.

What do we do with this information about when the dealer's vulnerable or formidable?

As you can see on the basic strategy charts, when the dealer has a weak card we let him take the chance of busting. Whenever we have either a stiff or pat hand, we stand when the dealer has 2 through 6. (There are exceptions when we have 12, which we'll cover later in the chapter.) Why should we take the chance of busting before the dealer plays out his weak

hand? The dealer has to draw to stiff hands, but the player doesn't.

But when the dealer has 7 through ace, he has a good chance of reaching a pat hand. Even with just a 7, the dealer will make a pat hand 74% of the time. That means he'll bust only one-quarter of the time. In that case, we hit our stiff hands, because it would be too risky to stand and hope the dealer will bust. The likelihood that the dealer will bust is too small; we must take the risk upon ourselves.

You can now see the basic strategy in its broadest terms. When we have a stiff and the dealer has a weak card, we stand and hope for the best. When we have a pat hand, we always stand because there's too much risk in hitting. When we have a stiff and the dealer has a strong upcard, we must hit and try to improve our hand, even though we'll often bust in the attempt. Also, we often double down and split against the dealer's weakest cards (check out those strategy charts!) so we can capitalize on his weakness.

The Rule of 10

Notice that when the dealer shows a 7, he's most likely to get a 17, a full 37% of the time. When he shows an 8, he's most likely to get an 18, and so on. This is no surprise since 16 out of 52 cards in a deck are 10s. Tens are by far the highest percentage cards in the deck, making up 30.8% ($^{16}/_{52}$) of a deck's composition. That's why it's so easy to assume—and the numbers bear it out—that the dealer will have a pat hand when showing a 7 through ace.

Probability of Dealer's Final Hand Based on Upcards (Excluding Blackjacks)

Dealer's Upcard	17	18	19	20	21	Bust
2	14%	13%	13%	13%	12%	35%
3	13%	13%	12%	12%	12%	38%
4	13%	12%	12%	12%	11%	40%
5	12%	12%	12%	10%	11%	43%
6	17%	10%	11%	10%	10%	42%
7	37%	14%	8%	8%	7%	26%
8	13%	36%	13%	7%	7%	24%
9	13%	10%	36%	12%	6%	23%
10	12%	12%	12%	36%	4%	24%
Ace	19%	19%	19%	18%	8%	17%

Although it's an oversimplification to say that the dealer's upcard is a "stiff card" or a "pat card," it's not totally amiss and it reinforces much of basic strategy.

This fact has led many blackjack players to rely on the informal "rule of 10," which generally assumes that every unseen card—particularly the dealer's downcard—is a 10. This rule of thumb is basically sensible and can help you get your bearings as you try to learn basic strategy. You look at the dealer's 6 and you say, "Hey, he probably has 16. He'll probably bust. There's no way I'm hitting my 13."

However, there are times when this rule of 10 will mislead you and take you away from proper basic strategy. For instance, you're supposed to hit 12 against a dealer's 2. If you're stuck on the 10 notion, you'll avoid hitting because you'll assume a 10 is waiting to bust you. You'll also think that the dealer has a 10 underneath and will receive another 10 to get his "bust deserts." It doesn't work that way. Remember that 10s make up *only* 30.8% of the deck. There are plenty of other cards that the dealer can use to improve on his 2—and there are plenty that won't bust you on a hit.

Furthermore, you can't blindly double down on every dealer's weak card, simply assuming that a 10 lies unseen and will give the dealer a stiff. For instance, doubling down on 7 against a dealer's 6 is not proper basic strategy—which means it's not the best way to make money.

Final Hand	Dealer's Probability
12–16	0%
17	14.52%
18	13.93%
19	13.35%
20	17.96%
21	7.29%
Total non-busted hands	
excluding blackjack	67.05%
Bust	28.20%
Blackjack	4.75%

Let's chew on the chart above for a moment. The first thing that we can take away from it is something that may seem obvious but is often unappreciated: The dealer will either have blackjack, end up with a final total

of 17 to 21, or bust. Therefore, all player hands of 16 or less are equivalent. Any time you stand below 17, your only hope of winning is to have the dealer bust. As you can see, this only happens 28.2% of the time. If the dealer has a weak card up (2–6), we can expect him to bust about 40% of the time. That's an improvement and incentive for us not to hit our hands—but it's still not even the majority of the time! When players complain (as we all do) that the dealer never seems to bust, they may not appreciate how under no circumstance does the dealer have a 50% chance of going over 21. More than two-thirds of the time we have to contend with a hand of 17 or above.

LESSONS THROUGH HANDS

In order to gain insight and comfort with basic strategy, it's useful to look at some hands, particularly the "troubling" ones. Included in these sections are some interesting hands and some of the misconceptions and common mistakes that plague players and please casino owners. We'll take a quick look at the general reasoning behind what we do and the math that assures us of our right move. (The costs for making certain playing decisions are based on a six-deck game. They are estimates based on data provided in *Professional Blackjack* by blackjack maven Stanford Wong.)

Stiff Hands

No one likes hitting a stiff hand. You have a 15 and the dealer has an 8. You know you have to hit, but you can't bear the thought of busting. Well, it has to be done. It's as much fun as going to the dentist. But, like that dental visit, sometimes it's the right thing to do, and, if you don't do it, it's going to hurt more in the long run.

Players who don't hit their stiff hands against the dealer's strong cards of 7 through ace are guaranteed losers. It doesn't matter if they complain that they "always" get a 10 and are afraid to bust. When the dealer has a 7 or higher showing, he will have a pat hand 74% of the time. That means we will win only one of four hands if we stand on a stiff hand—because our only hope is that the dealer will bust. That's too much to give away; we have to take a shot at improving our hand. Yes, we lose money when we hit a stiff against the dealer's strong hand, but we lose *less* than if we stood. Want a tired old aphorism to drive home this lesson? Here you go: "A penny saved is a penny earned."

In blackjack you sometimes have to settle for the lesser of evils; sometimes the best decision is only the best because all the other ones are worse. Let's look at some painful examples of your hand vs. the dealer's upcard:

16 vs. 7: Plenty of poor players fail to hit in this situation. It's almost understandable, but remember that the probability chart on page 50 shows that the dealer will bust only 26% of the time. We must chase him. On average, standing will cost us about $48 of every $100 we bet in this situation. Hitting will cost "only" $41 per $100. The hit decision saves us $7.

16 vs. ace: Okay, this is the kind of hand that makes the slot machines seem appealing. But that doesn't mean you go down without a fight. If you moan and stand, you'll lose $66.50 per $100 bet. If you moan and hit, you'll lose $51.60. That's an improvement of $14.90.

12 vs. 2 or 3: These are the only two exceptions to our perfect rule of never hitting a stiff when the dealer has a weak card. These hands reveal the flaws in the "rule of 10"—you can't assume that the dealer will have a 10 underneath and then get another 10 to bust. Tens are by far the most common value, but other values still make up nearly 70% of the deck. Enough good things can happen to the dealer's 2 (or 3) or to your 12 to make it worth hitting. The cold hard numbers? When you stand against a deuce, you'll lose $29.20 of every $100 bet in that situation. When you hit you'll only lose $25.30. The "odd" but absolutely correct choice will save you $3.90 per $100. Against a dealer 3, hitting will save you about $1.90.

16 vs. 2: You'll occasionally see a misguided soul hit this. The only explanation is that the player bought into a pseudo-profundity offered up by dealers and players: "A deuce is like an ace for the dealer." That bit of nonsensical wisdom likely derives from some of the arguments that tell us to hit 12 vs. 2. But if you look back to page 50, you'll see that the dealer busts 35% of the time with a 2, yet only 17% of the time with an ace. A hit will hit you for $47 per $100 bet, while standing sanely will only cost $29.

Heeding table chatter, instead of the strategy chart, wastes $18 in the long run.

Doubling Down

An examination of doubling down is the perfect antidote to our discussion of those depressing stiff hands. There will be no talk of cutting our losses here; this is where we get to stick it to the casino. Used according to basic strategy, doubling down will increase our profits in the long run.

Take a quick look back at the basic strategy charts (pages 48 and 49). There are two things to note about double down decisions. First of all, we double on our strong hands of 10 and 11 because if we get a 10, we have a very powerful hand. In that way, we capitalize on our strength. But we're also focusing on taking advantage of the dealer's weakness. We often double down against the dealer's weak cards—particularly the cream-puff 5 and 6. We can't be timid about putting more money out on the table in a favorable situation. The right doubles are crucial to your overall expectation.

It's important to note that some casinos restrict doubling down to hands of 10 and 11. This is an unfavorable rule that costs us 0.26%, but it still leaves us with the bulk of doubling down opportunities. Full loss of doubling privileges would cost us about 1.56% in expectation. That means correct doubling on 10 and 11 accounts for about 1.3% of our expectation. If you ever come across a game where you can't double at all, make sure you walk away on the double.

Interestingly, in terms of percentage, you often lose more when you double down than when you simply hit. Lose more? Didn't I just assure you that proper doubling down will increase your profits? Well, both statements are true. Let's say you make a $100 bet. You receive a 10 and the dealer gets a 7 up. If you simply hit (the wrong move), you'd have a 29% percent advantage, which means you'd expect to make a $29 profit on average. If you double down, you would only have a 23.5% advantage on your bet. Why the decrease? Because you're restricting yourself to only one card. In the case where you hit, you'd have the option to draw more cards if need be. However, the 23.5% double down advantage is on *twice* your bet. That means an average profit of $47 ($200 × 23.5%). A smaller edge on more money means more money in your pocket, which is what we count up (not percentage points) at the end of the session.

Let's look at a few hands that may make you do a double take (your hand vs. dealer's upcard):

11 vs. 10: This is a costly way to wimp out. Yes, the dealer has a big card, but so do you. Sure, you'll make $11.70 per $100 when you hit, but you'll turn that into $17.80 when you double down.

11 vs. 6: If you're afraid to put more money on the table for this hand, it's time to find another game—like tiddlywinks. Just hitting will profit you a cool $34 per $100 on average. Doubling makes a mockery of that decision: It earns you $68 per that same $100.

Splitting

One should learn all the split plays on the basic strategy chart, but there are a few mantras that even the rankest amateur must pick up.

Always split aces. This move has common-sense appeal. The split gives you two promising hands rather than a soft 12. (Remember, however, that you'll usually be able to take only one card on each ace.)

Never split 5s. The total of 10 will give you plenty of opportunity to get smart money on the table by doubling down. Who would get excited about starting with a hand of 5 anyway?

Never split 10s. Don't get greedy. Sure, a 10 is a nice base to work from, but it's not worth breaking up a powerful 20. Let the existing strong hand bring in the money. Some players think they're being clever by splitting 10s against a weak dealer card like a 6. That seems sensible—start with a 10, exploit the dealer's vulnerability. But, in this case, a bird in the hand is more valuable. Standing on 20 will make you a meaty $70 profit per $100 bet. The split will double your risk and drop your earnings down to $56.70.

Always split 8s. Oh sure, we split eights because … hmm … not so obvious is it? A lot of players, novice and veteran alike, are flummoxed by the obligation to split 8s. It's particularly a mystery against a strong dealer upcard. In some instances we can provide a common-sense rationale for splitting, but in others (like this one) we have to defer to the all-knowing computer.

There are three reasons why we split cards: We do it to win more, lose less, and, best of all, turn a loss into a win. A quick perusal of the strategy charts will bring some non-shocking news: We're aggressive with our splitting when the dealer has a stiff card, especially 5 or 6. Even among those splits, some are defensive in nature (lose less) while others are offensive (win more). Here's a bevy of examples that reveal how splitting has a split personality.

Lose Less

8†8 vs. ace: Is splitting this the essence of insanity? Nope. We know 16 is an awful hand. That's part of the reason why we always split 8s. Still, starting out with an 8 against an ace may not seem like a preferable alternative. Neither scenario is good, but yes, splitting is better. And here are the numbers to prove it: Playing it as a 16 we'd expect to lose 51.4%, which is $51.40 lost for every $100 bet. Playing it as two hands we'd expect to lose 19.3% on each hand. Multiplied by two (for our two hands), we get a net loss of 38.6% of the original bet. So we can save $12.80 in this unsavory situation.

9†9 vs. 9: A pair of nines sure seems formidable and, in most cases, it's a money-maker. However, against a fellow 9, we split in order to lower our losses. Standing on 18 vs. 9 will cost us $18.50. The split knocks that down to $9.50.

Win More

9†9 vs. 6: A hand of 18 is perfectly fine against a 6. Stand on it and you'll make $28 for every $100 bet. But split it and you'll be making $38.70 (when you can't double after split) or $43.90 (when the double after split option is available). All splits of 9s and aces against dealer's 3 through 7 improve on already profitable hands. And, yes, you have to split 9s versus 8. Playing for the "tie" by assuming the dealer has 18 will win you $9.90. Going for the jugular will improve that to $21.20.

4†4 vs. 6: Fours are in need of a little boost to make them worth splitting. That boost comes in the ability to double down after you split. When a split 4 is blessed with a 5, 6, or 7, you need the ability to cash in with the double.

SUPER NATURAL

Ah, blackjack. How do I love thee? Let me count the ways. First of all, a blackjack is a happy event because it's the most powerful hand one can get. You're guaranteed not to lose. But a natural's true delight comes from its 3-to-2 payoff. Much of this book's number-crunching is devoted to how various bets in the casino drain our money without our full awareness of why or how. Let's turn the tables a moment and discover just how valuable a blackjack is to the player's expectation.

Let's assume that you're playing the game in its pure (if not quite as prevalent) form: single-deck. What are your chances of getting a blackjack? To receive an ace as your first card, you have a chance of four (number of aces) out of 52 (total number of cards). To receive a 10-value card as your second card, you have a chance of 16 (number of 10-value cards in deck) out of 51 (total number of cards minus the first card you received). As we know from Chapter 2, the probability of both these things happening is $4/52 \times 16/51$. But that's not the only way to receive a blackjack; you can also get a 10 as your first card ($16/52$) and then an ace as your second ($4/51$).

So our total probability of getting a blackjack dealt in a single deck is both of these possibilities added together:

$$(4/52 \times 16/51) + (16/52 \times 4/51) = 32/663 = 0.0483 = 4.83\%$$

Thus, we have our first golden nugget of info about this glorious outcome. Overall, you can expect to receive a blackjack 4.83% of the time, or once in every 20.7 hands. (Remember that that's an average; don't assume the dealer, the house, and the fates are cheating you if you don't see a blackjack in 50 or 100 hands.)

Now we must consider the times when the dealer duplicates your blackjack and thus negates your 3-to-2 windfall (arrgh!). The chance of the dealer having an ace is $3/50$ (remember that your hand holds one ace and two cards from the deck), and her chance of then getting a 10 is $15/49$ (you have one 10 and three cards are gone from the deck). We also have to account for the reverse order: dealer gets a 10 ($15/50$) and then an ace ($3/49$). So we have the following:

$$(3/50 \times 15/49) + (15/50 \times 3/49) = 9/245 = 0.0367 = 3.67\%$$

Now we have another tidbit to keep in mind for a single-deck game. When you have a blackjack, the dealer will rain on your parade 3.67% of the time, which is once in every 27.2 hands in which you have blackjack.

To calculate our "natural" advantage, we need to know how often the dealer won't duplicate a blackjack. So:

P(dealer doesn't have blackjack when we do) = 1 − 0.0367 = 0.9633 = 96.33%

Now, we can see what the expected return is for our getting paid 3 to 2 on blackjack. Remember that the dealer has just as much of a chance to have blackjack as we do, but we don't have to pay the dealer 3 to 2. So here's how it breaks down:

Player advantage =
[(player bj) × (no dealer bj) × (payoff)] + [(dealer bj) × (no player bj) × (payoff)] =
[(.0483) × (.9633) × (+1.5)] + [(.0483) × (.9633) × (−1)] = 0.0232 = 2.32%

That 2.32% is a substantial part of why players have a fighting chance while playing blackjack. If you could remove all the other outcomes from the game and just alternate blackjacks with the dealer all day long, you would never have to work another day in your life. Alas, that's not the case, and the blackjack advantage is only a major part of your fight to get near even in the game.

Here is something to think about: Never play in a game where blackjack only pays 1 to 1. You'll usually see this in charity games, and you'd better be feeling very charitable if you're going to concede 2.32% to the house. By the same token, if you find a game that pays 2 to 1 on naturals (some casinos will run this promotion), grab a seat, because you're getting an extra 2.32%, which can result in a 1.5–2% overall advantage. Don't pass up an opportunity like this if you enjoy blackjack. These promotions don't come around often and they don't last long.

By the way, an excellent way to find out about blackjack promotions is to get on the mailing list of as many casinos as you can. An easy way to do that is to sign up for a slot card even if you have no intention of ever dropping a coin in a machine.

When you play your 4s as an 8 and hit them, you can expect to win $11.30 on average. Splitting *without* the ability to double after splitting will only get you $6.40. When the rule is in effect, you get bumped up to $19.30 on the split. In a single deck, you actually double down on the 4s when you *can't* double after split (worth $19.30), but you split when you can double after split (worth $24). It's these rule-dependent expectations that make a pair of 4s seem so fickle on the basic strategy charts.

From Loser to Winner

8†8 vs. 7: Here's a hand that goes from pitiful to profitable. Hit the 8s and you stand to lose $40.80. Split them and you're suddenly in the black with an average profit of $21.80. (That figure is based on being able to double after splitting, which is the norm in multiple-deck games.) That's a $62.60 about-face.

7†7 vs. 6: Here the 7s go from losers to bruisers. Standing on the anemic 14 and hoping for a dealer bust will cost you $15.60. Splitting will bring a profit of $19.30, for a gain of $34.90. (The split loses a lot of zip when doubling isn't allowed, with a win of only $5.90. That's still a lot more attractive than a loss.)

The Maverick

9†9 vs. 7: Basic strategy sometimes throws in a monkey wrench. You're cruising along the row of 9-9 basic strategy decisions (it's the same for multiple- and single-deck), and the general impression is that you split on everything from 2 through 9. But wait—there's an exception. You actually stand against a 7. Relying on logic, we can see that our 18 should hold up well against the 7. (Remember the chart on page 50: There's a 37% chance this will end up as a 17 we beat, a 26% chance it will bust, and a 14% chance that it will tie us at 18.) Relying on statistics, we learn that we win $40 when standing and earn only $36.90 when splitting. So resist the urge to split.

Soft Hands

A lot of players have a hard time with soft hands. It's not that the hands are bad to get—they're quite good in general—but they cause hesitation and consternation. To maximize their value, you have to know when to double down. Realize that the ace's flexibility leads to more aggressive play. You also must note that you always hit or double down on soft 17 or below. Let's look at some representative softies:

Soft 17 vs. 7: Too many players make the error of standing with soft 17. You *never* stand on soft 17. Even those who don't always make the mistake succumb to it against a 7 because they think they'll wind up with a push. Standing is not an "even" play. You'll lose $10.40 for every $100 risked in this situation. But a hit will bring a long-term expected profit of $5.50. That's a swing of $15.90.

Soft 17 vs. 6: Don't ever confuse soft and hard—you must read this as an action hand, not a "sit back and wait" hand of hard 17. You don't just hit this soft 17, you double it. Standing (heaven forbid) will get you $1.20, hitting $12.90, and doubling does its magic with a profit of $25.80.

Soft 18 vs. anything: Soft 18 has a unique status in the world of multiple-deck basic strategy. It's the only hand that has three different correct decisions: you stand against 2, 7, and 8; you double down against 3–6; and you hit against 9, 10, and ace (stand against ace in single deck).

You can't always be satisfied by the value of 18. (A side note of interest: The average winning hand in blackjack is a little higher than 18.) Sometimes you must make a pig of yourself to get all the hand's worth. You double down against 6, upgrading from a $28 win to a meatier $38.30. You're in trouble against a 9, but a hit (remember you don't have the bust problems that a hard 18 has) will leave you with an average loss of $9.80. Standing will cost you $18.30. Against a 7, don't mess with the status quo; you don't have anything to gain. Your 18 should dominate the dealer's 7 and it does: You'll win $40.20 on average. Messing around with doubling down will drop your win to $22.40.

SURRENDER
Surrender isn't always available, but you should know what strategy adjustments to make when you find it. The proper strategy for "late surrender" in multiple-deck games is as follows:
- Surrender 16 (but not a pair of 8s) against a dealer's upcard of 9, 10 or ace.
- Surrender 15 against a dealer's upcard of 10.

For single-deck games the rules are the same with one exception—don't surrender your 16 against a 9.

What's the reasoning for when to surrender? It's rather simple. Since you're giving up half your bet, you should surrender only in situations where your expectation is less than 50%. As the limited strategy shows, this doesn't happen as often as you think. In fact, surrender can be very detrimental to fatalistic players who use it every time they have a possibility of busting. I've seen players surrender 12 against the dealer's 8. If they decided to hit, as basic strategy dictates, their expectation would be a

loss of around $27 per $100 bet. That's a $23 improvement over just conceding $50 to the dealer.

Even a pair of 8s against a 10 isn't enough of a loser to warrant surrender. It's close—you'll lose about $49 on average—but it's still better than throwing in the towel. Here's another way to think about surrender: It applies only to hands that you win 25% of the time or less. This is just a different way of looking at the expectation. If you win 25% of the hands, the dealer wins 75%. Therefore, your net loss would be 50%, which is equal to the forfeit you make when surrendering.

It's highly unlikely that you'll find a casino that offers "early surrender," because it adds a sizable amount (0.62 percent) to the player's expectation. In early surrender, you can sacrifice your bet before the dealer checks for blackjack. If a casino runs a promotion offering this golden rule, add these moves to your basic strategy:
- Surrender any hard hand and pair totaling 5 to 7 or 12 to 17, against an ace.
- Surrender hard hands and pairs totaling 14 to 16 against a 10.
- Surrender hard 16 against a 9.

INSURANCE SCAM
The rule is simple for a player who does not count cards: Never take insurance.

First of all, realize that insurance doesn't actually "insure" anything. It's merely a side bet about whether or not the dealer has a 10-value card in the hole when he has an ace showing. The insurance bet is completely extraneous to your main bet. True, if the dealer has blackjack, you'll recover the loss (assuming you don't have a natural) of your main bet. But if the dealer doesn't have blackjack, you lose the insurance bet and you have no guarantee that you'll win your main bet. So don't think that your main bet is protected by this side bet. "Insurance" is just a clever title put on an unfavorable side bet.

But why is the side bet itself a bad proposition for basic strategy players? In order for insurance to be an even bet (with a correct payoff) one in every three cards (33.3%) must be a 10. But, in fact, only 16 out of 52 cards (30.8%) are 10s—that's one in every 3.25 cards.

Let's look at our expectation once some cards are dealt. We'll assume a single-deck game. You receive two non-10 cards and the dealer gets an ace. There are 16 tens among 49 unknown cards (52 cards minus the three you see). Therefore, you have a $^{16}/_{49}$ chance of the dealer having a 10 as the hole card, and a $^{33}/_{49}$ chance of the hole card being a non-10. We'll use a $1 insurance bet (which would win $2) for convenience sake. Our expectation is as follows:

$$E = [^{16}/_{49} \times (+2)] + [^{33}/_{49} \times (-1)] = -0.0204$$
House edge = 2.04%

That's the best-case scenario: a single deck and you have two non-10s. For a six-deck game, the house edge would jump up to 6.8%. (That's because the effect of removing three non-10s isn't as significant with multiple decks as it is with a single deck.)

Unfortunately, most players take insurance when they have a good hand, particularly a 20. When you have a 20, you're using up two 10s from the deck. Therefore, the expectation in a single-deck game is:

$$E = [^{14}/_{49} \times (+2)] + [^{35}/_{49} \times (-1)] = -0.1429$$
House edge = 14.29%

Whoa! And that's when people think they're being smart by "insuring" (see how misleading that term is?) a strong hand. The effect of having 10s in your hand is diluted with more decks, but the same situation in a six-deck game still grants the house a very hefty 8.7% edge.

Even Money

Now let's look at a situation that will consistently provoke incorrect advice from dealers, fellow players, and casino kibitzers. You have blackjack, and the dealer is showing an ace. It seems that everyone will tell you that you should take even money. Everyone is mistaken.

First, realize that taking even money is exactly the same thing as insuring a blackjack. The dealer may offer you even money instead of the insurance, but it's just two ways of reaching the same exact result. How so? Let's say you bet $10 and you're dealt a natural. The dealer shows an ace. You take insurance for $5.

There are two possible results:
- The dealer has blackjack. You push on your main bet, but you win $10 (2 to 1) on your insurance bet. You're up $10.
- The dealer doesn't have blackjack. You lose your $5 insurance bet, but you win $15 (3 to 2) for your natural. Again, you're up $10.

In either scenario, you're guaranteed $10. That's why many casinos will expedite the process by letting you take "even money" rather than actually placing the insurance bet.

Does this sound appealing? Tons of blackjack folk think so. Who would turn down a guaranteed payoff? You should—if you want to make more money in the long run. Here's why this isn't the "best bet" (as you'll often hear) in the casino. Assume a $10 bet and a single-deck game. We have 49 unknown cards: 15 of them are 10s and 34 of them are non-10s. Let's say we take even money/insurance for each of the 49 possible results. We'll end up winning $490 (49 × $10). Alternatively, we just play out the 49 possible hands without taking even money/insurance. We'll end up winning nothing on 15 hands (when the dealer has a 10) and winning $15 on 34 hands, which gives us an overall win of $510 (34 × $15). Last I checked, $510 feels better in your pocket than $490.

Here's the expectation calculation for a $10 bet when you have a natural and don't take even money:

$$E = [^{15}/_{49} \times (0)] + [^{34}/_{49} \times (+15)] = 10.41$$
E per dollar bet = $^{10.41}/_{10}$ = 1.04
Player Edge = 104%

Taking even money is a 100% return, and that's always nice. But a 104% return is even nicer. Why give up the 4% profit to the house? The "experts" who advise you take even money may be well-meaning, but they're well-meaning suckers. Sure, you may experience some short-term frustration when the dealer pushes your natural. But, over time, you'll make more money if you do what you instinctively do to insurance salesmen—ignore them.

(Card-counters know when there's a surplus of 10s remaining to be played. Therefore, they may know when insurance is a favorable bet. However, insurance should never be a consideration for the basic strategy player.)

HOUSE RULES AND THE HOUSE ADVANTAGE

Much of the house edge in blackjack is tied to the house rules. "What do you mean house rules?" I hear you cry. "I thought blackjack was blackjack." No need to panic. The general mechanics of play remain the same for all blackjack games. Once you know the protocol differences between a face-up and a face-down game, no blackjack game will play out in a strange or unfamiliar way.

Nonetheless, there isn't a "standard" blackjack game—no single form of the game is found in all casinos. In fact, you can often find several different forms within the same casino. The number of decks used in a game is but one variable. Scouting out the different games you'll find subtle and less-than-subtle differences in the playing conditions. Any change has some effect—large or small, positive or negative—on the player's expectation. (Remember the expectation is the house edge looked at from the player's perspective.)

How powerful a combo are favorable house rules and the proper basic strategy? Take a look at the rules for the old Las Vegas Strip game, which was the standard until the mid-1960s:

- Single deck
- Dealer stands on soft 17
- Double down on any two cards
- No doubling after splitting pairs
- Pairs can be split up to four times (except aces)
- Split aces only get one card
- No surrender

With these playing conditions, and using the strategy chart on page 49, you would be playing an even game. That's right—no house edge. (If you want to be precise, you would have a microscopic 0.01% edge.) That's why it's the "old" Las Vegas Strip game and an extremely rare offering these days.

The charts below will help you determine the value of a blackjack game. They show you the effect of various playing conditions on your expectation. Rules that increase your expectation (in other words, reduce the house edge) have a plus sign. Rules that decrease your expectation (in other words, increase the house edge) have a minus sign. The old-time Las Vegas Strip rules are used as the "standard rules" for the chart. They establish the player expectation at zero. All rule variations will change that for better or worse.

House-Favorable Rule Variations

Rule	Effect on Player Expectation
Two decks	−0.32%
Four decks	−0.48%
Six decks	−0.54%
Eight decks	−0.58%
Dealer hits soft 17	−0.20%
Double down only on 11 (no soft, no 10, no 9, no 8)	−0.78%
Double down only on 10 or 11 (no soft, no 9, no 8)	−0.26%
Double down only on 9, 10, 11 (no soft, no 8)	−0.14%
No re-splitting of any pairs	−0.03%
Dealer wins ties	−9.00%
Natural pays 1 to 1	−2.32%

Player-Favorable Rule Variations

Rule	Effect on Player Expectation
Natural pays 2 to 1	+2.32%
Double down on any number of cards	+0.24%
Double down after splitting pairs	+0.14%
Late surrender	+0.06%
Early surrender	+0.62%
Six-card winner	+0.15%
Player's 21 pushes dealer's 10-up blackjack	+0.16%
Re-splitting of aces	+0.06%
Draw to split aces	+0.14%

These percentages will vary slightly because the effects change based on the number of decks in play. Still, the charts will give you a good idea of how a particular game stacks up and what to look for (and look out for). Unless you're playing a blackjack variation game or are at a charity event, you're unlikely to encounter some of the ugliest rules, such as a natural paying even money or the dealer winning ties. But they're included for both their informational and shock value.

You can use the charts to estimate your expectation for a particular game at a place you like to play. Start from a base of zero (the standard rules) and then add in the effects of rule changes. Remember, any negative result means that you're at a disadvantage—but smaller is always better. If you get a positive result, stop calculating and start playing! Let's look at some examples of putting these charts into action.

Here's the breakdown on a typical Atlantic City game, where eight decks are used and doubling after splitting is allowed:

Standard rules:	0%
Eight decks:	−0.58%
Double after split:	+0.14%
Player expectation:	−0.44%

Here are the classic northern Nevada rules that you'll find in single-deck games all over Reno and Lake Tahoe:

Standard rules:	0%
Dealer hits soft 17:	−0.20%
Double down on 10 and 11 only:	−0.26%
Player expectation:	−0.46%

Yes, it's possible to locate a game where you would have the advantage without card-counting. There are small casinos in Nevada that offer low-stakes games where the player has the edge. Take a look:

Standard rules:	0%
Double after split:	+0.14%
Player expectation:	+0.14%

That was simple. Why can't every casino do that?

Here's a relatively lousy offering:

Standard rules:	0%
Six decks:	−0.54%
Dealer hits soft 17:	−0.20%
Double down on 10 and 11 only:	−0.26%
Player expectation:	−1.00%

Amazingly, the 1% house edge of this "awful" blackjack game is still better than almost every other bet in the casino.

As you can see from the above examples, blackjack games come in enough varieties to make Heinz jealous. It should also be clear that the standard advice of "play the game with the fewest decks" has to be qualified a bit. *All other things being equal*, it's always better to play in a game with the fewest decks. But casinos rarely make it that easy. They tend to mix and match the rules so that what appeals to the player is offset by something beneficial to the house. As a general rule, multiple-deck games have more liberal rules on splitting and doubling, while single-deck games are more restrictive and also have the dealer hitting soft 17.

There are so many blackjack offerings, you can't afford not to comparison shop. Legwork will pay off. I'm not even talking about scoping out a whole geographic region—you'll sometimes find variations of over one-half percent in the same casino. It's very important to ask what rules are in effect at the table you sit at, because the information is often not posted. Many of the recommended magazines and Internet sites in Appendix D will provide valuable information on where the best games are to be found.

Are these tenths of a percentage point really worth anything to you? The seemingly insignificant can add up. If you played 100 hands per hour at $5 per hand, each 0.1% reduction in expectation would cost you 50 cents (100 × $5 × 0.001). That doesn't sound like much? Let's compare the best game described above (+0.14%) to the worst (−1.00%). That's a difference of 1.14% if you choose the wrong game. For the 100-hand-per-hour $5 bettor, that's a loss of $5.70 per hour on average. I don't want to give that away. Do you?

WHY YOU ALWAYS USE BASIC STRATEGY

The blackjack table is not the place for hunches and intuition. The casino doesn't capriciously decide to change the way it plays the game— "oh, let's have the dealer stand on 15 today"— and neither should you. If you want to play a guessing game that uses cards, baccarat would be a better choice.

By deviating from basic strategy, you're giving money away to the casino. Some players balk at using basic strategy all the time because they're "not computers." Making wrong moves

SINGLE DECK VS. MULTIPLE DECK

If two games have the same exact rules, you want to play in the one with fewer decks. A single-deck game has nearly a 0.6% advantage over its overstuffed eight-deck counterpart, and a 0.3% edge over a double-deck offering. These are significant amounts in the battle for advantage. (However, casinos often burden the single-deck with unfavorable rules that neutralize its inherent advantage.)

But why should the number of decks make a difference? At first blush, it doesn't seem logical. It even seems anti-mathematical. After all, the playing cards occur in the same proportion in every deck—why should it matter if you use one deck or a hundred? The answer is that the effect of removing cards is much larger in single-deck games, and more beneficial to the player. Let's take a look at the different ways multiple decks corrode our advantage.

1. The player gets fewer blackjacks in a multiple-deck game. Blackjacks are very valuable because they pay us 3 to 2 whereas when the house gets a blackjack, we lose only our initial bet. We have already seen (on page 54) how a natural will, on average, occur once every 20.7 hands in a single-deck game. We can apply the same method to determine the likelihood of blackjack in a six-deck game:

$$(24/312 \times 96/311) + (96/312 \times 24/311) = 0.04749 = 4.75\%$$

Now we can only expect to receive a blackjack once every 21.1 hands. It's a small difference, but it adds up over time.

2. While the chance of getting a blackjack decreases with more decks, the chance of the dealer getting a blackjack when you do increases. Why? Because the effect of removing your blackjack cards is greater in a single deck. We saw that in a single-deck game, the dealer duplicates our blackjack once in every 27.2 of our blackjack hands. With eight decks, the same calculations lead us to the dealer having a 4.6% chance of copying our natural. Now, it's once in every 21.9 blackjack hands that we'll be deflated by a dealer duplication.

3. The offensive maneuver of doubling down at the right times is also hurt by multiple decks. Let's say you have a hand of 11 composed of the 3♦ and the 8♣. The dealer is showing the 6♥ as her upcard. (Suits are, of course, irrelevant in blackjack—you'll see why I included them in a moment.) As basic strategy dictates, you double down. What are your chances of receiving your ideal 10-value card?

Let's look at two scenarios: the one-deck game vs. the six-deck game. In both cases, we're working only with the knowledge of three cards removed from the deck. (In basic strategy, our actions are based only on our hand and the dealer's upcard.) The three cards are the 3♦, 8♣, and 6♥. (Again, suits are only relevant for this example—forget I mentioned them after this!) So the single-deck game has 49 unknown cards left and the six-deck game has 309 unknown cards left. The probability of receiving a 10-value card works out as follows:

Single-deck game: 16/49 = 32.65%
Six-deck game: 96/309 = 31.07%

So we have less of a chance to get our dream card in the six-deck game. Why is that? The number of 10-value cards is proportional, so it's not their fault. The problem is the multiples of the cards you've already seen. In a single-deck game, the 3♦, 8♣, and 6♥ are gone for good. But in a six-deck game, each of those particular cards has five "clones" living on in the pack. (Now you know why I emphasized the particular suits.) That means there are 15 extra cards that hurt your chances of getting a 10-value card. If we got rid of those 15 cards, our chances of getting a 10 would be $^{96}/_{294}$ = 32.65%. That, of course, is the same 32.65% chance that occurs with a single deck. Now you have a vivid example of why multiple decks dilute the impact of individual cards being removed—and why doubling down loses some of its oomph when more decks are in play.

4. In a multiple-deck game, standing with stiff totals (12†16) isn't quite as successful as it is in a single-deck game. The dealer has more ways to avoid busting when there are more small cards available. This reduction in busts helps the dealer more than the player because the house rules force the dealer to hit more often than the player does.

That's how more decks hurt us: It's the cumulative effect of fewer naturals, more pushes on naturals, less doubling down success, and less frequent dealer busting. The good news is that the damage levels off as decks increase. There's not a huge difference between playing six decks or eight decks. So we don't have to worry about the casino pitting us against a thousand-deck shoe anytime soon.

that cost you money in the long run is not a declaration of your free will; it's a declaration of foolishness. I can sympathize with players who don't want to feel like automatons, always making moves "by the book."

However, making plays automatically doesn't rob the game of its drama. There's still the mystery of the hole card and the tension of the particular hand's resolution. Think of every correct move you make in a supposedly hazy situation as a tribute to your mastery of the game and a display of your superior knowledge. If you want suspense, hesitate when you have 16 and the dealer is showing 7, and then hit it. Always.

Realize that basic strategy does not negate luck (or short-term fluctuations, as the mathematicians would call it). Do I know what will happen in one night of play? No. You may see your bankroll dwindle as you play perfectly, while the guy who doubles on 12 and stands on all 16s makes a fortune. That's the random nature of the cards. It won't last forever. Luck will conform to statistics, and skill makes long-term luck. If I had to bankroll a player, I would always put my money on the basic strategy player—not the willy-nilly player who's on a hot streak. (Of course, I'd really prefer to back a sharp card-counter.)

You must stick to basic strategy. You must be steadfast and consistent. Even if others make wrong plays and win, it can't sway you. Even if you bust 20 times in a row when you hit your 16 against the dealer's 10, you have to

hit that hand the next time it shows up. Even if the dealer is making six-card 21s, you can't get off your game. Feeling too flustered? Abandon the table before you abandon basic strategy.

YOU LOSE BUT WIN

It's sad to report, but basic strategy is not a magic key to the casino's coffers. It will not make you win every hand. Far from it—you'll only win 47% of hands that aren't tied. Yes, you lose more hands than you win. So how can you be just about even with the casino in terms of expectation? First, you get paid an extra half unit on blackjacks. Second, you get to put more money down on favorable doubles and splits.

BASIC TRAINING

In case you're tuning in late, the author has been incessantly urging all future, former, and current blackjack players to learn basic strategy. How do you go about that? You need to practice. You can deal out hands to yourself and check your decisions against the strategy chart. (The only caveat there is that some less common hands—soft totals and pairs—may not occur frequently enough to properly test-train you.) You can make flash cards—one side should have the player hand and dealer upcard while the other side shows the correct playing decision. Or you can join the silicon age, and pick up a software program in the store or download software from the Internet. (See Appendix D for recommendations.)

You can learn basic strategy in thematic groups. Based on frequency of occurrence, you should first learn strategy for the hard hands, then the split hands, and finally the soft hands. Keep in mind the patterns and reasoning we covered in earlier sections.

If possible, study the strategies that are specific to a particular game you plan to play. As was mentioned before, there is no one basic strategy that's exactly right for every game you play. (That's why I provided charts for single and multiple decks, as well as alterations for when doubling after splitting is allowed.) However, you won't lose much in expectation if you use the multiple-deck strategy as your foundation. We're often talking about small fractions of a percent. If you're unsure about what house rules you'll face when playing blackjack, learn the multiple-deck strategy. It will serve you well.

Ideally, you will memorize the strategy and it will become an automatic response. It won't take as long as you think to know the strategy cold and it will increase your confidence and enjoyment at the table. It's a lot of fun when you play without hesitation, wavering, or indecision. You can play each hand with the confidence of knowing you've made the best possible decision. You'll feel more in control than other players— and, truth be told, you'll feel a bit superior.

But this isn't parochial school. You won't get rapped on the knuckles if you want to play without being a basic strategy machine. Practice until you feel comfortable—then go out and play. If there are decisions that still confuse you (like those pesky soft totals), bring a photocopy of the charts to the table. No casino should have a problem with this. Just make sure you don't slow up play by having to refer to the chart *all* the time.

Basic strategy is the backbone of smart blackjack play. Learn it, love it.

WHAT NOT TO DO

If you spend some time at the blackjack tables, you'll no doubt run into a few players who promulgate the following approaches to beating the game. Some wrongheaded "strategies" for beating the game have become perennial favorites. Like urban legends, they always pop up now and again and they really don't make much sense on close examination. You'll see these approaches, but you shouldn't believe them.

Do as the Dealer Does

This strategy has a deceptive ring of truth. The reasoning goes as follows: "The dealer always takes my money. He doesn't even do any thinking—he just automatically follows the house rules. If I follow the same house rules, I'll be on equal footing with the dealer. Hey, I also get paid 3 to 2 on blackjack. All things being even, the money will really come pouring in." Well, all things are not even. The logic of this approach breaks down when *both* the dealer and the player bust. There is no symmetry in that case—the dealer always wins. As was shown in the analysis of the dealer's hand, the dealer will bust 28.2% of the time. A player mimicking the house will also bust 28.2% of the time. The player is hurt whenever there is a double bust, which will occur about 8% of the time (0.282 × 0.282). That leaves the player with an 8% disadvantage. The 2.3% payoff for naturals cuts into this house edge, but only reduces it to 5.7%. Leave the imitations to Rich Little. Giving up that much of an edge, imitation will be the sincerest form of stupidity.

No-Bust Strategy

No, this strategy doesn't involve only playing against male dealers. Using this strategy, players refuse to take a card if they have any chance of busting. That means never hitting with a hard 12 or greater. The appeal is apparent. It's very frustrating to hit your 13 against the dealer's 7, bust your hand, and then watch as the dealer proceeds to bust her own hand. Advocates of the no-bust approach often fall prey to the "a little knowledge is a dangerous thing" syndrome. They know that much of the dealer's advantage comes from winning double busts, and they submit this strategy as a way to negate that advantage.

However, you give too much away if you never try to improve your hand when you have a chance of busting. Using this approach, you'll end up with a stiff total about half the time. When you have a stiff total, your only hope is for the dealer to bust. But the dealer busts only 28.2% of the time. That's not enough. As was shown in the basic strategy discussions, it's often beneficial to take the chance of busting because it increases your long-term expectation. By "staying in the game" with the no-bust strategy, you'll be giving up a house edge that's been estimated at somewhere between 5% and 8%. With that kind of disadvantage, you and your bankroll won't be staying in the game for very long.

The Hunch Backers

The previous two strategies are certainly misguided, but at least they both have a pseudo-rational basis. However, such introspection and analysis elude the largest group of bad strategy players: the "hunch" players. These players rely on intuition, "a feeling," celestial signs, and biorhythms to guide their play. They just have a sixth sense about what the deal will bring, on how the cards are "running"—without any card-counting skills whatsoever. Or they use a flimsy "system" that was concocted by themselves or some charlatan.

Because they are essentially guessing, they are often wrong in their strategy decisions and perplexingly inconsistent. One time they'll double down on 11 against the dealer's 7, the next time they won't. Their ever-evolving approach to beating the game will lead to ever-mounting losses. They'll smile with satisfaction when their "feeling" is right and curse Lady Luck when their psychic powers are malfunctioning. We all have these feelings and impressions. We all occasionally think that we knew exactly what was going to happen—particularly after the fact. But those who indulge these feelings and fight against the "restrictions" of basic strategy are the casino's best friends. They play by their gut and their money ends up in the casino's stomach.

COST OF ERRORS

What if you ignored basic strategy and just went with the flow? Would the sky fall in? No, you'd just lose money. It's worth examining some of the most common errors to see how much they'll cost the average player. It adds up.

To determine the cost of errors, we'll assume $100,000 worth of play. Sound astronomical? Depends on how you play. It's interesting to see how the time and money add up at the blackjack table. Let's digress for a moment and look at that. At a full table with six or seven players, you can expect to play about 60 hands per hour. At a less crowded table with three or four players, you can assume about 100 hands per hour. Playing one-on-one against the dealer, you can get in over 200 hands per hour. The table below shows how quickly we get to $100,000.

It's quite revealing (and humbling) to see where you fit on this chart. Are you a black chip ($100) player who claims your own table and personal dealer? It's only five hours to 100 grand. Are you a $5 player who squeezes in at the crowded tables? It would take you about 333 hours to get your $100,000 played. That may cover a lifetime of blackjack for you or just be a year's worth of playing every weekend.

Now we go back to the issue at hand. How much will frequent errors eat into our $100,000 figure? That's what the chart on page 64 tells us. This chart uses the assumption that we'll always make the error when the hand comes up. We've already addressed many of these common (and not-so-common) errors in our discussion of strategy; however, shame does have a wonderful way of searing information into your neurons. To put it kindly, these moves are wrong and dopey. If you make them, you will cost yourself money and earn the scorn of the blackjack literate. However, don't expect

Number of Hands Required to Play $100,000				
Average Bet	Hands required to play $100,000	Hours needed to play $100,000 (60 hands/hour)	Hours needed to play $100,000 (100 hands/hour)	Hours needed to play $100,000 (200 hands/hour)
$5	20,000	333	200	100
$10	10,000	167	100	50
$25	4,000	67	40	20
$100	1,000	17	10	5

Cost of Basic Strategy Mistakes

Mistake	Correct Play	Cost per $100,000 Played
Always take insurance	Never take insurance	$279
Hit 16 vs. 2	Stand	$104
Split 10–10 vs. 6	Stand	$95
Hit 11 vs. 10	Double	$82
Stand 16 vs. 7	Hit	$67
Stand 12 vs. 2	Hit	$30
Stand 16 vs. 10	Hit	$27
Double 10 vs. 10	Hit	$24
Stand soft 18 vs. 10	Hit	$20
Double 9 vs. 7	Hit	$16
Stand 12 vs. 3	Hit	$15
Stand soft 17 vs. 7	Hit	$15
Stand soft 17 vs. 6	Double	$11
Hit 8–8 vs. 10	Split	$8
Double 11 vs. ace	Hit	$5

applause from the rank-and-file players when you avoid these mistakes; many of them don't know the correct play and may very well encourage you to make the wrong one.

The data for the cost of errors was taken from Don Schlesinger's *Blackjack Attack* (a bible of sorts for the card-counting crowd). The calculations are based on a four-deck game (some plays wouldn't be errors when playing a single-deck game), and take into account both the cost of the error and the frequency of receiving the particular hand. In other words, if a hand both occurs frequently and has a high penalty for making the wrong move, we're in trouble. (Sharp-eyed readers will note that the error costs don't jibe with the numbers provided when we discussed specific hands earlier— that's because the chart takes into account how often each hand actually occurs when you're playing. It's more of a "real-life" assessment.)

Some of these costs are substantial for any player—look at that insurance premium! Others aren't as impressive. A $5 player who overaggressively doubles 11 vs. an ace will sacrifice $5, but that may be over the course of 333 hours. That's a negligible cost of 1.5 cents per hour. Still, we must return to the theme of this book: Why give the casino anything extra? They have enough already.

As further insight into the chart, let's consider how much are we already giving to the casino. Let's assume a basic strategy player would face a typical house edge of 0.5%. After playing $100,000, the player's expected loss is $500. (That, in and of itself, is an interesting number to play with. Divide that by the hours of play for the various "players" in the chart on page 63, and see what the cost per hour is for those players.) The four most costly errors on the mistakes chart total $560. Consistently making those errors more than doubles the house edge. Granted, most players wouldn't make the mistake of splitting 10s. But you can take an assortment of errors and see how much they take from your pocket.

CARD-COUNTING

If you're like most casino players, you know *of* card-counting, but you don't really know anything *about* card-counting. Is it a myth? No, it's a skill used by thousands of players, and it's cause for (mostly undue) concern for the casinos. Does it work? Yes, the skilled application of a good card-counting system will give the counter a significant long-term edge over the casino. Does it require freakish mathematical ability or a photographic memory? No, just about anyone can learn how to count cards. Is it easy? Not as easy as falling off a log, but it is a skill that can be acquired with a lot of study and practice.

Card-counting is an advanced strategy and is unlikely to appeal to the average casino-goer. It would take a whole book (or several) to cover all the specifics and nuances of a card-counting system. We'll discuss the basics here; if you want to learn more about card-counting, there are plenty of suggested resources in Appendix D.

THE ORIGIN

The age of card-counting began with the publication of Edward Thorp's *Beat the Dealer* in 1962. His title wasn't hyperbole: He laid out specific methods (which earlier "counters" may have intuitively discovered) through which the player could make money off the casino. Thorp's system was actually quite unwieldy and difficult to master. But that didn't stop the casinos from being thrown into a tizzy.

Casinos quickly acknowledged that Thorp's strategy could be used to beat the game. Many casinos implemented very unfavorable rules, but these changes drove away all players, not just the supposed counters. In those early days, the casinos were essentially fretting over a "bogeyman"—there were probably only a handful of players who could successfully use Thorp's system.

The casinos restored better rules, but implemented changes that have remained with the game ever since. Typical games used to be played with a single deck dealt down to the very bottom. Players could raise and lower their bets wildly without the casino giving it a second thought. As we'll soon see, that's no longer the case.

Pit bosses may have been paranoid that a counter lurked in every seat, but the casinos were the ultimate beneficiaries of Thorp's book. They raked in the money as clueless players flocked to this hot and "beatable" game. Thorp's system was refined and ultimately replaced by other counting systems developed by the blackjack intelligentsia. The exploration of card-counting as an art and science has continued to this day.

THE CHANGING DECK

Blackjack isn't like other casino games. When you play slot machines, roulette, or craps, every outcome is independent of previous and future outcomes. Each time these games go into motion—the reels spin, the wheel spins, the dice roll—the outcome is completely random and unpredictable. The odds of a particular outcome are the odds, and they remain steadfast and true no matter what else has occurred.

A deck of cards isn't like any of the other gambling devices. A deck of cards has a "memory"; once a card is removed, the composition of the remaining deck changes. If you have a full deck of cards, you know that you have a 4 out of 52 chance of being dealt a king. What are your chances of getting a king after you see four kings dealt out? Zilch (unless there's something fishy with that deck). Those kings are gone. You *know* something about the deck. It's more than you'll ever know about dice or the random number generators in slot machines.

Here's another way to look at it. When you bet red or black in roulette, either color is equally likely to show up on any given spin. It doesn't matter if you've seen five blacks in a row or nine reds; each spin is a clean slate where red and black are equally likely. Now let's play roulette with a deck of cards. You have 26 red cards (diamonds and hearts) and 26 black cards (clubs and spades). A bet on what color card would come out of a freshly shuffled deck would be a 50–50 proposition—like its roulette equivalent.

Since we're making up this game, let's set out the rules: "Card roulette" is played in rounds, bets pay off even money, and seven players sit at the table. On the first round, six black cards and one red card are dealt. These dealt cards don't go back into the deck; they go into a discard tray. What color should you bet on in the next round? We have some information to work with. The remaining deck is composed of 20 black cards and 25 red cards. You have a $20/45$ chance of getting black and a $25/45$ chance of getting red. Choosing red is a no-brainer; you have a huge advantage. Unlike regular roulette, the odds aren't immutable; the odds shift, they're liquid.

Of course, the tracking of cards in blackjack is not this simple and it rarely brings such obvious advantages. But the point is the same: Cards already played affect your future prospects. Card-counters use information about cards that have been played to assess how favorable the remaining cards are.

Generally, high cards (10s and aces) favor the player while low cards (2–6) favor the dealer. Why do high cards favor the player? When there are more high cards in the deck, the player has a better chance of getting blackjack and having successful double downs. (Yes, the dealer is just as likely to get a natural, but the player gets the 3 to 2 payout.) Also, the player can make certain basic strategy changes, such as not hitting stiff hands. The dealer, however, always has to hit stiffs and therefore has a better chance of busting when a lot of high cards remain. Insurance can become an excellent bet for the counter (only for the counter!) when it's clear that more than ⅓ of the remaining cards are 10s. Conversely, an abundance of low cards deprives the player of high-card benefits. Even more dismaying, the dealer has less of a chance of busting when low cards abound. In those instances, you'll see more incidents of a dealer stringing out cards that benefit a weak upcard.

HOW CARD-COUNTING WORKS

A card-counter doesn't memorize the specific cards that come out of a deck. There's no need for a photographic memory or *Rain Man*–like ability. Card-counting systems simply keep track of the proportion of high and low cards remaining in the pack. The systems determine when the shoe or deck is "rich" in high cards or low cards.

Many systems have been developed. The Hi-Lo is a classic counting system and one often recommended for rookies. Every card is assigned a value as follows:

2, 3, 4, 5, 6 (low cards) = +1

7, 8, 9 (neutral cards) = 0

10, jack, queen, king, ace (high cards) = –1

Players keep a running total of all the cards that have been exposed by adding and subtracting the values of the cards. For example, a sequence of 4, jack, queen, ace, 8, 4, 2, 10, 7, 10 results in a total of –2. For a counter it's a sequence of $(+1) + (-1) + (-1) + (-1) + (0) + (+1) + (+1) + (-1) + (0) + (-1) = -2$. This is called the *running count*. When the count is negative, the deck is rich in low cards and favors the dealer. This makes sense because whenever a high card is played we subtract 1—its play means one fewer high card left in the deck. When the count is positive, the deck is rich in high cards

and favors the player. Similarly, this is sensible because the play of a low card has us adding to the count. A low card out of the deck increases the proportion of high cards remaining in the deck. The running count continually updates you on the composition of the remaining cards. (Notice that the numbers balance out in the Hi-Lo system. There are five +1 denominations and five –1 denominations. That means if you go through a whole deck and count properly, you'll end up with a value of zero.)

If this already seems like too much mental gymnastics to you, you should know that there's another step in most counting systems. Counters need a more accurate measure of the deck's favorableness. The *true count* is arrived at by dividing the running count by the number of decks remaining to be played. (Remember that most blackjack games are multiple-deck games.)

The fewer cards remaining, the stronger the likelihood that the effect of the count will be seen in the coming hand. A count of +6 at the beginning of a six-deck game doesn't mean much, but it's very significant when only two decks remain. That's why counters are always looking for good penetration. (That's not as obscene as it sounds.) Penetration is the measure of how many cards will be dealt before the dealer shuffles. The deeper into the deck that a game goes, the more potent and reliable the counter's information. Counters may tolerate other unfavorable conditions if the penetration on a game is good. If all the cards are dealt out, you would have 100 percent penetration. Such games don't exist anymore. The casino can't afford to have players so confident about the composition of the deck; the house doesn't come close to dealing that far in.

To drive home the message of penetration and general card-counting concepts, let's go back to our "card roulette" game. In this game, our counting system is as follows: All black cards are +1 and all red cards are –1. A positive count means a surplus of red cards remain; a negative means a surplus of black cards remain. If the first five cards dealt are black, we have a count of +5. In this simplistic example, we know exactly what we're dealing with: The chance of getting a red card next is ²⁶⁄₄₇ (55.3%). Red is an excellent bet. Imagine that the next 36 cards dealt split evenly between red and black. Our running count hasn't changed—it's still +5. But now our chances of seeing a red card are $\frac{8}{11}$ (72%). We'd want to make a huge bet on red. Our +5 is much more meaningful (and profitable) down at the end of the deck. The counting in blackjack is nowhere near this straightforward, but the principles remain the same.

How do you capitalize on the count? The primary method is quite simple: You bet more when the deck is favorable and you have the advantage. You want large bets out when the deck is "positive" and small bets out when the deck is "negative." The more positive a deck is, the larger your bet. The simple alteration of bets based on the favorableness of the remaining cards makes up the bulk of the counter's advantage. That's why it's essential for counters to have a sufficient "betting spread." A typical betting spread may move from one unit to five units based on the count. Of course, casinos keep an eye out for wild variation in a player's bets, knowing that it's a sign of a counter.

Counters can also profit from knowing when to deviate from basic strategy. For example, a high enough count could even make splitting 10s a profitable move. However, a smart counter doesn't want to draw attention to himself with too many unorthodox plays. Don't assume that the bozo who makes ridiculous plays at your table is actually a professional blackjack player. That's a generous thought, but counters play most hands according to basic strategy. Indeed, a perfect knowledge of basic strategy is considered a prerequisite for the card-counting craft.

DON'T COUNT ON IT

Card-counting has a certain mystique. It's perceived as a rogue pursuit worthy of Robin Hood, requiring smarts and an outlaw nature. The reality is not so romantic. Counters have to work hard for their money and deal with occupational woes that average folks would rather bypass.

Counters do not gain magical powers by virtue of their skill. They are not winning machines, who can sit at any table and quickly scrape together the down payment for a house. Counters, like mortal players, lose more hands than they win (they just have more money out on the table at the right time). Card-counting is a grind that takes smart, selective, and long-term play.

What can counters expect to gain for their efforts? That depends on the skill of the player, the system used, and the playing conditions. The edge for a capable counter is usually in the range of 0.5% to 1.5%. If a counter averages $25 per bet, plays 100 hands an hour, and has a 1% edge, his expected hourly win is $25 (100 × $25 × 1%). Is this a guaranteed hourly wage? Hardly. It's certainly not guaranteed in the short run. Counters suffer major fluctuations in their bankroll, and they have to have enough money to weather the bad times. In the long run, they should make money, but there are a lot of up and down streaks to contend with. These bankroll swings claim the careers of many an aspiring blackjack "pro."

Then there's the adversarial relationship with the casinos. Despite what the casinos would have you believe, card-counting is not illegal. Thinking is not against the law; when it is, we'll all be in trouble. However, Nevada casinos can *bar* (refuse service to) anyone for any reason because the casinos are considered private clubs. An identified counter may be asked to leave or be told that he can't play blackjack. It can be a badge of honor for the novice counter to hear these words: "Your play is too strong for us. You're welcome to play any of the other games in the casino."

By law, Atlantic City casinos may not bar players for skillful play. However, casinos use other countermeasures (called "counter counter-measures," perhaps?) to keep counters off their game. Some of the approaches to discouraging counters are: using more decks, early shuffling, shallow penetration, and raising the table minimum. It's a very real game of cat-and-mouse going on out there. Pit bosses sensitive to counters (tolerance varies from casino to casino) will do whatever they can to disturb and discourage counters.

That's why counters are preoccupied with real and imagined "heat"—unwanted attention from casino personnel. A major component of successful card-counting is disguising your skill. Counters come up with "acts" or "camou-flage" so the pit employees won't detect their

MYTHS AND MISCONCEPTIONS

Like anything that's popular and much-discussed, blackjack has inspired an assortment of incorrect assumptions and half-baked notions. Here are some of the more common cognitive errors:

The object of the game is to get to 21. You'll often see this written as blackjack's object, particularly in casino playing guides. By now (I hope), we know this to be patently untrue. The object is to beat the dealer. If our best chance of achieving that is by standing on 12, we do it. High hands are only worth pursuing when they lead to more winning hands.

Seat and table selection matter. Players sometimes switch seats at a table so that the cards will "run" better for them. There's no harm in this, but there's really no sense in it either. The order of the cards is random; there's no way of knowing where the good cards are going to come out. At tables full of players grumbling about the dealer's luck and a "bad shoe," I've often noticed there are one or two players who are conspicuously silent. They're making money as hard times have hit the more vociferous players. It usually has nothing to do with the quality of play; it's just that someone is in the right seat and the right cards are coming to her. There's no way of knowing if that luck will continue at that seat, move over two seats, stop completely, or bless the whole table. It's just random; there's no such thing as a "magic seat." For various reasons, card-counters may want to sit at first base or third base, but that's to gain tangible advantages.

On the subject of "hot" and "cold" tables, many gambling experts advise that you leave a table after losing a few bets in a row or don't sit at a table where players are flustered and frustrated by cold shoes. For psychological reasons, this advice is fine. For mathematical reasons, it's suspect. As we've seen, a card-counter could knowledgeably predict when a table will be "cold" (lots of low cards in the deck) or when it will be "hot" (a high proportion of high cards remain). However, the average player would have no concrete way of gauging these conditions. Any assessment for the non-counter would be based on essentially random events. Some writers claim that a "cold" table is telling the non-counter, in an intuitive way, that the deck is negative and laden with low cards. That doesn't seem to hold up under scrutiny. If things have been going poorly for the players, that might mean that a lot of low cards have been dealt. Consequently, there would be an abundance of high cards left in the deck. Instead of leaving the table, the smart move might be to raise your bets and capitalize on the "positive" deck! (I say that for argument's sake—don't follow that advice either.)

In a nutshell, if you don't count cards, you don't really know what's going on with the cards. That doesn't mean you shouldn't leave a table that's vacuuming up your money. You may not really "know" what's happening with the cards, but you know that you're depressed and frustrated. That's a good enough reason to take a break or play elsewhere. Bounce around seats and tables as much as you like. Just make sure that once you settle in you use basic strategy—that will change your overall outcome for the better.

A better system than card-counting. Successful card-counting systems have proven their mettle through mathematical analysis, computer simulation, and real-life play. The fact that the card-counting system works (for a dedicated minority of players) has led opportunists and the overly optimistic to create "better," "easier," and "more profitable" systems to beat blackjack, none of which work. Most of these approaches are just variations on classic betting progressions (which are covered in Chapter 16).

Others work at identifying "streaks" in shoes and clusters of cards without any solid mathematical basis or valid proof that they work. If you want to beat the game, look into a reliable count system and work at it. Other than that, use basic strategy. Don't bother with anything else.

Your fellow players and dealers know what they're talking about. I've been extremely snide and cynical about the advice you'll receive from other casino denizens. I apologize, but I'll continue to be so. Yes, some people know what they're talking about, but too many have too many bad ideas. My purpose is not to have you sneer at the ignorance of others or to make you smug (well, maybe just a little). Social pressures are very formidable, and it's very easy to be swayed into making the wrong move by those who proclaim to know it all—or, perhaps worse, by those who are gently well-meaning yet dead wrong.

Don't be surprised to find that dealers and pit personnel don't know (or don't advocate) basic strategy. It's not that they are aware of something that you aren't—they just never learned the proper play. Enjoy the company of those around you, but don't listen to them. Don't be pressured into taking insurance, sticking on 16 vs. 7, or any other basic strategy gaffe. It's your money on the table. Stay the course.

It's a team sport. You would think that players at a table would be comrades-in-arms, happily allied against the dealer. That notion is sometimes twisted into preoccupation with who's "hurting" the table. The focus of most in-fighting, moaning, and grumbling is when a player takes the dealer's bust card. If you don't want to be the object of constant scrutiny and you want to avoid peer pressure, avoid the "third base" seat. Remember the old "Who's on third?" Well, at the blackjack table the answer is, "Someone with thick skin." Since this seat plays immediately before the dealer plays his hand, it is considered the "anchor" position. It is the focus of much of the fuzzy thinking that pervades the table.

Some people will moan when a player makes a completely correct play, but ends up "taking the dealer's bust card." For instance, you hit your 12 against the dealer's 3. You get a 10 and bust. The dealer turns over a 10, giving him a total of 13. He hits, gets a 7, and has a total of 20. Suddenly, you're the boob who took the dealer's bust card. Even people who know better may groan in a way that you feel is a personal attack. Ignore it all. You're not a boob. Play that hand the same way always.

Even incorrect plays shouldn't draw the ire of other players. But they do—especially if someone loses his bet because of it. This may be human nature, but it's really irrational (perhaps that's also human nature?). The cards are random. No one knows exactly how they'll come out of the deck—not even card-counters. It shouldn't make a difference to any individual player what other players do. But it always seems to catch our attention when someone makes an incorrect play that leads to an unhappy result. Do we notice when the reverse happens? Probably not. Selective perception has us focus on the negatives.

Once you've digested the material in this chapter and are a blackjack whiz, you may find yourself a bit annoyed with other people's wrong moves, especially if they result in a loss for your hand. Don't be a griper or a know-it-all (unless someone specifically asks for help). Remember, those mistakes will help you as much as hurt you over the long run—they're irrelevant. I can remember many times when a "bad" play by someone hurt me. I can also remember many when it helped me.

Casinos cheat. This concern mostly arises out of the hand-held games where dealer manipulation is more plausible. It's extremely unlikely that there's any casino-sanctioned cheating going on in the major gambling markets; they're all highly regulated. Most accusations of cheating occur when players experience losing streaks that they feel are too severe to be purely random. These players usually don't appreciate how streaky the game can be. Your bankroll can go way down due to normal, albeit aggravating, fluctuation. If the casinos were cheating, they wouldn't need to bar card-counters. And the house doesn't need to cheat—it does well enough with the typical house edge against the average player.

ability. There's a lot to cope with for a 1% edge.

It's highly unlikely you'll become a pro, but if you want to make a hobby of learning this fascinating skill, then by all means pursue it. If your curiosity is piqued, you'll never have a shortage of reading. There are plenty of things to learn: optimal bets, risk of ruin, appreciation of risk, camouflage. It makes for fascinating study. In fact, it may be better enjoyed on paper than grinding it out in the casinos.

Don't assume you know anything about card-counting from what you read above. It could be just enough to get you into big trouble. You are not a counter simply because you "sorta" pay attention to how many high and low cards come out. It takes a great deal of practice and a full understanding of your betting system to become an effective counter.

THE CASINO STILL MAKES A KILLING

We've seen that blackjack can be played at a very small house edge with basic strategy. We've seen that blackjack can be played at an advantage by expert card-counters. But we haven't seen casinos remove their blackjack tables. The casinos can easily afford to offer this "beatable" game because very few players beat it.

Casinos don't really have to sweat (though they do) the losses imposed by proficient card-counters. Uninformed players, reckless players, and bad card-counters keep the blackjack tables quite profitable. Tables usually *hold* (win) about 20% or more of the money that players bring to the table. Why is that number so high when the house edge is so low? Because players rebet the money they buy in for. It's a phenomenon called churn. If you buy in for $100, you play through that amount many times—and each time it's exposed to the house edge.

Also keep in mind that a basic strategy player will be making an excellent bet, but will almost always be playing at a disadvantage. The expected losses, though tiny when compared to most other casino games, will add up. They'll add up faster the faster you play. For that reason, a slow, crowded table may be the best bet for the beginner (who doesn't demand too much elbow room). The chart below shows the breakdown of what the $10 bettor playing against a 0.5% house edge could expect to lose per hour under different table speeds.

The player at the ultra-fast table loses at over three times the rate of the player at the slow table. If both players made $25 bets, the difference would be even more striking: $7.50 versus $25. Unless you need your space or get a strong buzz from playing mano a mano against a dealer (put a price on that pleasure), you should opt for the slower table. As an added benefit, you have more time to think out your decisions or refer to a strategy chart at a slow table—provided you sit in a spot where there are some players who play before you.

Speed of Game and Cost per Hour

Kind of Table	Hands per Hour	Average Bet	House Edge	Expected Loss per Hour
Slow	60	$10	0.5%	$3
Medium	80	$10	0.5%	$4
Fast	100	$10	0.5%	$5
Ultra-fast	200	$10	0.5%	$10

Give some thought to your bankroll when you choose your table and your bet. As a rule of thumb, you'll want to have 100–200 times your basic bet available to give you some longevity. Blackjack, like all gambling games, will have wild fluctuations. You can't expect to lose at the tiny hourly rate. But you can expect to have more winning sessions than your comrades at all the other casino games.

BLACKJACK VARIATIONS

Thanks to its popularity, blackjack has inspired a variety of spin-off games and side bets. Many of these gimmick games vanish quickly. None have really improved on the original—certainly not in terms of house edge. You may find the following blackjack variations during your casino travels (Spanish 21 is currently the most popular). They're in a variety of casinos today. I cannot guarantee you about tomorrow.

MULTIPLE-ACTION BLACKJACK

Multiple-action blackjack is about as pure a variation as you can ask for. The rules are the same as traditional blackjack, but players can play three rounds of blackjack using one hand against a single dealer upcard. Players can make either two or three separate bets on the numbered betting spots at their seat. Each spot

represents a separate round of play. (See diagram below.) The player is dealt only one normal two-card hand. The dealer, however, initially receives only one single upcard and no downcard. Players decide how to play their hand against the dealer's upcard—just like normal blackjack. All the options are available: double, split, insurance, etc. If a player busts, all his bets are immediately collected.

After all the players have acted on their hands, the dealer plays out his first round. He draws another card to his one upcard. He then completes his hand following standard house rules (typically standing on soft 17). The dealer then compares his final hand to all the remaining player hands. First-round bets are paid out. The dealer then discards all cards but his original upcard, and proceeds to play out the second round. After the second hand is resolved, the dealer again keeps only his original upcard and plays out the final round.

Realize that each bet is resolved according to the result of its respective round. Suppose you made three bets and you were dealt a 14 and the dealer's upcard was a 9. You hit and receive a 5 for a total of 19. Your play is done. The dealer then plays out his first hand. He draws a king and has a 19. You push the first bet. He discards the king and begins his second hand. He draws a 7. He must draw to his total of 16 and he gets

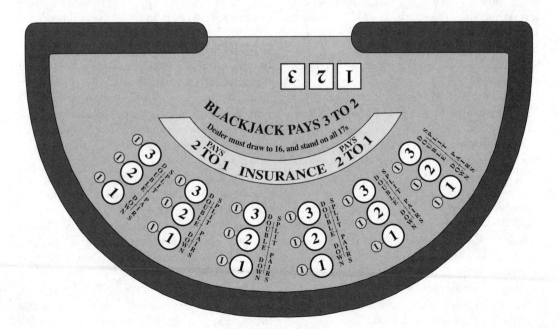

an 8. Bust. You win your second bet. The dealer discards the 7 and 8, and he begins his third hand. He draws an ace and, thus, has 20. That beats your 19. You lose your third bet.

The important thing to keep in mind with multiple-action blackjack is that you're really just playing three separate hands of regular blackjack. You must stick to basic strategy. If you do, the house edge will be the same as for a regular game. Unfortunately, many players change their strategy because they're afraid to bust and lose all their bets when they know the dealer has three different hands to play out. It's tough to lose two or three bets right away, but you still must hit your stiffs when it's called for. Imagine it's just three consecutive hands in a regular game; you would be consistent in that instance (I hope). If multi-action makes you too tentative to play out your hands properly, you shouldn't play it.

For multiple-action play your bankroll must be higher than in regular blackjack. You'll be getting in two or three times as many hands per hour. This will cause greater fluctuation than when you make single bets at a traditional blackjack table.

SPANISH 21

This exotic variation spares nothing when it comes to spicing up blackjack. Spanish 21 has caught on with the gaming public because of its "everything-but-the-kitchen-sink" approach. Take a look at this laundry list of rules and special payoffs:
- Player's blackjack beats dealer's blackjack. Still pays 3 to 2.
- Player's total of 21 beats dealer's total of 21. (In other words, your 5–9–7 beats the dealer's 10–6–5.)
- Double down on any number of cards.
- Split pairs, including aces, up to four hands.
- All split hands can be hit and doubled on two or more cards.
- Double down rescue. If a player is dissatisfied with the doubled hand, he can take back the doubled portion of the bet and forfeit the original bet. This doesn't apply to busted hands.
- Bonus payoffs on 6–7–8, 7–7–7, and 21s consisting of five or more cards.
- 7–7–7 of the same suit and a dealer upcard of 7 wins a jackpot of up to $5,000.

- Late surrender.
- Played with 6 "Spanish packs," each consisting of 2–9, jack, queen, king, ace (no 10s).
- Dealer hits soft 17.

Wow, this wild and crazy game seems to have everything. But did you notice that something was missing? The special 48-card "Spanish pack" doesn't have any 10s. We know that 10s are valuable for blackjacks, doubling down, and making the dealer bust. That difference alone wipes out the advantages of all those player-friendly bells and whistles.

Applying regular blackjack basic strategy to Spanish 21, a player will fight a house edge of over 2%. A basic strategy created specifically for Spanish 21 knocks the edge down to about 0.8%. That's very good, but it's still worse than the 0.5% we can expect in a regular game. In addition, the proper strategy is complex and differs significantly from normal basic strategy: You hit more hands, double less often, and must consider the specific composition of your hand because of the special bonuses.

Except as a novelty, I wouldn't recommend spending too much time or energy on this gimmicky game. Its simpler and more profitable parent is more deserving of your efforts. If you're intrigued and want to learn the right strategy, check out *Armada Strategies for Spanish 21* by Frank Scoblete. It seems to be the definitive (and only) book on the game at this time.

DOUBLE EXPOSURE BLACKJACK

In this variation, sometimes called See Thru Blackjack, both of the dealer's initial cards are dealt face-up. There's no mystery of the hole card. You know exactly when the dealer is stuck with a stiff or when you have to go against a pat hand. You know to hit 19 when the dealer is sitting with 20. Seem too good to be true? It is.

The house charges heavily for all the information it's sharing. The dealer wins all ties (except tied blackjacks—those the player wins). Blackjacks are only paid even money. Players can only double down on 9, 10, and 11. Pairs can only be split once. And, no, you can't take insurance (think about it).

The basic strategy for Double Exposure is, as you might suspect, much lengthier than that for normal 21. Much of it is intuitive, but it's still a lot to digest. Employing Double Exposure basic strategy will put you at a disadvantage of 0.6%–0.9%. It's nice to feel you've got the dealer's number, but the regular game will get you a lower edge with less effort.

SIDE BETS

Side bets are sometimes tacked on to blackjack to jazz up the game and attract more players. The trend in side propositions is to offer jackpot-type bonuses for certain card combinations. One hopes that this isn't the shape of things to come. A cerebral game like blackjack shouldn't be sullied by these silly sucker bets. (How's that for sibilance?) We're already inundated with poker variations that offer jackpot side bets. Call me a purist, but anticipating the next card after I'm dealt an initial ace is drama enough for me.

The only thing you need to know about side bets is that they almost universally carry a steep house edge. Take for example the high-tech 21 Madness that is trying to catch on with players and casinos. You make a one-dollar side bet. If you are dealt a blackjack, you get to press a giant button and a digital readout tells you what jackpot you've earned—between $5 and $1,000. To me, this seems equivalent to putting ketchup on filet mignon, introducing hip-checking to chess tournaments, or colorizing *Casablanca*. If one hadn't noticed, there are plenty of slot machines in the casino for those so inclined.

Stodginess aside, the real rap on 21 Madness is its house edge. Players can expect a blackjack about 1 in every 21 hands. The average jackpot on the side bet is said to be about $14. Shall we look at the expected return if we always make the $1 side bet?

$$E = [^{20}/_{21} \times (-1)] + [^{1}/_{21} \times (+14)] = -^{6}/_{21} = 0.2857$$
House edge = 28.57%

Gag. That is madness.

However, sometimes the suckers get their revenge. One of the first popular side bets was the over/under 13 bet. Players bet on whether their first two cards would be less than or greater than 13. The casino advantage was 6.5% on the over bet and 10% on the under bet. So why has this bet all but disappeared? Card-counters concocted a counting system that made over/under a very profitable investment. The casinos caught on and the bet went under for good.

The best way to find out about any side bet or newfangled twist that can be exploited is to be plugged into Internet discussion groups or subscribe to blackjack newsletters.

VIDEO BLACKJACK

Video blackjack has never caught on like its card-dealing cousin, video poker. One strong reason could be that most machines only pay back 1 to 1 on blackjack. That's a 2.3% bite out of your return. You may find the rare machine that offers the right blackjack payoff, but even then you'll be missing the social interaction that makes for much of blackjack's appeal. (Is it more fun to detest a live dealer than a heartless machine? Perhaps.)

In comparison to slot machines, video blackjack—even with the reduced pay of naturals—offers a better return. If you want to play for low stakes (nickel and quarter machines can be found) or practice your basic strategy in unintimidating conditions, the machines aren't a bad choice (although you can practice on your computer for free). If you play at dollar machines, realize that you're playing at a much faster rate than at the tables. Combine that increased speed with a bigger negative expectation and your losses can mount quickly. The crowded table may suddenly seem quite cozy.

THE ESSENTIALS FOR PLAYING BLACKJACK LIKE A GENIUS

- Blackjack is a game of skill. Played with skill, it's often the best bet you'll find in the casino.
- The object of the game is to beat the dealer. Whoever has a higher hand without going over 21 wins.
- Players who use basic strategy can play nearly even with the house. Blackjack games that carry a house edge of 0.5% or lower are very common.
- Basic strategy is the proper set of playing rules based on the cards in your hand and on the dealer's upcard.
- Basic strategy will maximize your earnings. Deviating from it will cost you money.
- If you don't know basic strategy, you can face a house edge of 2–3%.
- Learn, love, and listen to basic strategy. Sense a theme?
- Never take insurance unless you know how to count cards.
- Try to find the games with the most favorable playing conditions. Games vary in specific rules and the number of decks used. The right combination of rules can even give an edge to the basic strategy player.
- All else being equal, it's better to play against fewer decks.
- Card-counting involves keeping track of the proportion of high and low cards in the deck. Successful counters can gain a significant edge against the house.
- Most players would not want to take on the financial and mental commitment needed to make substantial money card-counting. It's very difficult and risky to pursue as a serious source of income. However, casual players may want to pursue it as a powerful skill.
- Although blackjack can be played close to even with the house or at an advantage, don't expect to win all the time.

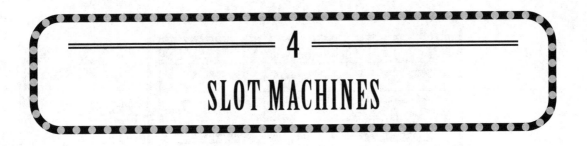

4

SLOT MACHINES

If, in addition to their usual clatter, slot machines could talk, they would probably echo John Lennon's irreverent comment about the Beatles, "We're more popular than Jesus." The slot machines are certainly the ruling deities in the world of casino gambling. They earn 60 to 70 percent of all gross revenue and take up, on average, a similar percentage of casino floors.

Slot machines are the cotton candy and the McDonald's of the casino. Everyone knows that they're bad for you, but few people can resist their junk-food appeal. And so the casino complies by providing rows and banks and carousels of simple-minded and greedy machines. The attraction of slots is self-evident: there's no skill or strategy or ego involved; it's immediately obvious what to do with the machine; and there is an ever-present fantasy that the jackpot will be bestowed on you.

There really shouldn't be much to say about slots. You put your money in and you take your chances. Yet this chapter doesn't end with this introduction. That's because slots are a gambling (and cultural) phenomenon and it's important to take a look at how they take your money as well as some common misconceptions about them. No one is going to be a professional slots player, but there are some smarter ways to play. It's hard to talk sense in the world of slots, because most people just hear "jackpot, jackpot, jackpot" ringing in their ears. Still, let's give it a try.

HOW SLOTS WORK

Slot machines came to the casino world as an unassuming side attraction to keep the wives busy while their more "sophisticated" husbands paid, er, played at the tables. Once on the floor, however, slots managed to stage a revolution of sorts that changed the way casinos viewed the machines—and the wives, too.

THE OLDEN DAYS

The current incarnations of the slot machine are all descendants of the Liberty Bell, created in 1899 by Charles Fey, a German immigrant working as a mechanic in San Francisco. The Liberty Bell operated the way many people still believe machines to work today. Within the casing were three *reels* or metal hoops, each with 10 symbols on it. The symbols were mostly suits from playing cards and, you guessed correctly, one Liberty Bell, crack and all, per reel. When the lever (*arm*) was pulled, the reels stopped sequentially and jackpots were awarded if three of the same symbol came up on the *payline* or row of symbols across the reels. The three Bells gave the largest prize— 10 nickels.

It is very simple to figure out the odds on this machine. Three reels each with 10 potential places to stop: $10 \times 10 \times 10 = 1,000$ possible combinations and only one of these combinations will yield the top jackpot.

It didn't take too long for our strait-laced ancestors to outlaw slot machines. In 1902 they were banned in their birthplace and, soon after that, in all of California and Nevada. But the slot manufacturers didn't give up that easily. First they set the jackpot to 10 free drinks and eventually they changed the coin machines to candy and gum machines, decorating the reels with images of fruit and packs of gum instead

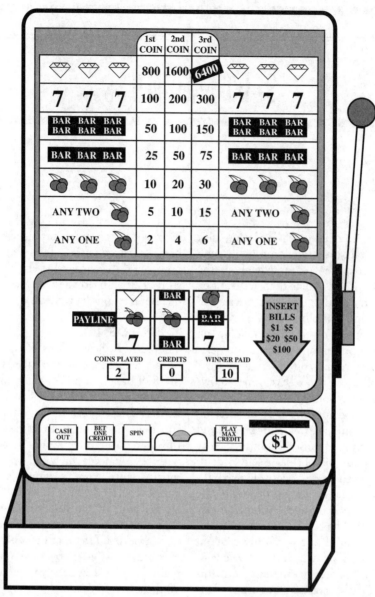

			1st COIN	2nd COIN	3rd COIN			
◇	◇	◇	800	1600	6400	◇	◇	◇
7	7	7	100	200	300	7	7	7
BAR BAR BAR BAR BAR BAR			50	100	150	BAR BAR BAR BAR BAR BAR		
BAR BAR BAR			25	50	75	BAR BAR BAR		
🍒	🍒	🍒	10	20	30	🍒	🍒	🍒
ANY TWO		🍒	5	10	15	ANY TWO		🍒
ANY ONE		🍒	2	4	6	ANY ONE		🍒

PAYLINE

BAR · 7 · 7

COINS PLAYED: **2**   CREDITS: **0**   WINNER PAID: **10**

INSERT BILLS
$1 $5
$20 $50
$100

CASH OUT   BET ONE CREDIT   SPIN   PLAY MAX CREDIT   **$1**

of the forbidden playing cards. We still have the ubiquitous cherries, and the gum labels eventually morphed into the bars we see on the reels today. Yet these symbols are pretty much the only thing old one-armed bandits share with their modern counterparts.

COMPUTER REVOLUTION

The children and grandchildren of the Liberty Bell, all variations of mechanical slot machines, weren't very popular with the players or with the casinos. Players didn't like them because they weren't a "serious" gambling alternative. But slots' popularity was most severely limited by the physical makeup of the machines. Each reel had, at most, 25 *stops* or positions to land on, and that fact alone kept the odds against reaching a jackpot at one level ($25 \times 25 \times 25 = 15{,}625$). Because the casino still needed to make money as well as cover its expenses, the top jackpot would necessarily have to be considerably less than the odds of attaining it. So the most a player might hope to win (betting the then-common nickel) was a couple hundred dollars. Obviously, anything that isn't popular with the players isn't going to be popular with the casino. Until the late 1970s, the largest casinos were home to only a few hundred machines. The picture is quite different today. Thousands of slots populate the casino floor.

Attitudes began to change when the machines began to change. Bally, the pinball machine manufacturer, developed an electro-mechanical machine which, as its name implies, had both electrical and mechanical parts. The betting functions and some aspects of the reel mechanism were electronic, but it was still the mechanical pull of the bandit's arm that wound the springs that turned the reels. Bally knew these machines were still limited by the limited number of possible reel outcomes. The solution was to have more money bet, allowing for bigger payouts. Along came dollar machines that accepted more than one token at a time and had larger *hoppers* (the machine's depository) to accommodate more coins.

That was good, but not good enough. The next modifications of the '80s went hand in hand. The reel mechanism became fully computerized and was thus capable of stopping all the reels quickly and accurately at any given point. How those points were determined is what really revolutionized the industry and made the slots what they are today. The technology that rang in the new age of slots is random number generator software or *RNG*.

The RiNG of Money

Whenever you play a slot machine today, you're playing against a mini-computer. Instead of being locked into one set of odds for payoffs based on the actual number of possible combinations of the stops on the reels, the RNG allows game manufacturers to design and customize the odds of each machine. This feat is accomplished through the use of what might be termed "virtual reels" that are much, much larger than the actual reels. For instance, a four-reel machine may have 20 symbols painted on each reel. But that's just for show. The "virtual" reel governed by the RNG may have 64 stops, making for much bigger jackpot possibilities ($64 \times 64 \times 64 \times 64 = 16,777,216$).

Sets of numbers are assigned to the virtual reel combinations. The RNG constantly—and I mean constantly—cycles through the sets, hundreds every second. When the SPIN button is pressed or the (now meaningless) arm is pulled, the computer chip is signaled to stop the reels at whatever combination of symbols corresponds to the set of numbers the RNG has picked at that millisecond. Most sets are given to the non-paying combinations. The least number of sets are given to the top jackpot reel results. Therefore, the RNG is much more likely to pick a losing combination of reel stops than a combination that pays the big bucks.

In essence, the reels are now simply something to watch for entertainment value. The outcome—a win or a loss—is determined long before the spinning reels stop, and over the long run will comply with the odds set by the casino for that particular machine.

With the possible outcomes increased, and therefore the amount of money to be won increased, the slot machine was no longer merely spinning its wheels. The fantasy of big money won on a single pull had arrived and was here to stay. It's important to remember that every slot machine on the floor today—as well as those that are likely to come in the future—is based on the principle of the RNG. So no matter if the machine has actual reels or a video display, no matter if you are running on a treadmill or being massaged by the chair as you play, no matter if the jackpot is $14 million or $14,000, no matter if you pull the handle or push the button, no matter if you just won on the last seven spins or if you just lost on the last seven spins … no matter what, the slot machine is governed by the microchip that has been preset to an exact, long-term pay schedule. Over millions of spins, the random results of the RNG will conform to the machine's expected probabilities (known to the casino, but not the player).

ENDLESS VARIETY: NAME YOUR POISON

The new technology allows slot designers to get creative at making it entertaining to lose money. In fact, manufacturers increasingly recruit Silicon Valley software designers to create more intricate and more mesmerizing machines with video displays, high-tech sound effects, and multiple games within one machine. All this eye candy is quite pleasing, but the machines still involve no skill. Although the casings and trappings of some of the machines currently on the floors of the

A LITTLE EXTRA SOMETHING

Many of today's cutting-edge machines have lots of entertainment features and additional bonus games. These can appear pretty complicated but the skill required to play (and even to win) still equals zero. You are treated to a lot of sound and fury signifying not much—except the ingenuity of the game designers.

Of course the purpose of the bonus games is to make it hard for you to get up from the machine with any money left. Pinball machines, rolling dice, miniature racing cars, LCD video screens with King Kong climbing the Empire State Building—this is the stuff dreams are made of, right? These machines tend to have lots of people gathered around them, rooting players on. Now, if we're noticing that effect, you can be sure the casinos have been watching as well. They know that while the bonus round entertainment is in effect, not only is the player at that machine not playing (from the casino's perspective read: paying), neither are any of those lollygaggers who are standing about cheering. It only makes sense that in the long run these machines would necessarily pay off less frequently or at a lower rate than "less exciting" ones—part of the payoff is the entertainment value.

Here's a little taste of the smorgasbord that awaits you on the casino floors:

• Multipliers get a little more revved up when bonus entertainment is added. An extremely popular, crowd-pleasing machine is Wheel of Fortune, based on the television game show. When the wheel of fortune symbols line up across the pay-line, the large wheel of fortune atop the machine starts spinning, complete with familiar sound effects. Similar to the TV wheel, there are dollar amounts in the spaces on this machine's wheel and the player wins the amount that it stops on.

• The Elvis slot machine features a CD-ROM player. When a Gold Record symbol on the third reel stops on the payline after three coins have been bet, you can press the PLAY ELVIS button and you'll be treated to live concert footage and a bonus of up to 1,000 coins. Just for fun, Elvis trivia questions appear on the screen when the bonus round is not in play.

• You'd like nothing better than to watch your coins pile up in the bank, right? Enter the "banking" machines. Piggy Bankin' slots feature animated piggy banks that burst open with coins. When enough credits build up in the "bank," (the piggy belly swells on the LCD screen) players *may* have the advantage. So if you want to play this type of machine, look for one where someone else has already made some "deposits."

• Then, of course, there is the run-of-the-mill, everyday, average, non-bonus slot machine—that costs only $1,000 to play a single game. Although on this machine you'd probably want to play maximum coin, which is $2,000, so you can rake in the million-dollar top prize. Here the entertainment is watching someone else actually put that kind of money into a machine.

casinos are quite involved, they all boil down to one of three basic varieties: *multipliers, buy-a-pays,* or *line games.*

Multipliers

Picture a slot machine in your mind and you are likely thinking of a multiplier machine. Perhaps the simplest concept of the different types of machine, multipliers pay for winning combinations across a single payline, usually the center row of symbols across three reels. They are called multipliers because the payback for additional coins is simply a multiple of the payback for a single coin. If, for example, three green bars lined up across the middle row of the reels pay off 100 coins with one coin played, a multiplier will pay 200 coins for two coins played, and 300 coins for three coins bet.

On some machines a bonus is paid for winning combinations hit with the maximum number of coins played. In our example above that would mean that instead of 300 coins for three green bars, you might win 500 coins. Paying for the possibility of this bonus by supplying the machine with the maximum coins is obviously something to consider. (Check out the Strategy and Smarts section on page 81 for a full discussion of when playing full coin is beneficial and when it might just be bogus.)

Buy-a-Pays

On a multiplier, payoffs are based on the same symbol combinations no matter how many coins are played. However, buy-a-pay games reward extra coins by making more symbols winners. For example, one coin on a buy-a-pay might get you in the running for the cherry jackpot, two coins would also give you a chance at winning if three bars come up, and you would need to bet three coins to win if three 7s appeared. Betting one coin on these types of machines could be very frustrating—with one coin in and three 7s on the reels you don't get a reduced payout; you get bupkis.

Line Games

In line games, the more coins you play, the more payoff lines are activated. In typical reel slots, this would include the three horizontal lines and perhaps the diagonals. Video slots have taken these games to a whole new level. Some games allow players to choose up to as many as nine paylines on which to wager. Just understanding all the paylines and payoffs would seem to require a Master's degree. Nonetheless, these video machines (affectionately known as Aussies since they originated in Australia) are gaining in popularity. One reason for this is that they often can be played for nickels. However, 45 nickels (playing maximum coins for nine lines) will cost you more per spin than your typical quarter machine.

Progressives

Yet another slot innovation of the late 1980s made possible by the RNG technology was the progressive. Progressives offer a top jackpot that continuously grows until someone hits it. After the payoff, the machine goes back to its reset value. (A nonprogressive machine is sometimes referred to as a *flat top* because it has a fixed amount as its top payout.) Some progressives are individual machines and others are banks of slot machines at one casino (or even across different casinos) electronically linked through phone lines to a central computer. In either case a small portion of each wager is channeled into the jackpot (the ever-growing amount of which is displayed over the machines with many a flashing light) and the rest is channeled into the pockets of the casinos. The Megabucks jackpot in Nevada starts at $7 million and connects more than 650 slot machines in 160 casinos. The odds against winning the jackpot are set at such an astronomical number that the amount to be won can grow to tens of millions of dollars—over $39 million at one point—much higher than individual casinos would be able to offer. Progressives like Quartermania and Nickels Deluxe offer lower-denomination players a chance, albeit a very, very small one, at hitting the life-altering score.

PLAYING A MACHINE

Once you pick your machine from the seemingly infinite selection, you'll see that the mechanics of play are mostly self-explanatory. But there are several physical aspects of the machines to keep an eye out for.

MEET THE MACHINE

Though the machine is really just a façade for the computer that runs it, it is the look of the machine that grabs you and makes you want to play. Slot machines have varying amounts of bells and whistles but most share the basic features shown in the illustration on page 76. On any machine, most important to note are the buttons. If you want to play something in between "max credit" and "one credit," insert the number of coins you want to play and press the SPIN button. Usually placed as far away as possible from the coin slot is the CASH OUT button. Press this when you are done playing and watch while the coins drop into the tray by

MAN VS. MACHINE

Computer chips dictate the payoff odds on slot machines, and casinos keep those odds somewhat secret. This situation might make one wonder if we are really getting a fair spin at the machines. Happily, our friendly neighborhood gaming regulators are on the case: Each jurisdiction sets its own limits on the length of slot odds and enforces casino compliance.

Meanwhile, the regulatory agencies are keeping an eye on the players, as cheaters are always testing their own technological advances. So if you win a sizable jackpot ($1,000 or more in most casinos), it is standard procedure for a slot manager to come over and congratulate you, but he will also check out the machine. He'll probably open up the casing and use the automatic reel respin feature to make sure that the last spin (your win) was legit. If you are concerned about losing your jackpot, rest assured that most machines today will lock up after hitting the top prize. So you can't accidentally spin your prize away before you get paid.

Occasionally, there might be a glitch in the casino's favor. Stories circulate about the unlucky lucky player who wins a jackpot but then loses it because the casino has determined that the machine was malfunctioning. Things can go wrong with a slot machine's innards—the wiring, the circuits—and legally it seems that a jackpot can be withheld if some aspect of the technology is amiss. In the extremely, extremely rare case that this should happen to you, see what the casino will do for you. If you're still not happy, call a lawyer and then the local news. The casino may not be forced by a court of law to rectify the situation, but they may very well be strongly encouraged to do so by the court of public relations.

your lap. There also might be a button that says CHANGE, which will summon a change attendant.

Slot machines come in all denominations—from a nickel to $1,000, though more than half of the machines you'll encounter will be quarter slots. On the floor, machines of the same denomination will usually be grouped together.

It Pays to Read the Pays

On the uppermost glass of the machine or the video screen the pay table will be given. This information is often presented in an easy-to-read grid and will tell you which symbols pay off how much for a given number of coins bet. Always read the pay tables; not only so you can know which symbols to hope for but also so you can better gauge how many coins you want to play based on the potential winnings.

Coins, Cash, or Credits?

In its infinite kindness, the casino makes it easier for slot players to play by having the machines accept paper money—from $1 to $20

and sometimes $100 bills. You'll likely see a bill acceptor on your right as you sit in front of a machine. Just below the reels (or the screen), on the shelf with the betting buttons, you'll notice a credit indicator. The number that appears here will show the number of "coins" you have to play with based on how much money you put in and the denomination of the machine. For example, if you sit down at a quarter machine and put in a $20 bill, the credit indicator will show 80 credits (20 ÷ 0.25). Always make sure the credits match the amount of money you have fed in.

On most machines this is also where your "coins" will accumulate if you win. Clever of those beneficent casinos—without coins in hand, you are more likely to play through your winnings until you are at a loss.

Of course, if you don't mind getting your fingers dirty, you can always feed in coins or tokens the old-fashioned way. No matter how you put in your money, don't forget to cash out what's left before you leave the machine. Hit the CASH OUT button and make sure that the credit window goes to zero.

Slot Club Card: Don't Play Without It

Often sitting just on top of the bill acceptor will be the slot club card reader. Check out page 87 for all you need to know about using this most valuable card—it's how the casino will track and reward your play with comps and possibly cashback. Suffice it to say that you should always sign up for a card at every casino you intend to play at and always put your card into the reader before one coin leaves your fingers.

Slots Etiquette

Slot players can be very territorial and many like to play more than one machine at a time. Make sure someone else isn't playing the machine you're about to sit down at. One way players indicate they are playing a machine is to put an empty coin cup or bucket in the coin tray. You can use this method if you've found a machine you're happy with and would like to take a short break. Just be sure you haven't left any coins or credits in the machine and that you can find your way back!

....

SLOT MACHINE STRATEGY AND SMARTS

So you make your way through the maze of machines and you find one that seems lucky to you. Would you like to increase your chances of being right about that hunch? Ah, wouldn't we all. The first rule of thumb about the slots is that there is no way to win consistently on them. But they do provide a certain mindless fun especially if you go into your playing session with full knowledge of how to decrease the risk in order to increase your time at the machine. And even if you can't make a living off of the slots, you can make a killing.

FINDING THE "RIGHT" MACHINE

There probably is a type of slot machine to suit just about everyone's temperament. After acknowledging that slots are totally a matter of luck—being in the right place at the right time—the trick to picking the right machine is to figure out what you want out of it. Will you be satisfied only going for a life-altering win no matter the cost? Check out the big progressive. Will you be satisfied with a potential total win

of just a bit more than you came in with as long as you get to hear the bells go off more frequently? Though there are no guarantees, your best bet would be to head to the stand-alone machines with lower top jackpots.

There are other considerations as well—your bankroll, the time you want to spend at the slots, the entertainment value. Since there is no skill involved in playing slots and it's next to impossible to know which machines will give you the biggest monetary payoff, only you can decide where you'd like to sit down and plunk in your coins. However, it is always good to know what's happening when you do just that.

SLOTS ON THE EDGE: PAYBACK PERCENTAGE

In this chapter, I refer to the house edge as payback percentage. These two terms are the same concept, just from an opposite perspective. The payback percentage, or the amount the player can expect to keep over the long run, is simply 100 percent (breaking even) minus the house edge.

Slots are the only game in the house where the casino advantage is a mystery. Minimum paybacks are set by the regulatory commissions in each jurisdiction—Nevada's is 75% and Atlantic City's is 83%. While competition has necessarily raised the average percentages in big gambling markets—Nevada, 95%; A.C., 92%—you never know exactly what is happening with the machine in front of you.

The theoretical *hold* or the percentage of money kept by the casino is programmed into the microchip that controls each machine. Slot managers set a total hold amount for all the casino's slots and then look to set gradations in hold across the floor. They also attempt to balance the hold of a machine with the amount of play that machine will see and the *hit frequency* desired. While entirely possible, it is unusual for a casino to change a machine's payback percentage while on the floor. Generally, the machines arrive from the manufacturer preprogrammed to the casino's specifications. Remember, two machines can have the exact same external appearance, yet have very different internal configurations, resulting in different paybacks and hit frequencies.

INSIDE THE NUMBERS

You walk into a casino with $100 and you play a machine that's programmed to return 93% (just to pick a typical payback). Will this cost you only $7 in the long run? That doesn't seem like an awful price for an evening's entertainment and a chance at a jackpot. But something rings false about this mathematical message, doesn't it? Experience tells us that the $100 will usually disappear over a playing session. So what's the deal? Why can't we take our 7% hit and—at least on average—saunter off with $93 in our pocket?

Well, the math is right. We would expect to lose only $7 over the long run on our $100—*if* we really played only the original $100. But nobody plays $100 worth of coins, cashes out, and walks away. What you do is constantly rebet the money that the machine pays off. This is known as churn. It happens in every casino game, but it is particularly nasty in fast-playing slots. The 7% house edge doesn't just apply to your original $100 stake; it eats away at every cent you put through the machine. For example, if you play three coins per spin on a quarter machine at a rate of 600 spins per hour, you'll put $450 (600 × $0.75) through the machine in an hour. With a house edge of 7%, your expected loss per hour will be $31.50 ($450 × 0.07). It's easy to see how the money evaporates as you pump away at the machines. The constant recycling of your money adds up and so does the house take. After three hours, your $100 will nearly be gone and so will your $7 fantasy.

Here's another way to appreciate how churn feeds into the house edge. A friend decides to tackle the $1 machines in Vegas. Let's assume a 95% return for a typical Silver State $1 machine. Your friend is equipped with $500; that may sound like a sum mighty enough to do long and brave battle with the one-armed bandits. Well, let's see. If your friend plays three coins per spin at 600 spins per hour, her cost per hour is: 600 × $3 × 0.05 = $90. So the $500 stake, on average, wouldn't last a full six hours. After six hours of play, $10,800 would be played through the machine and exposed to the house edge. Oddly, $500 goes a long way and yet not very far at all.

Given the inexorable casino grind, does it really make a difference what payback you pursue? Absolutely. Let's look at two machines. One is a certified 98% payback machine while the other is a "life-altering" jackpot progressive with a typical return of 88%. Assume that both are quarter machines on which you play three coins at 600 spins per hour. Here's what the 98% machine will cost you per hour over the long term (remember, the house edge is 2%):

Cost per hour = 600 × $0.75 × 0.02 = $9

Here's the average cost of the progressive with its 12% house edge:

Cost per hour = 600 × $0.75 × 0.12 = $54

That's some difference. If you started with $100, you shouldn't expect to last two hours on the progressive, while the 98% machine could carry you into the 11th hour. Of course, real life won't neatly conform to these mathematical expectations. You can win fast and lose fast on any machine in the short term. But if you want to extend your play, you have to rely on the long-term probabilities. Every percentage point in your favor will allow your bankroll to last longer, and that means you might still be sitting at the machine when the RNG comes up with a jackpot combination. At the very least, better payback will usually allow more time to go by before you're left scratching your head and pondering, "Where the heck did all the money go?"

The problem is that unless you are playing a *certified* machine—one that has a sign indicating the specific payback—you can't know the house edge that is eating away at your bankroll.

It's Payback Time

There are some ways to maximize your chance of getting a better payback:

- Las Vegas, simply because it has the most gambling competition, has higher slot paybacks than other casino locales. More specifically, the downtown Vegas casinos (local joints) generally pay back a slightly higher percentage than the Strip casinos.
- Stay away from restaurant, bar, supermarket, airport, and other store slot machines, since they are not known for advantageous payback. Since the proprietors are not generally interested in repeat business, there isn't much incentive to be generous.
- The most important way to guarantee the payback is to play on guaranteed machines. Sounds easy enough. Casinos will often advertise that they have machines that have a 98.5 percent payback or even better. However, this is a prime case of buyer beware in the belly of the casino. It's unlikely that machines will be specifically labeled with a payback or you might find just a bank of machines with a sign that says, "These machines are certified to pay up to 98.5%!" The "up to" is the key phrase. Sure, there is probably one machine in there with the high payback, but the rest are somewhere below the tantalizing percentage. You can't know which you've moseyed up to.
- Each month *Casino Player* magazine (and other publications) provide average payback percentages for the different machine denominations in the different gambling locations throughout the country. It may be useful as a rough guide—for instance, a recent issue clearly shows that the north Las Vegas casinos have paybacks up to five percent higher than most other gambling spots—but it can't be used to gauge how a particular machine within a given casino will pay back.
- Many magazines will "analyze" slots, listing a particular machine's features, gimmicks, and entertainment value. Fun? Yes. Useful? Rarely. The range given for the payback percentage of a machine is usually quite large (as much as 23 percent). You'll never know what part of that range applies to the machine you're sitting in front of.
- You must keep in mind that even if you were able to identify a specific payback percentage on a machine, there is no guarantee of winning. In fact, since the payback will always be less than 100 percent, there is a guarantee of long-term losing. In the short term, you might win on a 93 percent machine and lose on a 98 percent machine. In the short term, anything can happen, and that's why people play slots of every kind.

Denominations: How Much Do You Want to Play?

The average payback percentage generally increases as the denominations of the machines increase. This is not because casinos just feel better about higher stakes players. Any given machine takes up roughly the same amount of casino resources as any other. Consequently the casino must keep more coins in the lower-denomination machines to equal the hold on higher-denomination machines.

However, this is not to say that you should play above your means just for the chance to get a higher payback. While you may face a more negative expectation in percentage terms, lower-denomination slot play (nickels, quarters) will minimize your losses in absolute terms.

Let's compare a nickel machine that gives 90 percent payback to a $5 machine with 97 percent payback. On average, a slot player will set the reels spinning 600 times in an hour. So in one hour the nickel machine will cost you $3 ($0.05 × 0.10 × 600) while the $5 machine will cost you $90 ($5 × 0.03 × 600). Do you still play the $5 machine just because it has the lower house edge? Seems very questionable. The chart on page 84 shows the average cost of one hour of play playing different denominations. You can see that the $100 player is nearly six percent smarter than the nickel player, and $1,665 poorer for it.

TIGHT AND LOOSE MACHINES: HIT FREQUENCY

Slot fanatics constantly talk about machines being tight (holding on to their money) and

Average Cost of an Hour of Slot Play

Denomination	Average Payback	Cost/Pull/Coin	Cost/Hour/Coin
$0.05	91.55%	$0.004	$2.54
$0.10	92.10%	$0.008	$4.74
$0.25	94.81%	$0.013	$7.79
$0.50	95.72%	$0.021	$12.84
$1	95.67%	$0.043	$25.98
$5	96.47%	$0.177	$105.90
$25	97.19%	$0.703	$421.50
$100	97.22%	$2.780	$1,668.00

Based on 600 spins per hour.

loose (paying off frequently). "Oh, don't play there. Those machines don't hit," the kind sage next to you will say. But there really is no way to know. You and he and everyone are just dealing with perception and guesswork. Everyone, that is, except the casino.

A machine that has been programmed to pay back at a given percentage can fulfill that destiny in a variety of ways. The machine's *volatility* describes how the machine plays out a long-term objective (percent payback) in the short term. A machine with frequent hits of relatively small amounts could be programmed with the same payback percentage as a machine with large jackpots that are hit relatively infrequently. From the casino's perspective these two machines would be bringing in the same amount of money over the long run, but individual players would likely have very different views of the two machines.

A generalization: Machines that have higher jackpots—progressives are a good example—pay out other, smaller wins only infrequently, while flat tops pay off on their lesser wins more often. A higher jackpot machine will likely have you experiencing higher expected losses—unless you are the luckiest of lucky players and hit the top prize, an unlikely short-term scenario. Slot machines that have jackpots of 3,000 coins or less will likely have a higher hit frequency for smaller wins, which may make them a better short-term choice.

This doesn't mean you'll win more, but it does mean that you'll likely be able to play more. Hit frequency is an entertainment factor. Much of the time on high hit frequency

machines you will be "winning" an amount less than or equal to your bet and have no net monetary gain. Yet these hits allow you to continue to play and hope for the big jackpot. Also, part of the appeal of playing slots is to hear the machine make the noise of a winner—and then join in yourself.

FULL COIN PLAY

One of the longest-standing gambling tenets is "Always play the maximum number of coins allowed by the machine each and every time you play." Unfortunately, this pillar of gambling lore begins to break down under further scrutiny depending on the type of machine played. Let's see why.

When you are playing a straight multiplier machine with no bonus for playing maximum coin, the payback percentage does not change whether you put in one coin or multiple coins. However, we do know that the less money we expose to a given house edge, the longer we can stay in the game. That's the first reason to play one coin only. What happens when the machine pays a bonus for jackpots won with the maximum coins? This extra pay is figured into the total percentage payback for the machine, which means that playing anything less than full coin will be paying back at a lesser percentage rate. In other words, a machine might pay 91% with one or two coins played. The same machine might increase to 94% with three coins played because of the potential for more money being paid back through the max coin "bonus."

Also, you should only spend the amount of

IS THIS A LOOSE MACHINE?

Let's take a closer look at players' perceptions of tight and loose. You wander over to the latest and greatest slot machine to hit the floor—the MensaBucks machine. This is a traditional-looking slot machine with three reels. The only payout—when three brains line up on the payline—is $26,999,000. Each reel is programmed to have the equivalent of 300 stops, but only one with the winning brain. So 300 × 300 × 300 = 27,000,000 possibilities, but only one that will win. When the winning combination does hit, it pays over 99.99%. The casino would certainly think this hypothetical machine is incredibly loose, but no doubt every player save one exceptionally lucky one would think it is incredibly tight. Is it a smart bet? That depends on what you're after.

How 'bout this one? A pair of dollar machines sit side by side. One has winning combinations come up on each spin of the reels but pays back only a dollar on each; the other has one jackpot of $1 million but with odds set at one million to one. You *always* break even on the first one—that's not even gambling. On the second, you could lose a fortune before getting your "100%" payback—that's too much gambling for most of us. Which end of the spectrum do you gravitate toward? How much risk can you tolerate?

Of course this is all somewhat irrelevant since we would never know that such machines were actually set up that way, thanks to the slot shroud of silence. But these "thought slots" do give insight into the different desires and impulses of the player and the casino.

money you are comfortable spending, no matter the incentive to spend more. If you want to play full coin on this type of machine, make sure you can afford it. If not, go to a lower-denomination machine.

Progressives typically have payback percentages much lower than any other machine on the floor. Average payback for a multi-casino linked progressive like Megabucks is about 88 percent. Since these types of machines pay few jackpots other than the top prize, the only reason to play is for the big jackpot and you can win that only if you play full coin. So on these machines you must play maximum coin; you're playing for the fantasy. Otherwise, why would you be throwing money away on machines with lousy payback? Even if the return weren't so bad, you're not going to get much payback anyway because so much of the return is built into the huge jackpot. And you are not going to win the huge jackpot! Someone will, but you won't. That's the law of large numbers for you. It's like getting a trip on the space shuttle—it will happen to a few people on the planet, but it's very, very unlikely to be you.

Most slot players want to play slots for as long as their money will allow. If that's the case, you'd actually prefer to play max coin as infrequently as possible. Therefore, stick to one-coin multipliers that do not offer a bonus for the max coin jackpot. If you can't resist the progressives, you must play max coin. When you are playing a machine that rewards max coin play, it's really a tossup. Since each machine is programmed differently and we don't have the information about jackpot distribution, it's hard to make a steadfast rule about max coin in this last situation. So go with your gut, but first consult your bankroll.

MONEY MANAGEMENT: SLOT CENTS

Before you read further, I feel compelled to mention yet again that there is no method for beating slot machines. You might win big, you might lose big. There is no way of knowing or preparing in advance—it is a completely random outcome. That said, there are a few approaches to managing your playing stake to make the fun last a bit longer.

• Before hitting the machines in hopes of a big hit from them, decide on how much you want to put at risk in any one playing session. Based on that number, choose the denomination you want to play. A rough guideline: Two to three hundred dollars is the minimum stake you should have before staking out the $1 machines. If you've got less than $100 to spend, you'll be happier—and playing longer— at the nickel or quarter machines.

• If you slow down and stop your play often, you'll obviously slow down your losses. While that may be true for every casino game, slots are particularly mesmerizing and mindless, so self-imposed stopping points might be even more worthwhile.

• Cash out every so often. This is one way to slow down your play and the sound of the coins hitting the tray will surely make you feel like a winner—even if you're down.

• Perhaps the best advice, though the hardest to carry out, is to walk away with your winnings. Quit while you're ahead and don't give it back to the casino. Even though it looks like just red numbers on the credit indicator, it's actually your money. Take it and run. Or at least go get a bite to eat.

• Comps can be a powerful incentive to playing the slots, and indeed they can be a form of profit. (See page 87 for more on slot clubs, comps, and cashback.) Just make sure you are not spending hundreds at the slots to receive a $15.95 buffet meal.

• Think about moving over to video poker machines—after reading Chapter 5, of course. With a bit of skill at picking the machine and playing the cards, you can greatly improve your odds and possibly make it a positive expectation game. Add in your comps, and you've hit the jackpot.

Tax Tips

You wouldn't be playing if you didn't think you could win the (relatively) big one. Just remember to be prepared if you actually do.

Slot jackpots in excess of $1,200 are generally not paid directly through the machine. (The exception to this is on higher limit slot machines—you can accumulate more credits than $1,200 and then cash out, avoiding any official documentation. Of course you should report this anyway, but don't worry, I won't tell.) When the slot manager comes over to congratulate you and validate the jackpot by checking the machine, he'll also ask for some identification. Along with your cash (or, if you request, a check) you'll get the IRS's W2-G form for gambling winnings. Make sure you have ID on you at all times with your name and address, and that you have memorized your social security number or have your card with you.

Come April 15, you can offset the taxes on your winnings by also reporting your losses. If you use your slot club cards diligently, the casino can help you out with your record-keeping. They can provide you with a detailed summary of your play and how much you've lost over the year. Are you sure you want to know?

WHY PLAY?

You don't have to read between the lines of this chapter to realize that slots aren't the wisest gamble in the casino. Yet it's the rare casino visitor who doesn't succumb to the temptations of the slots at some point.

Blackjack and video poker players who look down their noses at slot players are not necessarily smarter gamblers. As long as you are playing within your limits with a full understanding of the cost of play, how you choose your entertainment is up to you. There is something undeniably appealing about the clank of the coins as they come pouring out of the machine just for you. Slots offer up instant gratification and demand an incredibly short attention span.

Let me tell you a little story. There once was a woman (okay, she's my mother) who liked to go on short jaunts to Atlantic City to play the slots. She headed down there about twice a year when the mood struck her. She's a smart woman, so her son, who knew a thing or two about gambling, constantly told her that she could do much better at games of skill like video poker or blackjack, or even games of pure luck like baccarat or craps. Ignoring him, she played mostly on the dollar machines and typically lost various undisclosed amounts of his inheritance. On a recent three-day trip to her casino of choice, where she smartly racks up her slot club points, she permanently sunk any attempts to talk "sense" into her. In a span of 24 hours, she hit not one, not two, but three sizable jackpots, for a total take of over $35,000. The odds of hitting just one of the jackpots? Large. The odds of one person hitting all three? Astronomical.

Nothing like your mother coming along to disprove everything you've been saying. Or did she? Part of the appeal of slots is the feeling that the impossible can and will happen to you. And sometimes, just by dint of luck, it does. Not to be a smart-alecky kid, but I also know that if my mother continues to play the machines, it is likely that much if not all of her phenomenal winnings will be drained away.

My next mission will be to dissuade her from playing the giant progressives. She'll likely ignore my good counsel. Knowing her, she'll hit the million-dollar jackpot just to further flummox her probability-spouting son.

....
SLOT CLUBS

Slot clubs are your passport into the culture of the slot players, allowing you to take full advantage of the entertainment value of your play. The first modern slot clubs to track players' play via computer appeared in Atlantic City in 1985. This was about the same time as slots were becoming increasingly popular, and provided the casinos with an opportunity to reward loyal players—and lure them back to play, and lose, some more.

Slot clubs—and their rewards, comps, and cashback—have nothing to do with whether you win or lose. The magnetic strip on the back of your card will tell the casino a lot about how you play: the denomination you choose, how long you play, how many sessions you play, how much money you put in, how much money you play through, how many coins you play on a typical spin, and also the total amount you win or lose. This last bit of information is the least important, however. Thanks to the computer programming of the machines, the casino knows it is going to get its projected win regardless of what individual players take home. As always, the casino is in it for the long run, so what they really care about is you coming back again and again and again.

SIGN ME UP!

Without question you should join the slot club at every casino you play. Yes, you should do this even if you are going to play only a few rounds and you know your points won't add up to a free meal, much less anything else. The reason is that you will be placed on the casino's mailing list, and you never know what other goodies might ensue.

Go directly to the slot club booth, which will usually be clearly marked. You'll fill out a short form, show some identification, and you'll generally be issued the card immediately. (The form will likely ask you when your birthday or anniversary is, so the casino can send you invitations to come back that seem personalized.) You can ask for duplicate cards if you like to play more than one machine at a time, or if you and a spouse or friend would like to accumulate points on one account. Two cards are also harder to lose than one.

COMPS

Once you've got your card, the next step is to use it. Insert it into the card readers that are attached to each machine. (Remember to remove it when you are done playing—it's so easy to forget!) The slot club offerings come in all varieties. With enough play you can look forward to meals, free or discounted hotel rooms, gifts, entry into slot tournaments, invitations to special events, and other freebies like a free pull for a chance to win $1,000,000.

This is all very exciting and certainly one aspect of slot play that is enormously appealing. Just one thing to keep in mind: Don't play beyond your means to get perks.

Details of how comps are awarded are a bit sketchy in many casinos. Nonetheless, you can speak to a slot club host and ask for the specifics on how comps are awarded. It can't hurt to ask. They might tell you, they might not. Usually the host will give you an idea of how much play you have to give in order to start getting freebies. (See Chapter 16 for more info on the benefits of having a host as your pal.) Most casinos want to see a few thousand dollars cycled through the machines (not lost!) before they take a personal interest in you. But don't undervalue your play. A dedicated quarter slots player has more value to the casino than a $25 blackjack player.

CASHBACK

What could be better than a free meal to go along with your fun at the slots? How about a free meal and some cashback also? The vast majority of casinos now offer this inducement to play. Some local Las Vegas casinos don't have cashback programs because they prefer to offer comps and machines, particularly video poker, with high payback. Most Native American casinos don't have these programs because they don't have enough competition … yet.

Each casino has a different formula for rewarding its customers. Here's what you need to know to figure out what a casino is offering you:

The system that points are based on. Most casinos base cashback/comp systems on total *coin-in*. This is the total amount bet including any winnings that you have played through. A few base the system on coin-out, which is better on those days where your wins are greater than your losses. In the long run, there isn't a difference between these two systems. Some casinos, especially in Atlantic City, use "theoretical casino win" instead. While this may be the basis for comps in some casinos, the mystery of this formula hasn't gone over well with the players, so it is used less often in cashback systems.

Amount of action necessary for one point. This is often referred to as the *countdown*. In most casinos, after you put your card into a reader, the display will welcome you by name and then give you three pieces of information: your total account points, your current session points, and the number of coins needed to get the next point. For example, a casino wants you to spend $3 in order to get one point. So, at a one-dollar machine the third number to come up might be a 3. This means that $3 (3 × $1 = $3) is worth one point. In a quarter machine, assuming the casino uses the same formula for all denominations of machines, the number of coins needed would be 12 (12 × $0.25 = $3). This will vary from casino to casino. Big Money Casino might set up a formula where one dollar coin-in equals one club point, while Lotsa Cash Casino might have one point equal to $50 coin-in. Now, Big Money sure sounds like they have a favorable system, but we don't know what it's worth yet.

The value of one point in cashback. This relationship will also vary widely among casinos. Look in the slot club brochure or ask a slot club host for the specifics at a casino. Big Money Casino's brochure tells us that we need 800 points to get $1 cashback. At Lotsa Cash two points will get us $1 back.

Now we can figure out the rebate percent and compare the casinos to see where we get the better deal.

Percent cashback =
$$1 \div [(\text{dollars played to earn point}) \times (\text{\# of points to earn dollar in cashback})]$$

Big Money Casino:
$$1 \div (1 \times 800) = 0.0013 = 0.13\%$$
Lotsa Cash Casino:
$$1 \div (50 \times 2) = 0.01 = 1.0\%$$

On the whole we'll get more money, at least more cashback, out of Lotsa Cash than Big Money.

Use this information as one factor to find a casino where you'd like to play. It isn't worth it to play at a casino where you can't find the games you like, the rooms are too expensive, and they are stingy with their buffet comps, all so you can get a bit more cashback. You need to look at the whole experience of playing.

Other aspects of cashback to consider:

When you get the rebate. Will the casino let you take your cash out of your account before you go home or will they mail it to you as a "bounce back" rebate? These mailings usually have a time limit (about two months), so you'll have to revisit the casino within that time to make good on the rebate. You might get a higher level of rebate from casinos that operate this way but it's still not so good if you are just spending a one-week vacation in Atlantic City from Florida.

The types of games you like to play. Some cashback programs award more points for $1 machines. Many give a reduced rate for quarter machines. Nickel machines weren't a factor at all until the Aussies, with their potential to play 45 to 90 coins, caught on. The rate of reward for the different denominations varies. This is all based on marketing and which players the casino wants to attract. You can decide how attractive each casino is to you.

SLOT MYTHS

Okay, so now we know that slot machines are just that: machines with slots for our money. Unless you see a sign posted on a specific machine indicating the payback percentage, there is no way to know how much you can theoretically expect to win on it. ("Expect to lose" is, sadly, more accurate, since no slot machine will have a positive payback.) But the fact that slots are controlled by computer chips doesn't stop slot fanatics from believing they are controlled by all sorts of other things, like …

The location of the machine.

There is a long-standing myth that loose machines are placed at the ends of aisles. There is a logic to this theory, but figuring out what the public perception of casino management theories are is part of the slot manager's job. So we're talking about a lot of second-guessing. Further debunking this theory is the fact that the casino floor is so jam-packed with slots of so many varieties, and there are so many aisles.

How hot or cold the machine is.

Every machine has a preprogrammed payback strategy. A machine is only "hot" or "cold" as each individual player perceives it as such. The microchip certainly doesn't care about our perceptions, nor about what happened on any previous spin. It is merely living out its destiny to constantly cycle randomly through however many millions or billions of combinations with which it has been programmed, stopping only for a millisecond when you push a button, and then continuing on. If the combination called when you push that button is a winner, good for you. If not, oh well. More than not caring either way, the machine is unaware of anything that happened in the past. No machine that you or anyone else sits down at will ever be "due." Observing a machine, we can only know what has happened in the past, and that is completely irrelevant to the future. If you were to watch a group of machines over the long haul, hundreds of thousands of pulls, maybe you could tell something about that machine's payback percentage or programmed hit frequency. But you wouldn't be able to take breaks over the course of several days and nights while you kept watch, you still might not be correct in your assumptions, you would most likely discover a typical negative expectation, and most important, you certainly wouldn't be having as much fun as if you just sat down and played.

The reliability of the slot personnel.

Since it is highly unlikely that many people outside slot management are privy to the configuration of high-payback machines, asking the slot machine personnel which machines are tight or loose is really an exercise in futility—and stupidity. They have no idea which machines pay off more than others. Even if they have seen a certain machine making a lot of noise on a certain shift, they are just observing a random fluctuation in the huge random cycle of the machine. Because a machine has "been hitting" is no reason to think that it will continue to hit—or that it won't. There is no way to know. This is not to say that every slot employee who points you to a machine saying that it is "hot" is only out to get a tip if you do happen to win. They might just be uninformed about the workings of the machines surrounding them and think they actually do know something. Good thing for you, you know better.

The temperature of the coins.

Just because the coins are warm as they come out does not mean the machine is "hot"; all those lights could certainly heat things up. If you were to warm up the coins or cool them down before you put them back into the machine, as some fanatics claim they do, the only thing that might happen is that you'll have hot or cold hands from handling them. The RNG is completely egalitarian: It can't be fooled by coins that blow hot and cold.

Pulling the handle or pushing the button.

Whether you pull the handle or push the button, put coins in or play credits, play max coins or one coin, or alternate these actions in some meaningful (to you) way, it just doesn't matter. The arm on the one-armed bandit has not been amputated simply for the sake of nostalgia. Now it merely acts as a signaler to the random number generator, and there is no way for you to control your fate.

The player's timing.

It happens all the time. You get up from a machine and watch someone else sit down in the abandoned seat and hit a jackpot. The head-smacking and the self-loathing ensues—"That would have been *my* jackpot if I didn't leave!" Wrong. Remember that the RNG is cycling through combinations every millisecond. The odds that you and the "jackpot-stealer" would have hit the button at the exact same millisecond are infinitesimal. There's no way of telling what "would have happened" when outcomes depend on milliseconds. Think about that the next time you sneeze, hit the button … and come up with a jackpot.

Gesundheit!

Most casinos offering cashback will have one rate for reel players and a separate rate—usually about half the reel rate—for video poker players. That's because the video poker machines generally have a much higher payback. Read Chapter 5 to take full advantage of these games. Adding 0.5% cashback can make a negative video poker game positive.

Location. Cashback exists because of competition among casinos, so it only makes sense that the best cashback would be where the competition is most fierce and where customers put the most value on it.

Las Vegas Strip: around 1%

Local Las Vegas: around 0.1%

Mississippi River: around 0.3%

Atlantic City: more secretive but generally around 1%

Casinos give you cashback expecting that you'll put it back in their machines and follow it up with money of your own. However, they do not hand it to you and then stand over your shoulder to make sure you fulfill their desire. Of course, if doing that also fulfills your desire, go for it. Just know that you can put it in your pocket and do with it as you please.

No matter what you intend to do with it, just make sure you get your cashback in your hot lit-tle hands. Don't leave it in your slot club account when you leave the casino, since you can lose it after a certain amount of time. Several casinos are trying creative ways to make sure you don't leave with their cash. Some give cashback only as machine credits (not so good) while others give you a choice of cash or double the amount in machine credits (slots better!).

PROMOTIONS

Always look for good promotions in your slot club mailings. Casinos that offer lackluster machines and comps can become very attractive with a worthwhile promotion. A typical promotion may offer double- and triple-point days where every point is worth two or three times its normal value. (So if you are usually getting 0.5% cashback, you'd get 1.5% on a triple-point day.) Some casinos try to snare new players with seductive promotions, such as refunds for losses (perhaps $100) incurred during the first hours of play. Such enticing deals are only for new slot club members, so be sure to take advantage of what's offered when you go to a casino for the first time.

TOURNAMENTS

Tournaments can be a fun way to wile away

some time you would otherwise use to spend even more money at the slots. You still have a chance to win a lot of money and you'll usually get plenty of freebies from the casino—meals, caps, T-shirts, etc.

In a tournament you're competing against other entrants for a set prize by attempting to rack up the most credits in an allotted period of time. Aside from an aching "spin" finger, tournaments can be a good deal. You want to look for contests that return all the entry fees as prizes. So if 200 entrants each pay $250, the prize schedule should equal $50,000. The tournament itself is then a fair game with a 100% return and merely a goodwill gesture on the part of the casino. You may not recoup your entry fee, but you'll know you had a fair shot at the money. These tournaments will generally seed a machine with some credits so you can get spinning away. When entry fees are in addition to the money that you play with, the casino gets its advantage, and at a fast rate.

As you might have guessed, the best way to learn about tournaments is to join slot clubs.

THE ESSENTIALS FOR PLAYING SLOT MACHINES LIKE A GENIUS

- Have fun with slots, but don't get sucked into the myths surrounding them. Slots are luck alone.
- As with any other game, divide your bankroll into playing sessions, set a total loss limit, and stick to it.
- To maximize your chances of playing a high-payback machine, play in northern Las Vegas casinos, look for certified machines, stay away from progressives, and play the highest-denomination machine you can afford.
- Know your machine. Check the denomination and pay table before you begin. Often you will be choosing between machines that hit smaller jackpots more frequently and ones that hit larger jackpots very infrequently.
- Always leave a machine with all your winnings—make sure to press the CASH OUT button.
- If you'd like to take a break, you can "reserve" your machine by placing an empty coin bucket in the coin tray.
- Join slot clubs and take full advantage of the comps, cashback, and special promotions and mailings you'll get from them.
- When you are feeling more sophisticated, give video poker a try.

5

VIDEO POKER

All casino machines are not created equal. It may look like a slot machine and it may sound like a slot machine, but a video poker machine is not a slot machine. Smart players often move away from reel slots and toward video poker. In casinos frequented by more discriminating "locals," video poker takes up as much, if not more, of the floor as slots. It's a game that rewards knowledge and skill: If you find the right machine, use the right strategy, and have the right bankroll, you will be a long-term winner. With casino comps factored in, video poker can be a profitable enough venture to attract pros. It's certainly a smart bet for the informed amateur. This chapter will fill you in on what you need to know to get the advantage.

Play video poker right and you'll be playing what many consider the best game in the casino. You can often find a machine that has only a 0.5% house advantage. That puts it in a league with the best craps bets and blackjack with perfect basic strategy. However, with video poker you get to play at your own pace and you also have the potential for big payoffs. All other games with jackpot offerings have big house edges.

I fear that people who are intimidated or bored by table games will think that slot machines are their only alternative. But the only input you have with slots is to pour in your money and pray for luck. Yet the slots' brethren—video poker—open up a whole other world of possibilities. It's a test of skill that no one is watching.

Video poker has enjoyed explosive growth throughout the '80s and '90s and it's not hard to see why it's the game of choice for knowl-edgeable players. Players make choices that affect their bottom line. Unfortunately, too many players make the wrong choices—either on what machine to play or how to play the cards that are dealt.

You do have the control in this game. You can pick the right machine and play the right way, and you can have a long-term edge over the house. This is a rare opportunity. But you do need the bankroll to weather the ups and downs of even the best machines. That's what makes it tough on the amateur. Visit for the weekend and you may bust your bankroll before the profits come in. Visit for a lifetime of weekends and you should end up ahead.

The length of this chapter and its breadth of information may seem overwhelming at first. Think of playing video poker as the start of an adventure. You can dive right into the strate-gies and get the gist of which are the good machines. You can then try to absorb some of the subtleties and more complex aspects of the game. There's a reason why this chapter and the blackjack chapter are bulkier than the oth-ers in the book: They are both games of skill that require some thought and study on the part of the smart gambler. So get comfortable, class is about to begin.

HOW VIDEO POKER IS PLAYED

There are many variations of video poker, but most machines are based on the classic poker game of five-card draw. You are dealt five ran-dom cards from a 52-card deck (or 53 cards if you're playing a machine that uses a joker). You get one opportunity to improve your hand by

♠ ◇ ♣ ♡	1ST COIN	2ND COIN	3RD COIN	4TH COIN	5TH COIN
ROYAL FLUSH	250	500	750	1000	4000
STRAIGHT FLUSH	50	100	150	200	250
FOUR OF A KIND	25	50	75	100	125
FULL HOUSE	9	18	27	36	45
FLUSH	6	12	18	24	30
STRAIGHT	4	8	12	16	20
THREE OF A KIND	3	6	9	12	15
TWO PAIR	2	4	6	8	10
PAIR OF JACKS OR BETTER	1	2	3	4	5

VIDEO POKER

PLAY 1 TO 5 COINS

WIN **4000** COINS ON ROYAL FLUSH WITH 5 COINS BET

25¢ PLAY 5 COINS

♠ ◇ ♣ ♡

HELD   HELD   HELD

INSERT BILLS $1 $5 $20 $50 $100

COINS IN 5

CREDIT 45

| CASH OUT | BET ONE COIN | HOLD CANCEL | HOLD CANCEL | HOLD CANCEL | HOLD CANCEL | HOLD CANCEL | DEAL DRAW | PLAY MAX CREDIT |

VIDEO POKER

drawing cards. You decide which of the five cards you want to keep and are dealt random replacement cards for those you choose to discard.

Video poker should not be confused with real poker. Yes, it does use the superficial mechanics of five-card draw, but the strategies and play have nothing to do with what you do at a poker table. Although you do need to recognize the ranking of poker hands (see page 183), your poker skills won't serve you well, and may hurt you more than help you. In real poker, your playing decisions and success are relative to the other players'. It doesn't pay to be second best. In video poker, your success is all relative to the *pay table* of the machine you've chosen—and your adherence to the strategy tables that we'll get to in a bit.

The payback for video poker machines is not programmed into a microchip as is the case with reel slots. The function of the RNG in video poker is to provide a randomly shuffled deck and random cards for each hand. The pay table determines the payback (in conjunction with the player's skill level).

As an extension of this, realize that the denomination of the machine is irrelevant when it comes to payback percentage. A quarter machine with the same pay table as a dollar machine has the exact same theoretical percent return. The only difference is that the dollar machine puts four times the stress on your bankroll.

MEET THE MACHINE

It's not difficult to find video poker machines among the sea of slot machines in the casino. Video poker makes up a sizable portion of any casino's floor and there will be entire sections devoted to these machines.

The machines share the look of slot machines: a colorful metal cabinet with a coin slot and bill acceptor. The gameplay results are shown on a video screen rather than on physical reels. Like slots, video poker machines come in all denominations, ranging from a nickel to $25. Quarter and dollar machines are by far the most popular and prevalent.

The Mechanics

The mechanics of playing video poker are incredibly simple and don't really vary from machine to machine.

As with any slot machine, the first thing to do as you sit down is to insert your slot club card. This is vital in video poker for ensuring that you get every possible bang for your buck. To start the game, insert the number of coins (or bills) you want to bet. A typical machine will accept one to five coins and the number of coins that you play acts as a multiplier of the payoff for a winning hand. Most machines will automatically deal the cards once the maximum number of coins has been inserted. Most players play maximum coins because that qualifies them for the jackpot hand, which awards a disproportionately greater amount for full coins played.

As we'll see on page 113, there may be occasions when you'll want to play fewer than max coins. In that case you'll press the DEAL button to receive your five initial cards. Most machines will indicate if these five cards already form a winning hand by making a sound and highlighting the hand type on the payout table. Some machines may automatically hold these winning cards for you, but you always have the option of holding and discarding whichever cards you want. (There are instances where you break up a winning hand to go for something higher, as will be shown later.)

Choose which cards you want to hold by pressing the HOLD button below the card, or, in some games, you can touch the image of the card on the screen. You can change your mind and "unhold" a card by pressing the button again; you can toggle the hold decision as much as you like. (It's unlikely, but you may run across an older machine in which you choose which cards to discard rather than hold. The buttons will say DISCARD. It's always good to check before you play.) The cards that you choose to discard will be replaced by new cards. You will then have your final five-card hand.

Always be careful about hitting the right buttons for the right cards. If you hit a big hand, make sure you hold what you need to hold. On many machines, if you hit the top hand, the machine will automatically go to the payoff mode. Winning hands are paid according to the pay table (or "pay schedule") on the machine.

VIDEO POKER STRATEGY AND SMARTS

A full understanding of how to play video poker well is beyond the scope of this chapter. It would take a whole book to give fair treatment to merely the most popular variations. But you can use the information here as a starter kit for appreciating the concepts and underpinnings of the game. You can also use the basic strategies given on pages 108 and 109 for Jacks or Better and Deuces Wild (two of the most popular games) to sample the machines and see if they appeal to you.

There are three things you need to do in order to strip away the mystery of a video poker machine and understand its value to you:

1. You must be able to read the pay tables and know which ones have the highest payback.
2. You must know the best strategies for the machines you choose to play.
3. You must know the *volatility* of a particular machine—what effect it will have on your bankroll.

Video poker is a lot more interesting than slot machines; it is worth learning the basics (there's money in it for you), and—while some strategy is complex—it isn't quite differential calculus. If you're only interested in getting an edge over the slot zombies while playing an intriguing game, you can jump ahead to the strategy tables for Jacks or Better and Deuces Wild. However, stick around and read the following sections if you really want to understand what makes video poker tick and how a basic aptitude can make you a smart video poker consumer.

UNDERSTANDING THE MACHINES

Based purely on the mechanics, playing video poker is simplicity itself. However, playing it well entails a bit more effort. Video poker is one game where the house advantage is definitely affected by how much knowledge the player has. The two main skills involved—proper machine selection and knowing the proper strategy for the machine you're playing—get complicated because video poker comes in a never-ending variety of games.

How do you navigate this sea of machines? First, let's look at them in the broadest terms. There are non-wild card games such as Jacks or Better and Double Bonus. Then there are wild card games such as Deuces Wild or Joker Wild. Within these two general types, there are many varieties. Some of these will be to your favor, some won't. Payout schedule return rates vary from below 90% to above 100%.

While video poker can seem mysterious with its many versions and options, for the knowledgeable its appeal lies in its lack of mystery. Every machine can be deciphered, so you'll know exactly where you stand (granted, you may need some computer software or reliable information to accomplish this).

The best place to start your video poker conquest is with the machine that started the whole phenomenon: the Jacks or Better game. When video poker first appeared in the 1970s, it had a problem. The first machines paid off only on two pair or greater, which quickly drained players of their money and enthusiasm for the game. Then the Jacks or Better machine was introduced, which paid off for a pair of jacks or higher. Video poker hasn't looked back since. The classic Jacks or Better machine is still very popular and considered the "standard" game,

particularly good for beginners because of its easily understandable strategy.

Better yet, the best version of Jacks or Better has a 99.5% payback percentage when played with expert strategy. That means it has only a 0.5% house advantage. In other words, in the long run, you can expect to lose only 50¢ of every $100 you play. This is one of the best bets in the casino. A few video poker games actually give you an advantage over the house when played expertly; their strategies are a bit more complicated.

Consider Jacks or Better as the Hershey bar of the video poker candy store: classic, reliable, straightforward, and simply satisfying. You may want to move to more newfangled and exotic confections, but Jacks or Better will always be the most accessible and understandable treat. We'll use Jacks or Better as our standard game to explore the principles that underlie smart video poker play and to gain insights into the concepts that make the game so compelling and unique.

The Pay Table

The most important thing that we look at on our machine is the pay table. The pay table strips away the game's mystery; it's our window into knowing whether the game is worth our money. Unlike slot machines, the pay table isn't just there for us to ooh and aah over all the pretty payoffs; it can reveal how much a game pays back if played perfectly. Granted, this information isn't printed explicitly on the pay table. You'll know it either through what you've read (in this chapter and other sources) or through analyzing the pay table on video poker software (see Appendix D).

Pay tables like the example on page 96 can be found on the screen or written on the machine's glass (sometimes both).

The first thing you'll notice is that all the payoffs are scaled according to how many coins are played; that is, you get twice the payoff for paying two coins, three times the payoff for three coins, etc. So the odds don't change: Throughout the pay table, a flush will pay six coins per coin played. This is true for all the hands *except* the royal flush. Notice that the royal flush payout takes a big leap on the fifth coin played. For the first four coins, you receive

Jacks or Better Pay Table

Hand	1st Coin	2nd Coin	3rd Coin	4th Coin	5th Coin
Royal flush	250	500	750	1,000	4,000
Straight flush	50	100	150	200	250
Four of a kind	25	50	75	100	125
Full house	9	18	27	36	45
Flush	6	12	18	24	30
Straight	4	8	12	16	20
Three of a kind	3	6	9	12	15
Two pair	2	4	6	8	10
Pair of jacks or better	1	2	3	4	5

250 coins for every coin played if you hit a royal flush, but if you play five coins, you receive 800 coins for every coin played (4,000 ÷ 5 = 800). This sort of bonus on the highest hand is typical for all video poker games. That's why nearly every author advises readers to always play max coins, and that is usually the right play. A little later we'll discuss when you might want to choose otherwise.

It's worth noting that the payoffs are in an "A for B" format rather than "A *to* B." That means that the cost of your bet is included in the amount that is paid off to you. So if you receive a pair of jacks (or a pair of queens, kings, or aces—that's what the "or better" means), you only get back your bet. You don't make a profit unless you hit a hand of two pair or higher. (Still, "merely" getting your bet returned to you isn't a bad thing—that common payoff is crucial to allowing you to live and fight for many hands.)

Also realize that the payoffs are in terms of "coins," not dollars. These coins are the denomination of the machine you're playing on. If you're on a quarter machine and betting max coin, you'll be betting $1.25 per hand (5 × $0.25). Dividing all the payoffs on a quarter machine by four will give their dollar value. If you make a flush, it will pay $7.50. If you hit the royal flush, you'll make $1,000. On a nickel machine, dividing the payoffs by 20 will put them in terms of a dollar. Obviously, on a dollar machine the payoffs don't have to be translated. Of course, you don't have to worry about this math while playing any machine; it just helps to keep things in dollar-and-cents perspective (and prevents you from thinking you can win $4,000 for a royal flush when heading over to a quarter machine).

Full Pay

For Jacks or Better, 9/6 machines are known as *full-pay* machines. Let's examine these terms in reverse order. First, full pay does not mean that you will get 100% (or more) of your money back—we already established that the 9/6 machine will return only 99.5% to skilled players. In video poker jargon, full pay means that you are getting the highest standard pay table for a particular machine. In other words, alterations haven't been made in the payoffs that would shortchange you and lower your overall expectation for the game.

When examining the Jacks or Better pay table, the area you should concentrate on is the payoff for the full house and the flush. For one coin played, full-pay machines return 9 coins on a full house and 6 coins on the flush. These machines are known as 9/6 machines. Congratulations—knowing this bit of lingo is your first major step into the world of discriminating video poker play.

Casinos are full of *short-pay* (as opposed to full-pay) machines; this may be frustrating but it isn't exactly devious on the part of the casino. After all, the information is right there on the pay table (if you know what you're looking for). In the realm of Jacks or Better, 8/5 machines are much more common than 9/6 machines. As you may have guessed, these 8/5 machines pay only 8 for the full house and 5 for the flush. These reductions hurt your bankroll—8/5 machines return only 97.3% when played expertly. Seemingly small changes can make a big difference. That's over 2% that you'll needlessly give up to the casino if you don't shop for a 9/6 machine.

Another number to check carefully on the pay table is the return on two pair. If the machine returns only one coin on two pair, you're probably looking at a Jacks or Better variation that has other differences in payouts and requires different strategies and analysis (such as Double Bonus, which we'll address later). If all else were the same and it paid only one coin on two pair, you'd be looking at a machine that rips you off.

Notice that the payouts for playing one coin are used to distinguish the machines. Since the pay table is proportionate throughout, you can use the one-coin payout as a reference. You don't need to be burdened by the whole pay table. "But wait," cry out the perceptive readers, "what about the jackpot hands that are disproportionately large when max coins are played?" Yes, sometimes that needs to be mentioned separately to distinguish one machine from another. Even so, we can forgo the whole pay table grid presented on page 96 and give a single line that presents all the essential info for a machine based on one coin. The only tricky thing is the payoff on the jackpot hand: Keep in mind that it is the payoff on a single coin, *given* the fact that you played maximum coins. So the quick and easy way to show all the essential info for Jacks or Better would be as follows:

HAND	PAYOFF
Royal flush	800*
Straight flush	50
Four of a kind	25
Full house	9
Flush	6
Three of a kind	3
Two pair	2
Pair of jacks or better	1

*(Five coins must be played for this per-coin payback.)

What a Difference a Pay Makes

When learning to love and appreciate pay tables, you'll soon realize that every coin counts. Take a look at our old pal Jacks or Better. I've said that the 9/6 full-pay version has a payback of 99.54% with *expert play*. Knock one coin off each of those payouts, bringing the machine down to 8/5, and the best you can do is a 97.30% payback. But it gets worse: Plenty of casinos have 7/5 machines (96.15%) or 6/5 machines (95.00%) out on the floor. Let's not shrug off a few percentage points. Take a look at the chart below, which is based on playing a five-coin quarter machine at a rate of 600 hands per hour (600 × $1.25 = $750).

As you can see, it's essential to know what you're getting into. Of course, once you're aware that it pays to read the pay table, the choice is rather obvious. Even if you don't know the percentages, all else being equal, you would naturally play the game that gives greater pay for the same hands.

But comparison shopping won't always bring such clear-cut decisions. Very often, all things *aren't* equal on two games, with the payoff going up on some hands and down on others. Then it's tough to know which machine is more attractive—if either. In that case, you'll want to stick with what you're sure of. Or, if you're so inclined, you can take some notes on the machine and do some analysis at home with a program you'll find listed in Appendix D.

Another popular machine is Deuces Wild. Its strategy is a bit more complicated than Jacks or Better but it can pay more than 100 percent. That's right, a positive expectation, a *player's* edge—but only if you know how to pick the machine. Compare the pay tables of the two Deuces Wild machines on the next page.

Comparison of Different Jacks or Better Machines				
Jacks or Better Version	Expert Payback	Hourly Play	Expected Hourly Loss	House Edge Increase Compared to 9/6
9/6	99.54%	$750	$3.45	——
8/5	97.30%	$750	$20.25	5.9 times
7/5	96.15%	$750	$28.88	8.4 times
6/5	95.00%	$750	$37.50	10.9 times

HAND	MACHINE #1	MACHINE #2
Natural royal flush	800	800
Four deuces	200	200
Wild royal flush	25	25
Five of a kind	15	17
Straight flush	9	13
Four of a kind	5	4
Full house	3	3
Flush	2	2
Straight	2	2
Three of a kind	1	1

So which machine is better? Well, machine #2 looks attractive. Sure, you sacrifice a coin on the four of a kind payoff, but the straight flush and five of a kind payoffs are pumped up by four and two coins, respectively. Forget about it—it's not even close. Machine #1 is a classic full-pay Deuces Wild machine and will return a gaudy 100.76% with expert play. Machine #2 is a Deuces Wild variation that won't make anyone wild—its return is a relatively anemic 97.08%. Why the big discrepancy? It's that one itsy-bitsy coin on the *quads* (four of a kind) payout. You'll see a lot of quads in Deuces; on average, they'll show up about one time in 15 hands. In full-pay Deuces, the four of a kind accounts for a massive 32% of your total return. On machine #2, the lowered four of a kind payout delivers only

THERE'S HOMEWORK?!

An informed discussion of video poker tends to elicit a two-stage response in the uninitiated. First, there is a great enthusiasm—perhaps seasoned with skepticism—that there are actually machines where you can have a long-term advantage against the house. Next come glazed looks and mild resentment when people learn that it takes a certain amount of study to obtain the edge. Well, that's how it is. Like any game of skill, video poker demands effort and time devoted to acquiring proficiency. People seem to accept this—though rarely execute it—for a well-known "beatable" game like blackjack, but they're a bit surprised that much thought goes into beating a "glorified slot machine."

Video poker machines are open books for analysis. But you have to know how to read them. Thankfully resources abound to help you decipher, learn, and practice video poker strategies. You can purchase books and/or strategy cards by established experts such as Bob Dancer, Dan Paymar, and Lenny Frome.

You'll also have to invest time into playing. Practice software is perfect for this purpose—allowing you to increase your learning curve without decreasing your bankroll. I don't want to sound like a shill for these software makers, but if you want to explore video poker seriously, the programs are indispensable. (Shareware versions are also available.) Some software wonders: You'll be shown the correct play, a hint/warning, your strategy errors, and the *expected return* (that will be made clear shortly) on all the 32 possible ways to play each hand. The programs will track your whole session and show you how close to perfect you played. In addition, you'll be able to see what your mistakes cost you.

You also may want to check out newsletters, magazines, and Internet newsgroups. Once the video poker bug bites you, you'll probably want to sample much of the useful information and advice available. You may be surprised at how quickly you become a strategy gourmand.

For specific recommendations and ways to acquire any of these materials, look in Appendix D. If the thought of investing too much thought and effort into video poker disagrees with you, you can just pick up the essentials by reading the rest of this chapter. Follow the strategy listed for either Jacks or Better or Deuces Wild—and you'll be ahead of 90% of casino visitors.

about 25% of the total return. The increased payouts on the less frequent straight flush and five of a kind just don't pick up the slack.

One more example will suffice to show that pay table scrutiny is worthwhile (and tricky). Check out this pay table for a Double Bonus machine:

HAND	PAYOFF
Royal flush	800
Straight flush	50
Four aces	160
Four 2s, 3s, 4s	80
Four 5s–Ks	50
Full house	9
Flush	6
Straight	5
Three of a kind	3
Two pair	1
Jacks or better	1

Hmm, looks like this Double Bonus machine is a tantalizing takeoff on the already appealing 9/6 Jacks or Better. We're getting huge bonuses (thus the name) on four of a kind hands and we even get an extra coin on the straight. Okay, you know there's a catch. Here it is: Two pair pays only one coin instead of two. How big a catch is that? It offsets the other inflated payoffs to such a degree that the expert payback is only 97.81%. That's more than 1.5% less than ordinary, unbonused 9/6 Jacks or Better. Two pair is such a common hand—it accounts for over 25% of the payback in regular Jacks or Better—that cutting it in half is a real bankroll killer.

So is every Double Bonus really Double Bogus? Not at all. If you go from a 9/6 to a 10/7 payout on the full house and flush, this game becomes a profitable 100.17%. In fact, 10/7 Double Bonus is one of the favorite targets of knowledgeable players (though its strategy is tough to master).

PICKING THE RIGHT MACHINES

What have we learned so far? Every coin paid out is critical and every distinct pay table warrants its own analysis.

Here are some more tips that will steer you away from the duds in the video poker world and toward the gems.

• Casinos have no qualms about setting payoffs on certain hands lower than the "standard" full pay, and the change can come anywhere on the pay table. So read what's in front of you. If it seems like I'm pounding this point to death, it's because I am.

• Be very wary of cuts to the payoffs for the more common hands. Extravagant jackpots for high hands are appealing, but they may not be enough to offset even the most seemingly innocuous dent in your lower payoffs. Then again, sometimes it may be enough. That's why, as a beginner, you should stick to the conventional, oft-discussed games that you have strategies for. After that, you'll need to read the experts' analyses of more obscure games or run your own analysis on your faithful software.

• As a general rule, you should avoid new machines. Newer machines may have more high-end jackpot hands or imaginative card combinations, but the entertainment value usually conceals a lower payback. Also, you won't know the proper strategy for the machine. Generally, the more exotic the pay table is, the more counterintuitive a strategy will be. Most pros stick to tried-and-true machines. Unless you're a free-spending adventurer, you should do the same. (At least until you get reliable info on the new machine.)

• Sometimes it's easy to be drawn in by the marketing lure of a game's title, but don't judge a game by its name. Bonus Poker Deluxe pays back only 98.5%. Double Double Bonus is a lower-paying game than Double Bonus.

• Making the effort to look for a good machine is half the battle. You have to remind yourself that in reel slots you're mostly playing blind, but in video poker it's quite the opposite. Exercise that free will. One Jacks or Better machine can be different from the next (sometimes literally next to each other!). You'll always find people playing short-pay machines like 8/5 Jacks or Better (with no *progressive*) when there are nearby machines that offer full pay. Look around the casino or the casino next door.

• Seek and ye shall find—but it may not be easy. The quality of games varies from geographic region to geographic region—even from casino to casino. Some casinos may have one kind of full-pay Jacks or Better and Joker Wild

THE BEST FULL-PAY MACHINES

Below are the pay schedules for some of the best full-pay machines around. Don't forget that the payback percentages assume maximum coin and perfect play. (Also remember that the payouts are per coin, but the royal flush payout is the payout per coin when max coins are played.) It is well beyond the scope of this chapter to even touch on strategy for some of these games; instead, this is a public service announcement. If you come across one of these games, you can make it your mission to learn the strategy and make some money. (Some of the Web sites in Appendix D have listings of full-pay machine locations.)

Jacks or Better

Royal flush	800
Straight flush	50
Four of a kind	25
Full house	9
Flush	6
Straight	4
Three of a kind	3
Two pair	2
Jacks or better	1

Payback: 99.54%

Double Joker

Royal flush	800
Wild royal	100
Five of a kind	50
Straight flush	25
Four of a kind	9
Full house	5
Flush	4
Straight	3
Three of a kind	2
Two pair	1

Payback: 99.97%

Double Bonus

Royal flush	800
Straight flush	50
Four aces	160
Four 2s, 3s, or 4s	80
Four 5s to kings	50
Full house	10
Flush	7
Straight	5
Three of a kind	3
Two pair	1
Jacks or better	1

Payback: 100.17%

All-American Poker

Royal flush	800
Straight flush	200
Four of a kind	40
Full house	8
Flush	8
Straight	3
Two pair	1
Jacks or better	1

Payback: 100.72%

Loose Deuces

Royal flush	800
Four deuces	500
Wild royal flush	25
Five of a kind	15
Straight flush	10
Four of a kind	4
Full house	3
Flush	2
Straight	2
Three of a kind	1

Payback: 100.97%

Deluxe Deuces

Royal flush	800
Four deuces	200
Natural straight flush	50
Wild royal flush	25
Five of a kind	15
Natural four of a kind	10
Wild straight flush	9
Wild four of a kind	4
Full house	4
Flush	3
Straight	2
Three of a kind	1

Payback: 100.34%

Deuces Wild

Royal flush	800
Four deuces	200
Wild royal flush	25
Five of a kind	15
Straight flush	9
Four of a kind	5
Full house	3
Flush	2
Straight	2
Three of a kind	1

Payback: 100.76%

Joker Wild

Royal flush	800
Five of a kind	200
Wild royal flush	100
Straight flush	50
Four of a kind	20
Full house	7
Flush	5
Straight	3
Three of a kind	2
Two pair	1
Kings or better	1

Payback: 100.65%

Jacks or Better (rare 9/7)

Royal flush	800
Straight flush	50
Four of a kind	25
Full house	9
Flush	7
Straight	4
Three of a kind	3
Two pair	2
Jacks or better	1

Payback: 100.80%

while another has only full-pay Deuces Wild. Try not to get defeated and give in to the temptation of the flashing lights and glitz by just sitting down anywhere.

- In the quest for good machines, there's always one answer: Go to Vegas. It's video poker heaven and sets the standard for the rest of the world. You'll find the greatest selection and variety of full-pay machines throughout Nevada. The "local" casinos off the tourist-infested Strip tend to have the best machines. You'll find forms of video poker generosity in the desert that will never appear anywhere else.
- I must reiterate that, although machine selection is crucial, knowing how to play the machine with a quality strategy is equally important.

DECISIONS, DECISIONS, DECISIONS

Okay, you've identified a good machine and want to sit down to play. Wait a minute. You've only fought half of the good fight. Now you need to know the expert strategy for that machine.

But where do the strategies come from? How much can there be to picking some cards and trying to get the best hand? Well, it isn't rocket science but there is a science to it that involves, yes, mathematics.

Let's look at the basics. You're dealt five cards in your initial hand. For each card, you have two alternatives: hold or discard. That leads to an overall choice of 32 ($2 \times 2 \times 2 \times 2 \times 2 = 32$) different "hold" combinations, ranging from holding none of the cards to holding them all. Each of these combinations has its own payoff potential. The correct play—always and as a certainty—is to play the combination with highest expected return (see page 102 for the explanation of this concept).

If you had a psychic vision and knew what the next cards in the deck were, then you would know the "correct" play for any hand. As was true in blackjack, you have to trust that there is a correct, irrefutable way to play each hand that will result in the greatest winnings for you over the long run. Just as with any other information in this book it's based on math and probability. But whenever you don't get the cards you need, you may feel that there was a better way to play the hand. There's not.

The information in video poker is even more clear-cut than other gambling situations. There is no ambiguity: You know what five cards you see and you know what potential they have with the other cards in the deck. The deck is random but honest; that allows us to use probability to guide us. To a certain extent, the pay table lets us take control of our gambling destiny; it allows us to learn what the smart choices are for every hand that's dealt out.

How important is it to play the games with correct strategy? If you care about your bankroll, very important. Game manufacturers estimate that casinos should expect to hold between two and four percent more than the payback with optimum play. The difference is attributable to one thing: player error (players either not playing max coin or playing the game imperfectly). Is it really so hard to decide what cards to hold or discard? Sometimes not: no one will be unsure to keep three of a kind or a full house when it's dealt. But there are many card combinations that can be played several ways. Look at the following hand:

10♠ 9♥ J♥ 6♥ Q♥

Do you hold the four-card straight (9♥ 10♠ J♥ Q♥)? Or the four-card flush (6♥ 9♥ J♥ Q♥)? Or a three-card straight flush with a gap in it (9♥ J♥ Q♥)? Or just a two-card royal flush (J♥ Q♥)? The answer depends on what kind of game you're playing. But there will be only one right choice. (Turn to page 108 to see what you do with this hand when playing 9/6 Jacks.)

Expert Play

When talking about the payback on a 9/6 Jacks or Better machine, I have said that you can expect to get back 99.5% of the amount you play (over the long term) with expert play. But what exactly is expert play? Absolute expert play is determined by the calculations of the software programs mentioned earlier. The expected return for each hand is calculated and then strategies are distilled from this information. For our purposes, the definition of expert play will be playing in an informed way that uses strategies that come very close to computer-like perfection.

The thing to realize is that you have to learn the strategies. You can't assume that intuition or your "poker smarts" will lead you to make the right plays in video poker.

Common sense may often guide you correctly, but sometimes the right decision will not be obvious. On any individual hand, your "gut instinct" choice may lead to success, but if you want long-term success you need to use consistent strategies.

EXPECTED RETURN

Thus far, we know that you need two things to have success in video poker: a healthy respect for understanding pay tables and for learning proper play. But what lies at the heart of these two fundamental points? That core component is a topic that is near and dear to all video poker aficionados: expected return. The concept of expected return is just another form of the mathematical principle of expectation, which was discussed at length in Chapter 2 and which is referred to throughout the book. Expectation, in regard to gambling, is the dollars-and-cents result you can expect to achieve over the long haul when you take a certain course of action. For our discussion of video poker, expected return (ER) *is the long-term dollars-and-cents result expected of each different combination of hold/discard.*

The ER is our way of quantifying how correct a particular play is; it tells us what our long-term payback will be when we play a hand a particular way. The calculation of the ER—and therefore the correct play—depends entirely on the specific payoffs for winning hands.

Let's look at a simple example of expected return. We're playing 9/6 Jacks or Better and we're dealt the following hand (of course the actual order in which the cards appear doesn't matter): 2♥ 6♥ 7♥ 8♦ 9♥

Do you go for the flush or the straight? Well, the pay table gives us 6 for 1 for a flush and only 4 for 1 on a straight so the answer may be intuitive, but let's break it down in terms of expected return. Say you go for the flush and discard the 8♦. There are 47 cards left in the deck (52 – 5 = 47) and nine of those are hearts you need to fill the flush (that's 13 heart cards minus the four that you're holding). So the probability of getting the flush (which will pay six coins) is 9/47. The probability of not getting a flush (these hands pay nothing) is 38/47. The ER looks like this:

$$ER = [9/47 \times (6)] + [38/47 \times (0)] = 1.1489$$

Very nice. You have yourself a winning play in the long run. How do we know that? The expected return is greater than the amount bet—a bet of 1 coin will, on average, return 1.1489 coins.

Now let's look at the straight draw. You discard the 2♥. There are eight cards out of the 47 in the remaining deck that can fill the straight: the four 5s and the four 10s. A straight pays out four coins and thus we have this calculation:

$$ER = [8/47 \times (4)] + [39/47 \times (0)] = 0.6809$$

We can clearly see this is a much weaker choice than the flush draw. In fact, it's a long-term loser. On average, you'll get back only 0.6809 coins for every one you bet.

Every time we make the decision to go for the flush instead of the straight, we are making a move that is better by 0.468 coins (1.1489 – 0.6809). Look at it in terms of real money. If you're playing 5 coins on $1 machine, the right choice is better by $2.34 ($5 × 0.468). On a quarter machine at max coin, it's worth about 59¢ ($1.25 × 0.468). You don't want to throw that money away by making the wrong choice. Short-term experience and regrets should not factor into the equation. If you go for the flush 10 times and each time you pull a card that would have filled the straight, that's just too bad. It's no excuse for following the wrong strategy. You must adhere to the best move for the long term—if you want to be a winner. (Ten times or 1,000 times—frustrating as it may be—is still the short term.)

What if we decided to hold all five cards? Obviously, the ER would be 0—it's not a paying hand. If we discard only the 7♥, the ER would still be 0. Nothing we could draw would make a winning hand. Remember that there are 32 ways that this hand can be played. Every one of these ways has its own ER. The correct play is the one with the highest ER.

This illustration was very simple. With this hand, 2♥ 6♥ 7♥ 8♦ 9♥, the best choices involved drawing only one card, and only one winning hand could be made in each case (either a flush or a straight). But what if the 2♥ were a Q♥? This would further increase the flush draw's ER because now we have the possibility of getting another queen and making a paying hand of a high pair.

Calculations get very complex—that's why we rely on our friend the computer. If you decided to throw away all five initial cards, the remaining 47 cards could form 1,533,939 unique hands. Despite this wondrous variety, the ER of discarding all five cards comes out to a paltry 0.3623.

It's important to understand that the pay table and ER are inextricably linked. In our example above, if a straight paid 7 coins instead of 5, the ER for a straight draw would be higher than for a flush draw. (No machine actually has this particular kind of topsy-turvy payout, but any change in the pay schedule will affect all the expected returns and, consequently, the strategies.)

It's also important to realize that very often the best decision for a hand will have an ER that is less than the bet. But it is essential in these cases to choose the best bad choice— the hold combination that has the highest ER and will therefore minimize your losses in the long run.

Does all this seem very impractical to you? Last you checked, you didn't have a microprocessor implanted in your head that runs ER calculations. Don't worry; it's fine to let all the video poker pundits and their computers do the work for you. But an understanding of ER is the foundation of your understanding of the game. And it's ER that gives rise to the more general (and practical) rules you use when playing. You need to know the strategy for your predraw hands; behind that strategy is ER, but you don't have to know the specific ER. Let's review what we've covered:

- There are 32 ways to play any five-card draw hand.
- The only way to know the best play is to calculate the ER for each of the 32 possibilities based on the machine's specific pay table.
- The correct play will be the one of the 32 possibilities with the highest ER.
- Strategy recommendations incorporate the correct ER choices in as general a way as possible, which may sacrifice some of the computer perfect exactitude for more manageable and enjoyable play.

TOTAL RETURN

Now that we have an understanding of expected return, we have the ability to know what a particular video poker game will return to a player who uses perfect play. You were wondering where the payback percentage claims were coming from, weren't you? That 99.5% for 9/6 Jacks or Better wasn't just pulled from thin air. The curtain is pulled back and we reveal *total return*: the number that has the video poker cognoscenti either drooling or running in the opposite direction. The total return, commonly called the payback percentage, is the expected return for the whole game when played perfectly over the long run.

Total return (TR) allows us to compare different games with different pay tables. It is analogous to expected return, but it applies to an entire game rather than a specific hand. TR for a machine is arrived at by adding together the ERs for the correct play of each unique hand (there are 2,598,960 different hands in a 52-card deck).

Knowing the total return is incredibly empowering. A machine that pays back 100% allows you to play even with the house—with a 0% house edge. If a machine pays off less than 100%, then you will eventually lose money to it (not including slot club perks). If a machine pays over 100%, playing expertly over a long period of time should lead to profit. It's essential to note that the total return percent will be achieved over a huge number of hands; whether the average player can stick around long enough to be guaranteed the success of a positive return machine will be discussed later.

Remember that we are talking about the long run and averages. In any given session, it's highly unlikely that your return will be in line with the machine's total return. But if you play the best machines with expert play, you will give yourself the best chance to come out ahead.

When you're playing with the advantage, building up your playing speed will help you as long as it's not at the cost of accuracy. If you have a 0.5% edge and you play a $1 machine at 500 hands per hour, you'll bet $2,500 and have an expected win of $12.50. If you play at 700 hands per hour, you'll bet $3,500 and have an

9/6 Jacks or Better

Hand	Frequency	Percent Probability	Payout	Return
Royal flush	1 in 40,390.55	0.002%	800*	1.98%
Straight flush	1 in 9,148.37	0.011%	50	0.55%
Four of a kind	1 in 423.27	0.236%	25	5.91%
Full house	1 in 86.86	1.151%	9	10.36%
Flush	1 in 90.79	1.101%	6	6.61%
Straight	1 in 89.05	1.123%	4	4.49%
Three of a kind	1 in 13.43	7.445%	3	22.33%
Two pair	1 in 7.74	12.928%	2	25.86%
Jacks or better	1 in 4.66	21.459%	1	21.46%
Nothing	1 in 1.83	54.543%	0	0.00%

*Royal flush payout is based on max coins (4,000 coins for 5 coins played).
Total return: 99.54%

expected win of $17.50. Plus you'll earn more slot club points. (Practicing at home on the computer will help speed up your play.)

Above are the results of an analysis of 9/6 Jacks or Better run on the WinPoker software.

The frequency of each paying hand is based on the long-term results of playing each of the initial hands with perfect strategy. The overall return for each kind of winning hand is calculated by multiplying the percent probability by the payout. A quick look at this table gives us some essential info and insight into the game of Jacks or Better:

• You can "expect" to get a royal flush only once every 40,390 hands. However, the royal accounts for nearly 2% of the machine's total return. Without hitting the royal, the machine pays back only 97.5%. (This is still better than most slot machines.)

• Nearly 55% of the hands you play will produce nothing. You can't expect to win all the time. On the contrary, you'll lose most often.

• A pair of jacks or better accounts for over 21% of the game's return. Even though this hand is a push, it is essential to keeping your bankroll going as you pursue the bigger payoffs.

• Contrary to normal poker odds, the frequencies of final hands in video poker are not set figures. They are predicated on the strategy used. For example, the full house occurs more often than the flush or straight in Jacks or Better. That's because the higher-paying full

house is pursued more often when using perfect strategy.

• Don't ignore the little hands. Jacks or better, two pair, and three of a kind make up nearly 70% of the total return.

The next step is to create a reasonable strategy that can be used to come close to those computer-perfect results.

STRATEGY TABLES

Once you know what games have a positive expectation, you'll know—from a mathematical point of view—what the best games are. It's like comparison shopping for the best car. But, in this case, you have to learn how to drive the specific car. That's learning the strategy.

In order to get the maximum payback from video poker machines, you need to make the choices that will get you the best expected returns on each hand. Since you're not a computer nor can you have a computer with you in the casino, you'll need to use general strategy rules to guide your play. Strategies are ways to generalize what to do with each hand.

Since there are over 2.5 million starting hands, you could have 2.5 million rules. That would be just a bit unwieldy. Strategies work from general hand patterns and what the best average return would be for certain decisions. The more complex a strategy table is, the more precise it likely is, but it's also more difficult to use. The time wasted splitting hairs might not be worth it when you're playing on a profitable machine.

Most strategies are created by calculating the average expected returns for different types of hands. For instance, in Jacks or Better the average expected return of all the hands where you start with a four-card flush is lower than the average expected value for a high pair (jack, queen, king, or ace). Therefore, the high pair is the preferred predraw combination to hold and is listed higher on a strategy chart.

The reason you'll find different strategies from different experts is that they're dealing with an art, rather than a science. Each analyst tries to create the smallest number of rules that will encompass all the hands and lead to nearly computer-perfect results. You'll find that most strategies from the top experts are pretty similar—but the presentation (or the level of detail) will differ. Some are more concerned with practical application and ease of use; others want to take you into the land of many decimal points.

Many things will affect the purity of your payback percentage: the compromises of the strategy, your flawed human memory, fatigue, distractions, etc. Suffice it to say that accuracy is important, but being off by hundredths of a percent is nothing to lose sleep about.

When you go to play, bring your non-electronic strategy aids with you—charts, cue cards, your own personal notes, whatever. Make copies of the Jacks or Better and Deuces Wild strategies in this chapter. Don't worry that the casino will trouble you; I have never heard of a patron being banned from a casino because of a video poker strategy sheet.

LEARNING TO READ

Obviously, in order to use the charts on pages 108 and 109 and any other strategy charts, you need to know the poker hand rankings. See page 183 in the poker chapter if you need to get acquainted with them or would like a refresher. On the charts you'll see things like "three-card straight flush." This has no meaning in table poker, and also has no place on the pay tables of video poker machines. What it means is that you are holding three cards that have the potential to be part of a straight flush, should the draw go your way.

AN OPEN-BOOK TEST

The more you use the chart, the more you'll memorize it. Test yourself with these Jacks or Better hands:
1. 8♣ 9♣ J♥ 10♣ J♣
2. 10♥ J♥ 4♥ Q♥ K♥
3. 9♠ 10♦ J♣ Q♣ 10♥
4. 7♣ 8♦ 3♣ 10♥ 5♣
5. 10♠ 5♦ 7♦ Q♠ J♣
6. Q♦ Q♥ J♥ K♥ 5♠
7. 9♠ 4♦ 4♠ J♠ 2♠
8. A♠ K♣ J♥ 4♦ 6♦

And the answers are:
1. Keep 8♣ 9♣ 10♣ J♣ over J♥ J♣ because a four-card straight flush is higher on the chart than a high pair.
2. Keep 10♥ J♥ Q♥ K♥ over 10♥ J♥ 4♥ Q♥ K♥ because a four-card royal takes precedence over a made flush.
3. Keep 10♦ 10♥ over 9♠ 10♦ J♣ Q♣ because the low pair comes one spot ahead of this four-card straight on the chart.
4. Keep 3♣ 5♣ 7♣ rather than discarding the whole hand because a "double inside" straight flush (one with two gaps) is better than drawing five new cards. You did spot that double-gapper, didn't you?
5. Don't hold a 10 and a high card of the same suit when there's another high card. It's better to keep the two high cards, because you'll have more chances for paying pairs. Don't just dream of the royal flush. Hold: Q♠ J♣.
6. Hold: Q♦ Q♥. Don't break a high pair to draw to a three-card royal. Just hold the high pair.
7. Keep 9♠ 4♠ J♠ 2♠. A four-card flush is stronger than a low pair (but weaker than a high pair).
8. Keep K♣ J♥. Don't keep the ace as a "kicker"—it's the weakest of your high cards. You never hold three high cards of assorted suits including the ace; that is, you only hold an unsuited J-Q-K.

ARE YOU IN THE MONEY?

VOLATILITY

So you've got strategies and you've done some practicing. Now let's talk about the money. Assume you have found a positive expectation (over 100% payback) video poker machine that you like. Assume that you play the game with the right strategy. You're on easy street, right? But then you sit down to play and you lose during your first five sessions. You're down hundreds of dollars. What happened? Wasn't the money supposed to come pouring in? Have I been deceiving you about video poker, claiming that it's a game where you can get the "edge"? No. You've simply been a victim of the game's—and really this applies to any gambling game—short-term fluctuations.

Volatility is a measure of the roller coaster effect that a game will have. It is the mathematical concept that makes it a little nerve-wracking to try to walk away with the casino's money, even when you have the advantage. Some games have greater fluctuations than others and are considered more volatile. What makes a game volatile? Hit frequency, which is the percentage of hands with winning outcomes, is the first determinant. Obviously, the more frequently that a machine gives some sort of significant payback, the better chance you have of keeping your playing stake going.

Second, as a general rule, the more that your return is concentrated in the rare hands, the more volatile the game will be. (In order to determine that, you need to have a sense of the machine's payback analysis—again, the books and software will come in handy.) Let's look at the relatively volatile Deuces Wild. Below is the WinPoker software analysis of the game.

You'll learn to love this stuff if you catch the video poker fever. The thing that makes Deuces Wild volatile is that nearly 6% of your total return is concentrated in the royal flush and four deuces hands. These aren't common hands. Assuming that you play 500 hands per hour, the four deuces should show up once every 10 hours, and the royal flush about once in 90 hours. Without those two hands, the machine pays back only 95%. If they don't show up for obscene lengths of time, you'll likely be losing quite a bit of dough.

This isn't a game where you hover around being "even"; you'll likely lose hundreds before hitting the one or two big hands that put you ahead. Here's another sobering way to look at it: Hands of four of a kind or less account for 99% of the hands you'll end up with. However, they account for only about 82% of the total return. That means you're playing against an 18% house edge when the top hands aren't appearing.

Not surprisingly, the games with the highest returns have the highest volatility. That means you and your money might not be able to stick around long enough to reap the profits. However, a less volatile game like Jacks or Better will usually let you play longer, but ultimately has a (slight) negative expectation. That's the bind the casino puts you in.

Even a relatively non-volatile game like 9/6 Jacks or Better will put you through the wringer

Deuces Wild				
Hand	Frequency	Percent Probability	Payout	Return
Royal flush	1 in 45,281.93	0.002%	800*	1.77%
Four deuces	1 in 4,909.10	0.020%	200	4.07%
Wild royal flush	1 in 556.84	0.180%	25	4.49%
Five of a kind	1 in 312.34	0.320%	15	4.80%
Straight flush	1 in 239.53	0.417%	9	3.76%
Four of a kind	1 in 15.40	6.494%	5	32.47%
Full house	1 in 47.11	2.123%	3	6.37%
Flush	1 in 59.39	1.684%	2	3.37%
Straight	1 in 17.86	5.598%	2	11.20%
Three of a kind	1 in 3.51	28.471%	1	28.47%
Nothing	1 in 1.83	54.691%	0	0.00%

*Royal flush payout is based on max coins (4,000 coins for 5 coins played).
Total return: 100.76%

AT THE VERY LEAST

The strategy for any video poker game can get very complex with many rules, rankings, and exceptions to rules. I find that using a hand-ranking table works best for me as I try to master a game. However, many people prefer "plain English" rules. The full hand-ranking charts are on pages 108 and 109, but here are some rules of thumb that will let you dive right in and have you playing Jacks or Better and Deuces Wild at a higher level than most players.

JACKS OR BETTER
- Never keep a "kicker"—an extra high card along with a pair.
- You will never draw to an inside straight unless you have three or four high cards. Four high cards? Realize that J–Q–K–A is an inside straight. Only one rank of card can complete it—the 10.
- You never keep three cards to a straight or flush, but you do keep three cards to a straight flush in some circumstances.
- When you start using the full strategy table, take it at its word. Don't defy the chart because you need to hit a "big" hand. Don't break up a full house or two pair because you're itching for a four of a kind.

DEUCES WILD
- The only single card you hold is a deuce. Translation: Don't hold a single ace or any "high" card—it does nothing for you. There is no such thing as a high card in Deuces Wild.
- Never discard a deuce. The only time you might even think of this is if you have a shot at a natural royal. It's the wrong move; don't do it.
- You will never hold only one other card with a single deuce. Again, don't think that holding a high card with a deuce adds any value; it only hurts.
- A pair is always preferred to a four-card straight or flush.
- Never hold two pair. You must discard one pair (it doesn't matter which) and draw three cards.
- Don't worry about which of the two pair to discard when you have that decision. Sometimes you'll curse your choice; other times you won't. It evens out overall and you have no power to make the "right" choice.
- As a rule, you don't want to play a machine that has less than a five-for-one payout on four of a kind.
- Four of a kind is your sustenance in this game. It accounts for nearly one-third of your total return. This clarifies certain strategy decisions such as keeping a pair over a four-card flush. It also explains why a lull in quads (which, on average, should show up once in 15 hands) can make your money dwindle fast.

at one point or another. Let's pretend that we're at a Jacks or Better machine that pays off in a perfect cycle according to its expected payback. (I must emphasize that this is not how a real machine works; there are no patterns or cycles to detect.) A royal flush should come once in every 40,390 hands and it will account for 1.98% of the game's return. So we dutifully play our "for-argument's-sake-only" machine at $5 a hand for the 40,389 hands before our royal is "due."

(Okay, if the machine were really that predictable, we would be playing only $1 per hand before the royal was due—just indulge me!) That means we have put $201,945 in the machine ($5 × 40,389) and we have been getting a total return of 97.56% (the machine's normal 99.54% minus the 1.98% for the royal). In total, we will have lost $4,927.46 ($201,945 × the house edge of 2.44%). That's quite a price to pay on the path to the royal. Then on the next hand, we hit the

JACKS OR BETTER STRATEGY TABLE

These tables list the best hold combinations in order of decreasing expected return. Work from the top of the chart down until you find the first description that matches your hand. Once you find a match, don't look further down the chart; you are always looking for the highest possible choice. Just keep the combination of cards that matches the strategy listing and discard the rest.

You'll also need to learn some lingo. What is typically called an "inside straight" in poker (four cards of a possible five-card straight, with only one rank of card able to complete the straight) is often referred to as a straight with a "gap" in it. For example, 2♥ 6♠ 8♦ 9♦ 10♣ is a "four-card straight, one gap" hand. By holding the 6, 8, 9, 10, you can complete the straight only by drawing a 7. This is as compared to an "open" straight, which would allow for one of two ranks of cards to complete it. For example, discarding the 2 in this hand, 2♥ 7♠ 8♦ 9♦ 10♣, gives the opportunity to draw a 6 or a jack to complete the straight. The more gaps a hand has, the more limited are the options to complete it. Two last linguistic lessons: "T" is sometimes used for a 10 and "suited" means all the cards have the same suit and is indicated on the chart with an "(s)."

- Royal flush
- Straight flush
- Four of a kind
- Four-card royal flush
- Full house
- Flush
- Three of a kind
- Straight
- Four-card straight flush
- Two pair
- Pair of jacks or better (high pair)
- Three-card royal flush
- Four-card flush
- TJQK: unsuited
- Pair of 10s or less (low pair)
- 9TJQ: unsuited
- 89TJ: unsuited
- 9JQ (s)
- 9TQ (s)
- Four-card straight, open, no high cards
- Three-card straight flush, two gaps, two high cards
- Three-card straight flush, one gap, one high card
- Three-card straight flush, open, no high cards
- JQKA: unsuited
- Two-card royal flush, two high cards
- Four-card straight, one gap, three high cards
- Three-card straight flush, two gaps, one high card
- Three-card straight flush, one gap, no high cards
- JQK: unsuited
- Two high cards: unsuited (when you have three don't keep the ace)
- Two-card royal flush with 10 and no ace
- One high card
- Three-card straight flush, two gaps, no high cards
- Nothing (draw five cards)

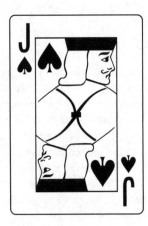

DEUCES WILD STRATEGY TABLE

The strategy table for Deuces Wild is broken up into four separate tables based on the number of deuces (or ducks as they are often called) that appear in the initial hand. Some people find this helps them to memorize the possibilities.

No deuces in initial hand:
- Royal flush
- Four-card royal flush
- Straight flush
- Four of a kind
- Full house
- Three of a kind
- Flush
- Straight
- Four-card straight flush
- Three-card royal flush
- One pair
- Four-card flush
- Four-card straight; open, but not 3456
- Three-card straight flush
- 456(s)
- 345(s)
- TJ(s)
- Three-card straight flush; two gaps, 7–K high
- TQ(s), JQ(s)
- 346(s), 356(s)
- Four-card straight; one gap, includes 3456, but not A345
- Nothing (draw five cards)

One deuce in initial hand:
- Wild royal flush
- Five of a kind
- Straight flush
- Four of a kind
- Four-card wild royal flush
- Full house
- Four-card straight flush; open, 2 & 567(s) to 2 & 9TJ(s)
- Three of a kind
- Flush
- Straight
- Four-card straight flush; one gap, includes 2 & 345(s), 2 & 456(s)
- Four-card straight flush; two gaps, 7–K high
- 2 & A34(s), 2 & A35(s), 2 & A45(s)
- Three-card royal, no ace
- Three-card straight flush; open, 2 & 67(s) to 2 & 9T(s)
- Three-card royal, with ace
- Deuce only (draw four cards)

Two deuces in initial hand:
- Wild royal flush
- Five of a kind
- Straight flush
- Four of a kind
- Four-card wild royal flush
- Four-card straight flush; open, 2, 2 & 67(s) to 2, 2 & 9T(s)
- Two deuces only (draw three cards)

Three deuces in initial hand:
- Wild royal flush
- Five of a kind: 2, 2, 2, pair of T–A
- Three deuces only (draw two cards)

Four deuces in initial hand:
- Four deuces (draw one card)

THE DOLLARS AND SENSE OF THE STRATEGY CHART

Why are there so many distinctions on the strategy chart? Is it really worth it? Yes, following the chart will help you make (or save) money. (If we really wanted to squeeze every cent out of the machine, there would be quite a few more headache-inducing rules.) The only way to convince you that the decisions have a rhyme and reason is to look into the mathematics. For any possible card combination, we have to look at its expected return, which reveals what our choice will be worth on average. So let's take a look at the mathematics behind the strategy chart's sometimes cryptic guidance.

We're dealt this hand in 9/6 Jacks or Better:

10♣ 10♥ J♥ Q♥ K♠

We have, as always, 32 different ways to hold these cards. But it's safe to say that even the most casual player would consider only three possibilities: hold the pair of 10s; hold the three-card royal flush; or hold the four-card straight. What to do? Let's break down the expected return for each of the possibilities. (The calculations were done with the ever-handy WinPoker software.)

• We hold the 10♥ J♥ Q♥ K♠. There are 47 different cards that we can draw. Our highest possible hand is the straight, which we can get with one of eight cards (the four 9s and the four aces). But we can also make a high pair with one of nine cards (three each of the jack, queen, and king). The chart below reflects the expected distribution of the 47 hands.

Final Hand	Number of Occurrences	Payout per Coin Played	Total Value (number of occurrences × payout)
Pair of jacks or better	9	1	9
Straight	8	4	32
Nothing	30	0	0
Total hands = 47		Total payout = 41	

We calculate the expected return by dividing the total payout by the total number of hands.

The expected return of 10♥ J♥ Q♥ K♠ = $^{41}/_{47}$ = 0.8723

• When we hold 10♣ 10♥, we have a three-card draw. The number of possible combinations on a three-card draw is 16,215. (In other words, there are 16,215 distinct three-card groupings of the remaining 47 cards in the deck—that's combinatorial math for you.) Let's look at all the expected results.

Final Hand	Number of Occurrences	Payout per Coin Played	Total Value (number of occurrences × payout)
Four of a kind	45	25	1,125
Full house	165	9	1,485
Three of a kind	1,854	3	5,562
Two pair	2,592	2	5,184
Nothing	11,559	0	0
Total hands = 16,215		Total payout = 13,356	

Expected return for 10♣ 10♥ = $^{13356}/_{16215}$ = 0.8237

• Holding 10♥ J♥ Q♥ gives us a two-card draw and 1,081 possible hands. The breakdown is as follows:

Final Hand	Number of Occurrences	Payout per Coin Played	Total Value (number of occurrences × payout)
Royal flush	1	800	800
Straight flush	2	50	100
Flush	42	6	252
Straight	37	4	148
Three of a kind	7	3	21
Two pair	21	2	42
Pair of jacks or better	243	1	243
Nothing	728	0	0
Total hands = 1,081		Total payout = 1,606	

Expected return for 10♥ J♥ Q♥ = $^{1606}/_{1081}$ = 1.4857

Hey, the three-card royal hold is actually a money-maker. In the long run, we'll get back 1.4857 coins for every one we bet. The chart also reveals how much of a hand's expected return comes from results other than the big hand we fantasize about. The smaller winning hands make up much of the potential return. For instance, if the 10♥ J♥ Q♥ gave us only a royal flush payout and no other intermediate returns, it's ER would be an anemic 0.7401 ($^{800}/_{1081}$). Blecch. Much of its strength comes from the other paying results.

Now we have enough information to guide our strategy decision. What do we know? We know that the three-card royal hold is much more valuable than the four-card straight (0.8723), which in turn is preferred to the pair of 10s (0.8237). Lo and behold, all this ugly number-crunching is reflected on the strategy chart. The three-card royal comes before 10-J-Q-K, which comes before a low pair. Notice that it isn't just any four-card straight that has higher value than a low pair—it's only the specific combo of 10-J-Q-K. The expected return guides our way and makes these distinctions.

How much is it really worth to us? Let's assume that we're playing five coins on a $1 machine. By choosing the three-card royal, we will on average get back $7.43 ($5 × 1.4857). Going after the 10-J-Q-K straight will bring us $4.36 ($5 × 0.8723). The wrong choice will cost you $3.07 ($7.43 – $4.36) in the long run—for each time you make the blunder. That's a significant cost, and such mistakes can add up quickly when you're playing by intuition alone.

Let's say that we're at the same machine spending $5 a hand, and our only choice is between the 10-J-Q-K straight and the pair of 10s (as would be the case if the hand were 10♣ 10♥ J♦ Q♥ K♠). Expected return is, of course, still our wallet's ally. We follow the strategy and keep 10-J-Q-K and its $4.36 expected return. Were we to keep the pair of 10s, our expected return would be $4.12 ($5 × 0.8237). In the long term, that mistake would cost us about a quarter each time we made it. Although both of these choices are "losers"—meaning they have a negative expectation—the better choice is clearly a winner because it minimizes our losses. Every cent saved gives us a chance to still be playing when the big hands roll around. In that way, expected return and its strategy offspring can lead us to long-term success.

royal, win $4,000, and are somewhat restored to health. But not completely—we're down money even after the royal arrives! That's because 9/6 Jacks is a negative expectation game and when everything goes according to plan, you end up a loser. Okay, we'll give ourselves the benefit of the doubt and say that our make-believe machine was part of a slot club that gave 0.5% cashback. So we made a profit. But—and that's the point of this whole exercise—we plummeted way down before we got most of the way back up. You just have to be prepared for the wild swings.

Of course, the hands won't show up in predictable patterns. Anything can happen in the short term. In fact, it's safe to say that in any given playing session, you will end up doing better or worse than the game's expected total return. That's "luck"—we don't know what will happen over hundreds or even thousands of hands. It would not be shocking to go 100,000 hands without a royal. Then again, you may hit three royals in 40,000 hands or make an unusually high number of straight flushes and quads to keep you pink and profitable. What you need to remind yourself of is that all the ups and downs will average out over the long term. The end result will fall in line with the game's payback percentage based on your ability—that's skill.

Volatility and the Long Run

Video poker is streaky. Take some consolation that a losing session doesn't mean that you're playing poorly. You can't start altering your strategy because you're feeling desperate to hit a royal or four deuces or four aces. It's all one long session and it can span years.

So now you're asking yourself just how long is the long run? How many hands must you play in order for everything to "even out" and thus be assured that your advantage will fill your wallet? Some say one million hands will do the trick. At 500 hands per hour, that works out to 2,000 hours. We're not talking about a weekend's stay. If you're serious about playing video poker, you can't worry about the short-term results. This is true for the most casual recreational player. If you know that you're playing a particular game well, you shouldn't worry. You are in it for the long run. Of course, that long run may be hard to reach if you're playing only two weekends a year. If that's the

case, don't assume that you'll see the royal. Eight hours of play at 500 hands per hour gives you only a 9.4% shot of nailing a royal.

Your success is based not only on the machine's total return, but on your skill in achieving the return. All the discussion thus far may convince you that video poker is very royal-centric. Well, it is, but the jackpot hands aren't the whole story for the skilled player. The big hands will come one way or another. What the skilled player does is play all her cards for the maximum expected return and therefore sustain her bankroll for when the big hands do come around.

No matter who you are—pro or piker—you will lose more sessions than you will win. Again, that's because you need the higher payouts to get you winning and they are more rare. Even pros say they lose two out of three sessions. (However, on average, the losing sessions should be significantly smaller than the wins. If they're not, then you're playing the wrong machines and/or playing them with inadequate skill.)

BANKROLL

So what does all this mean in terms of bankroll requirements? For the casual and recreational player, the bankroll message is always the same: Be prepared to lose and play only at a level at which you're comfortable. In video poker you must be financially and mentally prepared to lose half the value of a royal flush during a session. That means $2,000 on dollar machines, $500 on quarter machines, and $100 on nickels.

It's not just a matter of dollars and cents, and how much you need to ride out the vicissitudes of the game. It's also a matter of psychology. If what you may lose makes you too uncomfortable, you're playing at too high a level. In that case, you can't afford to be drawn in by the lure of having the edge against the house. Drop down in denomination, play slower-moving games with reasonable house edges (blackjack for example), or just set a stop-loss limit for your video poker play. Accept that someday all your play on the best machines will win you some money, but you can't afford to "force" it to happen. Realizing you have a theoretical advantage can be dangerous. Remember that the casino gives away a lot of money in games where they have the mathematical edge (of course, they take in more than they give away), but the casino has a huge bankroll to weather fluctuations in fortune. The same may not be true for you.

But what if you want to play the games in serious pursuit of getting the edge; not with the time and dedication of a pro, but with the long-term intent of coming out ahead. You want to know what you need to survive long enough to win. The answer would require a lengthy discussion and some serious math; such information can be found in books dedicated to the game. The rule of thumb is that you should have a bankroll equal to three royal flush payouts. So that's $3,000 for the quarter player and $12,000 for the dollar player.

The more volatile the game, the bigger a bankroll you'll need. Try to be realistic. An undercapitalized player with a small edge is a casino's best friend.

ONE COIN VS. FIVE COINS

Many introductory gambling books will tell you to always play the full five coins on any video poker machine. Many seemingly knowledgeable players will shake their heads in disgust if you aren't playing "max coin." The reasoning is obvious: Playing max coin qualifies you for the higher pay on the jackpot hand (typically the royal flush). This in turn leads to a higher percentage payback. But that doesn't mean it's the right play for everybody—particularly a beginner.

Let's look at 9/6 Jacks or Better. With five coins played and perfect play, the game will return 99.54%. If you play only one coin, the game will return 98.37%. Wouldn't you always want to qualify for the higher payback? We need to go beyond the percentages and check out the actual money involved in two scenarios. Both assume a $1 machine, 500 hands per hour, and 2 hours of play.

Scenario #1: Max coin
Total amount played: $5,000
    (500 hands/hour × $5/hand × 2 hours)
House edge: 0.46%
    (100% − 99.54%)
Expected loss: $23
    ($5,000 × 0.46%)

Scenario #2: One coin
Total amount played: $1,000
    (500 hands/hour × $1/hand × 2 hours)
House edge: 1.63%
    (100% − 98.37%)
Expected loss: $16.30
    ($1,000 × 1.63%)

So the one-coin scenario has you coming out ahead by $6.70. This result often comes as a surprise to those fixated on percentage. Of course, it makes perfect sense. Even at a higher house edge (up to a certain point), when you risk less money you stand to lose less money. This will almost always be true in video poker when you face less than a 100% return.

Of course, if you based your play on money and not time, then you should always play max coin. If you knew you wanted to play exactly $1,000 worth of hands then you should play the max. But very few people would have the patience or discipline to do this. It would mean playing 200 hands and then stopping, and having only one-fifth of the play compared to playing one coin. This isn't very realistic because most players want to increase their time at the machine. By playing one coin when the house has the edge, you will increase your playing time and slow your losses.

But haven't I been saying what a good opportunity video poker is? Yes, it can be, but you have to find the right machine and you have to know how to play it properly. Any time you're stuck below 100%, the less money you risk the better. If it's a losing proposition, you shouldn't expose five times your money to make it a "better" losing proposition.

Of course, you also have to put a price on the psychological and entertainment value of getting the big jackpot—if and when it comes. It may hurt to have only one coin deposited when you hit the royal flush. Still, your one-coin choice would be a wise one. You may bemoan your one-coin royal, but in the long run you would be ahead—well, to be precise, losing less. (That doesn't mean that full-pay Jacks or Better should only be played at one coin. Slot club benefits can bring the game over 100%.)

If you're playing a machine that returns 100% or more, and you know near-perfect strategy, then you should definitely play max

THE ROYAL FOLLIES

From all the discussion of how important a royal flush is to your payoff, you might think that the royal should be pursued at all costs. Many players have this mentality, and it's a losing one. Let's compare some expected returns when you play five coins in Jacks or Better. You'll see the royal pursuit can often be a royal flop.

Take a look at this one:

2♠ 2♥ J♣ K♣ 7♦

Expected return on holding 2♠ 2♣ is 4.1184, while the expected return on holding J♣ K♣ is 2.9439. Not even close. You hold the two 2s.

Next question: Would you give up the 250 coin payout on a straight flush to pursue the royal?

9♦ 10♦ J♦ Q♦ K♦

You shouldn't. The straight flush has an ER of 250 (since we don't discard anything). The ER for dumping the 9 in pursuit of the ace is 93.0851. Again, not even close. Take the money and celebrate.

Let's look at something more tempting:

J♥ J♦ Q♦ K♦ 3♣

Holding the high pair will earn you more than holding the three-card royal in the long run, with an ER of 7.6827 versus 7.4422.

All of these tidbits are incorporated into the strategy tables, so holding on to the tables will always be the right move.

coin. Whenever you have the advantage, you need to exploit it. Do you know expert strategy for full-pay Deuces Wild? Then you would be foolish not to play max coin. With five coins, the machine returns 100.76%. With anything less than five coins, it returns only 99.25%.

There's another smart choice to preserve your bankroll, increase your payback percentage, and give you a shot at the max jackpot: Step down in denomination. Rather than playing one coin on a $1 machine, you can play max coin on a quarter machine for only a 25¢ increase (you would play $1.25 per hand rather than $1). Or drop down to playing max nickels instead of a single quarter. The problem is that you have to make sure you find a machine with the same pay table at the lower denomination. Particularly for nickels, it's hard to find full-pay machines.

Also, remember that the return percentage increases only on the fifth coin. If you play two, three, or four coins, you're playing at the lower percentage. Therefore, playing two, three, or four coins would be very foolish—you're putting more money at risk for a lower percentage.

Let's recap:

• When you have the edge, bet max coin.

• When you don't, bet only one coin—don't give away more money chasing a few percentage points and a more "satisfying" royal.
• Either play one coin or five—don't mess with the in-between.
• Consider stepping down in denomination.
• Don't forget to factor in slot club benefits.

SO MANY GAMES, SO LITTLE TIME

The popularity of plain vanilla Jacks or Better has led to many offspring.

COMMON VARIATIONS OF JACKS OR BETTER

When you encounter an unfamiliar Jacks or Better, read the pay table. If you find something good, it doesn't mean that there's a catch. (But double check.) You might find an uncommon 9/6 machine that pays 4,700 for a royal instead of 4,000. If all else is the same, that's great—it pays back 99.9%! Why the weird number for the royal jackpot? Because on a quarter machine the payout would equal $1,175, just below the $1,200 mark where you would have to fill out a tax form.

A typical reduction in the pay table comes in the form of 8/5 Jacks or Better, which obviously pays 8 for the full house (instead of 9) and 5 for the flush (instead of 6). The reduced payoffs make this only a 97.28% return with perfect play.

Bonus games are very popular with players because they offer bigger payoffs for high hands. These machines pay out more on four of a kind, particularly four aces. There are different bonuses based on the particular ranks of the four of a kind. The game of choice for some video poker pros is Double Bonus Poker because perfect play will lead to a payback of 100.7% and $1 machines are widely available.

Be careful because some Double Bonus machines have 9/6 payouts. That's not what you want! You want 10/7. You need the increase on the full house and flush because the payout on two pair is reduced to one coin instead of two. The playing strategy differs greatly from plain old Jacks or Better and is tough because of penalty cards and lots of special cases. If you don't take the time to learn the strategy, you'll probably be playing the game in the same payback range as 9/6 Jacks or Better, but with greater volatility.

Triple Play Poker

Triple Play Poker allows players to play three hands at once with bets of up to five coins per hand, for a maximum of 15 coins. The game displays three poker hands—one face-up and two face-down. The face-down hands contain the same five cards as the face-up hand. As you choose each card to hold in the face-up hand, the exact same cards appear in the two other hands. When you draw, you draw to all three hands at once, but the draw cards for each hand come from separate, independent decks (minus the original five cards). Each hand is paid off according to its results. Popular games like Jacks or Better, Bonus, and Deuces Wild are offered in this format, but not often at full pay.

There's no reason to change your playing strategy in this format. All it's doing is allowing you to play at three times your normal rate. So, in Triple Play Jacks or Better, a pair of queens is still preferable to a three-card royal. Whether you play the hands consecutively, as on a regular machine, or at the same time, the expected return remains the same. So don't chase the three-card royal just because you seem to have three times the chance of hitting it.

Should you play this variation? If you can find a game where you have the edge, the simple answer you might glean from the rest of this chapter is: "Absolutely!" Mathematically, it makes sense: When you have an advantage, you want to run as much money as you can through the machine so you can earn your long-term percentage on that money. Indeed, playing three hands at a time will let you reach the long-term even faster. But that's a theoretical argument.

As I've also tried to stress throughout the chapter, real people play with real dollars and cents. Your bankroll might not be able to handle three times the risk per hour. Increasing your risk will make the game more volatile and your swings of fortune will be both extremely good and bad. It's great when a strong hand shows up in the first five cards and you know that you will have triple delight. But if you hit a short-term fluctuation of bad "luck"—which might involve thousands of hands—you'll be heading up to your room a lot sooner than you anticipated. Even in an advantageous game, there's no guarantee that your advantage will kick in when you need it. As was said in the section on bankrolling video poker, don't bet your house on the edge.

So there isn't a clear-cut answer. You have to know your bankroll, delve even further into the math of volatility, and know your stomach's tolerance for good and bad swings. This game is best if you know what you're doing and if you're playing for the long haul; or if you want to move up from simple quarter play, but don't feel ready for dollars. A quarter triple-play will have you playing $3.75 per hand rather than $5 per hand on the dollar machines. Something more to contemplate: There are also five-play and ten-play machines!

DEUCES WILD

Deuces Wild is an exciting game because all the wild cards make for big hands. It's also exciting because the full-pay version has a return of 100.76%. Players like that they can receive a sizable mini-jackpot by hitting four deuces, which occurs once every 4,900 hands on average. However, the game is more volatile than Jacks or Better. Another possible drawback: If you fall in love with this game, you'll have to move to Nevada. It's the only place you're sure to find the full-pay version of Deuces Wild. High rollers should be aware that almost all the machines are of the quarter variety.

Common Variations of Deuces Wild

There are many variations on traditional full-pay Deuces Wild. The pay table has been altered in many imaginative ways and has led to a wide variety of payback percentages. The most typical reduction in an unfavorable pay schedule is a reduction on the four of a kind payoff from five coins to four coins. This deviation alone plummets a normal full-pay return from 100.76% down to 94.27%! However, most manufacturers are smart enough to increase the payouts on other hands so that you have some compensation. Most often that compensation isn't enough. Hand frequencies are not what you're accustomed to from non-wild poker. Four of a kind is a lot more common than full houses and flushes.

JOKER WILD MACHINES

Joker Wild machines (also called Joker Poker) insert a joker into the mix (thus making a 53-card deck). The game had its heyday in Nevada, but now has lost its luster among the masses and the intelligentsia. This fall from grace can mainly be attributed to the scarcity of full-pay machines available. Not only that, the game is rather volatile and demands a complex strategy.

For some inexplicable reason, Atlantic City gamblers are either unperturbed or unaware of Joker Poker's shortcomings. The game, in its myriad short-pay forms, is quite popular in New Jersey. One nasty reduction from the full-pay version (listed on page 100) is a drop from 20 coins to 15 coins for four of a kind. This little casino tweak alters the payback from 100.65% to 96.38%. Also, there are Joker games that start paying back only on two pair rather than a pair of kings. The supposed compensation comes with the big hands—the royal often pays 1,000 coins for 1 and five of a kind pays 800 coins. That's not enough. An additional and more frequent jackpot hand is nice, but not if your expectation is still markedly negative and almost 70% of your hands are non-payers.

However, one of the best A.C. casino offerings is a Joker Poker variation. The game of Double Joker uses two jokers in a 54-card deck and returns 99.97% with perfect strategy. The danger of the game is its volatility; it will put you through the wringer because nearly two-thirds of your final hands will pay nothing. You have to hit some quads to keep you healthy in this game. Still, this is one of the best East Coast offerings.

PROGRESSIVES

Progressive jackpots constitute another major part of the video poker puzzle. These machines are very common, popular, and potentially profitable for the player. Progressives usually involve a bank of 10 or 12 machines that are electronically linked. A small portion of each bet made at the machines—usually about 1%—goes toward the jackpot on the royal flush (or whatever is the top hand). A large meter above the machines displays the current level of the jackpot. (There are also stand-alone progressive machines.)

A standard progressive is an 8/5 Jacks or Better game. The pay table is the same as a typical 8/5 pay table except that the royal flush pays a jackpot that is displayed on the meter above the machine. Maximum coins must be played to be eligible for the jackpot. After the jackpot is hit, it is reset to a certain value, which is normally the standard nonprogressive value.

Remember that a normal 8/5 machine has a payback percentage of only 97.3%. If the game is at its reset value, you're much better off with a standard 9/6 machine instead. How high does the jackpot have to be to make the game have a 100% payback? The break-even point is a return of 8,665 coins when 5 coins are played. But that's not the amount you'll see on the meter; the meter shows dollar value (it catches the eye much better!). So the dollar value to look for on a quarter machine would be $2,166.25. On a dollar machine, it would be $8,665. But even at these levels, you could still make more of a return on nonprogressive Deuces Wild and other high-return machines if you played them well.

While it's exciting to find a machine that has reached the 100% level or beyond, there are a few caveats to keep in mind. (You knew it couldn't be too easy.) The value of the royal dictates your strategy and that means that you should be making strategy changes when the royal hits certain values. Knowing what to do will require—you guessed it—study and computer practice. Strategy for an 8/5 progressive is different from standard 9/6 strategy. For example, you never hold an A–10 of the same suit in regular 9/6, but on a high progressive that option enters the strategy chart. If you use 9/6 strategy, you won't be losing much of an edge, but it would be enough to make video poker pundits turn pale.

Also, since so much of the payback is confined to the rare royal, the game is more volatile (see discussion on page 105) than your standard game. As the royal flush gains value, proper strategy will have you sacrifice the short-term payouts to go after the disproportionately big jackpot. That means you might lose quite a bit of dough in pursuit of your theoretical advantage. Another thing to be aware of is that, although 8/5 at a certain level is a rather attractive progressive machine (9/6 progressives would be better but are scarce), you can really be creamed by the giant linked progressive machines that have 6/5 pay tables. That game would require a jackpot of 12,350 coins ($3087.50 on a quarter machine) to be beneficial to the player and it would be even more streaky to play.

Jackpots can grow quite large if no one hits them for some time; it's not unheard of for the growing jackpot to make a game's total payback over 102%. If this happens, you'll probably end up encountering the ever-opportunistic pros. Very often, a team of pros will try to occupy every seat at a carousel when the progressive gets high enough to pique their interest. Stories are told of pros using their cell phones to call up fellow players to take over their seats. These "tiger teams," as they're called, will attack jackpots, seeking to walk away with the profit (and, of course, hoping that they will hit the big jackpot sooner rather than later). Progressives have been known to make some vultures overly aggressive, hovering over players' shoulders and waiting to leap in. This isn't common and you shouldn't be intimidated.

If you see a video poker progressive that enters the stratosphere of the "mega" slot machines, you've probably come across Five Deck Frenzy. It's a wide-area progressive (which means the machines are linked at multiple casinos) that uses a separate deck for each of the five cards dealt. Naturally this makes for much stranger strategies and winning hands than any other video poker game. The jackpot hand is five aces of spades—the probability of landing that combo is a not-in-this-lifetime 14,896,150 to 1. (Okay, that's a slight exaggeration. If you expertly played 600 hands an hour, 40 hours each week, you could expect to get this hand once every 12 years.) At the jackpot's reset level of $200,000, the game has a return of only 98.3%. Yes, the game does go positive at $518,000, but that's about as theoretical as you can get. It's extremely unlikely you'll get the hand and neither you nor your bankroll has enough long-term in you to cash in on that advantage. The verdict: Novel, but of no value to the serious player.

DOUBLING UP

Some video poker machines offer an option that allows you to risk the payout on a winning hand for the chance of doubling the payout. This side proposition will pop up on every winning hand. If you agree to do it (you don't have to), the typical play mechanic is to have a random card revealed on the screen. You then pick one of four random face-down cards. If your card is higher, you double your winnings. If it's lower, you lose your winnings. If it's the same rank, it's a push. If you win, you can keep on going with the double-or-nothing offer until you lose, decide to stop, or reach the machine's limit (sometimes 10,000 coins).

Many players believe that this is a scam to deprive them of their winnings—especially when they see too many aces pop up as the card they have to beat. In reality, there is no trick; the cards are completely random, just as they are in the regular part of the game. This is a purely 50–50, even-money bet, a casino rarity in which there is no house edge whatsoever.

Heavy breathing generally ensues when the phrase "no house edge" is uttered in the casino, so why isn't the double-up option much appreciated by video poker players?

It has some drawbacks. Although it's a fair bet, it compels you to put your winnings at stake. Those winnings are part of your payback percentage for video poker and by risking them, even in a purely "even" bet, you're increasing the volatility of the game. It's not like you're playing a completely separate even-money game where you can control your stake—that would be very nice.

Also, the bigger the fantasy you have of doubling your winnings into a fortune, the less chance you have of achieving it. Yes, you have a 1-in-2 chance of succeeding on any particular double. But if you're planning on turning your 10-coin win on two pair into a 1,280-coin bonanza, you'll need to successfully double 7 times in a row. You have a $\frac{1}{128}$ chance of that happening—that's about 0.8%. Try it enough times and you'll succeed, but your bankroll might not let you last long enough when you keep wiping out your normal hand winnings.

Most important, if you're playing video poker the way you want to play it—at over 100% return—this feature hurts you. Why would you want to make an even bet when you can play with an advantage? Once you have the edge, you want to get in as many hands as possible; you don't want to be slowed down by doubling up, which will just result in a "push" with the house in the long run.

However, it can be a smart bet if you're playing a less than 100% return game. The even-money double-up bet will slow down your play and expose less of your bankroll to the house edge. The bet won't win you more money, but it lets you lose less—and that's especially good if you enjoy the feature. However, realize that using the feature often may, as explained above, cause your bankroll to fluctuate more.

Most machines are equipped with the double-up feature, though it is rarely turned on. It seems neither players nor casino management have much enthusiasm for it, but you might be able to get a slot attendant to turn on the feature if you're fond of it. Be aware that you won't accumulate slot club points for any double-up action.

Essentially, the double-up feature doesn't change anything in the long term. But it will make your money come and go faster, and it will slow down your regular play—a benefit when the house has the edge and a detriment when you have the edge.

....
THERE'S STILL MORE TO KNOW

We've certainly covered a lot. And this is just the beginning of what you'll need to know to conquer video poker. You'll definitely want to factor casino perks into your play, no matter what your level. As you get more advanced, you might want to consider adding penalty cards to your strategy. Let's discuss both these ideas.

SLOT CLUBS

To get the most out of playing video poker, you must join a slot club. You must join all the slot clubs at all the places you play. For more information on what slot clubs are and how they work, see page 87 in the slot machine chapter.

Putting a value on everything you receive from a slot club can become an obsession. And why not? The benefits come in multiple forms and vary based on your play and the casino: room, meals, merchandise, cashback. In my mind, it's even more important for the smart video poker player to analyze and understand what a particular slot club delivers than it is for the reel slots player. A savvy video poker player has a very good understanding of what to expect (at least in the long term) from the machines he plays. The slot club benefits will be another crucial part of the equation for a game's expectation.

For the serious video poker player, valuing casino perks is an essential science. For the number lover and bargain hunter, it can be quite an intriguing pursuit. For example, let's say one casino offers only a measly 0.1% percent in cashback, but is happy to provide a free room and meal if you play $5,000 in the machines per day. If the room has a value of about $80 and the meal $30, then your rate of return on the machines has just risen by 2.2% ($\frac{110}{5000}$). Of course, that's only if you stop playing after putting $5,000 through the machines—which is unlikely. And if you don't care about the room and the meal, then you would want to find a place that offers more cashback.

Be aware that many slot clubs require more play on video poker machines than slot machines, due to the fact that video poker generally has a smaller house edge. Inquire at the slot club to see if they make a distinction. It used to be that only $1 players got the best slot club benefits, but that seems to be changing.

IT'S NOT TABLE POKER

Before you discard any cards at the video poker machine, the first thing you should discard are all the lessons and assumptions you have from playing real poker. The only thing to carry over from the poker table is a knowledge of the hand rankings. After that, you have to learn the proper strategy for the type of machine you choose to play. Here are some of the ways that the video poker and live poker logic diverge.

- Don't hold a *kicker*. A kicker is a high card that's held with a lower pair. This tactic is questionable for live poker and it's certainly wrong for video poker. For example, you have: 6♦ 10♠ A♥ 6♥ 4♣. Don't hold the ace along with the pair of sixes.
- If you go for the inside straight in live poker, you're considered a chump. However, in many versions of video poker it's the right move to make. In Deuces Wild, you'll always draw to the inside straight over drawing five new cards. In Jacks or Better, inside straights with three or more high cards can be drawn to.
- In many video poker games, the ace is not the best card in the deck. The best card (if you don't have wild cards) is the lowest card that qualifies for a winning pair. For instance, in Jacks or Better games that card is the jack. Why? The lower the "high" card is, the more ways it can be used as part of a straight. A jack can be used in any straight from 7-8-9-10-J up to 10-J-Q-K-A. An ace can be used in only two straights: A-2-3-4-5 and 10-J-Q-K-A. Remember, a pair of aces doesn't pay any more than a pair of jacks. It's the straight limitations that always make the ace the card to chuck when you have three mixed-suit high cards. Bonus games, though, put a higher value on the aces.
- In video poker, a hand's worth is determined only by the pay schedule. Hands that receive the same pay have no strength relative to each other; that is, a pair of jacks is just as good as pair of aces, and a king-high flush is no better than an 9-high flush. That's why the term "high card" in video poker is defined only by the pay table. If a game were to pay money for a pair of nines or more, then every card from nine to ace would be a "high card."
- In regular poker, you would never think of two or three cards to a royal flush as having any meaning. Learning how to value these holdings in video poker is essential for success. How and when you pursue the royal takes up a decent portion of the video poker player's brain.

Promotions

Special promotions are another thing to keep an eye out for in your quest for the ever-larger edge. Typical promotions might be bonus payouts of 20,000 to 50,000 coins for royal flushes in a particular suit or sequential royal flushes. (A royal flush is sequential when the cards appear on the screen in exact order from left to right or right to left.) We already discussed how rare royals are; getting a specific kind is obviously tougher. There are 120 ways to order the cards in a royal flush, but only two of them are sequential. So only one in 60 of the already unlikely royals will pay off the super bonus.

Other promotions or specials include double or triple slot club points, scratch tickets for a four of a kind (providing a chance at even greater winnings), and extra pay on heart flushes on Valentine's Day. You have to know how to evaluate the offer based on its value to you and then adjust your strategy accordingly. Yes, that means you'll have to break out the calculator and the computer if you really want to know the precise value. Pros and video poker geeks thrive off this stuff; don't be embarrassed if you do too. If you're really serious, you should even calculate whether the extra time it takes to get a bonus payout paid by hand or a ticket scratched or a drawing entry filled out is worth it when playing a positive expectation game. Sometimes you're just better off playing as fast as you can.

Like slot clubs, these promotions are worth keeping an eye on because any extra return, no matter how small, is a good extra return. But you shouldn't play lower-quality machines at a casino just to say you were in on a promotion. You have to look at the whole picture.

PENALTY CARDS

Some simple strategies—such as the ones in this chapter—won't give any consideration to *penalty cards*. A penalty card is a discard that can affect the expected return of the cards you hold. As such, it affects your decisions on what cards to keep. For example, suppose you hold a jack and queen of the same suit. Any discards in that suit will reduce the number of possible flushes you can draw. Also, any discards of a value of 8, 9, 10, king, or ace will reduce your chances of getting a straight. And if you discard a card that could both be in the flush and straight (such as an 8 of the same suit), you reduce the number of obtainable straight flushes.

Penalty cards can be a major headache and major disincentive to learning strategies. They are the main reason why a game like Double Bonus is difficult to master. In games where straights and flushes have higher relative value, the significance of penalty cards increases as does the complexity of the strategy.

When using computer software, you may have an error message pop up that says you didn't make the choice with the highest expected return even though you followed the standard strategy rule. A penalty card is often to blame. It's good to grasp why one play is more accurate than the other, but it does slow down your learning process and very often the differences are insubstantial.

Many pros and pundits analyze penalty card situations to death. Very often they are of more academic than practical importance. If you take too much time to think about fractionally important correct plays, you'll lose money in the long run because you won't play as many hands. On Jacks or Better, you can get within one one-hundredth of a percent of computer-perfect play without penalty cards.

If a strategy cheat sheet without penalty cards can get you within 0.01%, then the difference at a $1 machine at 600 hands per hour will be only 30¢. With a strategy that is simple yet accurate, you'll play faster, make fewer errors, and have more fun.

TIME TO GO PRO?

So you've assimilated all the harsh realities about volatility, playing expertly, and needing a substantial bankroll. Still, your mind keeps returning to the fact that you can play this game at a profit over the long run. I don't blame you—that's a very exciting proposition. And there are a number of video poker pros. Should you ditch the job and head to the glittering casino? Unadvisable.

Let's look at your profit per hour (normally we talk about cost per hour, but we're in the lovely realm of positive expectation here). Once you get comfortable, you can assume 600 hands per hour (novices may play only 300 and some pros claim 1,000). You have mastered Deuces Wild, which gives you a 0.76% edge, but you're confined to quarter machines because those are the most widely available full-pay versions. So:

Profit = 600 hands per hour × $1.25 ×
0.76% = $5.70 per hour

That's not much more lucrative than working at your favorite fast food joint. Well, we'll throw in 1% worth of comps and cashback from the slot club. So that adds $7.50 to your earnings for a grand total of $13.20.

Your profits (including the slot club) will ultimately amount to 1.76% of what you bet. This pay won't be consistent. You'll never know what your short-term hourly return will be. If you're playing dollars, you may lose $1,000 in five hours or make $4,000 in ten minutes.

There are other drawbacks to professional video poker. It can get pretty unstimulating when it's a daily grind. You have to eat casino food all the time to get your comp value. Do you really want to sit in a casino chair for an eight-hour workday? That can be pretty hard on your back. And we haven't even mentioned hemorrhoids.

Yes, you can move on up to other machines

at higher denominations. Profits on $1 and $5 machines can become pretty enticing. But then you have to deal with the inevitable losing streaks and have a working bankroll of $10,000 to $100,000. You would need millions of hands to be assured of your profit. It's a hard way to make an easy living.

For most of us, it's best to think of video poker as a recreation, but a potentially profitable one. At the very least, it can be an inexpensive form of gambling—over the long haul—if you make the right choices.

VIDEO POKER MISCONCEPTIONS

In addition to feeding their quarters and dollars into the machines, many video poker players like to put their two cents in. Although video poker is a solitary activity, the aisles are filled with a mix of friendly sages and irksome know-it-alls. Don't count on much of the input being accurate. Here's the real deal:

• Prepare to meet many a good Samaritan who will warn you not to play a certain machine because it just paid off a royal and is therefore no longer "due." Or perhaps he'll tell you that a certain machine is "hot." Smile benignly and pay no heed. This kind of short-term observation is nonsense with reel slots and it's even bigger nonsense with video poker where skill and knowledge affect the outcome. Nothing is "due." Every hand is a fresh start where the pay table and your skill will reveal a machine's value to you. The machine will just go about producing its random results. If you hit a half-dozen four of a kinds in an hour that doesn't mean that the machine is tapped out. The odds remain about 1 in 425 for quads. Yes, some machines will seem hot and some cold, but those streaks can be recognized only when they're behind you. Karmic readings from your fellow patrons have no bearing on the matter.

• Good machines are not determined by how often they "give" royals. Using proper strategy on a 9/6 Jacks or Better game, you will hit a royal about once in 40,400 hands. The worth of a machine is determined by its pay table. You don't want to give away money on the more common hands. You'll make, on average, 465 full houses and 445 flushes in those 40,400 hands. Any reduction in the payout for those will greatly reduce your payback and might knock you out too soon to even see the royal.

• Playing with good strategy on a good machine is preferable to playing with perfect strategy on a lousy machine. For example, using standard Jacks or Better strategy on a Double Bonus machine will get you a return of 99.6% as opposed to the optimal return of 100.17%. (That's actually better than the Jacks or Better return! But the game is much more volatile.) Playing perfectly on a 7/5 Jacks or Better machine will return only 96.15%.

• Leave a machine because someone obnoxious is next to you, or because the smoke is too heavy, or because the buttons stick, but don't do it because you think the machine has a master plan to bankrupt you. Of course, if your superstitious nature and psychological distress cause you to play poorly or unhappily, then move to another machine—that doesn't make a difference either (as long as the new machine has the same pay table).

• The RNG will determine what cards are dealt. Just like the name says, the results will always be random. It's as if you are sitting at a table and dealing the cards from a well-shuffled deck, and then, after the hand, all the cards are reshuffled. The results have nothing to do with good vibes or what color your socks are.

• There's nothing to be gained from inserting coins as opposed to playing credits. The RNG doesn't care. The only thing this does is slow down your play.

• Some players will say that you have to play higher-denomination machines in video poker because the cheaper machines are tight. The coin amount has nothing to do with it. It's the pay table that determines the machine's return, not its denomination. The randomly shuffled cards aren't "set" for a certain return; they return what they do because of the pay schedule. The only partial truth in this myth is that you usually won't find good pay tables on nickel machines.

• Quarter machines may be perceived as a low-stakes choice; however, they can consume a lot more than chump change. If you play five coins per hand and 600 hands per hour, you'll play $750 through the machine in an hour. In comparison, a $10 blackjack player who plays 60 hands an hour is playing only $600 per hour. Look for the best pay tables on quarter machines or it may cost you more than you may think.

• All generalities have exceptions in video poker. There's certainly no one-size-fits-all rule that applies to all different types of games. Depending on how certain hands are rewarded, your guiding strategies will change.

COMMON QUESTIONS

Do the machines really provide a random deal?
Nevada gaming regulations very specifically state that any machine that represents a card game must be completely random. All cards must have the same probability of appearing. In other words, you get a fair deal. Also, all machines manufactured in Nevada must meet the Nevada standards before they're shipped to another locale. The big brands such as IGT, Bally, and Williams should be trusted; if nothing else, the big manufacturers want to maintain the integrity of their names.

That doesn't mean the microchip can't be tampered with at the destination spot, but it's unlikely. Gambling in the U.S. is well regulated and most jurisdictions reinforce the Nevada standards. The more off the beaten track you go—obscure Native American casinos, cruise ships, laundromats—the more potential there is for concern. But these locations will probably hurt you with poor pay tables rather than microchip chicanery.

It's very easy to suspect that the machines are programmed to defeat you when things are going poorly. You'll notice all the flushes, straights, and full houses that refuse to fill in. That's just it—you notice it because it's frustrating, especially when you're on a bad streak. You probably don't notice all the times that you hit these hands. Have faith. The machine is a blind dealer. Over the long run, all the cards will fall as one would expect from a random deal.

How does the machine shuffle the deck?
A video poker machine is shuffling continuously through the use of its microprocessor and its random number generator. The RNG is always at work, even when the machine is seemingly idle. Hundreds of numbers are generated by the RNG per second and they correspond to cards to be dealt. Each card has an equal chance due to the way it's mapped onto the RNG results. For more on the RNG, see the slots chapter.

When does the shuffling stop?
Most sources indicate that the continuous shuffling stops when you drop in your fifth coin, bet max credits, or press deal. In other words, when the machine is forced to deal, it stops shuffling and has a fixed deck. It doesn't matter how long you take to make your discards; everything is already set. So you can stare and pray and hesitate before drawing the one card to your four-card royal, but your fate has already been decided. By the way, you do know that you have a one in 47 shot to pump your arms in the air in this situation, don't you?

Are the draw cards from the top of the deck or lined up behind the first cards?
The better question is "Why is this question so often raised?" I think the answer to that query is that human beings have an infinite capacity to torment themselves for no good reason. The answer to the first question is that most every current machine has the cards come off the top of the deck. That means that if you discard one card, you will get the same new card no matter what position your discard came from. Why do so many second-guessing players want the scoop on this? Take a look at this situation in Jacks or Better: J♠ J♥ Q♥ K♥ 3♣. The proper play is to hold the pair of jacks. Let's say you end up with: J♠ J♥ 10♥ A♥ J♣. Do you see why the regret-prone might regret? If the three-card royal were kept and the cards came off the top of the deck (as they do), then the 10♥ and A♥ would have filled in the royal. If machines had one draw card lined up behind each initial card (that is, the 10♥ behind the Q♥, the A♥ behind the K♥), then the royal couldn't have happened and your choice would be regret-free. You know what? The real lesson in this is to follow the right strategy, have faith in its long-term results, and don't irritate yourself with what might have been.

Are the casinos nuts?
In other words, how can casinos afford to offer games that pay back over 100%? We know that casinos aren't known for their philanthropic natures. Indeed, the casino would lose money if every player played at 100+% return machines and played expertly. However, that's not the case. Only a small subset of all video poker players know how to play with the full advantage. Most video poker players play by "intuition" and thus assure that the machines will pay 2% to 4% below maximum return. In addition, the best machines have to be identified by informed players. They're often hidden among the throngs of machines whose inferior pay tables guarantee casino profits. Casinos benefit from a reputation of having generous machines, as more players are drawn in without the necessary skills to capitalize on the casino's supposed beneficence. However, there are times when casino management removes games that prove to be too player-friendly. Some machines have been produced with such extreme player advantages that the pros would hit them nearly 24 hours a day until the casinos finally pulled the games. Lose no sleep over the casino's profits; as soon as a machine doesn't pull its weight in earnings, it will disappear. So, in a twisted way, one must hope that the majority of players never drink from the cup of video poker knowledge. After all, they're the ones subsidizing the profitable play.

So if I'm selective and skilled, I'll win every time I play?
No, no, no. A thousand times no. Go back and read the section on volatility again. Video poker pros lose more sessions than they win. Sometimes you'll lose a lot. Sometimes you'll win a lot. In the long run, you should come out ahead if you are playing a positive expectation machine properly.

None of the gambling sites in my region offer the best paying games. So do I now have to feel dopey if I choose to play video poker?
No, not at all. If you enjoy video poker, then the pleasure you get from playing can make it a wise choice. It's almost a certainty that the video poker machines will be a better choice than reel slots. Even below-average video poker games will return more money than your average slot machine. You should still seek out the games that have the highest return (the best of the bad) and play them with expert strategy. You will lose money playing a negative expectation game in the long run, but you can keep those losses to a minimum. If you're playing at more than a 1.5% house edge, though, you may want to check out blackjack, the pass line bet at craps, and baccarat.

THE ESSENTIALS FOR PLAYING VIDEO POKER LIKE A GENIUS

- Learn which machines have the highest mathematical payback. Anything over 100% means you would have the long-term edge if you played the game expertly.
- Learn the strategy of the machine you wish to play. This can be done through books and other expert sources. Practice your strategy on computer software.
- It's smart to start on lower-denomination machines while you're still mastering the strategy, as long as those machines have a full-pay schedule.
- Always check the pay table to make sure you're playing a full-pay version of the machine you like.
- When you're starting out, it's best to stick to one kind of machine. By specializing, you'll master the game faster and you won't be confused by the strategies of other games.
- You don't have to play perfectly to do very well. You don't need to be a computer.
- You shouldn't be obsessed with penalty cards and errors. Remember to enjoy yourself.
- Scout around your gambling destinations for the best machines. Keep in mind that Nevada has by far the greatest selection of machines that are favorable to the player.

6

CRAPS

Craps is the fastest, most thrilling table game in the casino. When you pass by a noisy craps game, you can almost smell the adrenaline as the dice fly through the air. The game induces the giddiest highs and the most miserable lows in its players.

Craps once ruled the roost at the casino. This was the game of choice for inveterate gamblers and thrill-seekers. Unfortunately, the game has steadily lost its popularity over the last 20 years, most likely because new players don't want to take the time to figure out the game. The problem with craps is that it's not a game that a newcomer feels comfortable joining; the intimidation factor is very high. The layout is complex, the jargon incomprehensible, and the chaotic activity calls to mind the floor of the New York Stock Exchange.

Relax. It's really not that scary. If you stick to the simple bets—which, happily, are the ones with the best odds—you can quickly get a grip on craps and discover its incredible appeal. You won't find a spot in the casino with more personality and camaraderie: Players let it all hang out at the table as they celebrate and despair together. If you give this exhilarating and streaky game a try, you may find yourself hooting, hollering, and high-fiving like an old pro. However, if you become part of the craps clique, you'll also experience the doldrums and lifelessness of a "cold" table.

One must approach craps with some caution—not because it's innately difficult, but because it's a fast and volatile game. Money can be won and lost very, very quickly at these tables. The game also has a split personality—there are a few excellent bets (with a low house edge) and a whole array of awful ones. After you've read this chapter, you'll be able to distinguish the savvy wagers from the sucker bets.

HOW CRAPS IS PLAYED

THE SCENE

You can't miss the craps table in the casino. It's large—about three times the size of a blackjack table—with high sides and a sunken layout. Take a look at the craps table on page 125. Kind of makes you dizzy, doesn't it? Have no fear—all will be explained soon. Two quick notes to reassure you: 1) Notice the layout is the same on the right and left, allowing bettors on both sides of the table; 2) The bets in the middle of the table are all lousy and should be ignored. See, it's already less intimidating!

The table can accommodate 10 to 12 players—and they'll all be standing. Generally players don't get a seat unless they have a physical impairment or untold wealth.

A craps table is usually run by four casino employees known as the *crew*. Two dealers stand on the inside of the table (bordering the pit). They are each responsible for changing cash into chips and collecting and paying off bets on their half of the table. In between the two dealers sits the *boxman*. He oversees all the actions, settles any disputes, and keeps an eye on the other three employees. He also examines any dice that go off the table. The *stickman* stands across from the boxman on the other side of the table and handles the dice with a long, curved stick, pushing them toward the player who's rolling and retrieving them. The stickman controls the tempo of the game, calls out the rolls, attends to the *center bets* (the lousy ones in the middle), and maintains dice security. The stickman also acts as a salesman, using entertaining patter to hawk some of the worst bets on the board. (Find out what he's talking about in "Dice Dialogue" on page 138.)

You should be able to find $5 minimum craps at just about any casino. Sometimes you'll find tables at $3 or even less at the less ritzy casinos. Find an open area on the rail to set up shop. If you need to buy in for chips, put your money down on the table. It can't go directly into the dealer's hand. You should wait until the dice are at the center of the table before taking any actions. It's considered unlucky and bad form to have the dice hit your hands while you're fussing over the table. It's almost time to introduce you to the table action, but first let's take a quick look at dice and the not-so-awful mathematics needed to really understand craps.

DICE 101

The easiest way to get comfortable with craps is to get comfortable with the dice. In case you're dropping in from Mars, a *die* is a cube with one to six dots (*pips*) on each of its sides. Thus, there are six possible outcomes for the roll of a single die (1, 2, 3, 4, 5, or 6). Craps is played with a pair of dice; this makes for 6 × 6 = 36 possible combinations on each roll. Since only one combination of the dice can give you a total of 12 (6–6), the probability of this occurring on any given roll is ¹⁄₃₆. On the other hand, you have six ways to make a total of 7 (1–6; 2–5; 3–4; 4–3; 5–2; 6–1); this gives you a probability of ⁶⁄₃₆ (or ⅙) to get a 7 on any roll.

Get acquainted with the chart on page 126—it summarizes all the combinations for two dice and supplies just about all the "dice sense" that you'll need. (Note: One white die and one black die are used to distinguish between different combinations. In other words, a roll of 1–2 is distinguished from a roll of 2–1.) Looking at the chart you'll see that everything is symmetric around the number 7. A 6 is as likely to come up as an 8, a 5 is as likely as a 9, etc. This "pairing off" will make figuring the odds and probabilities for different rolls twice as fast. For instance, the odds against rolling a 10 are 33–3 (3 ways to make 10, 33 ways not to), which reduces to 11–1. The odds

against rolling a 4 are the same: 33–3, or 11–1.

Even more essential for craps is the ability to calculate the odds of any number being rolled before a 7. The odds against rolling a 5 before a 7 are 6–4 (six ways to make the 7 versus only four ways to make the 5). A little further on in this chapter, I'll give examples of how this chart can be used to calculate the house advantage on

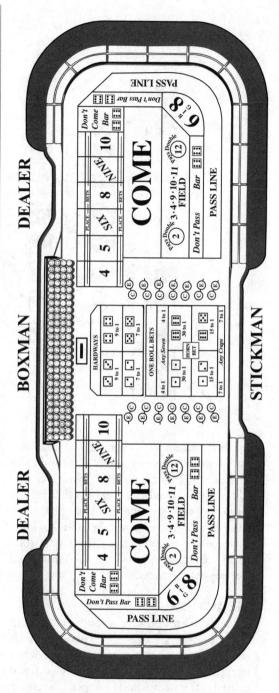

DICE CHART

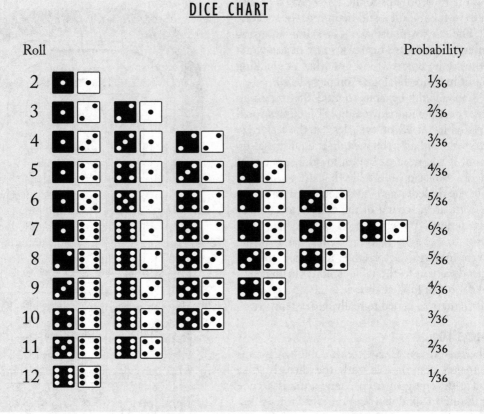

Roll		Probability
2		1/36
3		2/36
4		3/36
5		4/36
6		5/36
7		6/36
8		5/36
9		4/36
10		3/36
11		2/36
12		1/36

craps bets. Although it's perfectly acceptable to just follow the advice by rote, it is my hope that you'll become conversant with these basic probabilities. Such knowledge will help you if a casino runs any special promotions that tinker with paybacks and odds—you'll be able to see if you're getting a good deal. More important, mastery over the "guts" of the game will increase your enjoyment.

THE ACTION

Although there's always activity at a craps table, the best place to begin to understand the game is with a new "round" of play, which begins when one of the players is offered five or so dice by the stickman. If the player wants to roll, he selects two of them, and becomes the *shooter*. This player then generates all of the action the other players will bet on.

In order to roll the dice, the shooter is required to make a line bet—on either the *pass* line or the *don't pass* line. (See the diagram on page 127.) The other players at the table will also be placing bets on the layout. Shooters most

commonly bet the pass line; most of the other bettors will make this bet as well, in "support" of the shooter. The alternative is to bet don't pass, which is a bet against the shooter's success. The payoff for either a pass bet or a don't pass bet is even money, meaning if you bet $5, you'll win $5 plus get your original $5 bet back.

In order for any roll to be considered legal, the shooter must fling/throw/roll the dice so they rebound off the opposite wall. The shooter's first roll of the dice during a round is known as the *come-out roll* and there are various ways for players to win and lose on this roll.

Let's look at the rules governing a come-out roll. These rules never vary, no matter what bets are placed on the layout.

- If the come-out roll is a 7 or 11 (a *natural*), the pass line wins and the don't pass loses. The round is over.
- If the come-out roll is a 2, 3, or 12 (collectively known as *craps*), the pass line loses and the don't pass line wins or ties. The don't pass bet will be a tie when the come-out roll is 12 (sometimes 2); the don't pass line will "bar" the

roll that is treated as a tie. The round is over.

- If the come-out roll is a 4, 5, 6, 8, 9, or 10, then that number becomes the shooter's *point*. The dealers will then take a *puck* (button) that says OFF on its black side and ON on its white side, and place it ON side up on top of that number on the layout. This reminds all players what the point is. The outcome of the pass line and don't pass line bets is yet to be determined. The shooter will keep on rolling until one of two things happen: He rolls the point number (*makes the point*) or he rolls a 7 (*sevens out*). If the point is rolled first, pass line bettors win and don't pass bettors lose. If the 7 is rolled first, the reverse is true—pass loses and don't pass wins. In either case, the round is over.

A new round always begins with the same shooter until he sevens out. If the shooter rolled a natural or craps on the come-out roll, or if the shooter made his point, he gets to roll again. Only when the shooter sevens out are the dice offered to the next player clockwise at the table. And the process begins anew.

Here are a couple of points to spare you confusion:

1) Yes, 7 is a winner on the come-out roll for pass line bettors and 7 is a loser for those bettors on any subsequent roll. The reverse is true for don't pass bettors.

2) The numbers 2, 3, 11, and 12 have no meaning for pass or don't pass bettors after the come-out roll.

The above sequence is the crux of craps and the engine that drives the game. Of course, there are many more options to cover—some essential, most worthless—but if you grasp the come-out roll and its various outcomes, you're well on your way to becoming a smart craps player.

THE BETS AND THE ODDS

Where you bet your money is what will make or break you at the craps table. The house advantage can range from less than 1% to over 16%. For the mathematically inquisitive, the analysis of the bets below will provide some calculations for the house advantage. It would be repetitive to do this for all the craps bets, but you can try it yourself if you're so inclined.

THE PASS LINE BET

Let's refresh our memories about the mechanics of the pass line bet: It is placed immediately prior to the come-out roll. If the come-out roll is 7 or 11, you win. If it's 2, 3, or 12, you lose. Any other number becomes your point. If your point rolls before 7, you win. If 7 rolls before your point, you lose.

This is the bread-and-butter bet for most players. It's readily accessible to all bettors around the whole length of the table. Most players bet the pass line because it means they are going "with" the shooter, hoping that she gets a pair of hot dice and rolls all night.

Keep your eyes on the point markers, which

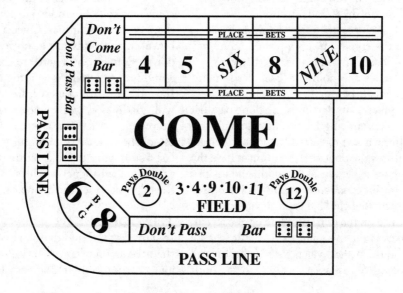

indicate the come-out and point rolls. If the current roll is a come-out roll, the disks are on OFF and off to the side of the betting layout. When a point is established, the disks are placed in the appropriate *point boxes* (the numbers above the come line). These point markers clue you in to whether the next roll is a come-out roll or a point roll.

The house edge for pass line bets is 1.41%. This is one of the best bets in the casino—especially because it requires no skill. Rarely do you find such a low house advantage on bets that are pure luck.

Bets on the pass line cannot be removed or reduced after a point is established; they can, however, be increased. You *do not* want to increase the bet. The biggest advantage for the pass line player is on the come-out roll where you have a better chance of winning than losing ($\frac{8}{36}$ chance to roll 7 or 11; $\frac{4}{36}$ chance to roll 2, 3, or 12). Once a point is established, the odds are against the pass line bettor. Along the same lines, the casinos, in their never-ending generosity, will let you bet on the pass line in the middle of a round, after you have missed the come-out roll (this is called a put bet). Again, it would be foolish to do this because your advantage has been sacrificed.

DON'T PASS LINE

We also covered this bet above. In summary: This is an even-money bet that must be placed before the come-out roll. It's the opposite of the pass line. On the come-out roll, don't pass bettors lose on the 7 and 11 and win on the 2 and 3. If a 12 (or the 2 in a few casinos) is rolled on the come-out, it's a push—no money is won or lost. On point rolls, the bet wins if 7 appears before the point; it loses if the point number appears before a 7.

Some players are drawn to the don't pass bet because of an enticing bit of faulty logic. They figure, "If the house has an advantage on the pass bet and this is the opposite, then I must have the advantage over the house." Uh-huh, and casinos are run by independently wealthy philanthropists. The catch is the "bar" number indicated by a pair of dice on the don't pass line on the layout. All it takes is for this number to result in a tie and the house magically gets its edge back. Let's take a look. We can assign a value to the don't

pass bet winning by subtracting the chance of getting a 12 (assuming that's the bet that ties) from the chance of a pass line bet losing. The chance that a pass line bet loses = 0.507071 (see page 129 to learn how this is calculated).

Chance of rolling 12 on come-out roll =
$\frac{1}{36}$ = 0.027778
True probability of winning don't pass =
0.507071 − 0.02778 = 0.479293
House edge = P(pass win) − P(don't pass win)
= 0.492929 − 0.479293
= 0.013636

Thus, the house edge for the don't pass is 1.36%. It's another excellent wager that is slightly better than the pass line bet, but only marginally. If you bet $2,000 an hour, the don't pass bet would save you $1 an hour over the long run compared to the pass bet.

Despite the allure of a quality bet, don't pass bettors are rare birds in the casinos. Why? Because most bettors crave the action of a hot shooter. They want to see naturals and points made, not craps. It takes some fortitude of character to withstand social pressures and make what is often referred to as the "wrong" bet; of course, there is nothing inherently wrong with the bet. Occasionally, you'll see a pessimistic shooter bet the don't against himself. (Of course, it's not really "against" himself because if he wins, he wins. Why should it matter how he does it?)

For the don't bettor, the hard part is the come-out roll. The odds are against him with the 7 and 11 as winners. Once a point is rolled, however, the odds are always in favor of the don'ts. Remember: There are six ways to make 7 and fewer to make any of the other numbers. It won't surprise you to learn that the casino will gladly let you remove (*take down*) or decrease a don't bet after a point has been established. *Never* do this unless you realize the last $20 to your name is on the table (in which case, you have bigger troubles). When you have the edge, don't let the casino off the hook.

THE COME BET

If craps only offered up the pass line bets, even the greenest novice could walk over to a table and be confusion-free after a few minutes of

INSIDE THE NUMBERS

You can win a pass line bet in one of two ways—winning the come-out roll or making your point—and both ways need to be factored into the total probability of winning this wager.

Probability of Winning Come-Out Roll

Roll	Probability
7	$^6/_{36}$
11	$^2/_{36}$

Probability of Making a Point

Point	Probability of Establishing Point	Probability of Passing	Probability of Making the Point
4	$^3/_{36}$	$^1/_3$	$^3/_{108}$
5	$^4/_{36}$	$^2/_5$	$^8/_{180}$
6	$^5/_{36}$	$^5/_{11}$	$^{25}/_{396}$
8	$^5/_{36}$	$^5/_{11}$	$^{25}/_{396}$
9	$^4/_{36}$	$^2/_5$	$^8/_{180}$
10	$^3/_{36}$	$^1/_3$	$^3/_{108}$

$$P(\text{win pass line bet}) = P(\text{win come-out roll}) + P(\text{win by making point})$$
$$= (^2/_{36} + {}^6/_{36}) + (^3/_{108} + {}^8/_{180} + {}^{25}/_{396} + {}^{25}/_{396} + {}^8/_{180} + {}^3/_{108})$$
$$= 0.492929$$

Once we have the probability of winning a pass line bet, we can find the probability of losing the same bet.

$$P(\text{lose pass line bet}) = 1 - P(\text{win}) = 1 - 0.492929 = 0.507071$$

The house edge is then calculated by subtracting the probability of winning from the probability of losing.

$$\text{House edge} = 0.507071 - 0.492929 = 0.014142 = 1.414\%$$

observation. However, the craps veterans would be bored to tears. Dice players want betting action and, in that regard, the casino always aims to please.

Thus, we have the *come* bet. The come bet (note the large betting box marked COME on the layout) allows a bettor to make a "virtual" pass line bet even after a point has been established. The come bet turns the next roll of the dice into a come-out roll and starts its own round of play, separate from the original pass line activity of the shooter. To clarify: If the shooter is rolling the dice in pursuit of a point and you place a come bet, the next roll of the dice will affect your come bet as if it were the come-out roll for a pass line bet.

The same rules apply to the come bet as to the pass line bet. If a point is rolled, the come bet is moved to the point box of the specific number rolled. This will be resolved just like a pass line point number: If the specific number is rolled first, the bet wins; if 7 is rolled first, the bet loses. The dealer orients your come bet in the place bet box so that it corresponds to your position at the table.

Let's look at an example. You have a $5 bet on the pass line and the shooter establishes 8 as the point. You take another $5 chip and place it in the come box. Here are the possible outcomes of the next dice roll:

1) The shooter rolls a 7. You lose the $5 pass line bet. You win the $5 come bet.

2) The shooter rolls 11. You win the $5 come bet. The pass line bet is unaffected.

3) The shooter rolls 2, 3, or 12. You lose the $5 come bet. The pass line bet is unaffected.

4) The shooter rolls an 8. You win the $5 pass line bet. The come line bet is moved to box 8 on the layout and becomes the "point" of your come bet. It will be resolved only when a 7 (lose) or an 8 (win) is rolled.

5) The shooter rolls a 4, 5, 6, 9, or 10. The pass line bet is unaffected. The come line bet is moved to the specific number on the layout and that becomes the point for your come bet. It will be resolved only when a 7 or the specific number is rolled.

Since it is exactly equivalent to the pass line wager, the come bet has the same house edge of 1.41% and it also can't be removed until it is resolved. You can bet on come as often as you like after the come-out roll. It will allow you to put a lot of money in action.

THE DON'T COME BET

As you might expect, the *don't come* bet is the opposite of the come. That is to say, the don't come bet is a "virtual" don't pass bet. It is independent of the actual don't pass bet and can be put into action only after a point is established. The exact same rules apply to the don't come bet as apply to the don't pass bet. There's a relatively small box on the layout for this bet, but it will still indicate what number (2 or 12) is barred on the come-out roll. The house edge is, of course, 1.36%.

If a point number is rolled on the come-out roll of a don't come bet (got that?), the dealer moves the bet to the specific number on the layout. Notice that the bet goes into the smaller box above the main place bet boxes. Don't forget: This bet *wins* if a 7 is rolled before the point number is repeated.

TAKING ODDS

Okay, strap yourself in. Taking odds causes the greatest confusion and headaches among rookie craps players, but—and this is a big but—it is the best bet at the craps table and integral to increasing your chances of winning. For a negative expectation game (like craps), taking *odds* (also known as *free odds*) is the best bet available.

Now that I've scared you, let me provide some reassurance. Taking odds only looks mysterious. Once you're familiar with the concepts, you'll make this bet with the greatest of ease. Part of the reason that the odds bet seems so strange and daunting is that it's not advertised anywhere on the craps layout. Why? Because the casino has no advantage on this bet—that's right, zero house edge. However, you must make a negative expectation bet—pass, don't pass, come, don't come—in order to take odds. An odds bet combined with one of those bets makes the house edge lower than 1%.

Here's how taking odds works. Casinos allow a player to take odds on pass, don't pass, come, and don't come bets after a point has been established. These additional wagers can be made any time after a point is established—as long as you made an original wager. If the bet on which odds are placed wins, the odds bet is paid fairly.

Let's look at this in terms of the most common bet—the pass line. If a point is rolled on the come-out roll, you can bet additional money that the point will be rolled again before a 7. You place this bet next to your pass line bet, but just behind the pass line itself. The amount you win if the point is rolled before a 7 is the true odds.

You can also take odds on a come line bet. This is logical since the come bet is really an independent pass line bet. But you can't physically place the bet yourself; to take odds on a come bet, put down the chips you want to bet, and announce your intention to the dealer. Since there is not much room in the place bet box (that's where your come bet went after a point was established), the dealer will place the odds bet on top of the come bet, offset just a little to indicate that it is payable at true odds.

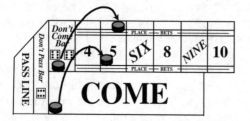

Examples of Taking Free Odds

Point	Probability of Making Point	Pass Line Bet	Pass Line Bet Pays	Double Odds Bet	Double Odds Bet Pays	Total Potential Win	Total Potential Loss
4 or 10	1/3	$5	$5	$10	$20	$25	$15
5 or 9	2/5	$5	$5	$10	$15	$20	$15
6 or 8	5/11	$5	$5	$10	$12	$17	$15

When you take odds for don't pass and don't come bets, it's called *laying odds*. You can lay odds on the don't come bets the same way you take odds on come bets. Examine the chart below and you'll realize that you are putting up more money than you are paid off. For example, when the point is 8, you must put up $6 in order to win back $5. (Keep in mind, you'll be getting back $11—the $6 you bet and your $5 in winnings.) Is this some sort of rip-off? Absolutely not. You're getting the true odds. As a don't bettor, you have the advantage once a point is established. There's a better chance that 7 will be rolled than the point number. That's why you are paid off "less" when you lay odds than when you take odds. It's perfect odds. Neither you nor the house is the favorite.

The chart below summarizes what the true odds are for each point. Get comfortable with this chart—as has already been mentioned, the odds bet is your best bet in craps. This chart is derived using the probabilities established in the dice chart on page 126. For example, how do we know the true odds of getting a point of 4 before a 7? There are six ways to make 7 on any roll and three ways to make 4. Thus, the odds are 6 to 3, which reduce to 2 to 1. Voilà! The same reasoning is used for all the odds bets.

Not surprisingly, you may remove your odds bet at any time. No house advantage, no restriction. Come odds are inactive on a shooter's come-out roll (when the puck is in the OFF position). This is a superstitious tradition, based on the notion that since the table wants a 7 (to win the pass line bets), it's a bad time to have your odds working on a point established previously. Come odds that are "off" will be returned to the player if the shooter rolls a 7. Of course, the dice don't care about the table's karma and if your come point is rolled, you'll miss the payoff. The bettor can request that the odds be *on* or *working* during the come-out roll. Don't come odds, unpopular with the crowd but unburdened by silly superstition, are always working.

How Much Can I Bet on the Odds?

Casinos advertise the maximum odds bets they allow as a maximum multiple of the original bet. A sign at the craps table will usually indicate the odds bet. It may say "2× odds" (read as "two times odds") or "5× odds." If you don't see a sign, go ahead and ask one of the crew members at the table.

The majority of casinos allow you to take at least double odds ("2× odds") on each pass line or come bet. Let's make sure we know what this means. If you bet $5 on the pass line and a

Points and Their True Odds

Number	Point Probability		Win Payoff Odds	
	Pass Line: Point Before 7	Don't Pass: 7 Before Point	Payoff for Pass Line or Come	Payoff for Don't Pass or Don't Come
4 or 10	1/3	2/3	2 to 1	1 to 2
5 or 9	2/5	3/5	3 to 2	2 to 3
6 or 8	5/11	6/11	6 to 5	5 to 6

point is established, you can bet *up to* $10 on the odds. For example, you make a $10 pass line bet, and the shooter has a come-out roll of 6. The casino offers double odds. You make a $20 odds bet (double your original wager). If the shooter passes (makes his point), you win $10 for your original wager (1 to 1) and $24 for your odds bet (6 to 5). Of course, if the shooter rolls a 7, you lose the entire $30.

The manner in which don't pass and don't come bettors lay free odds is slightly different. The bettor is allowed to back up the original wager with an amount that will produce *winnings* that are a multiple of the original bet (as opposed to pass and come odds bets where the bet itself is a multiple of the original). This multiple is determined by the odds offered by the casino. For example, you have a $10 bet on don't come and 5 becomes the established point. The point of 5 lets you know that you can lay odds at a payoff of 2 to 3. (Check out the chart at the bottom of page 131.) The casino offers double odds. Therefore, you can make a $30 odds bet in order to win $20 (two times your original wager of $10). If a 7 shows up before a 5, you would win a total of $30: $10 for your don't come bet and $20 for your odds bet. Note: If the casino offered only single odds, you could make only a $15 odds bet in order to win $10.

You should make odds bets that can be paid exactly, or the dealer will pay off by rounding down. This means that if you bet $2 on the pass line and the shooter comes out with a 6, you shouldn't back up the bet with $4 (assuming double odds). Why? Because if the shooter passes, the proper payoff on the odds bet would be $4.80. The craps table, however, doesn't deal in dimes, so your payoff would be rounded down to $4 (or maybe $4.50). The house gains back its advantage. Therefore, if the point is a 6 or 8, you should bet increments of $5 on the odds so you can be paid off in even dollars. If the point is a 5 or 9, you should bet a dollar amount that is an even number. If the point is 4 or 10, it doesn't matter what increments you take odds in, because the bet is paid off 2 to 1.

Most casinos will allow you to increase your odds bet over the advertised maximum—just enough to have it be paid off as a round number. For example, you would probably be allowed to take 2.5 times odds on a $2 bet if the point is 6 or 8. Dealers will often let you know what the optimal amount to bet on the odds is; in this way, they can be both helpful (since this will whittle down the house edge even further) and spare themselves annoying calculations. Any time you have trouble figuring out odds, ask the dealer.

Odds bets are often used as a marketing tool for casinos to attract savvy dice players. Scout around for the best offers. In Las Vegas, some local casinos offer 100× odds for low limit games. In this case, the maximum allowable odds bet may be $25, based on a 25¢ wager. Do as much comparison shopping as possible in choosing your gambling destination. In general, the smaller or more "local" the property, the better the odds. Occasionally, you may find a casino that offers 3, 4, 5 odds, where 3× odds are allowed on 4 and 10, 4× on the 5 and 9, and 5× on the 6 and 8.

What's So Great About Odds Bets?

In isolation, odds bets have you playing "even" with the house. No advantage either way. But the reality is that you must first make a negative expectation bet in order to place the odds bet. Nevertheless, odds bets "chew into" the house edge on your total wager. The negative expectation on your original bet (pass, don't pass, come, don't come) doesn't change, but the fact that you're increasing your wager *without* further exposure to the negative expectation decreases the house advantage on your total wager. Think of it this way: The house always has a 0% percentage advantage on your odds bets and it always has a 1.41% advantage on your pass line wager. Where do you want to put more of your money? That's why bettors love it when casinos offer high multiple odds.

A simplified way of seeing the benefit of taking odds is to look at how you can apportion your money. For example, let's assume you're willing to risk $30. Let's also assume that the shooter ends up with a point of 8. (It could be any point, but this will make the numbers easier for our analysis.) Look at the chart on the next page to see the different ways you could apportion your money and the difference in the payoffs.

Even without crunching numbers, you can see the benefits of minimizing your pass line bet and increasing your odds wager: bigger

Bet Allocation for Pass Line with Odds

	Pass Bet	Odds	Pass Win	Odds Win	Total Win
Pass Only	$30	None	$30	None	$30
Single Odds	$15	$15	$15	$18	$33
Double Odds	$10	$20	$10	$24	$34
5× Odds	$5	$25	$5	$30	$35

$30 total bet in each case.
Assumes point of 6 or 8.

payoffs when the point is made and a smaller pass line bet exposed to the ever-present 1.41% house edge. The factor that this table doesn't take into account is when you win on the come-out roll; obviously, in that situation, you would wish that you had as much on the pass line as possible. While this may cause occasional regret, don't let go of the fact that larger pass line bets mean a larger amount exposed to a negative expectation. The reduction in house edge for your *total wager* is summarized below for various odds offerings.

BET	HOUSE EDGE ON TOTAL WAGER
Pass Line	1.41%
Single odds (1×)	0.85%
Double odds (2×)	0.61%
Triple odds (3×)	0.47%
5× odds	0.33%
10× odds	0.18%
20× odds	0.10%

The Odds Must Not Make You Crazy

Although I'm promoting the odds bet, there is a danger you must take note of. No, it doesn't involve nefarious doings by the casino; it has to do with your own bankroll and mentality. The free odds bet will cut into the house's edge, but it shouldn't tempt you into making bets that are out of proportion to your bankroll. If you're a $10 craps player (that being your comfortable bet on the pass line) and you see a table offering 10× odds, you shouldn't start backing up your pass line bet with $100 in free odds. "But I'm dwindling that house edge just like you keep nagging me to do!" you protest. That's true, but you have to realize that craps is a very volatile game. If you bet $100 more on each come-out roll than is comfortable for you, a bad run of dice will leave you broke and frustrated, quickly. You have to be able to sustain your play at a comfortable level. Also realize that you're still facing an overall negative expectation no matter what odds are offered.

The smart way to approach 10× odds as a $10 player would be to place $1 on the pass line (if that meets the table's minimum) and then back it up with $10 in odds. That way you're still in your comfort zone monetarily and you're minimizing the edge. Remember that more is not always better—you must consider your own circumstances. Suppose you come across a wondrous 100× odds table that requires only a 50¢ pass line bet. Oh my, the house edge is only 0.02%! But does the thought of betting $50 makes you break out in a sweat? Does $5 sound okay? Then take 10× odds and know you're getting a good deal for your risk of $5.50 on each come-out roll.

PLACE BETS

The pass, don't pass, come, and don't come bets with odds should be your mainstays at the craps table. If you're craving a little more action though (and what craps player isn't?), the only other bet to consider is the place bet.

A place bet can be made on any of the point numbers—4, 5, 6, 8, 9, 10—at any time. If your number rolls before 7, you win. If 7 rolls before your number, you lose.

You make a place bet by putting your chips down on the table and telling the dealer which number you want to bet on. For instance, you can put down $10 and say, "Place the 5." The dealer will take your bet and put it on the appropriate point box number. He places the chips in a corresponding position to your playing position at the table, so he can easily identify which bets belong to which players. The

Place Bets to Win (Number Before 7)			
Place Bets (to win)	True Odds	Casino Odds	House Edge
4 or 10	2 to 1	9 to 5	6.67%
5 or 9	3 to 2	7 to 5	4.00%
6 or 8	6 to 5	7 to 6	1.52%

dealer must take the chips from you at the come line and place the bets. The player never reaches above the come line—it is the dividing line between players and dealers.

Place bets are very popular because they can be made at any time and allow players to bet multiple numbers at a time. Also, many players indulge in the flimsy reasoning that a place bet only has to hit once while a come or pass bet has to hit a number twice to be a winner. The drawback of this instant gratification is that the bets are paid at less than correct odds.

Since everything in craps is reversible, you won't be surprised to discover that you can also make place bets to lose. In this case, you're betting that a 7 will come up before the number you are placing. Again for reasons of table tact, not too many people make these bets. And the bets are, of course, paid at less than correct odds, but are always working.

Place bets can be taken down at any time. Simply ask the dealer to "Take me down," and you'll get your entire bet back. Place bets are also "off" or "not working" on the come-out roll unless the player requests them to be "on."

The tables above and on the facing page provide a breakdown of the place bets and the house edge on each. (Check out the Inside the Numbers sidebar on page 136 for how the house edge is figured.)

I advise placing only the 6 and 8 because of their moderate house edge. The fact that the numbers are the second most likely combinations to show up is a bonus. If you do bet these numbers, you must wager the exact amount to insure receiving the full payoff. In other words, if casino odds are A to B, place bets in multiples of B. The dealers should help you out in this regard. All you really need to know is that you must bet $6 to win $7 on the 6 or 8 because those are the only place bets worth making.

Speaking of all you need to know, you now

are in command of the full repertoire of worthwhile craps bets. I recommend you make only six wagers: pass with odds, don't pass with odds, come with odds, don't come with odds, place the 6, or place the 8. That's it! But to satisfy your curiosity and for a sense of completeness, here are the rest of the bets at the table.

BUY AND LAY BETS

The buy bet is exactly the same as the place bet except you pay a 5% *vig* or commission to receive the true odds. The dealer places a small "buy" button on your chips to indicate that it is a buy bet.

The rationale for buying numbers is that you get the true payoff. However, the 5% vig gives all the buy bets a 4.76% house edge. The only attraction of the buy bet is that if you must bet on the 4 or the 10, buying them at a 4.76% house edge is preferable to placing the same numbers at a 6.67% disadvantage.

If you want to buy the 5, for example, you'd give the dealer $21. The dealer will place $20 on the number, and put $1 into the bank. Since many craps tables will charge you a minimum of $1 no matter how small your bet is, you should bet at least $20 on the number you buy since $1 is five percent of $20. Some casinos collect the commission only on winning bets, while most collect it at the time the bet is made. This creates a rather large difference in the house edge. Buying the 4 or 10 in a casino where the vig is only on the win takes the edge from 4.76% (vig on win and lose) all the way to 1.67%. An ugly bet becomes much more attractive in this situation. Buy bets are inactive on the come-out roll unless called "on" by the player.

A *lay* bet is merely the opposite of the buy bet. It is a bet that a particular number (4, 5, 6, 8, 9, or 10) will not be rolled before a 7 comes up. The casino also takes a 5% commission on these bets.

Place Bets to Lose (7 Before Number)

Place Bets (to lose)	True Odds	Casino Odds	House Edge
4 or 10	1 to 2	5 to 11	3.03%
5 or 9	2 to 3	5 to 8	2.50%
6 or 8	5 to 6	4 to 5	1.82%

PUT BET

A put bet is a bet made on the pass line after the come-out roll. The appeal of this bet is that you get to "choose your point." If you must do that, make a buy or place bet. It is foolish to bet this way, because 45% of pass line wins are made on the come-out roll that you're bypassing with this bet. The put bet isn't even allowed in Atlantic City and Connecticut.

A MULTITUDE OF LOUSY BETS

Take a look at the layout on page 125 again. Much of the table, particularly the center, is devoted to advertising *proposition* bets. Most of these bets are one-roll bets, which means the next roll of the dice determines their outcome. They all carry large house edges and are intended to generate two things: excitement for impatient bettors and big revenue for the casino. Unless you request otherwise (by saying "take it down"), when these bets win, they remain in action.

In some casinos, the odds are printed in an unscrupulous—er, ingenious—manner. They are shown as "A for B," rather than the more typical, and less misleading, "A to B." This means that on a "5 *for* 1" bet, the casino pays you $5 and keeps your $1 bet. The more common way to show this would be "4 *to* 1." (Thankfully, most casinos have switched over to the less deceitful "A to B" layouts.)

So cast your eyes on these bets as you read this section and then promise to never look their way again. Once we eliminate these billboards for financial ruin, the smart player's layout is very manageable: the pass line, the don't pass box, the come area, the don't come area, and the point number boxes.

The Field Bet

The *field bet* is designated on the layout by a large box with FIELD written in it and a whole slew of numbers. The bet is that the next roll will be 2, 3, 4, 9, 10, 11, or 12. It pays even money for 3, 4, 9, 10, and 11, and usually pays 2 to 1 for 2 and 12. Some casinos pay 3 to 1 for either the 2 or 12 (but not both) and some replace the 9 with the 5 in the field (this makes no difference).

This is a popular bet for inexperienced players. You get to bet on seven out of twelve numbers and you're paid even money or more! Well, take a closer look. If we refer back to the dice table, we see that the probability of getting 3, 4, 9, 10, or 11 is $^{14}/_{36}$. The probability of rolling a 2 or 12 is $^2/_{36}$ and the chance of rolling a 5, 6, 7, or 8 is $^{20}/_{36}$.

Now we have the info to figure out the expectation for a $1 bet:

$$E = [^{14}/_{36} \times (+1)] + [^2/_{36} \times (+2)] + [^{20}/_{36} \times (-1)]$$
$$= -^2/_{36} = -0.0556$$

Therefore, the house edge works out to a hefty 5.56% advantage. If either the 2 or 12 pays triple, the house edge is 2.78%. Better, but not good. The advice for keeping your money and marriage intact is the same: Don't play the field.

Big 6 and Big 8

I happen to like casinos so I try not to view the existence of this bet as proof that they are evil incarnate. This sexy-looking wager takes up two meaty corners of the layout. The bet is that the 6 (or 8) will appear before a 7. Sound familiar? This is the *same exact* thing as a place bet on the 6 or 8, but instead of getting paid 7 to 6, you get paid even money. This decrease in payoff translates to a house edge of 9.09%! The house edge on the place bet is only 1.52%. (Translation: With the Big bets, you'll lose $1 out of $11; with place bets, you'll lose $1 out of $66.) Thank goodness this bet isn't offered in

Atlantic City. And remember, there's a third way of making this same wager. You can buy the 6 or 8, but that leads to a 4.76% house edge. (Still much better than this nonsense!) For 6 or 8, place or face disgrace.

Center Propositions

Hardways: These are bets on the exact combinations of the dice pictured at the center of the craps table. There are four hardway combinations: Hard Four (2–2), Hard Six (3–3), Hard Eight (4–4), and Hard Ten (5–5). These are not one-roll wagers. Hardway bets win if the selected hardway is rolled before a 7 appears or an "easy" version of the number appears. For example, if you bet the Hard Eight, you win if 4–4 comes up before a 7 or an "easy eight" (5–3 or 6–2). The payouts for Hard Four and Hard Ten are 7 to 1 and the true odds are 8 to 1. The house edge is 11.11%. The payouts for Hard Six and Hard Eight are 9 to 1 and the true odds are 10 to 1. The house edge is 9.09%. Hardway rolls are inactive on the come-out roll unless called "on" by the player.

Any Craps: A one-roll bet that the next roll will be 2, 3, or 12. It pays 7 to 1 and has a house edge of 11.11%. True odds are 8 to 1.

Any Seven: A one-roll bet that the next roll will be 7. It pays 4 to 1 and has a whopping house edge of 16.67%. True odds are 5 to 1.

Eleven or *Three*: Two separate one-roll bets that the next roll will be 11 (or 3). It pays 15 to 1 and has a house edge of 11.11%. True odds are 17 to 1.

Twelve or *Two*: Two separate one-roll bets that the next roll will be 12 (or 2). It pays 30 to 1 and has a house edge of 13.89%. True odds are 35 to 1.

Horn Bet: A one-roll bet on four numbers: 2, 3, 11, and 12 (horn). It's made in multiples of four, with one unit on each number. If any one of these numbers is rolled, you win. If any other number is rolled, you lose. If a winner appears, the bet is paid at the posted odds of the individual number. House edge is 12.50%.

Horn High Bet: A one-roll bet made in multiples of 5 with one unit on three of the horn numbers, and two units on the "high" number of the bettor's choosing. For example, a $5 horn high eleven would put $1 each on 2, 3, 12, and $2 on the 11. The house edge varies, depending on what number is "high," but it's always huge. There's no secret to this bet; it's just an opportunity for a bettor to show flash rather than substance.

C & E: A one-roll bet that the next number will be 2, 3, 11, or 12 (craps and eleven—thus the initials). Same thing as the horn bet, but can be made in those cute little circles. More silliness.

Hop Bet: A one-roll bet that the next roll will result in one particular combination of the dice, such as 2–2 (called a "hopping hardway") or 3–5. Most hop bets are paid 15 to 1, but 2–2, 3–3, 4–4, and 5–5 are paid 30 to 1. The house edge on the 15 to 1 bets is 11.11% and the house edge on the 30 to 1 bets is 13.89%. These bets aren't even on the layout and are made orally. Run—don't hop—away from them.

There are other arcane and unusual ways to make and combine proposition bets. The only interest they have to you, the intelligent gambler, is to add Damon Runyon-esque color to the proceedings. No need to put money on any of these wagers. No matter how you dress them up, bad bets are bad bets.

INSIDE THE NUMBERS

Using a $6 place bet on the 6, we can see how the house edge on placing the 6 (or 8) is calculated from the expectation (E):

$$E = [(\text{probability of getting 6 before 7}) \times (\text{win})] +$$
$$[(\text{probability of getting 7 before 6}) \times (\text{loss})]$$
$$E = [(5/11) \times (+7)] + [(6/11)(-6)] = -1/11$$
$$E \text{ per } \$1 \text{ bet} = (-1/11)/6 = -1/66 = -0.01515$$
House edge = 1.52%

CRAPS VARIATIONS

You might find a Mini-Craps game in a casino. This is craps, simply played at a smaller table with seats (aah!) and only one dealer. You get the same odds and a more relaxed approach to the game. However, these tables tend not to do well for the casino and are disappearing.

A few casinos have tables offering Crapless Craps (sometimes called Never Ever Craps). In this variation, the numbers 2, 3, and 12 don't make you lose on the come-out roll. They become point numbers instead. A roll of 11 on the come-out won't win you anything; it too becomes a point number. These alterations bring the house edge up to 5.4% on the pass line bet. We'll pass.

You may also come across a video version of craps. This electronic version is played the same way as Crapless Craps. That means the house has the same unacceptable 5.4% edge on your pass bet. You can play a quarter at a time, but it's a dull and, uh, crappy investment.

STILL NERVOUS?

Let's take a walk-through. Find a spot at a table that's not too empty (you need that energy) and not too crowded (you don't need frenzied players or dealers who are too harried to help a rookie). It's likely that the game will be in the middle of a round—you'll know this is true if there are a lot of chips on the layout and the white puck (the ON/OFF marker) is ON on a number.

Wait for this round to end. When the marker is moved to OFF (its black side), a new round begins. If you need chips, put your cash down on the table and let the dealer take care of you. The stickman will give the dice to someone to roll. Place the chips you want to bet—let's say $5—on the pass line. You're in the action!

The shooter has a come-out roll of 11. Pass line winner. You're up $5. You take your $5 profit and keep $5 on the pass line. Same shooter has a come-out roll of 3. Oops, craps. Lose your $5 pass line. Place another $5 on pass. Same shooter has a come-out roll of 5, making the point now 5 and so the ON marker is put on the 5. You're thinking about taking odds. You'll do it. You scratch your head and recall that the free odds on a 5 pay 3 to 2. The table offers double odds (you can wager two times your pass line bet). So you put $10 behind your pass line bet. The shooter rolls a 6, 11, 2, 8, 6, 11, 6, 9. All meaningless to you. Then the shooter rolls a 5. Winner! You just won $20—$5 on your pass line bet and $15 on your odds.

Feeling good, you keep $5 on the pass line. The same shooter comes out with a 10. That's the point. You back up your pass line bet with $10 in odds (which pay 2 to 1 on a 10). You also decide to try the come bet. You place $5 in the come box. The shooter rolls an eight. That's meaningless to your original wager. Now the $5 come bet is moved to the place bet box 8 on the layout, oriented in a way so that the dealer knows it's yours. You decide to take odds on the come bet—meaning you're taking odds on the eight. The odds are 6 to 5. You put down two $5 chips and tell the dealer, "Odds on the 8," and he puts the chips on top of your original come bet, offset a little so that he knows that it's an odds bet. Feeling lucky, you place another $5 come bet. The shooter rolls a 7. Say good-bye to your pass line wager and its odds and to your come wager on the 8 and its odds. That's $30. But you do win $5 on your last come bet (7 was a winner for this "virtual" come-out roll). Net loss: $25. It adds up in craps!

You keep on playing and the dice come around to you. Don't panic! You can decline them, but there's no need to. Just make either a pass or don't pass bet and then select two of the five (or six) dice the stickman will push your way. You don't have to wait for a signal; since the dice were offered, it means that all bets are down and you can roll. A few protocol tips:

DICE DIALOGUE

Part of the charm of craps is its lively patter and alleyway lingo. On the other hand, all the rapid chatter coming from the stickman and the players can make rookies feel like they're in a foreign country. Here's a brief guide to some of the table talk.

The Basic Bets

Pass line bet: The "front line" bet. Make this bet and you're a "right bettor." You're betting with the "do's" and "with" the dice.

Don't pass bet: The "back line" bet. Justly or not, this bet makes you a "wrong bettor." You're betting with the "don'ts" and "against" the dice.

The Table Action

Working: A bet is "working" if it's "on" or "live" for the next roll. Generally, place bets, come odds, and buy/lay bets are not working on the come-out roll unless a player says to the dealer to have them work.

Press: Raise a previous bet, typically by doubling it. For example, after winning your place bet on the 6, the dealer may ask, "Do you want to press the 6?"

Take down: Remove a removable bet from the table.

Throwing numbers: Tossing an abundance of point numbers (4, 5, 6, 8, 9, 10) and not being struck down by the 7. A shooter who does this inspires much joy, as in, "This guy kept throwing numbers and I made a killing."

Natural: A term for the 7 or 11 being thrown on the come-out roll.

Two ways: A method of tipping. The player will bet one chip for the dealer along with his own bet. If a player says, "Hard Eight, two ways" and gives $2, then $1 is a bet for the player and $1 is a bet for the dealer.

The Numbers

There's a seemingly limitless variety of calls for the various numbers. Some may be unique to a particular casino—and only understood by the stickman and his cohorts. Others are universally known. Be warned: The lingo is frequently off-color as well as colorful.

Two: Craps; snake eyes; rat's eyes; two aces.

Three: Craps; ace deuce, no use; Joe Louis—the old one-two; winner on the dark side.

Four: Little Joe; little Joe from Kokomo; hit us in the tutu.

Five: Little Phoebe; five fever; we got the fever; fiver, fiver, racetrack driver.

Six: Pair of treys—waiter's roll; two trees—Brooklyn forest; sixie from Dixie; catch 'em in the corner; the national average.

Seven: Big red; six ace, in your face; six ace, out of the race; five two, you're all through; cinco dos, adios; front line winner, back line skinner.

Eight: A square pair; Ozzie and Harriet; the windows.

Nine: Nina from Pasadena; center field; center of the garden—home of the Rangers; What shot Jesse James? A forty-five.

Ten: Puppy paws; pair of sunflowers; pair-a-roses.

Eleven: Yo leven; yo levine the dance hall queen; six five, no jive.

Twelve: Craps; boxcars; all the spots we got.

Keep the dice in plain view at all times (casinos are paranoid), throw the dice hard enough so they bounce off the end wall of the table, and use only one hand. Now go shoot some numbers!

CRAPS STRATEGY AND SMARTS

YOUR BETS AND BANKROLL

The basic wisdom in craps is the best: Keep your pass line bet as low as possible and take odds. More important, you want to maximize your odds while maintaining a level of risk that's acceptable to you. If the casino offers double odds, determine what you want to wager, divide it by three, and put that much on the line. Then, when you've backed up the bet with 2× odds, you have placed your full wager and knocked down the house's edge.

No matter how smart you bet, craps is a fast and volatile game. Even if you shave the house edge to nearly nothing by taking free odds up the wazoo, you must be prepared for losing streaks. Because of the nature of dice, you can lose your entire stake even when playing close to even with the house.

Be aware of how much money you have on the table. Craps players' fortunes swing so wildly because their bets run rampant. Watch those come bets; they can add up quickly, especially when you're taking odds. A shooter gets hot and keeps making points—the money comes pouring in. A shooter sevens out at the wrong time—a small fortune disappears off the table.

That's the double-edged thrill of the game. If you want to get your feet wet and keep your money under control, just make a pass bet and take odds. See how that feels. Then you can move up to adding come bets with odds. Perhaps, you might place the 6 or 8. Progress at your own pace. Until you get comfortable with all the goings-on, I would suggest not having more than three bets riding at any one time.

Craps is home to a peculiar phenomenon: The more a person plays, the more he tends to make the occasional sucker bet. Blame it on the rhythm of the game, the salesmanship of the dealers, or the seductions of Lady Luck, but try not to be led unto temptation. You may hit a proposition bet at times, but, guaranteed, they will drain your money in the long run.

SYSTEMS

As always, be very wary of systems. When a game has as many bets as craps, there are a mind-boggling number of ways to mix and match bets. But one fact is unchangeable: You can't turn a negative expectation game into a positive expectation game. System devotees—both hucksters and true believers—will push ways to "insure" your bets and make sure you're an odds-on favorite to come out ahead on a particular roll. Be careful: A certain style of betting may win you money 9 out of 10 times, but the tenth time will cost you more than the nine wins combined. Refer to the dice chart on page 126 and calculate the numbers when something sounds too good to be true. If you don't have the patience for that, just ignore the system. You won't regret it.

Let's look at a "system" a friend of mine enthusiastically championed. It isn't inherently awful, but it illustrates many of the pitfalls and faulty premises of systems players. My friend called the system the "quick cash system" because it makes the bettor a 5-to-1 favorite to make some money on any given roll.

The system works like this: Take $22. Place the 6 and 8 for $6 and place the 5 for $5. (Put $17 down and tell the dealer to "Place six on 6, six on 8, and five on 5.") You bet the other $5 on the field (it's "ideal" to find a field bet that pays double on 2 and triple on 12 or vice versa). The only number not covered is the 7. That means on the next roll you have 30 ways to win and only 6 ways to lose. Remember, the field bet is a one-roll-only bet and that the place bets can be removed at any time. Let's look at your overall expectation (see chart on page 140).

Some points to consider about the "quick cash system":

- You're risking $22 to win—at most—$15. More than one-third of the time ($14/36$), you'll win only $2.
- The house edge is a respectable 1.136%. But you could put $11 on pass and take single odds for an edge of 0.85%. Or you could put $7 on pass, take double odds for $14 (or $15 if the point is 6 or 8), and reduce the house edge even further.
- If you don't find a field bet that pays triple on either 2 or 12, the house edge jumps up to 1.768%. A straight pass line bet is better.

Faulty System Example

Result	Probability of Result	Net Profit or Loss	Outcome
2	$1/36$	+10	$10/36$
3	$2/36$	+5	$10/36$
4	$3/36$	+5	$15/36$
5	$4/36$	+2	$8/36$
6	$5/36$	+2	$10/36$
7	$6/36$	−22	$−132/36$
8	$5/36$	+2	$10/36$
9	$4/36$	+5	$20/36$
10	$3/36$	+5	$15/36$
11	$2/36$	+5	$10/36$
12	$1/36$	+15	$15/36$

Total expectation = $-9/36$ = −0.25

Expectation per dollar = $-0.25/22$ = −0.01136

House edge = 1.136%

- My friend insists that this is a one-roll-only deal. He takes his profit (of course, in his mind, the 7 won't show) and he moves on. This doesn't hold water: If you play once in 10 sessions, or 10 times in one session, it's the same thing.
- He also plays at higher stakes of $110 (the system can be played in multiples of 5). It's volatile—a couple of sevens and your quick cash system is a quick drain.

If this kind of number play amuses and distracts you—and the house edge isn't outrageous—go ahead and enjoy. But you must also think about the potential impact on your bankroll.

Some "systems" are designed to slow down your play. Take the patently superstitious system in which you don't bet on the pass line until the shooter makes one point. This only "works" in that it keeps your bankroll under control. Fewer wagers, less exposure to risk. But I'd be reluctant to call this a system; I'd say it's a betting style or money management technique.

SUPERSTITION

Be prepared to encounter all kinds of fuzzy thinking and bizarre bugaboos in the world of craps. Every veteran dice player will warn you about "cold" tables where the dice only allow for craps or sevening out. They will testify in court that this is a real phenomenon. It is—in the past tense. That table *was* cold or *was* hot; no one,

including the dice, knows what the future holds.

Some players chart tables and scout out good shooters. Another pal of mine believes he can look in someone's eyes and tell whether he'll be a "quality" shooter or not. Need I say that no individual can influence the randomness of the dice? Some other favorite superstitions:

- If the dice are thrown off the table or they hit somebody's hand, a 7 will surely come on the next roll. The cost of taking this chestnut seriously: a bet on "any seven" and a house edge of 16.67%.
- A woman shooting for the first time ("a virgin") will have a great roll and win a lot of money for the table. A man shooting for the first time will do the exact opposite.
- Never mention the word "seven" after a come-out roll. The dice will hear you.

The rituals and hang-ups of craps players are pretty amusing and add to the atmosphere. The best advice is to enjoy the camaraderie, make your solid bets, and don't try too hard to talk much sense into the other players. The major downside to the craps mentality is that don't pass bettors are often looked on with disdain. Shooters take offense if you bet against them and other players have the misguided notion that you're betting "with" the house. Playing the don'ts is a fine approach, but you may want to hold off on it till you feel comfortable in your own status as a craps player.

THE ESSENTIALS FOR PLAYING CRAPS LIKE A GENIUS

• Get comfortable with the following bets before you play: pass, come, and free odds.
• The only good bets at craps are: pass, don't pass, come, don't come, free odds, and placing the 6 and 8.
• Stick to the pass line and a come bet or two (with odds) at the beginning.
• The house advantage is good for pass (1.41%) and don't pass (1.36%) wagers. These numbers are reduced even further by taking (or laying) odds.
• Make sure you take what's coming to you. Payoffs on winning bets will be considered active bets if you don't remove them from the betting layout.
• Take advantage of free gaming classes at casinos to get comfortable with the mechanics of the game. Just don't take the betting advice at face value.
• Ignore the proposition bets that the dealers are always hawking. They're sucker bets.
• Ignore all systems.
• Bet a comfortable wager and bet as much of it as possible on the odds. For example, if a casino offers double odds, bet one-third your normal wager on the pass line and two-thirds on the free odds.
• Beginners may want to avoid the don't pass and don't come bets because they might be seen as "confrontational."
• There are no professional craps players. This is a negative expectation game with fairly high volatility. Enjoy, but watch your bankroll.

7

BACCARAT

Casino patrons are often intimidated by baccarat because it has a reputation as a game of wealth and mystery. Played in a roped-off area called the pit, baccarat is perceived as the exclusive province of the highest rollers—aristocrats, business magnates, celebrities, or perhaps men who introduce themselves as "Bond—James Bond."

Baccarat (pronounced bah-kah-rah) is the game favored by the *whales*—the wealthiest gamblers in the world. There are a few private games in plush baccarat pits that require minimum bets of $500 and put a maximum of $250,000 on wagers. The casinos cater to these high rollers' every whim; every high-priced hunger pang or thirst is met with instant gratification. Many legends circulate about the millions lost in a single evening by Middle Eastern sheiks or Asian tycoons. It's also true that a lucky streak by a high-rolling billionaire can negatively affect a casino's quarterly report.

Yes, the game can be extravagant and elitist. But for all its impressive trappings, baccarat is merely a guessing game. No matter how many bettors sit at a baccarat table, only two hands are dealt: the *Banker* hand and the *Player* hand. You bet on which hand will come closest to a total of 9. There are absolutely no strategic decisions to make and there is no skill involved. You don't have to be particularly clever, knowledgeable, or cultured to participate.

Baccarat is also accessible to the "masses" in the form of *mini-baccarat*. This democratized version has the same rules as the original game, but is played on smaller tables located on the general casino floor and typically has a $5 minimum bet. It's the same game the rich have

been indulging in for years, merely stripped of some of its glitter.

Most important, no matter what size table you play baccarat on, the house edge is one of the smallest you'll find in the casino. It's still a negative expectation game so you'll lose in the long run, but you may be able to give the house a decent fight.

HOW BACCARAT IS PLAYED

Classic baccarat and mini-baccarat have exactly the same rules, but the physical setup, betting limits, and procedures differ for each. I'll focus on the full-scale version and then point out mini-baccarat's differences further on.

THE SCENE: CLASSIC BACCARAT

Don't be deterred by the mystique of the baccarat pit. The atmosphere is usually quite relaxed and friendly, and very few pits are "exclusive" in any sense. They subscribe to the universal casino credo: Anyone with money is welcome to play. And you don't necessarily have to wager huge amounts to get in on the action. You can find baccarat pits that offer tables with minimum bets as low as $25.

When you play in the pit, you get to indulge in (or at least observe) all the niceties and privileges geared toward the high rollers: an elegantly appointed room; tuxedo-clad dealers; extremely attentive service; and a disproportionate number of beautiful women. (Very often, they're *shills*—casino employees who act as players to attract high rollers to the game.) Plus, you can handle the cards and even mangle them if you're displeased.

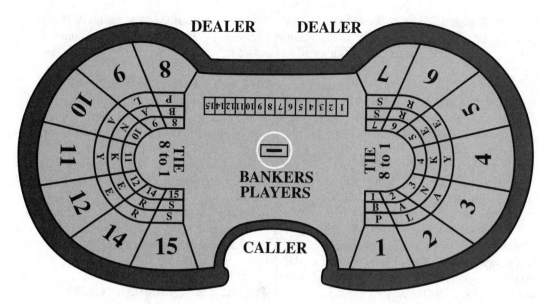

The Table and Crew

The full-sized baccarat table (see illustration above) is about three times the size of a blackjack table and typically seats 14 players (sometimes 12). At each end of the 14-seat table, there are seven numbered positions, each of which correspond to a player. You'll notice that these player positions are numbered from 1 through 15; casinos oblige superstitious players by omitting 13. At each position, there are sections to place the three possible bets: Banker, Player, or Tie.

Three dealers service each table. The dealer who stands in the middle of the table (between positions 1 and 15) is known as the *caller*. He runs the game and makes sure all the correct procedures are followed. The two other dealers, each working a particular end of the table, pay off the winning bets and collect the losing ones.

Before a new game starts, all three dealers perform an elaborate ritual of shuffling eight decks of cards. After one of the players cuts the cards, the decks are placed in the *shoe*. More ritual: The dealer reveals the top card from the shoe and proceeds to *burn* (discard) the number of cards equivalent to the card's value. All discards are literally discarded, sent through a slot in the table, never to be used again.

THE ACTION: CLASSIC BACCARAT

Baccarat is the only game in the casino where the players get an opportunity to actually deal the cards. The player seated at the number-one position is given the first chance to be the banker. Players don't have to accept the shoe and are free to pass the offer to the next player. If you do take the shoe, there is no particular advantage or disadvantage; dealing merely adds to the flair of the game. You are not obligated to bet on the Banker's hand even if you choose to deal and be the banker. But if you bet Player, you may get some good-hearted—and not-so-good-hearted—flak about "betting against yourself" from players who don't appreciate the game's random nature. Once a Banker hand loses, the shoe is offered to the next player counterclockwise at the table.

Players bet by placing their chips in the appropriate box on the layout opposite their seat. Bets made on the Player or Banker are paid off at even money (1–1). If the Banker wins, players who made this bet must pay a 5% commission on their winnings. For example, if a player had a $100 bet on the Banker's hand and it won, $5 would be owed to the house. Rather than collecting this commission (also known as the *vigorish*, or vig) after each game, the dealer keeps track of your commission in a box in front of the chip rack by using plastic markers designating the amount owed. You may pay this commission at any time, but it must be collected after the shoe is completed.

A Tie bet is also available and pays 8–1 (sometimes 9–1) if the Player and Banker hands are tied. The tie carries a large house edge and should be avoided, as will be explained later on.

After all bets are placed, the player with the shoe deals two cards for each hand. This entails more arcane ritual. The first card to come out of the shoe is the first Player card, and it is slid face-down to the caller. The next card is the first Banker card and it is placed face-down next to, or slightly under, the shoe. The third card (the second Player card) is slid face-down to the caller. The initial part of the deal is completed with the fourth card (the second Banker card), which joins the first under the corner of the shoe. The caller then passes the Player's cards to the player at the table who has placed the highest Player bet. (If no one has bet on the Player, then the caller reveals the cards himself.) The player then examines the cards either quickly or in a variety of elaborate, amusing, and sometimes excruciating ways. The Player cards are then returned to the caller, who places them face-up in the center of the table on the area marked PLAYERS. Next, the Banker cards are flipped over and placed on the area marked BANKERS.

The caller determines the values of the hands and sees if another card must be taken according to the rules discussed on the next page.

THE SCENE: MINI-BACCARAT

Mini-baccarat plays like its big brother; it's just more humble. You can feel comfortable dressing as casually as you like. (Haute couture is rarely expected even in full-scale pits.) The blackjack-style table of mini-baccarat usually seats seven players. (See illustration below.) There is only one dealer and she is the only one to handle the cards. Players can't deal or butcher the cards as they do in the classic version and commissions on winning Banker hands are settled more often.

THE ACTION: MINI-BACCARAT

Basically, the low roller sacrifices some solitude and pampering for less fuss and lower stakes. Limits are usually from a $2 or $5 minimum up to a $500 maximum. However, it's important to note that mini-baccarat moves much faster than the large version. You may get in an extra 50 hands per hour. This is not necessarily a blessing for the casual gambler. The amount you wager per hour could be comparable to what you wager in the full-scale game. Be aware of this because baccarat, though a good bet, still has a negative expectation.

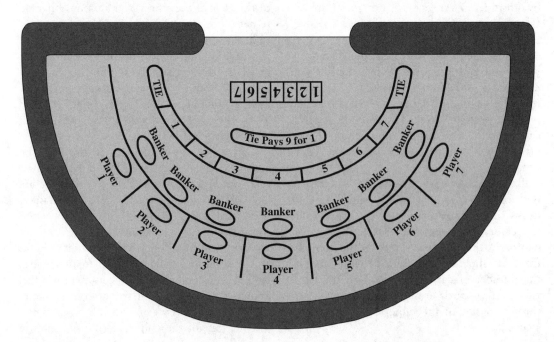

HOW THE HAND PLAYS OUT

Baccarat is often compared to blackjack because you are hoping the hand you bet on gets as close as possible to a certain total—in this case, 9, rather than blackjack's 21. But in baccarat you're not playing your own hand, you're betting only on one of two hands dealt to the table. More important, you have no decisions to make about the play of the hands. The dealer acts according to predetermined rules without consulting players at the table. Players can control only how much they wager and whether they bet on the Player hand or Banker hand. This lack of decision-making can actually be quite a comfort to novices.

CARD VALUES

All cards 2 through 9 count as face value. Aces count as one. Tens, jacks, queens, and kings all count as 0. When the total of the cards is more than 9, the first digit in the total is dropped. This means all hands will have a value from 0 to 9.

For example: King + 4 = 4
$$9 + 3 = 2$$
$$Ace + 9 = 0$$

DRAWING CARDS TO THE HANDS

Following the house protocol the dealer reveals first the Player hand and then the Banker hand, determining whether the hand wins on the first two cards or whether cards will be drawn. No baccarat hand will ever have more than three cards. This means that at most one card can be drawn to a hand.

As we know, the highest total any hand can have is 9. A two-card total of 9 is called a *natural* or *le grand naturel* and cannot lose. A total of 8 is the second-best hand and is also called a natural or *le petit naturel*. It loses only to a 9. An 8 or 9 on the first two cards ends the game. If both Player and Banker are dealt identical natural hands, the game is a tie. If either the Player or the Banker has a natural 8 or 9, the other hand cannot draw a third card, and, therefore, loses. Both Banker and Player also stand on a hand totaling 7 (even if it doesn't earn an elegant French name). The Player hand also never draws on 6.

The table below summarizes the rules for when Player and Banker take a third card. The rules are nonintuitive and appear rather arbitrary. Of course, it is not necessary to memorize these "third card rules." You can blithely ignore them and just wait for each hand's outcome. But I don't recommend this approach (at least not for long) and it probably won't appeal to you once you sit down at the game. It's worth absorbing the rules for two reasons: 1) It will increase the drama of the game and thus

Baccarat Drawing Rules		
When the Player's first two cards total:	**Player's hand ...**	**and Banker's hand ...**
0, 1, 2, 3, 4, 5	Draws a card.	Draws according to the rules below.
6, 7	Stands.	Draws when first two cards total 0, 1, 2, 3, 4, or 5, and stands on 6, 7, 8, or 9.
8, 9	Natural stands.	Never draws.

When Banker's first two cards total:	**Banker's hand draws when Player's third card is:**	**Banker's hand stands when Player's third card is:**
0, 1, 2	Anything.	——
3	1, 2, 3, 4, 5, 6, 7, 9, 0	8
4	2, 3, 4, 5, 6, 7	1, 8, 9, 0
5	4, 5, 6, 7	1, 2, 3, 8, 9, 0
6	6, 7	1, 2, 3, 4, 5, 8, 9, 0
7	Always stands.	
8, 9	Natural stands.	
Naturals immediately win or are tied. A 9 beats an 8.		

your enjoyment; 2) You may catch dealers' mistakes. This latter possibility is not so remote, because mini-baccarat's popularity has led to inexperienced casino personnel dealing the game.

....

BACCARAT STRATEGY AND SMARTS

THE HOUSE EDGE

The house edge in baccarat is among the lowest of any casino game. The casino advantage is only 1.06% on the Banker wager and 1.24% on the Player wager. The Tie wager should be avoided by those who don't normally flush or burn their money. One of the worst bets in the casino, it carries a whopping 14.36% house advantage! The giddy, independently wealthy players around you may throw some money on the Tie bet. Don't follow suit. Even if you find the rare game that pays 9 to 1 for a Tie bet, you'll still be giving up 4.84%.

WORKING ON COMMISSION

Some players feel resentful about the 5% commission on Banker wins and suspect that they are being "gypped" by the casino. The numbers don't support this innate resistance to being taxed. The casino charges the commission in order to give the house an advantage. But, as we just learned, the Banker bet still enjoys a smaller house edge (1.06%) than the Player bet (1.24%).

Some casinos offer 4% commission on Banker wins, either as a special promotion or on a regular basis. Such a rate would most likely only apply to full-size tables. But if you enjoy baccarat and feel comfortable with the higher stakes of the pit game, don't pass this opportunity up. The house edge on the Banker bet is reduced to 0.60%. Some casinos will even flash the occasional 3% commission to draw in the baccarat cognoscenti. The house edge then is a mere 0.14%

PATTERN SPOTTING

The first thing you'll notice when you sit down to play baccarat is that most—if not all—of your fellow players are tracking the results of each hand on scorecards. An "X" may be placed for a winning Player hand and an "O" for a winning Banker. They're all looking for "patterns" in the outcomes of the hands. Why? Excellent question. Let's just chalk it up to tradition, ritual, and superstition.

There is certainly no rational reason to think that a randomly shuffled shoe of eight decks is going to follow distinct patterns. But veteran (and very high-spending) baccarat players will swear until they're blue in the face that the heart of the game lies in patterns and streaks. The patterns even have names, such as when the shoe is "choppy" (alternating between wins for the Player and the Banker) or when there are "skip ties" (a couple of instances where a tie is followed two hands later by another tie). Many baccarat players will buy in, then sit and wait while the game is being dealt, searching for trends, waiting patiently, then picking their spot.

As will be discussed in Chapter 16, patterns and streaks are only identifiable after the fact; you have no way of knowing in advance whether a pattern will start, continue, or end. Still, baccarat buffs are a superstitious lot, relying on intuition and pseudo-scientific clairvoyance. It makes for entertaining company. You may want to mark up your own scorecard just for the sake of camaraderie. You will start seeing patterns. *Don't* exceed your normal bets in pursuit of these ephemeral streaks and trends. Would the casino provide everyone with pencil and chart if there really were anything to it?

WHAT ABOUT CARD-COUNTING?

You may be wondering if *card-counting* could give you an edge while playing baccarat. Card-counting involves keeping track of cards that have been played from the shoe in order to gain an advantage against the house. This is discussed in greater depth in the blackjack chapter.

On the face of things, card-counting sounds promising because each hand in baccarat is not a completely independent event. As more cards are played from the shoe, the more you know about the cards left.

However, while individual cards can be shown to be mathematically favorable or unfavorable (depending on if you bet Banker or Player), each one's effect is minuscule. You also can't increase your bet in mid-hand like in blackjack. The baccarat card-counter so rarely

INSIDE THE NUMBERS

Thanks to the wonders of modern computing, we can ascertain the chances of the three baccarat wagers occurring in an eight-deck shoe. They are as follows:

Player wins   44.625%
Banker wins   45.860%
Tie   9.516%

We can use these percentages to determine the expected outcome of the various baccarat bets.

Expected Outcome for $1 Bet on Player Hand

Outcome	Result of Bet	Frequency	Expected Earnings
Player wins	+1	0.44625	+0.44625
Banker wins	−1	0.45860	−0.45860
Tie	0	0.09516	0
	Total expected outcome		−0.01235
	House edge		1.24%

Expected Outcome for $1 Bet on Banker Hand

Outcome	Result of Bet	Frequency	Expected Earnings
Player wins	−1	0.44625	−0.44625
Banker wins	+0.95 (5% vig)	0.45860	+0.43567
Tie	0	0.09516	0
	Total expected outcome		−0.01058
	House edge		1.06%

Expected Outcome for $1 Bet on Tie

Outcome	Result of Bet	Frequency	Expected Earnings
Player wins	−1	0.44625	−0.44625
Banker wins	−1	0.45860	−0.45860
Tie	+8	0.09516	0.76128
	Total expected outcome		−0.14357
	House edge		14.36%

If you do further reading on gambling, you will frequently come across writers who state the house edge as 1.17% for Banker bets and 1.36% for Player bets. This number is arrived at by ignoring ties. If ties are not taken into account, the Banker will win 50.7% of the time and the Player will win 49.3% of the time. Although it's true that a Banker or Player bet is resolved only when one or the other wins, you are putting money at risk on every bet, even when a Tie occurs. Therefore, I believe it is more accurate to base the house edge on the money you can expect to be returned to you over the long run—including every bet you make, not just the ones with a Player or Banker win.

finds a situation where he has the advantage against the house that his efforts are worthless. Systems have been developed that are theoretically intriguing, but are, in the final analysis, thoroughly impractical.

BETTING WISELY

Baccarat can be considered a coin toss played with a lot of fanfare, ritual, and wealth. But don't let this comparison lure you toward betting "systems" that involve doubling up your

CHEMIN DE FER

Chemin de fer (French for "railroad") is essentially the same game as today's casino game of baccarat, but one of the players banks the game, rather than the casino. The other players compete against the banker. The "banker" designation rotates around the table. The casino takes no risk and merely charges a fee from each banker. Another difference between baccarat and chemin de fer is that the banker and player (the player who bid highest against the banker) can make decisions about drawing a third card in certain situations. If you want to be precise, it's chemin de fer, not baccarat, that Agent 007 plays.

bets until you win. Check out Chapter 16 for a thorough debunking of those systems.

Streak analysis is also hogwash, but it makes things more interesting when you've got only two bets to choose from.

The savvy player will ask, "Shouldn't I always make the Banker bet since it has the smallest house edge?" The short answer is yes. But you also have to ask yourself why you're playing baccarat. It's a negative expectation game and you will lose money in the long run. Do you want more entertainment out of it than just monotonously placing your bet on Banker time and time again? I don't think yes is a foolish answer to that question.

If you made 100 bets of $10 on Banker, your expectation would be a loss of $10.60. If you made 100 bets of $10 on the Player, your expectation would be a loss of $12.40. That's only a $1.80 difference—not an unreasonable amount to put at risk for some variety. (And you wouldn't be placing *all* your bets on the Player.) This is *not* an argument to throw your money around haphazardly. If you made those 100 bets of $10 on the awful Tie bet, you'd have an expected loss of $143.60. Big difference.

Since the casino has the edge, it will have the upper hand over the long term. But since the edge is small, you have a better chance for short-term success. Try to escape with your winnings when you can and don't chase after your losses. Remember that although mini-baccarat has lower stakes, it does play at a faster pace. Don't lose track of how much you're risking per hour.

THE ESSENTIALS FOR PLAYING BACCARAT LIKE A GENIUS

- Baccarat is an excellent choice for anyone who wants to play a simple guessing game that requires no playing strategy. The only decision is whether to bet on the Banker or the Player.
- The house edge is very small: 1.06% for Banker bets and 1.24% for Player bets.
- Never, ever bet on the Tie with its larcenous 14.36% house edge!
- Look for games with 4% commission on the Banker bet. At such tables, make only the Banker bet because the house edge on it is a measly 0.60%.
- Don't forget to keep enough money in reserve to settle up your commissions on winning Banker bets. It can be a bit embarrassing if you don't.
- The rules for full-scale baccarat and mini-baccarat are the same. The protocol, table limits, and surroundings differ.
- Start off with the less formal and less intimidating mini-baccarat tables.
- Don't deny yourself the pleasures of the baccarat pit. Go see how the casino royalty live!

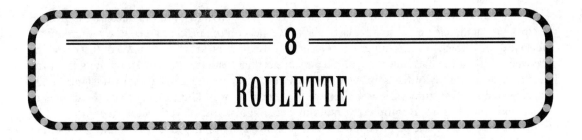

8

ROULETTE

The classic game of roulette has charms that soothe the savage gambler. This slow-paced game tends to attract a more subdued, sophisticated—shall we say—*civilized* crowd. In European casinos, roulette is associated with tuxedoed men and stylish women; it has an air of elegance and nobility, grace and dignity. The exact origins of the game are hazy (some attribute its invention to the 17th century mathematician Blaise Pascal) but it became a fixture in European casinos by the mid-18th century.

The roulette wheel is considered the most instantly recognizable symbol of gambling in the world. This is somewhat ironic because, although the game is extremely popular throughout Europe, it has never been a big draw in the United States. It earns significantly less than the other table game heavyweights: blackjack, craps, and baccarat.

This second-class status can be attributed to the fact that American roulette wheels are "impure" in comparison to their European brethren. They contain "00" as well as "0." This addition makes for a bigger casino advantage, thereby discouraging those who might enjoy the breezy simplicity of the game. A few American casinos offer single-zero wheels. Unfortunately, roulette tables with these wheels often have minimum bets as high as $25. That may put too much pressure on a recreational gambler's bankroll, even considering the lower house edge. Conditions do change, though, and it's always worthwhile to ask around.

Another explanation for roulette's relative lack of success in the U.S. might be its personality—it's a tranquil and passive game in a nation of ever-on-the-go movers and shakers. Still, roulette does have its devotees and it's easy to see why. It's a perfect game of chance, instantly comprehensible, requiring neither skill nor strategy. It's a clean guessing game, in which you can't really make a dumb bet, but you can't really make a smart one either.

HOW ROULETTE IS PLAYED

THE SCENE
Roulette is a slow and relaxing game with momentary jolts of excitement. After all, everyone wants to know where the heck that little ball is going to land.

The Wheel
Nearly three-feet in diameter and about 100 pounds, the wheel is the star of the show. This finely tuned piece of equipment contains 38 numbered compartments or *pockets*. The pockets are colored red, black, or green. Numbers 1 through 36 are divided evenly among red and black pockets; "0" and "00" get green pockets.

Rather than being distributed haphazardly around the wheel, the numbers are ordered to achieve as much balance as possible among high and low, red and black, odd and even. Look at the diagram on page 150 and you can see the wheel is quite masterfully laid out. Directly across the wheel from every odd number is the next highest even number. Black and red alternate; pairs of even numbers alternate with pairs of odd numbers (with some variation around the 0 and 00). This design is standard for all 38-number wheels.

The *croupier* (dealer) spins the wheel counterclockwise and releases a small plastic ball clockwise on a track on the upper portion of the wheel. When the ball slows down, it leaves the track and eventually finds its way into a pocket after running into various buffers and ornaments that ensure a completely random result. Be prepared for the ball to bounce out of several pockets before it finds its final destination.

The Table and the Chips

The long roulette table can usually accommodate six to eight people. On the table is a layout containing all 38 numbers (see page 151). As with any table game, check the minimums before sitting down. If you're playing a $5-minimum table, you must place at least $5 for every bet you make on the *outside* bets. (Outside and *inside* bets are explained in detail below.) For instance, if you bet black or red, odd or even, high or low, you must place at least a $5 chip on the bet. However, your inside bets on specific numbers and combinations only have to total $5. In other words, you can make five individual $1 bets on the inside to meet the minimum.

Beginners are sometimes confused by the fact that roulette uses different chips from the rest of the casino. Each player is assigned a different color of chip; this enables the dealers to distinguish one player's bet from another's. The chips are purchased at the table with either cash or regular casino chips. These chips have no value at other gaming tables—they are for roulette use only. When you have finished playing, the dealer will exchange your roulette chips for casino chips.

When you sit down and buy in, the dealer will ask you what value you want your chips to be. For a $5 game, the minimum value for chips is usually $1. For a $1 minimum game, chips will probably be worth 25¢. Your choice should be based on the size and kind of bets you plan to make on each spin. The dealer keeps track of the value of each player's colored chips by placing a *lammer* (a marker with an amount on it) on top of a chip of that color. All your chips will be worth the same amount—

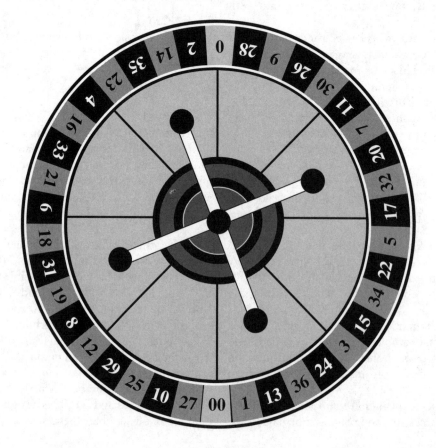

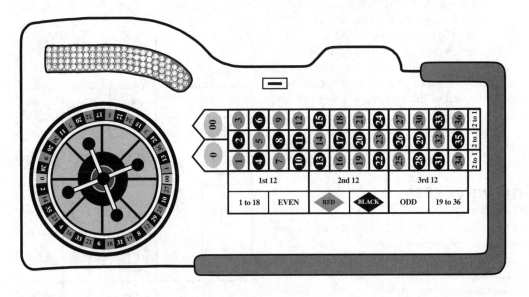

25¢, $1, $5, etc. A stack of chips generally contains 20 chips. The stacks are then defined by the lammer that tops them. For instance, a 100 lammer indicates $100 per stack (meaning $5 chips) and a 20 lammer indicates $20 per stack (meaning $1 chips). So you may be playing the blue chips worth 25¢ (the dealer has a 5 lammer on a blue chip) when you notice the woman next to you is playing red chips worth $25 (a 500 lammer on a red chip).

THE ACTION

Roulette moves at a leisurely pace as players place their bets down on the table's layout. Different players' chips often share the same position (no problem—thanks to those differently colored chips). Feel free to stack your chips right on top of other players' chips. The dealer can tell them apart by the color. You have plenty of time to place your bets; you can still bet while the wheel is spinning and after the dealer releases the ball, but not after he announces, "No more bets" and waves his hands over the table.

When the ball comes to rest in a pocket, the dealer calls out the winning number and places a clear cylindrical marker on the number's spot on the layout. The table is swept clean of losing wagers before winners are paid. The dealer will pay the bets furthest away from him (the outside bets) on the table and work in, until he gets to the inside bets, which get paid last.

Don't touch the table to collect or place chips until the dealer removes the marker from the layout and announces, "Place your bets." Remember to pick up whatever chips you don't plan on betting again. And then it's time for the next spin.

THE BETS

A multitude of roulette bets are illustrated by lettered chips in the diagram on page 152. The bets are quite straightforward, but make sure you position your chips precisely. You don't want to miss a payoff because of an errant chip. Quick review of how payoffs work: The odds are stated as A to B, which means you'll win A dollars for every B dollars you bet. For example, a $1 bet on a single number pays 35 to 1; if the number hits, you'll win $35 and get back your $1 bet for a total of $36.

THE OUTSIDE BETS

These wagers are placed "outside" the 38 numbers of the layout, and refer to groups of numbers or colors. All outside bets lose if the ball drops into the 0 or 00 pocket.

Red or *black:* A bet that the winning number will be the color you bet on. Pays even money (1 to 1). *Chip A on diagram.*

Odd or *even:* A bet that the winning number will be either—surprise—odd or even. Pays even money. *Chip B.*

Low or *high:* A bet that the number will either be low (the 1–18 spot) or high (the 19–36 spot). Pays even money. *Chip C.*

Columns: A bet on the 12 numbers contained in any one of the three long columns on the layout. Just place your chip on the "2 to 1" spot at the end of the column you want to bet. Yes, it pays 2 to 1. *Chip D.*

Dozens: A bet on either the first dozen numbers (1–12), the second dozen (13–24), or the third dozen (25–36). Pays 2 to 1. *Chip E.*

THE INSIDE BETS

These bets are made on specific numbers or combinations of numbers either within the number layout or on its border.

Straight-up bet: A bet on a single number (including 0 or 00). Place your chip(s) squarely in the center of the number you want. This is the longest shot in the game and it pays 35 to 1. *Chip F* is a straight-up bet on the number 8.

Split bet: A bet on any two adjoining numbers (including 0 and 00). Place your chip on the line separating the two numbers. If either of the two numbers shows up, this bet pays 17 to 1. *Chip G* is a split bet on 29 and 32. By the way, a split bet on 0 and 00 can be made at the border of the two numbers *or* on the line separating the second and third dozen. Apparently, this is a labor-saving device for those at the far end of the table.

Street bet: A single bet, paying 11 to 1, that covers three numbers in a row. Place your chip on the outside line of the row you want to bet. *Chip H* is a street bet on the row containing 13, 14, and 15.

Corner bet: Also known as a square bet or quarter bet, the corner bet is a single bet on four adjoining numbers that form a square. Place your chip at the point where the four numbers converge. If any of the four numbers show up, the bet pays 8 to 1. *Chip I* is a corner bet on 2, 3, 5, and 6.

Five-number bet: There's only one five-number bet, and that's fortunate because it's the worst roulette bet you can make. (This will be explained further in the odds section.) *Chip J* indicates this horrible bet, which covers 0, 00, 1, 2, and 3. Place your chip at the corner intersection of 0, 1, and the first dozen. It pays 6 to 1.

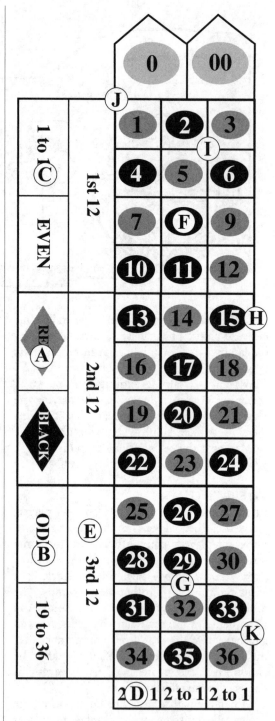

Six-number bet: Also known as a *line* bet. This bet covers two adjacent rows of numbers. Place your chip on one of the outside lines at the intersection of two rows. The bet pays 5 to 1. *Chip K* is a line bet on 31, 32, 33, 34, 35, and 36.

ROULETTE STRATEGY AND SMARTS

The mathematics of roulette is elegant and simple. If you're not interested in the whys and wherefores of roulette's odds, just know that all the bets in American roulette except one give the house a substantial 5.26% advantage. The one exception is even worse—the five-number bet, which has an edge of 7.89%. For those who would like to know how these numbers come about, check out the Inside the Numbers sidebar on page 154.

SURRENDER

Surrender is a beneficial rule found in Atlantic City casinos and in some other areas. (Inquire at the tables before you play.) The rule applies only to outside bets that pay even money; that is, red/black, odd/even, high/low. If the ball lands on 0 or 00, you lose only half your bet rather than the full amount. This knocks down the casino's advantage on even-money bets to 2.63%. Even-money bets become twice as good as other bets; you're just sacrificing the chance of a big payout. The numbers work out this way:

$$E = [^{18}\!/_{38} \times (+1)] + [^{18}\!/_{38} \times (-1)] + [^2\!/_{38} \times (-0.5)]$$
$$= -^1\!/_{38} = -0.0263$$
House edge = 2.63%

If an American casino should happen to have a single-zero wheel, it will rarely offer the surrender rule.

THE EUROPEAN WHEEL

European fondness for roulette is not without cause. Things are different over there: The tables are usually run by two croupiers, a rake is used to clear losing bets, and players use standard casino chips rather than the nontransferable ones used at American tables. But, of course, the big difference is the wheel, which has only 37 numbers, including a single 0. For gamblers, this is certainly addition by subtraction. The absence of 00 drops the house edge down to 2.70% on all bets. (And thank goodness there's no five-number bet!)

The payoffs for all the bets on the European wheel are the same as for the American wheel.

Let's look at the house edge for a dozens bet (notice how the number of possibilities is 37, not 38):

$$E = [^{12}\!/_{37} \times (+2)] + [^{25}\!/_{37} \times (-1)]$$
$$= -^1\!/_{37} = -0.0270$$
House edge = 2.70%

EN PRISON

The roulette picture is even rosier overseas because most European roulette tables offer a rule called *en prison*. This is similar in spirit to the surrender rule discussed earlier. In this case, if you make an even-money bet and the ball lands on zero, your money isn't removed from the table. Instead, it is considered "in prison" and its fate is to be determined on the next spin. If the en prison bet comes in on the next spin, your original wager is returned to you, without winnings. If your bet loses, you lose the original wager. If zero should happen to show again, the bet remains in prison.

With en prison, the house edge on even-money bets is sliced in half to a very appealing 1.35%. With a little European twist, roulette goes from one of the poorer bets in the casino to one of the most respectable. That will certainly make a game popular on a continent. A look at the numbers for the even-money bets:

$$E = [^{18}\!/_{37} \times (+1)] + [^{18}\!/_{37} \times (-1)] + [^1\!/_{37} \times (-0.5)]$$
$$= -0.0135$$
House edge = 1.35%

We consider a half-dollar lost (−0.5) every time 0 comes up (¹⁄₃₇) because half the time the dollar will be lost and half the time it will be returned with no winnings.

CAN ROULETTE BE BEATEN?

The short answer to the above question is no. Make that an emphatic no. Yet, for some reason, this simple game of chance attracts an inordinate amount of attention from system gurus, con men, dreamers, and number-crunchers. The various approaches range from mostly ridiculous to occasionally sublime.

Systems

Maybe it's the unyielding clarity of roulette's odds that drives certain people to vainly chal-

INSIDE THE NUMBERS

Let's look at what's happening on a straight $1 bet on a single number. Since there are 38 numbers on an American wheel, the probability of a particular number coming up on a spin is $\frac{1}{38}$. The true odds, therefore, are 37 to 1. But you're paid only 35 to 1 when you hit a single number. That's a $2 shortfall. On average, over 38 spins, you'll lose $2, which is 5.26% of the $38 you bet over those 38 spins. The same result is revealed by the expected outcome (E) formula that was discussed in Chapter 2:

$$E = [\tfrac{1}{38} \times (+35)] + [\tfrac{37}{38} \times (-1)] = -\tfrac{2}{38} = -0.0526$$

House edge = 5.26%

But what about all the other bets? Same story. If you look at the casino's payoff odds, you'll realize they all pay off the "correct" odds ... if you were playing on a wheel with only 36 numbers. The 0 and 00 are the monkey wrenches that always lead to a $\frac{2}{38}$ disadvantage. Here's how a $1 bet on "black" (18 of the 38 numbers) shapes up:

$$E = [\tfrac{18}{38} \times (+1)] + [\tfrac{20}{38} \times (-1)] = -\tfrac{2}{38} = -0.0526$$

House edge = 5.26%

Want one more? Let's look at the line bet that covers six numbers:

$$E = [\tfrac{6}{38} \times (+5)] + [\tfrac{32}{38} \times (-1)] = -\tfrac{2}{38} = -0.0526$$

Once again, 5.26% of every dollar is removed from your pocket.

And then there's the really awful five-number bet. Notice that the casino odds of 6 to 1 aren't quite right even if the wheel had only 36 numbers (that payoff would be an impractical 6.2 to 1). So the casino gets an extra edge beyond the 0 and 00.

$$E = [\tfrac{5}{38} \times (+6)] + [\tfrac{33}{38} \times (-1)] = -\tfrac{3}{38} = -0.0789$$

House edge = 7.89%

lenge the laws of mathematics. Or maybe there are just too many rip-off artists in the world. Whatever the case may be, roulette systems are legion. They are sold (or promoted) in books, pamphlets, magazines, newsletters, and in every nook and cranny of the Internet.

They are all worthless. Well, let me be more magnanimous. Some are relatively harmless ways to fiddle with your chips and spread around your bets while facing the never-altered house edge of 5.26%. Others are very dangerous concoctions that may lull you into a false sense of security and then devastate you with a huge loss (or losses). Don't spend a cent to purchase any of them.

Many systems are variations on the "double-up until you win" Martingale system that we'll discuss and dismiss in Chapter 16. Essentially, this approach will lead to many small wins and some catastrophic losses. There are some betting progressions on single numbers that will leave

you with a small win and keep you under the table limit if the number hits within 200 spins. Not good enough. About one in every 200 sessions you'll end up with a whopping loss, and you never know when it will actually show up.

Other systems promote ways to "hedge" your bets so that you "guarantee" yourself winnings. No combination of bad bets is going to magically turn into a good bet. This couldn't be clearer than in American roulette, in which every bet (except for the lousy five-number bet) has a 5.26% edge (unless you are playing at a table that has surrender). Any way you slice or dice it, you're left with that same casino advantage.

Not long ago, I was treated to an example of the fuzzy and rather nonsensical thinking that typifies "systems" players. While playing at the roulette table, a friendly college student excitedly told me about his system. His "steady" bets were $100 on red and $10 on the split bet covering 0 and 00. He explained to me that he was "taking the edge away from the house." He conceded that he "might lose a little more for a short time," but that when 0 or 00 showed he "would be ahead of the game instead of behind."

The kid wasn't trying to sell anything; he was just enthusiastic about an approach his friend gave him. But you can see how some hazy double-talk and some misapplied knowledge can set you on the wrong path. If you know that 0 and 00 somehow give the house an advantage, then, heck, maybe betting on them would lessen that advantage.

We can easily see how this "system" ends up with our old predictable house edge. If the ball lands on a red number (probability of $^{18}/_{38}$), then the kid wins $90 ($100 for the red bet minus $10 for the split bet). If the ball lands on 0 or 00 ($^2/_{38}$), the kid wins $70 ($170 for the split bet minus $100 for the red bet). If the ball lands on a black number ($^{18}/_{38}$), the full $110 bet is lost. Therefore, we have the following equation:

$$E = [^{18}/_{38} \times (+90)] + [^2/_{38} \times (+70)] + [^{18}/_{38} \times (-110)] = -^{220}/_{38} = -5.7895$$

E per dollar bet = $-5.7895/_{110}$ = −0.0526

House edge = 5.26%

I tried to explain to the kid that the overall edge wouldn't change. He just grinned at me and said, "I dunno, it seems to be working so far tonight."

Don't be taken in by a free demonstration of a roulette system. Success in any particular session (or several sessions) proves nothing. The scam artist would have to be very unlucky to suffer the inevitable, gargantuan loss on the night of an "exhibition." If they played their system all the time, they would lose. That's why they make their money selling systems and not playing roulette.

It's impossible to beat roulette with a betting system because the bets can't be tricked into paying off at their true odds. That's why casino owners count systems players when they're trying to relax and fall asleep at night.

Biased Wheels

Roulette wheels are expertly crafted, finely tuned pieces of equipment. Unlike the other "random event" generators of the casino—dice, playing cards—wheels are not replaced every couple of hours (or less). The wear and tear on a wheel's parts can lead to mechanical imperfections: warped wood, slight tilts or imbalances, worn or loosened dividers between pockets, etc. These defects could theoretically lead to a wheel being *biased*—meaning that it isn't providing completely random results.

Let's assume we found a truly biased wheel. This wheel has a section of four numbers (perhaps 19, 8, 12, and 29) that show up more frequently than expected. One would expect, on average, that one of these four numbers would appear once per 9.5 spins ($^4/_{38}$), but instead we find that the ball lands in this section once per 8 spins ($^1/_8$). So we place a dollar on each of the four numbers. (We'll ignore the $5 table minimum for this example. If you found a true bias, you'd be betting a lot more than $1 anyway!) If one of the numbers lands, we win $32 ($35 minus the three $1 losers). If the section misses, we lose $4. Here's the expected outcome:

$$E = [^1/_8 \times (+32)] + [^7/_8 \times (-4)] = ^4/_8 = +0.5$$

E per dollar bet = $^{0.5}/_4$ = 0.125

Player's edge (!) = 12.5%

You can see how finding a wheel that favors numbers could be quite lucrative. Over the long run, for every $1,000 bet, you'd expect to make $125. Nice return. Nice fantasy. But don't quit your job and stake out the nearest roulette table.

While I have heard legitimate tales of biased wheels, I suspect they are discovered as frequently as holy grails and open bank vaults. There are many obstacles to finding a biased wheel. First of all, you need to know statistics rather intimately and be able to gather tons of data. Tens of thousands of spins may be needed to detect a weak bias. If a wheel has blatant imperfections and a whole section is favored, perhaps you would have statistical "confidence" in one or two thousand spins. At 40 spins per hour, it would take 50 hours to record 2,000 spins. Second, many casinos swap wheels around so you're not always seeing the same wheel at the same table. And finally, after all your time and effort, the wheel may not be biased or it may not be biased enough to overcome the house edge. In fact,

A FRENCH TWIST

This chapter demonstrates a strong bias toward the European approach to roulette. So much so, I'm sure you're booking tickets to Monte Carlo right now. (Perhaps not.) Before you go, you'll want to familiarize yourself with the French terms for the bets. How else are you going to impress the croupier with your worldliness and sophistication?

En plein: Straight-up bet
À cheval: Split bet
Transversale: Street bet
Carré: Corner bet
Sixaine: Line bet
Rouge/noir: Red/black
Impair/pair: Odd/even
Passe/manque: High/low
Douzaine: Dozen bet
Colonne: Column bet

Here are some other bets primarily available in European casinos:

Quatre premiers: The first four numbers (0, 1, 2, and 3).
Quatre derniers: The final four numbers (33, 34, 35, and 36).
Voisins: A "neighbor" bet. A number and the two numbers on either side of it on the wheel.

with increased computerization and electronic displays, the casino will most likely detect a bias before you do.

Of course, the logistical difficulties of detecting wheel bias don't inhibit the system hucksters. Many systems are based on the notion that short-term observation can lead to long-term riches. Don't fall for it. Just because a number shows up three times in 50 spins doesn't mean that it's a "dominant," "hot," or "streaking" number. This is just normal random fluctuation. Systems players will often eye the electronic tote boards found at many tables that reveal the last 15 numbers hit. If a number appears twice on the board, they'll bet it with vigor. But there's no significance to this. A little math reveals that there's a 96% chance of two numbers matching among 15 shown.

You will divine nothing meaningful from examining 15, 50, or 100 spins. Let's look at this from a purely pragmatic standpoint: Would the casinos put up those electronic tote boards if they really thought they gave the players an edge? The house is very happy to have studious roulette players who sit and record numbers, as long as those players are laying down bets and getting chewed up by the 5.26% house advantage. Perhaps the casino would get uptight if you recorded numbers for two full days and nights, started betting a bundle, and then won like crazy. If this happens, please give me a call.

Dealer Tracking

Dealer tracking is essentially the same concept as wheel bias, only here the flaw is in the dealer rather than the wheel. Advocates of dealer tracking argue that they gain an edge by observing dealers who consistently and unconsciously spin the ball at exactly the same speed. By noting exactly where the dealer releases the ball, these players believe that they can predict, within a few numbers, where the ball is going to land. Remember, bets can be laid down while the ball is spinning.

One basic assumption about this approach can't be denied: Dealers are human—they daydream and fall into absent-minded routines just like the rest of us. But, other than that, I see too many obstacles to making this a feasible strategy. First of all, you would have to track not only how fast the dealer spins the ball but also how fast he spins the wheel. Already this task would induce nausea and headaches in me. But even if you have the observation skills of Hercule Poirot and the instincts of Michael Jordan, you still would have to contend with the random scatter of the ball caused by the ornamentation, ridges, and dividers on the wheel. Many trackers claim it's possible to account for the randomness and achieve advantageous predictions. I remain skeptical.

THAT'S THE WAY THE BALL BOUNCES

In summary, roulette isn't a game you should expect to win. But it is a relaxing and mesmerizing game. Although I've attacked systems, I don't want to discourage players from betting on loved ones' birth dates, athletes' jersey numbers, number of teeth remaining, or any other lucky digits. That's part of the pleasure.

It's difficult to control your bankroll when you're playing against a large house edge. One way to slow down your losses is to bet less. (Not too shocking!) Also, realize that, although

the house edge is the same for outside and inside bets, you have less of a chance of consecutive losses if you make the even-money bets. As an extreme example, let's say you have only $25 to wager and you want to play five rounds. In each round, you can make a $5 bet on red or five $1 bets on individual numbers. Either way, the long-term expectation is the same. But the chance of losing all five of your red bets is 4% (about 1 in 25 times); the chance of losing five rounds of straight-up bets is 49% (about 1 in 2). Only you can decide the trade-off between playing longer with smaller payouts or going for the big payoffs. Just know that, in the long run, it equals the same thing anyway.

Now let's see if you've been listening. Quick quiz: A roulette wheel lands on black eight times in a row. What do you do? 1) Bet on black because it's hot. 2) Bet on red because it's due. 3) Bet on whatever you want because it doesn't matter. Did you pick number 3? Good, you passed the chapter. However, if number 17 came up eight times in a row, I'd say bet 17. There is something very wrong with that wheel.

THE ESSENTIALS FOR PLAYING ROULETTE LIKE A GENIUS

- Roulette in the U.S. is not a terrific proposition. The house advantage for a standard 38-number American wheel is 5.26%.
- Never make the five-number bet (0, 00, 1, 2, and 3). Its house edge is 7.89%.
- Look for casinos that offer surrender, which cuts the house edge to 2.63% on even-money bets.
- Search for European-style wheels (37 numbers including single 0). The house edge on all bets is 2.70%. If en prison is offered, the edge falls to only 1.35% on even-money wagers.
- "Professional roulette player" is an oxymoron. No betting system will change the casino's advantage.
- A fair roulette wheel cannot be beaten in the long term and finding an unfair (biased) one is highly unlikely.

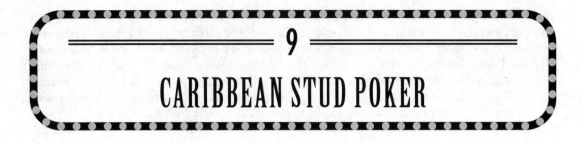

9

CARIBBEAN STUD POKER

Most new table games come and go—and are hardly missed when they're gone. Caribbean Stud Poker is an exception to this rule. It is one of the fastest-growing table games today. It was born, appropriately enough, in the Caribbean islands, spread to cruise ships, and has become a mainstay in casinos throughout the United States.

The game's appeal is that it's easy to understand, has the promise of big payoffs, and is based on our much-adored game of poker. Beyond that, it's a little difficult to comprehend why the game has caught on so fast. Did I mention that it has a house edge over 5%? That would be enough to force most new table games into extinction. Perhaps it's clever marketing. Perhaps it's the noncompetitive, congenial atmosphere among players. Since the object of the game is to beat the dealer's five-card poker hand with your five cards, the only opponents at the table are the dealer and the house.

HOW CARIBBEAN STUD POKER IS PLAYED

THE SCENE
Caribbean Stud is played on a blackjack-type table with up to seven seats for players. The game is run by one dealer and uses a standard 52-card deck. The cards are usually shuffled by an automatic shuffling machine, which spits out five cards at a time. At each player's position on the Caribbean Stud Poker table is an area marked ANTE, an area marked BET, and a drop slot between the ANTE area and the dealer. (See diagram on page 160.) The table minimum for the *Ante* bet is usually $5 or $10.

THE ACTION
Play begins after all players make the mandatory Ante bet in the designated ANTE area in front of them. The dealer takes sets of five cards from the automatic shuffling machine and places one before each player as well as herself. She reveals one card of her set and places it on top of her remaining four cards. The dealer then pushes each set of cards closer to the appropriate player. That is the time to pick up your cards and look them over—don't do it beforehand. (In the unusual instance that the game is dealt by hand, you should still wait for all cards to be dealt before picking up your hand.)

You are now going to evaluate the value of your hand and decide whether to stay in against the dealer's hand. This doesn't require much poker skill, but it does require knowledge of the poker hand rankings. (Consult the chart on page 183.)

After evaluating your hand, you have two choices:

1) If you decide not to continue with your hand, you can fold by placing your cards face-down towards the dealer. The dealer will collect and remove your cards—and your Ante.

2) If you decide to play out the hand, you must place a bet on the BET area of the table. The Bet wager must be exactly twice the Ante wager. If you made a $5 Ante bet, an additional $10 bet completes the hand.

After all the players have made their decisions, the dealer turns over her four remaining cards and makes the best possible poker hand out of her five cards. The dealer *qualifies* by receiving a poker hand that ranks ace-king or higher. This means the dealer's hand must contain an ace and king or it must be strong enough to beat a poker hand that contains an ace and king.

Here are the possible outcomes for the players:
- If the dealer qualifies, she compares her poker hand to each player's poker hand. If the player's hand is higher, the player wins on both his Ante and his Bet. If the player's hand is lower, the player loses both his Ante and his Bet. If the two hands are identical in rank (a very unlikely event), the hand is a tie and no money is exchanged.
- If the dealer's hand does not qualify, all players who stayed in win. But they *only* win on their Ante. This is important to note. The Bet is considered a push and is not paid off.

Winning Ante bets are always paid even money, no matter what hand you have. If the dealer qualifies and a player has a stronger hand, the Bet wager is paid off according to the following schedule (although these odds may vary).

HAND	PAYS
One pair or less	1–1
Two pair	2–1
Three of a kind	3–1
Straight	4–1
Flush	5–1
Full house	7–1
Four of a kind	20–1
Straight flush	50–1
Royal flush	100–1

Be prepared for some frustration. You can have a beautiful hand and if the dealer doesn't qualify, you get paid only even money on your Ante. So don't get too excited about your flush until you see what the dealer turns over. You may end up with nothing for your Bet wager.

The Progressive Jackpot

There is a way to get paid off on big hands, even if the dealer doesn't qualify. It's Caribbean Stud's progressive jackpot feature and it's the dangling carrot that keeps players coming back for more. For an additional $1 on each hand, you become eligible to win a top prize that generally exceeds $100,000. The typical reset level for the progressive jackpot is $50,000.

This $1 side bet is placed in the drop slot in front of a player's betting position. (You were wondering what that was doing there, weren't you?) After all bets are made, the dealer will press a button that causes the $1 chips to drop below the table. A small red light will glow next to your drop slot to indicate that you made the optional bet. If your acceptor light is not lit, let the dealer know right away.

This side bet gives the player a (slim) chance at the amount on the progressive payout meter, regardless of the dealer's hand. Although values for flush, full house, and four of a kind vary from casino to casino, the typical progressive jackpot payoffs are:

Royal flush	100% of jackpot
Straight flush	10% of jackpot
Four of a kind	$100–500
Full house	$75–250
Flush	$50–100

Don't forget that the payoffs occur whether or not the dealer qualifies. Sometimes dealers who don't qualify will absentmindedly fold up players' hands and just start paying off the Antes. If you win a jackpot bet, make sure the dealer knows!

In the *extremely* unlikely event that more than one player at a table gets a royal flush on the same hand, most casinos will have the players split the jackpot. But a few casinos have a stated policy that pays the player nearest to the dealer's left the whole jackpot, and the other player(s) only the reset value of the jackpot. So make sure you grab the seat directly to the dealer's left. Next, I will explain what to do if you are simultaneously struck by lightning and attacked by a shark.

EXAMPLE OF PLAY

Let's look at a Caribbean Stud Poker hand in action. You place a $5 chip in the Ante box. The dealer deals everyone five cards and reveals her top card as a 10. You look at your cards: you have two 2s, two 8s, and a king. Two pair. Good hand. You *call* the dealer by placing $10 in the Bet box and you place your cards face-down to the left of your bet. Here are three possible scenarios:
- The dealer turns over her cards. She has 9, 4, jack, and ace along with her upcard of 10. She fails to qualify because she doesn't have

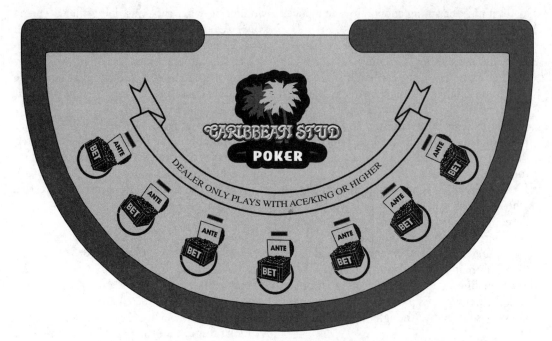

ace/king or better. No payment for your two pair. You get even money for your original $5 Ante. So you end up with your $5 Ante, your $10 Bet, and $5 in profit.

- The dealer reveals ace, queen, jack, and a 10 along with her 10 upcard. Whew! She almost had a straight. The good news is that she qualified with the pair of 10s. Therefore, you get paid even money for your Ante and you win $20 (2–1) for your Bet. You have your $5 Ante, your $10 Bet, and $25 in profit.
- The dealer turns over 10, 5, 5, and 4. She has two pair (10s and 5s) that beat your two pair. You lose your Ante and Bet. Down $15.

CARIBBEAN STUD POKER PROTOCOL AND ETIQUETTE

The following rules of etiquette are in place to prevent players from cheating or getting an "edge" on the house by seeing extra cards.

- Players cannot exchange or communicate information regarding their hands.
- A player may play only one hand per round of play.
- Players must keep their five cards in full view of the dealer at all times.
- Once a player has examined his cards and placed them face-down on the layout, the cards may not be touched again.

CARIBBEAN STUD POKER STRATEGY AND SMARTS

THE BIG EDGE

Why does Caribbean Stud have a sizable house advantage of over 5%? The dealer doesn't have any advantage in terms of cards; it's a 50–50 chance as to who will have the better hand. The disadvantage for the player comes from the betting structure. You must bet three times your Ante (your Ante plus the Bet) in order to stay in a hand. And on the occasions where the dealer doesn't qualify (about 44% of the time), you win only the amount of your Ante. You also must sacrifice your Ante if you decide to fold. The bonus payouts for winning hands don't offset these betting inequalities.

Some players think they can win a few extra bucks by "bluffing" on occasion. First of all, realize that there's no such thing as true bluffing in Caribbean Stud—nothing you do will affect the dealer's play. A bluff in this case means a player makes the Bet wager with a lousy hand and hopes to "steal" a win on the Ante when the dealer doesn't qualify. This is an awful move. The dealer will qualify about 56% of the time. If we assume a bluff hand is always weaker than ace-king (the dealer's qualifier), then the bluffer will lose 56% of the time. Remember, the bluffer loses not only the Ante but also the Bet,

INSIDE THE NUMBERS

You can calculate the expected return (and thus the house edge) of any Caribbean Stud jackpot as long as you have a calculator, the jackpot's current payouts, and the probabilities in the chart below. The example shows a jackpot of $352,146. At this level you're playing "even" with the house—neither a negative nor a positive expectation. Any jackpot higher than this and the edge goes to the player. Anything lower and the edge returns to the house.

Hand	Probability	Payout	Expected Return (Probability × Payout)
Flush	0.001965402	$50	0.0983
Full house	0.001440576	$75	0.1080
Four of a kind	0.000240096	$100	0.0240
Straight flush	0.000013852	$35,214	0.4878
Royal flush	0.000001539	$352,146	0.5420
Total expected return (sum of all expected returns)			**$1.26**

You may be wondering why the total expected return is $1.26. If we're "even" with the house, shouldn't the expected return be $1 for our $1 side bet? Yes, $1 would have you even on the side bet, but I'm taking into account the 26¢ you sacrifice on the $5 Ante bet since it's the most common table minimum. It's based on a house edge of 5.22% on every dollar of your Ante dollar. (5.22% of $5 is 26¢.) Thus, we need to make back $1.26 to get even.

One more thing for you math mavens to keep in mind. The payouts for flush, full house, and four of a kind are the typical minimums. Higher payouts obviously mean a better return and a lowering of the jackpot requirement for a positive expectation.

which is worth double the Ante. Let's look at the expected outcome of this "gutsy" move:

$$E = [0.44 × (+1)] + [0.56 × (−3)] = −1.24$$

The bluffer loses 24¢ more than he would if he just sacrificed his $1 Ante by folding his worthless hand. May as well go play keno!

BASIC STRATEGY

Does a strategy exist that will make the house's edge reasonable? No—unless the progressive jackpot is at very high levels, as explained in the sidebar above. But "basic strategies" have still been developed by gambling experts and mathematicians. In a paper entitled "An Analysis of Caribbean Stud Poker," Peter Griffin and John M. Gwynn Jr. determined that the most manageable strategy is to make the Bet wager with a hand of A–K–J–8–3 or better. By following this strategy, the house edge is 5.32%. Olaf Vancura, in his excellent book *Smart Casino Gambling*, offers five rules that bring the house edge down to 5.22%. They are:

• Always fold if you hold nothing.
• Always make the Bet with a pair or better.
• If you hold ace-king, make the Bet if one of your other three cards matches the dealer's upcard.
• Make the Bet if you hold ace-king-queen or ace-king-jack when the dealer's upcard is any of your five cards.
• Make the Bet if you hold ace-king-queen-x-y (x greater than y) when the dealer's upcard is less than x.

Vancura's strategy isn't very complicated, but for the 0.1% that it saves you, it may just be easier to remember to stay in with A–K–J–8–3 or better. No matter how you play it, the house takes a huge bite out of your money. It should be noted that the house edge discussed here is in terms of your Ante wager. For your average total wager (including the times you make the Bet wager), the house edge is around 2.8%. Since the Ante wager is the amount you will commit on every hand, I believe it is more sensible to consider 5.32% as your disadvantage.

THIS IS PROGRESS?

So what about the progressive jackpot bet? No doubt, much of Caribbean Stud's popularity is due to this optional bet that feeds into the slot-machine mentality of a "life-altering" payoff. Is your $1 going to a worthy cause? Very rarely.

Look at the chart on page 170 to see the probability of getting a particular five-card poker hand. As you can see, the odds of getting the hands that pay out on the side bet are pretty slim. Unless the jackpot gets very high, the house edge is huge on this bet.

Let's assume the minimum payoffs on flush ($50), full house ($75), and four of a kind ($100). Even if the jackpot gets as high as $200,000, the house still has an advantage of 20% on every dollar bet. Need a concept refresher? The 20% advantage means that if you made this bet an infinite number of times while the jackpot was at that level, you would earn back an average of only 80¢ on each dollar. Yes, that takes into account the times you win that big, big jackpot. Of course, someone could sit down and get a royal flush on her first hand ever—bad odds don't rule out an individual getting lucky. But we know for certain that if we looked at all the players making all the $1 side bets at this jackpot level, they would be losing 20¢ on each of their dollars.

The jackpot needs to be $352,146 for the player's overall expectation to be positive in a game with a $5 Ante bet. The negative expectation of the Ante wager is taken into account. (See the sidebar on page 161 if you want to know how the numbers break down.) If you can find an Ante of $1, the jackpot needs to be only $281,000 to make it a positive expectation game.

But just because something has a positive expectation doesn't mean you are wise to chase it. As we saw in the discussion of house edge and expectation in Chapter 2, having a positive expectation doesn't guarantee winnings in all circumstances. When the jackpot's positive expectation depends on a 649,739 to 1 long shot (the chance of being dealt a royal flush), your advantage will most likely turn out to be theoretical—and not deposited in your savings account. Also, keep in mind that you're compelled to make the heavily negative Ante wager if you want to make the $1 side bet, and you can't redistribute your risk like you can with free odds in craps.

The above analysis is purely logical, rational, and accurate. However, if you play Caribbean Stud at all, it's safe to assume you place a higher value on the chance of a big payday than on getting the most bang for your buck. In that case, you have to do what supplies the most excitement and enjoyment. In other words, if you land a royal flush and you didn't deposit your $1 in the slot, don't blame me.

THE ESSENTIALS FOR PLAYING CARIBBEAN STUD POKER LIKE A GENIUS

- This is a slow and social game that promises large payouts, but has a big house advantage. Determine if its pleasures offset its cost for you.
- To reduce the casino's edge to 5.32%, always make the Bet wager with A–K–J–8–3 or better.
- Never, ever "bluff" by playing a hand worse than ace-king high.
- The side bet on the progressive jackpot is the show's main attraction, but it often carries a gigantic house edge. You have to factor in the table minimum and the jackpot payouts before you'll know if the side bet is a positive play. Realize this as your dollars disappear.
- If the jackpot goes over $352,150, you almost certainly have the "edge" statistically. This doesn't mean you'll win it!
- Try other table games with much lower house edges such as blackjack, baccarat, and craps.

10

LET IT RIDE

Let It Ride is another young gun in the world of table games. Much like the slightly older Caribbean Stud Poker, the game owes its success to poker-style play and the promise of big payouts.

Let It Ride didn't evolve naturally as a game of chance—it's a designer diversion (as is Caribbean Stud). Let It Ride was introduced in 1993 as a proprietary game created by Shuffle Master Gaming—the same company that makes all those automatic shuffling devices you see at card game tables. In fact, Shuffle Master specifically created Let It Ride in order to produce a larger market for its card shufflers.

Let It Ride doesn't require a player to beat the dealer or other players. Players simply hope to achieve a winning poker combination (pair of 10s or better) using the three cards they are dealt and two cards shared by the table. (If you are not familiar with the rankings of poker hands, check out page 183 and all will be made clear.) The house advantage in Let It Ride is slightly better for the player than Caribbean Stud's, but it's still a rather hefty 3.5%.

Aside from the potential for big payoffs, much of Let It Ride's appeal is its laid-back atmosphere—since there's no competitive aspect to the game, there's no need to spew venom at the dealer or fellow players. Another attraction is that you can pull back two of your three initial bets (as will be explained below), which gives at least the illusion of control. The game doesn't offer the best (or worst) odds in the house, but it is a simple, pleasant "transition" game for slot and keno players who want to hit the tables.

HOW LET IT RIDE IS PLAYED

THE SCENE
Let It Ride is played at a blackjack-size table that can seat seven players. (See diagram on page 164.) The game is run by one dealer and uses a standard 52-card deck. The cards are, of course, shuffled up by an automatic shuffling machine, courtesy of Shuffle Master. Each player's position on the table has three betting areas (the "$," "2," and "1" circles) and a payout schedule. Table minimums are usually $5 or $10, although you may be able to find $3 tables in the smaller casinos during non-peak hours. Let It Ride Bonus tables feature electronic "sensor" circles that each player can use to make a $1 side bet on the bonus payoffs.

THE ACTION
Casual observers of Let It Ride may initially think the game is complex because of the three betting circles, but nothing could be further from the truth. The play is very simple.

To begin, all players place a bet in each of their three betting circles. All bets *must* be of equal size; that is, if you bet $5 on the "$" circle, you must bet $5 on the "1" and "2" circles as well. Once all the bets are down, the dealer deals each player three cards face-down. The dealer then places two more *community cards* face-down in front of him. These last two cards will be used by all players in conjunction with their own three cards to form a five-card hand. Players hope to a have a final hand that is a winner as determined by the payout schedule.

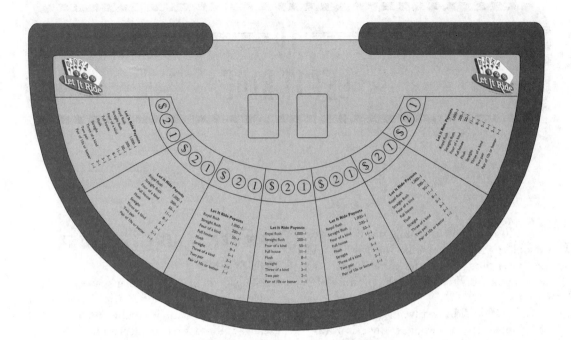

The first action of the play sequence occurs after the three cards are dealt. You evaluate your three cards, and, without knowing the identity of either community card, decide whether or not to keep the bet in circle "1." If you don't like the prospects of your three cards, you can withdraw the "1" bet by scraping your cards toward you on the surface of the table (like asking for a hit in face-down blackjack) or by any hand motion toward yourself. The dealer will remove the bet from the circle and slide the chips toward you—the bet is no longer at risk for this hand. If you like your three cards and want to "let it ride" (now the name makes sense, right?), you put your cards under or behind the first ("1") bet (like standing in face-down blackjack).

After all players have made their decisions on the first bet, the dealer exposes one of the two community cards. Now you must make a decision on bet "2" in the same manner as you did for bet "1." Of course, now your choice to keep or remove the wager is based on four cards—the three in your hand plus the community card. Don't forget the following: *Your decision on the second bet is completely independent of your decision on the first bet.* If you removed the first, you can still keep the second—and vice versa. A lot of beginning players needless-ly get tripped up on this.

After all the players have made their decisions on the second bet, the dealer exposes the second community card. This completes your five-card poker hand—your three cards plus the two face-up community cards. At this point, you have no more decisions to make. You're stuck with that last bet on the "$" circle no matter how miserable your hand may be. (Hey, we wouldn't want the casinos to go broke, would we?)

The dealer turns over each player's three cards in turn, checking for a winning hand—meaning one that qualifies for a payout. You must have a pair of 10s or better to get some money. Since Let It Ride is a proprietary game, the following payout schedule should be found at every casino offering the game.

HAND	PAYOUT
Royal flush	1,000–1
Straight flush	200–1
Four of a kind	50–1
Full house	11–1
Flush	8–1
Straight	5–1
Three of a kind	3–1
Two pair	2–1
Pair of 10s or better	1–1

If a player's hand qualifies for a payout, the dealer will provide the payout for *each* of the bets that were kept in the betting circles. For example, if you have three of a kind (paying 3 to 1) and you kept a $5 bet in the "2" circle in addition to one in the "$" circle (for which you had no choice anyway), you would win $15 on each bet, for a total of $30. The bet in circle "1" that was removed does not get a payoff. Of course, if your hand does not qualify for a payout, all the bets you kept in the circles are lost.

THE BONUS GAME

Let It Ride Bonus has become a very popular version of the original. The bonus version offers up an optional $1 side bet that qualifies players for seemingly huge payoffs on rare hands. (We'll discuss the reality of the numbers in the Strategy and Smarts section. So the suspense doesn't kill you, I'll let you know that this side bet usually has a huge house edge.) The bonus bet has nothing to do with your regular bets during a hand. That means you only place the $1 side bet once for each total hand—it's not offered up in triplicate, nor do you have the option of removing it during play. And it is just a side bet: You must play the regular hand in order to shoot for the bonus.

Bonus payouts vary significantly from casino to casino because Shuffle Master offers many variations. A typical bonus pay table is below. Before you salivate at the numbers, realize the house advantage in this case is 25.6%. The payouts aren't shown on an odds basis because they are all based on a $1 bet—you can't bet more and you can't bet less on the bonus.

HAND	BONUS PAYOUT
Royal flush	$20,000
Straight flush	$2,000
Four of a kind	$400
Full house	$200
Flush	$50
Straight	$25
Three of a kind	$5
Two pair	No bonus
Pair of 10s or better	No bonus

If you look at some "ancient" gambling references from all of two or three years ago, you may be confused by references to a tournament version of Let It Ride. This predecessor to Let It Ride Bonus allowed players to win bonus payouts on a $1 side bet and potentially qualify for a nationwide tournament. Qualifiers had to have one of the top hundred hands among all players in a three-month period—the bare minimum was usually a high straight flush!—and they were given $3,000 in "travel money" to get to the tournament. Plenty of prize money was awarded these lucky souls and the grand prize winner could snare anywhere from $500,000 to $2.5 million depending on what the game pulled in during the three-month period. It was an exciting and attention-getting format, but alas, it was snuffed out. Why? It was costing Shuffle Master too much money to run. Maybe it's a good thing though; only 39¢ of every dollar side bet was being returned through the normal bonus payouts and only 22¢ went to the playoff fund. With the new bonus payouts, sans tournament, the expected return is a bit better.

EXAMPLE OF PLAY

You arrive at the Let It Ride Bonus table, sit down at an open spot, and wait for the current hand to finish. You decide to just go with the table minimum and place a $5 chip in each of the three circles in front of you. You decide against the $1 bonus side bet this round. The dealer sends three cards your way—you pick them up and slowly peek at each one. You squeeze out a J♦ J♣ 4♥. You smile because you have a delightful no-brainer—the pair of jacks is a guaranteed winner and you know you'll keep all your bets up. You place your cards facedown under the "$" chip to indicate you're "letting it ride" the whole way.

The other players make their decisions and the dealer turns up one of the community cards in front of him. It's the 7♠. Doesn't help you, but you're sitting pretty anyway. The other players decide what to do with their second bets. The dealer then turns over the second community card. It's the 7♣. That just improved your payout. You now have two pair—the jacks and the 7s. That's 2 to 1 on all three bets. The round is over and you're up $30.

One more hand? Again you go with the $5 minimum and you also put $1 on the red circle for the bonus payout. Your first three cards are

INSIDE THE NUMBERS

For a simple game, Let It Ride has a fairly complex house-edge computation. Derived from number-crunching using the payout schedule, true odds, and perfect strategy, the actual house edge is 2.86%. How does that relate to the 3.5% edge mentioned in this chapter? It all has to do with the variability of the number of bets in play on each hand.

For simplicity's sake, let's assume a player's base bet is $1—this means he would have to put up three $1 bets at the start of a hand. When using proper strategy, the player's average bet per hand will be $1.2237. "Huh? What the heck does that mean?" you may ask. The following chart shows how we get this number. The frequency of occurrence for different decisions is a probability dictated by proper strategy. The numbers come from Jim Kilby's and Jim Fox's informative book *Casino Operations Management*.

Amount Being Let Ride	Frequency of Occurrence	Expected Amount (Amount × Frequency)
$3 (3 bets)	0.069358	$0.20807
$2 (2 bets)	0.084990	$0.16998
$1 (1 bet)	0.845652	$0.84565
	Total	$1.2237

So, if you apply the "true" house edge (2.86%) to the average bet ($1.2237), you arrive at a casino earning of 3.5¢ per hand ($1.2237 × 0.0286). And that means for every $1 base bet, you're expected to lose 3.5¢. Lo and behold, 3.5¢ is 3.5% of $1. That's why it's more accurate to say that the house edge on your base bet is 3.5%. Don't you feel better knowing that? (This same reasoning applies to Ante and subsequent bets in Caribbean Stud Poker and Three Card Poker.)

9♦ 4♦ Q♦. A potential flush is tempting, but you decide to take your first bet down. (By the time you are sitting there you will, of course, have read the strategy section below.) The first community card is a 3♦. You keep your second bet up. You wait for the second card to be turned up by the dealer. 9♥. Ouch, a useless pair of nines—no payout. If your flush came in, you would have made $40 for each bet (8 to 1) and $50 for the side bet in this casino. Instead of raking in $130, you're down $11 on this hand. So it goes.

LET IT RIDE STRATEGY AND SMARTS

THE HOUSE EDGE

It's tempting to see Let It Ride as a good gamble. It's simple to understand, you can "spare" two of your bets if you have lousy cards, and you have the promise of giant payouts. In reality, the game isn't so beneficent. The house edge compares favorably to Caribbean Stud, craps proposition bets, and American-style roulette, but it comes up well short when compared with blackjack, quality video poker machines, baccarat, and good craps bets.

For those who use the proper playing strategy as shown in the next section, the house edge in Let It Ride is 3.5%. This requires some clarification. The 3.5% edge is on the amount of your single bet, not on the total of your three bets. In other words, if you make three $5 bets on each hand and use the proper strategy, you should expect to lose 17.5¢ per hand ($5 × 0.035) in the long run. You wouldn't be losing 52.5¢, which is $15 × 0.035. It still adds up. If you get in 45 hands per hour, your expected loss would be $7.88 ($5 × 0.035 × 45 = $7.88).

BASIC STRATEGY

What to do, what to do? That's the nagging question in Let It Ride when you have one of those hands that fall between being a "no-brainer" and a "no-hoper." Usually, straight and flush possibilities put you into this hazy territory and it pays to know the right move. The mathematics of analyzing five-card hands isn't obscure, but it can be exhausting. Luckily, all the hard work has been done already. In his book *Mastering the Game of Let It Ride*, Stanley Ko worked out a basic strategy that has held up under analysis. The strategy works as shown in the chart below.

BETTING MENTALITY

Blame it on the big payouts, but Let It Ride feeds right into the slot-machine dream of hitting the big one. Many players feel the Let It Ride basic strategy seems a bit conservative and perhaps—dare they say it—wimpy. They claim the fun of the game is to go after the winnings, not to minimize their loses. (As if the two were mutually exclusive!) So they chase payouts with small pairs or three-card flushes or even a single high card. As smart players could tell them, these "gamblers" will come out losing more than they should in the end. The point of using the strategy chart is to minimize your losses according to the rules of probability, and thereby keep you in the game as long as possible, just in case the big royal flush does miraculously descend on you.

Some players also mistakenly believe that having the option to take back two bets gives them license to "take a chance" when they feel like it. After all, since they *usually* take back their bets when they have a weak hand, they *save* money in all those situations. Why not get risky when the mood strikes? This sort of erroneous thinking does have a certain appeal and is attributable to the clever betting structure of Let It Ride. The more accurate way to think about the bets in the game is that they're not already "spent." Being able to have one or two of the three bets returned is the logical equivalent to having only one bet and being allowed to put out one or two more. So rather than thinking

Three Card Playing Strategy (Bet #1)	
Let the first bet ride if you hold:	**Examples**
A winning hand	4♣ 4♥ 4♦; Q♦ Q♣ 5♥
Three to a straight flush (three suited cards in a row), *except* ace–2–3 or 2–3–4	4♣ 5♣ 6♣
Three to a straight flush with one gap in the sequence *and* at least one high card (10 or higher)	7♠ 9♠ 10♠
Three to a straight flush with two gaps in the sequence *and* at least two high cards	8♣ 10♣ Q♣; 9♥ Q♥ K♥

Four Card Playing Strategy (Bet #2)	
Let the second bet ride if you hold:	**Examples**
A winning hand	6♣ 6♦ 6♥ 6♠; K♦ K♣ K♥ 8♣; 7♣ 7♥ 9♦ 9♣; A♠ A♥ 4♣ 5♥
Four to a straight flush	5♦ 6♦ 7♦ 8♦
Four to a flush	2♣ 4♣ 7♣ 9♣
Four to an outside straight (one that can be completed by a card on either side) *and* at least one high card (10 or higher)	7♦ 8♣ 9♦ 10♣

You have the option of keeping the following hands because they leave you even with the house (no advantage either way):

Four to an outside straight *without* a high card	2♦ 3♥ 4♥ 5♠
Four to an inside straight (a card of only one rank can complete it) *and* four high cards. Described another way: all four cards 10 or higher.	10♣ J♥ Q♠ A♦

INSIDE THE NUMBERS

You can calculate the expected return (and thus the house edge) of any Bonus Pay Table as long as you have a calculator, the pay table, and the probabilities that we plucked from the five-card poker chart on page 170. This is just one example of a typical pay table. The house edge ends up a whopping 25.54%. Unfortunately, you'd be hard pressed to find one much better than this.

Hand	Probability	Payout	Expected Return (Probability × Payout)
Royal flush	0.00000154	$20,000	0.0308
Straight flush	0.00001385	$2,000	0.0277
Four of a kind	0.00024010	$400	0.0960
Full house	0.00144058	$200	0.2881
Flush	0.00196540	$50	0.0983
Straight	0.00392465	$25	0.0981
Three of a kind	0.02112845	$5	0.1056
Two pair	0.04753902	No bonus	0
Pair of 10s or better	0.16252655	No bonus	0

Total expected return on your $1 bet (sum of all expected returns): $0.7446

How big a dent is the side bet putting in your bankroll? Let's look at the numbers. As we discovered earlier, if you're a regular $5 bettor (three bets of $5) using basic strategy and playing 45 hands an hour, you should expect to lose $7.88 an hour. Let's add the side bet at a not-atypical edge of 25.54%. Now you're betting an additional $45 per hour on the bonus game ($1 × 45 hands). The expected loss is: $45 × 0.2554 = $11.49. Thus, your $1 side bet is costing you $3.61 more per hour than your regular $5 wager. Your total expected losses are brought up to $19.37 ($7.88 + $11.49). Doesn't sound like the road to riches. But then you have the classic conundrum: If you're playing a game like Let It Ride, are you worried about your bottom line or are you dreaming of royal flushes? You have to pick your thrill. But there are better places to go dreaming in the casino. For royal flushes, check out the video poker section.

they are already spent, the more sensible way to look at the "1" and "2" bets is that you're given the opportunity to triple or double your initial bet (your base bet) *when the situation favors you.* (It's somewhat analogous to doubling down in blackjack.) Otherwise, you just want to hang tight with your "$" bet and hope for the best.

WHAT ARE MY CHANCES?

Unfortunately, the best isn't usually that great. It pays to look at the numbers and put our fantasies in perspective. Although five-card stud isn't a poker game that's much in favor these days, looking at the realities of five-card poker hands will help your card sense and your

appreciation of Let It Ride and Caribbean Stud Poker. The chart on page 170 gives some very useful info about Let It Ride and poker hands in general.

As the chart reveals, 76% of the hands dealt to you in Let It Ride are going to be losers. That's three out of every four hands! It is not uncommon to go 15 or 20 hands in a row without getting a paying hand. A glance at the cumulative probability column highlights the harsh reality that your hand will be a straight or better less than 1% of the time. If you're in it for the big money, the wait can be exasperating and tedious.

Realize that basic strategy won't change the

outcome of your hands—your five cards are your five cards. Over the long term, your hands will adhere to the expectations of the chart on page 168. What basic strategy does is tell you when to risk more money because the odds favor you and when to risk only the minimum because they don't. Yes, it's true that you don't keep your bets riding often. Let's take a look:

BETS PLAYER LETS RIDE	PERCENTAGE OF THE TIME
3 bets	6.9%
2 bets	8.5%
1 bet	84.6%

Nearly 85% of the time you're pulling your money back. Boring? Maybe. But this is a lesson most Let It Ride players learn quickly and intuitively. Devoted players emphasize that this is a game of patience, patience, and more patience. The basic mentality—and not a misguided one—is to hope for a quick hit when you sit down, relax and enjoy your fellow players, and then hope that a *really big hit* comes along. Of course, the problem is that you can sit and lose 20 hands in a row. The flaw with playing the waiting game in Let It Ride is that the longer you play, even if smartly, the longer the 3.5% house edge will have a chance to work on you.

Nonetheless, you can see why people get hooked on the game. It's a very warm and cozy feeling when you get an automatic winner on your first three cards and only have to contemplate what improvements the community cards may bring. Also, it seems that most fans of the game have made big hands. If your early experiences with Let It Ride lead to long dry spells, you'll probably end up hating it. If you try it and land some good winning hands, you'll end up loving it—or at least being inexorably drawn back to it.

Bonus Betting

Does the $1 side bet in the bonus game make the picture more rosy? No, for the most part, it makes it much worse. As mentioned before, bonus pay tables vary from casino to casino. They can range from having a keno-esque house advantage of 35.14% to a rather reasonable 3.05%. (For the inside scoop on calculating a bonus game house edge, see Inside the Numbers on page 168.) Why do I call 3.05% reasonable when there are so many better bets in the casino? (I generally disdain any house edge over 1.5%.)

Just over 3% seems reasonable if you're a slot machine devotee who chases big payoffs, though you have no idea what percentage you're facing on any given machine. Here's a chance to sit at a table, know what you're up against, get comfortable with table games, exercise a little playing strategy, and still have a shot at the big money. Don't get me wrong—I'd rather see someone who wants to pursue a mega-payout play Caribbean Stud progressives when they reach the right levels or, better still, video poker. But the Let It Ride Bonus option isn't awful—except it's nearly impossible to find a payout table with an edge of only 3.05%.

ALSO TO KEEP IN MIND

Many casinos put a limit on the payout for any given hand. Some may set it at $25,000, others at $75,000. Although the chances are very slim, you don't want to be shortchanged if you do hit a big hand. Since the casino is holding back on the dollars already, you want every single one you earn by getting lucky. Let's look at this unlikely, yet conceivable, scenario.

You have three $10 bets riding and a $1 side bet when—what do you know—you hit that royal flush. Your three bets pay 1,000 to 1, adding up to $30,000. The side bet kicks in $20,000. That's $50,000 you have coming to you. But at Casino X, with a 25 grand limit, you get only half your earnings. Casino Y, with a $75,000 limit, will pay you out in full. It's worth inquiring because, should the impossible happen, you don't want to suffer a coronary from combined excitement and disappointment. Also, as a smart gambler, it's your obligation to get every dollar that's coming to you in a payout.

So how should you bet? First of all, don't let the following calculations lead you to bet *more* than you're comfortable with. Second, find out the maximum payout and don't bet more than that number divided by 3,000 as your single bet. If the limit is $25,000, don't bet more than $8 as your base unit. If you're making the side bet, subtract the royal flush award (often

What to Expect from Five-Card Hands

Hand	Number of Ways to Get Hand	Odds of Receiving Hand	Probability	Cumulative Probability
Royal flush	4	649,739 to 1	0.00000154	0.00000154
Straight flush	36	72,192 to 1	0.00001385	0.00001539
Four of a kind	624	4,164 to 1	0.00024010	0.00025549
Full house	3,744	693 to 1	0.00144058	0.00169606
Flush	5,108	508 to 1	0.00196540	0.00366146
Straight	10,200	254 to 1	0.00392465	0.00758611
Three of a kind	54,912	46 to 1	0.02112845	0.02871456
Two pair	123,552	20 to 1	0.04753902	0.07625358
Pair of 10s or better	422,400	5.15 to 1	0.16252655	0.23878013
Nonwinner	1,978,380	1 to 3.19	0.76121987	1
Total	2,598,960		1	1

$20,000) from the table max and then divide by 3,000. Let's look again at the $25,000 limit with a side bet.

$$\$25,000 - \$20,000 = \$5,000$$
$$\$5,000 \div 3,000 = \$1.67$$

Oops—you won't find a casino that lets you bet that low. In that case, find a casino that has a higher payout limit!

Here's another thing to keep in mind if you play Let It Ride: the availability of information about other players' cards. The official rules stipulate that players aren't supposed to disclose their three-card hands to each other. However, some casinos are very lax about this rule and some seem to encourage mild kibitzing among players as part of the congenial atmosphere. While I don't advocate cheating, I also think it's foolish not to take advantage of any edge given by the casino.

I certainly don't recommend that you actively try to gain an illicit edge here. But if there is a laissez-faire attitude, take serious note of whatever card information is available. Will this really help? To take full advantage of additional information, you would have to get very comfortable with the relationship between the payoff odds and the true odds. If you are already comfortable with these concepts, you probably don't need me to tell you to be aware of freely given card info.

Let's take a relatively simple example of how information is power. First, look at the basic strategy chart. You see it says it's an even-money move to keep your second bet up when you have a four-card outside straight with no high cards (for example: 4, 5, 6, 7). Why is it even money? The chance of you filling the straight is 40 to 8; there are 8 cards that will make the straight—the four 3s and the four 8s—and there are 40 cards that won't help you at all. These odds, 40 to 8, can also be stated as 5 to 1. That's the exact payoff on a straight—5 to 1. Therefore, there is no advantage or disadvantage in keeping your second bet up.

But, if you happened to know that another player had a 3 or an 8, you would be at a disadvantage pursuing the straight. You would know that one of the cards you could use is not available to you. Take your bet down. This is an illustrative example, but don't stray from basic strategy until you know the true effects of card information.

THE ESSENTIALS FOR PLAYING LET IT RIDE LIKE A GENIUS

• Remember you are not competing against the dealer or other players. You're simply hoping to get a winning five-card hand.
• The house edge is 3.5% for those who adhere to the basic strategy.
• The side bet for the bonus game generally carries a massive house edge, but it varies. Compare payout tables if you're going to make the side bet.
• Players must be willing to cope with major swings in their bankroll. Three-quarters of hands played are not winners.
• Use Let It Ride as an alternative to slot machines, but also as a steppingstone to games with lower edges such as video poker, blackjack, and baccarat.

PAI GOW POKER

Pai gow (pronounced pie gow) poker is a leisurely paced card game that rewards player skill and patience. Occasionally referred to as Asian poker or double-handed poker, it was first introduced in California card rooms in 1986. This game combines principles from the ancient Chinese game of dominoes known as pai gow (see sidebar on page 176 for a brief explanation of this mystifying game) and the all-American game of poker.

Pai gow poker is certainly a "sleeper" among casino table games. This is not to say that it has a soporific effect on players (although some speed junkies may argue this case), but rather that it has enjoyed growing popularity despite being neither a perennial favorite (blackjack, craps) nor a flashy newcomer with eye-catching payouts (Caribbean Stud, Let It Ride).

The object of pai gow poker is to make two poker hands that beat the banker's hands. The player is dealt seven cards that he makes into a five-card hand (*high hand*) and a two-card hand (*low hand*). Some observers find pai gow poker extremely complex at first blush. In fact, the game is rather simple and straightforward for those gamblers who feel comfortable making decisions and exercising a little skill. Perhaps most important, it offers players a reasonable chance to win, at least in comparison to other new table games. The house advantage is about 2.5%.

Since the game evolved out of the Asian domino game, its strongest popularity is among Asian players, but its appeal is growing among a broad-based clientele. Three elements have led to its small but significant celebrity:

You can handle the cards, you can make strategic choices, and a player with a big enough bankroll can act as the bank and play against both the house and other players. You'll often find high rollers at the pai gow table who casually bet hundreds or thousands of dollars. The fact that it's rather slow-moving allows newcomers to get comfortable and veterans to control their bankroll. Pai gow players are generally a congenial lot—perhaps as an outgrowth of the game's relaxed pace.

HOW PAI GOW POKER IS PLAYED

THE SCENE
Pai gow poker is played at a blackjack-sized table with betting spots for six players (see diagram on page 174). Each betting area consists of a circle to hold the wager, a horizontal rectangle for the player's two-card hand, and a vertical rectangle for the player's five-card hand. The game is run by one dealer and uses a standard 52-card deck, plus one joker. The joker is a limited wild card and its function will be fully explained shortly.

An automatic shuffling machine is most often used to mix and deal the cards into packets of seven. Two decks of cards alternate between being in play and being shuffled by the machine. The table minimum is often $25 because many free-spending players are drawn to this game, but you should be able to locate $10 games in some casinos.

THE ACTION
Before any cards are dealt, players make their wagers in the betting circles. For purposes of

our introduction to the game, we'll assume that the dealer is the banker. The majority of the time, this will be the situation at the table. Since the object of the game is to beat the banker, this means all players will be playing against the dealer.

What's the Deal with the Deal?

Dealing involves a bit of arcane ritual carried over from the original Asian game; it serves to satisfy the superstitious players who want a "random distribution" of cards (and it also serves to thoroughly mystify newcomers). The contrivances of dealing have nothing to do with the play of the game, but you'll feel more comfortable if you understand the ritual.

If you're playing at a low-tech table, dice will be used to determine the order in which hands will be dealt. The dealer shakes a dice bowl containing three dice and the total determines who receives the first hand of seven cards. It is necessary to know who the banker is in order to understand how the cards are dealt out. (Remember, sometimes the banker may be a player instead of the dealer.) The banker's position has a value of 1, 8, or 15 in relation to the dice roll. The dealer then counts counterclockwise from the banker's number until he reaches the total on the dice. That player position is where the deal will start. Empty betting positions and the dealer's spot are included in the counting.

Look at the diagram on page 174. If the dealer is the banker and the dice total 6, the dealer will count five spots counterclockwise from himself and give position 5 the first hand. The deal then continues clockwise (perplexing, isn't it?) so position 4 gets the second hand, position 3 gets the third, and so on. If the dice total 10, the first cards will be dealt to player 2. Why? Because 8 (the dealer/banker's number) plus 2 is equal to 10. As a final example, if the dice total 15 the deal will start with the dealer.

Many casinos forgo the exotic and time-consuming dice ritual and instead have a random number generator and an LED readout. The readout provides a number from 1 to 7 which shows where the deal starts—the banker is assigned the number 1 and the other numbers are relative to him counterclockwise.

On each and every deal, 49 of the 53 cards will be dealt out. (The remaining four cards go to the discard rack.) As each player's hand is dealt, the dealer removes it from the automatic shuffler machine and places it face-down on the appropriate area. Hands are dealt to all seven betting areas (which includes the dealer), whether they are occupied by a player or not. A small plastic marker called a *chung* is placed on top of the banker's hand to indicate its status. You should not touch your own hand until all hands have been dealt out. It's always "safe" to look at your hand when the little green light on the automatic shuffling machine goes on—this means all seven hands have been dealt out. After the hands are dealt, the dealer will collect the hands dealt to empty betting areas and discard them.

Playing Your Hand

Of course, the mystery of the deal is not the substance of pai gow poker; the play of the hand is. Each player must arrange her seven cards into two separate hands: a five-card hand and a two-card hand. The five-card hand must have an equal or higher poker value than the two-card hand. The five-card hand is also known as the *back hand* because you place it on the back rectangle which is usually marked "High" or "Highest"; the two-card hand is, not surprisingly, also called the *front hand* because it goes on the front rectangle generally marked "2nd Highest."

Five-card hands are ranked and evaluated just like traditional five-card poker hands (see page 183 for poker hand rankings). The two-card hand also has a traditional poker rank, but realize it can only be one of two rankings: a pair or high card. There are no flushes and straights with two cards! The highest possible two-card hand is a pair of aces.

Standard poker knowledge will allow you to determine the rank of your hand, but you must be aware of a few of pai gow's quirks. There is one joker in the deck. Be careful: It is not a completely wild wild-card. The joker can only be used as an ace or to complete a flush or straight or straight flush. The joker will assume the highest rank possible in filling these hands. This means if it is used to complete a flush or straight, the joker replaces the highest card absent from the flush or straight.

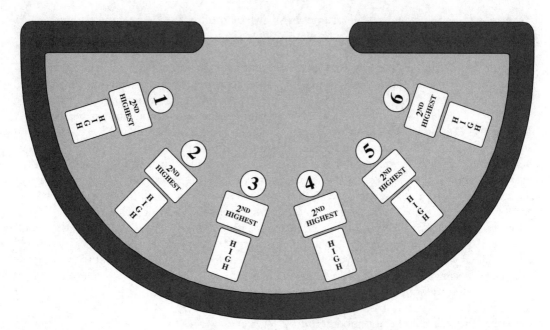

For example, in a five-card hand of joker, 9♦, 7♦, 10♦, 2♦, the joker will be the A♦. In a hand of joker, A♦, Q♦, 3♦, 2♦, the joker will be the K♦. In a straight such as joker, 8♣, 9♦, 10♥, J♥, the joker would automatically fill out the straight as a queen, rather than a 7. The joker *never* forms pairs, three of a kind, four of a kind, or five of a kind with any cards other than aces.

The only other departure from poker norms is that the second-highest straight is A, 2, 3, 4, 5. (The highest, of course, is A, K, Q, J, 10.) This curious exception to traditional poker rankings is in effect at most casinos, but not all—make sure to ask when you sit down or when the situation arises. It could make a difference.

PAI GOW POKER
HAND RANKINGS
Five aces (including the joker)
Royal flush
Straight flush (A, 2, 3, 4, 5 is the highest)
Four of a kind
Full house
Flush
Straight (A, 2, 3, 4, 5 is the second highest)
Three of a kind
Two pair
One pair
High card

Again, your five-card hand *must* be of equal or greater value than your two-card hand. It's fine to have a five-card hand that is equal in rank to the two-card hand (for example, they both can contain a pair of 8s).

Resolution of the Hand
After all the non-banker players have set their hands, the banker turns his cards over and sets his own hands. Whether acting as a player or banker, the dealer always sets his hands by using a set of rules known as the *House Ways* or the House Rules. These guidelines dictate how the dealer creates his two hands and leave him no options. At many casinos, you can request a copy of the House Ways.

The players' hands are turned over one at a time by the dealer and compared to the banker's hands. As you would expect, the five-card hand is compared to the five-card hand, and the two-card is compared to the two-card. If the player and banker have exactly the same hand (let's say K, J in the two-card hand), it's called a *copy*. Important: All copies are considered won by the banker.

The player vs. banker showdown can have three results:
• Both of the player's hands beat both of the banker's hands. This means that the player's front hand beats the banker's front hand and the player's back hand beats the banker's back

hand. This win pays even money, but a 5% commission is collected. A $10 bet earns you $9.50 ($10 minus a 50¢ commission).

- Both of the banker's hands beat both of the player's hands. Player loses her bet. Remember, a tie between hands is as good as a win for the banker.
- The player wins one hand and the banker wins the other. This is a push and no money changes hands. It doesn't matter whether the five-card hand or the two-card hand is the winner (or loser) for the player. Both have equal significance in determining the outcome of the wager.

Unlike baccarat where you can have a running tally of your commissions, the commission on winning wagers in pai gow must be paid immediately. You can either put it out next to your bet or the dealer will subtract it from your payoff. No commission is charged on losing or pushed hands.

PAI GOW POKER PROTOCOL AND ETIQUETTE

As with most casino games, the pai gow poker rules of etiquette are in place to keep players from cheating or getting an "edge" on the house.

- Once your two hands are placed face-down in their appropriate areas on the layout, you are not allowed to touch them anymore.
- Make sure your second-highest hand doesn't beat your highest hand. If you accidentally set a stronger front hand, your hand is considered *fouled* and you automatically lose your bet. However, if the banker makes this mistake, the dealer will reset the hands according to the casino's House Ways.
- Don't be afraid to ask for help. If you're unsure of what to do, the dealer will advise you on how to set your hand. He will tell you how the house would do it using the House Ways.
- The pai gow atmosphere is usually relaxed with advice flowing freely (if you ask for it). However, casinos will vary in their tolerance of shared card information. Some casinos (or dealers) don't mind players kibitzing with each other and consulting on how to set their hands. Other casinos (or dealers) prohibit a player whose cards aren't already set on the layout from looking at another player's cards.
- If you play more than one player spot at a table, the first hand you play must belong to the spot with the largest of your bets (if the amounts vary). This rule is supposed to minimize the benefit of seeing a larger percentage of the deck; although, this would rarely change your strategy anyway.
- Your seven cards should be in full view of the dealer at all times. If you hold them away from the table, you'll probably get a mild reminder not to do so. I've seen a player accidentally drop a card and the casino made him forfeit his hand because it was considered fouled.

PAI GOW POKER STRATEGY AND SMARTS

THE HOUSE EDGE

Unlike its older brethren blackjack and baccarat, pai gow poker has yet to earn intense scrutiny and analysis by a wide variety of gambling experts and mathematicians. The most thorough treatment of the game and the current bible on the subject is *Optimal Strategy for Pai Gow Poker* by Stanford Wong.

Wong estimates that the average non-banking player will buck a house edge of 2.84% (you'll discover why I use the qualifier "non-banking" shortly). The game would be a 50–50 proposition—and therefore without an edge—if not for two factors: the commission on winning bets which, according to Wong, turns out to be about 1.57% over the course of all hands, including losses and pushes; the other factor is that the banker wins all copied hands, which Wong estimates to be a 1.27% advantage.

A skilled player using the proper hand-setting strategies can shave the house edge by a measly 0.3%, down to 2.54%. That means a savings of $3 for every $1,000 played. However, it is still worthwhile to become acquainted with the hand-setting strategies offered on page 178. First of all, they will give you a sense of the game's logic, so you have something else to go on instead of your "gut instinct." Second, they'll prevent you from making costly errors.

The house edge for the non-banking player

WHAT'S WITH THE DOMINOES?

In casinos that cater to Asian gamblers, you may stumble across the real McCoy that inspired pai gow poker—the ancient Chinese dominoes game of pai gow. And you will have absolutely no clue what is going on. Actually, the broad strokes of the game will be familiar to a pai gow poker player: Dice to determine who starts the deal, two hands high and low (made from dominoes, of course), players as bankers, the 5% commission, etc.

The bewilderment is in the details. The 32 dominoes (also called tiles) have both numerical and symbolic values. Simple observation will not help you decipher how players take their four dealt dominoes and turn them into two hands of two dominoes. For instance, the best hand is a pair that Westerners wouldn't readily identify as a pair: the 1–2 tile combined with the 2–4 tile. This isn't a criticism of the game; it just makes it difficult to learn initially. If a person never saw a deck of cards, I'm sure the ace being both high and low would seem contrived and bizarre.

Pai gow has a house edge similar to that of pai gow poker and it does reward skilled play. For those who want to enter into this cryptic but intriguing world, most casinos have ranking charts that explain the permissible pairs and the rankings of the dominoes. If you take it as a challenge to learn the puzzle of the dominoes and become conversant in terms such as "gee joon," "wong," and "bo," then I applaud you. Although I'm not xenophobic by nature, I find the strangeness of the hand-setting and the lack of a significant advantage to be sufficient discouragement from exploring it further (plus it's not available in many casinos). Personally, I prefer to stand on the sidelines and admire the dealers' dexterous "shuffling" of the dominoes. Apparently, many cowardly non-Asians feel like I do, since the game is almost strictly played by Asians.

in pai gow is not minimal, especially for a game that requires a bit of skill and thought. Still, it compares favorably to roulette, Caribbean Stud Poker, and Let It Ride. But, without a doubt, the best way to cut into the casino's advantage is to enter into the world of banking. As the next section shows, playing as the banker is the smart way to play.

BANK ON IT

First off, let there be no confusion. In pai gow poker, the role of banker is not just a ceremonial title as in baccarat. If a player wishes to bank, she must be able to cover all the player bets made during that round of play. In theory, the banking option should be offered—at least in a token manner—to each player at the table before a round. In reality, a player usually has to ask for the bank because it's not offered.

Why do you want to bank? One reason is immediately obvious—you get to win all copied hands. That's a 1.27% advantage you take back

for yourself. You still have to pay a 5% commission on your wins, but even accounting for that, if you can use skilled play against unskilled players, you'll be just about even with the house. That's right—no house edge. The casino, in its infinite wisdom, will not allow you to consistently take advantage of this situation. Most casinos will allow you to bank for only one or two hands before relinquishing the bank to the dealer or some other player.

Let's see what you bring the house edge down to if you're capable of banking every other hand. Half of the time the house edge is 2.54% (when you're the player) and the other half the house edge is zero. Therefore, the total house edge is around 1.27% (2.54 ÷ 2 = 1.27). That's not too shabby—actually better than a straight pass line bet in craps.

In his book, Stanford Wong analyzes banking situations where the player can actually break even overall or perhaps get a small edge on the house. He recommends banking at a table with multiple players whose total bets equal six to fourteen times the minimum bet you make as a player. (You only want to make the minimum bet when you're a player.) For example, if the minimum bet is $25, you want the other players to bet a total from $150 to $350 when you are banking. This may not be such an easy situation to find, or to bankroll.

Since you want to bank as often as possible, try to find games that will allow you to do so. One out of two times is typical; two out of three is harder to find. It also depends on whether other players are taking advantage of the banker benefit—the more who are, the longer the wait until it's your turn again.

But before you leap into the land of the chung, decide whether you can afford the bad streaks that will befall you as banker. If many players are betting or just a few have really big bets out, your bankroll can suffer greatly. Remember, you must have enough chips and/or cash on the table to cover all wagers placed in the round. But the one hand isn't really the worry (especially since you won't be allowed to bank if you can't cover the bets); the problem is exposing yourself to multiple losses in pursuit of a small advantage. This can be dangerous territory and shouldn't be entered into recklessly. If you have plenty of money and a good understanding of the game, this is the smart move. Otherwise, be cautious.

A good compromise for the casual but intelligent gambler is to find an empty table and play head-to-head against the dealer. Although this isn't socially enticing, you'll be able to alternate banking with the dealer. You'll be working at a 1.27% disadvantage, but you'll be able to control your spending. When you're banking, the dealer will wager an amount equal to the last amount you bet against the house on the previous hand. You could have the dealer bet less, but you wouldn't want him to since you want as much money put up as possible when you're banking. If you're comfortable in this scenario, next try banking at a table where one or two players are making bets you can handle.

Some other banking notes:
• In order to bank, a player must have wagered in the previous round against another banker (whether it was the dealer or another player).
• The dealer combines the banker's wins and

losses before calculating the amount of the commission.
• A player who banks can't foul his hand. If he doesn't set his cards right, they will be reset according to House Ways.
• Some casinos allow players to co-bank. In this case, the player and the dealer share the responsibility for the wagers. The player must cover half of all the wagers. The dealer's hand is discarded and the player's hand is the official bank hand and it is set according to House Ways.

SETTING YOUR HANDS

How should you manipulate those seven cards into two hands? That's where the pleasure and the occasional befuddlement of pai gow poker lie. If you're comfortable with poker rankings, your instinctive decisions probably won't lead you too far astray. As mentioned before, pai gow expert Stanford Wong believes skilled play earns you only about 0.3% over the "average" player. But why be average? And you certainly don't want an inflated sense of your "card smarts" to translate into below-average play, do you? So read the basic strategy recommendations here and if you discover you enjoy pai gow, move on to Wong's book.

The simple strategy for setting your hands boils down to this: Make the highest two-card hand possible that still is less than your five-card hand. This sounds like common sense. You want to win money, which means you want to give yourself the best shot of winning both hands. One great hand won't do it—that will just leave you with a push.

For example, you don't want a powerhouse hand like a full house for your high hand when it leaves you with something anemic like 8, 7 for your second highest. Sure, a full house will nearly always beat any other five-card hand, but the 8, 7 will only beat another two-card hand about 2% of the time (one in 50 times). Much better to split that full house into a three of a kind and a pair. The worst three of a kind (2, 2, 2) wins over 80% of five-card hands and the worst pair (2, 2) wins over 70% of two-card hands. Now you have a good chance of making some moolah.

A more subtle example of overkill occurs with hands that contain three pair. Rookie players will

Pai Gow Poker Hand-Setting Rules

If you hold:	Set your five-card hand as:	And your two-card hand as:
No pair	Highest card.	Second- and third-highest cards.
One pair	Pair.	Next two highest cards.
Two pair (with pair of aces)	Pair of aces.	Other pair.
Two pair	Generally split. But if your high pair is jacks or 10s *and* you have a side ace, keep the two pair together and put the ace in the two-card hand. If your high pair is nines or lower *and* you have a side ace or king, keep the two pair together and put the ace or king in the two-card hand.	
Three pair	Second- and third-highest pairs.	Highest pair.
Three of a kind	With three aces, split them by playing one ace in the two-card hand and the pair of aces in the five-card hand. In all other cases, keep the three of a kind together in the high hand.	
Five-, six-, or seven-card straight	Keep the lowest complete straight.	Two highest cards that preserve five-card hand's straight.
Straight and two pair	Ignore the straight and play as two pair.	
Five-, six-, or seven-card flush	Lowest complete flush.	Two highest cards that preserve five-card hand's flush.
Flush and two pair	Ignore the flush and play as two pair.	
Flush with full house (including joker)	Ignore flush and play as full house.	
Full house	Three of a kind.	Pair.
Three of a kind and two pair	Three of a kind and the lower pair as a full house.	Higher pair.
Four of a kind (2s through 6s)	Four of a kind.	Next two highest cards.
Four of a kind (7s through jacks)	Split them unless you have a king or ace that you can play in the two-card hand.	
Four of a kind (queens, kings, aces)	Always split them.	
Straight flush	Use the strategy for straights.	
Five aces (with joker)	Put a pair of aces in the two-card hand.	
Five aces with a pair of kings	Put the kings in the two-card hand. Then pinch yourself and wake up.	

often leave the highest pair in the back hand and put one of the two weaker pairs up front. Foolish. Perhaps the reasoning is that one pair is basically as good as another or that the back hand is "stronger" by having the high pair. Alas, this is quite wrong. Almost any two pair will hold up equally well in the five-card hand, but a high pair is significantly better than a low pair in the two-card hand. Just remind yourself that you want to be as competitive as possible in both hands.

Even given this advice, there will be times when all you can do is make one of your hands as strong as possible and hope for a push. This is accounted for in the strategy chart above. You'll notice in the chart that the presence of an ace or king is often integral to how aggressively you will set your hand. When you can put a high card up in the two-card hand, you have more flexibility with your five-card hand. And, of course, there are times when you have completely lousy cards and you just have to pray for the banker to have something even more awful.

Always take a moment to pause and think about your hand. For example, you have a hand like this: A♣, K♠, Q♥, J♥, 10♦, 9♣, 3♣. Your instinct may be to place that ace-high straight as your five-card hand and leave 9-3 as your two-card hand. Bad, bad move. You have a king-high straight (going down to the 9) and a chance to put an ace up top in the two-card hand. Or let's say you have this hand: K♠, J♠, 9♠, 8♠, 5♠, 4♦, 2♠. Don't absentmindedly resign yourself to a push by keeping the king-high flush and putting up the lousy 4–2 combo. That last 2 is a spade! Give yourself a jack-high flush and put up the king in the front hand. In other words, look before you leap. You can always ask the dealer for help.

MORE PAI GOW POKER KNOW-HOW

Pai gow can be a terrific game if it suits your temperament. It moves slowly and many hands—around 30 to 40 percent—will result in a push. While this might seem coma-inducing to high-adrenaline craps and slots players, it is a nice atmosphere for those who enjoy cards and other people's company. Moreover, the pace of the game keeps it from being very volatile—you can stick around for a long time with a modest bankroll. It's unlikely that a prudent gambler will feel "out of control" while playing pai gow. It just doesn't move fast enough to generate that sort of dizziness. But, as we discussed, if you choose to bank and a lot of money is being wagered on the table, you're exposing yourself to greater short-term risk.

As with every casino game, you'll see a lot of superstition crop up at the pai gow poker table. Players may change seats to get better hands and they are often preoccupied with the ritual of the deal.

You will see enough bizarre hands in pai gow to make you believe higher powers are at work. Let's look at two extremes. You have A♠, A♦, A♣, A♥, joker, 9♠, 7♥. Wow! Up go your pair of aces, back go your three bullets. Dealer/banker shows this: 3♣, 7♣, 5♥, 9♣, 2♦, 4♣, 10♣. That's junk, isn't it? Nope. The dealer has a club flush for the back hand and a sorrowful 5, 2 to put up front. You push and curse the fates. Then this happens to you: 10♠, 8♥, 7♥, 6♣, 4♣, 3♦, 2♠. You put your 8, 7 in the front hand and get ready to hand over your bet. The dealer has the same hand as before: 3♣, 7♣, 5♥, 9♣, 2♦, 4♣, 10♣. Your 8, 7 beats his even more pitiful 5, 2. You push and thank the fates. That's pai gow. (Remember, the dealer has no choice in setting his hand. Even if he were playing one-on-one against you, he couldn't break his flush and put the 9 and 5 in the low hand and leave his high hand with 10, 7, 4, 3, 2—a combo that would beat you both ways.)

Speaking of player laments, I'll give you the scoop on the term "pai gow" itself. You'll often hear players refer to junk hands with no pair as a "pai gow." Anxious players will wish a "pai gow" on the dealer. Some erudite gamblers will even inform you that the term pai gow means "no pair." Well, as you may have suspected, the casino isn't the place to learn Chinese linguistics. The proper translation for pai gow is "to make nine"—this makes sense as applied to the original Chinese dominoes game of pai gow because players hope for a valuable score of nine. So not only is the translation wrong, but the flavor of the phrase is lost as well—it's supposed to be a good thing, not a bad one. The real phrase to use should you wish evil on others' hands is "lop-lop," which means "nothing-nothing." Don't feel compelled to educate your fellow players about their inaccurate lingo. They may not appreciate the foreign language lesson—especially if they're losing.

THE ESSENTIALS FOR PLAYING PAI GOW POKER LIKE A GENIUS

- Pai gow poker is a slow, sociable game that is easy to play once you understand its fundamentals.
- The five-card hand must always be equal or greater in value than the two-card hand. Take your time when setting the hands. A fouled hand will cost you your bet (and a little pride!).
- If you forget the strategy tips, ask the dealer for help.
- The house edge is about 2.84% for unskilled players and 2.54% for skilled players who follow the tips on hand setting.
- To give yourself the best chance to make money over the long term, you must bank. If you play as the banker under the right conditions, you can be even with the house or perhaps have a slight edge.
- Banking will require that you have a larger bankroll. Be aware of what you're risking and that banking for large amounts can turn this non-volatile game into a volatile one.
- If you are alone at a table with the dealer, always alternate as the bank. This doesn't put any extra stress on your bankroll and gives you the advantage of ties half the time, reducing the overall house edge to a respectable 1.27%.

12

POKER

Poker holds a unique spot in the world of casino games: It could be your best shot to earn money in the casino or it could be an exercise in humiliation.

Poker is a rich, complex game that combines skill, luck, and intense psychological warfare. Every player competes against and interacts with every other; each player's actions influence each other player's actions. In other casino games, you play against the house and its predetermined, unchanging rules. Or you face a machine whose microprocessor controls your fate. Poker does have similarities to sports and race betting where your success comes from outsmarting the oddsmakers and the rest of the betting population, but in poker it's personal. The opponent you need to outsmart sits at the table with you.

Whether played as a casual recreation or as a cutthroat profession, poker endures as America's most popular card game. It's been estimated that 70 million Americans are familiar with the standard rules of poker, marking it as quite the socially acceptable gambling activity. The game is incredibly adaptable: It may come in the form of bidding pennies at a favorite aunt's kitchen table, or playing quarter-ante, wild-card-infected games in a dorm room, or getting together with some buddies for serious stakes one Thursday night a month.

In the past decade, legalized poker has seen explosive growth. There are currently more than 1,000 poker rooms across the United States—not only in casinos, but also in states that don't have legalized casino gambling, but in which public card rooms are legal (notably California).

Almost every casino of any significant size has a poker room. Modest poker rooms contain a few tables while giant ones reverberate with the action of dozens of games. The rooms are often cordoned off in a back area of the casino where players are deprived of—or spared—the glitz and activity of the other casino areas. Poker rooms aren't big revenue producers for the casinos; instead, management generally offers poker as a gesture of goodwill toward card players. A few casinos cater to the poker player; at other casinos, it's apparent that the rooms function as a minimal customer service concession and may not even be open 24 hours a day. In any case, the casino's hope is that poker players (or their spouses) will play more revenue-enhancing games in their hours away from the card table.

You'll find many differences between a casino poker room and the all-night card-fest with which you may be acquainted. In a casino, you'll probably have only two games to choose from (typically seven-card stud and Texas hold'em), you'll be hard pressed to find draw poker, you won't find games with wild cards, and you will be bound to follow the proper procedures and etiquette that may elude your grasp after your sixth beer when playing in your den. These differences will be further discussed later in this chapter, but it's good to be prepared for the culture shock.

The essential first step to playing casino poker comfortably and successfully is to have poker experience, which, unfortunately, cannot be taught in a book. To become a proficient poker player, one must play, play, and then, for a change of pace, play some more. To gain a further edge, the most skilled and knowledgeable professional (and amateur) players study books on poker that detail the strategy, math, psychology, and nuances of the various games. Poker is extremely complicated and subtle once you attempt to understand it in-depth. Such insights are beyond the scope of this book. If you want to delve more deeply into the science of poker, check out the books in Appendix D.

In this chapter, we will cover the mechanics of the most popular casino poker games: seven-card stud and Texas hold'em. We will also examine some rudimentary strategies and key differences between home and casino poker. For those who are unacquainted with even the basics of poker, we'll start with a brief introduction to the game. Caution: If you need to read the introduction to the game, you ought to start your poker career in nice, friendly, low-stakes games at home with your friends and family. After you become fluent in the game, you can make your first foray to the casino.

A QUICK POKER PRIMER

Poker is not one game, but a large family of related games. There are so many variations that it sometimes seems a new "family member" appears every time someone picks up a deck of cards. Still, there are general principles that unite almost all games that fall under the name of poker.

GENERAL OBJECT AND PROCEDURES

The object of poker is deceptively simple: Win the money in the *pot* during a round of play by either having the best poker hand (highest ranking five-card hand) when the wagering is done or by forcing all other players out of the hand. The pot contains all money contributed during a hand, including *antes*, which are used to seed the pot before each hand begins.

Almost all poker games use a regular deck of 52 cards, comprised of four suits (clubs, diamonds, heart, and spades) that each have 13 cards ranked as follows from highest to lowest: ace, king, queen, jack, 10, 9, 8, 7, 6, 5, 4, 3, 2. (Note that in most games the ace can also be counted as the lowest card.)

Each hand of a poker game is, in essence, a self-contained game in which someone will be awarded the pot. A new hand is initiated by the dealer, who—as you might suspect—deals out the cards according to the rules of the particular game. Each player in turn, proceeding clockwise from the dealer, may either bet or *check* (also known as "pass"). If a player makes an opening bet, the next player clockwise has three choices: *fold, call,* or *raise.* (Players can no longer check once a bet has been made.) A fold means that the player does not want to spend more money to vie for the pot; therefore, he discards his cards and is no longer part of the hand. A call means that the player stays in the hand by betting an amount equal to the current bet. A raise means that the player increases the current bet. A *reraise* is a raise of a previous raise. Betting ends when all who wish to call the highest bet have done so or when all but one player has dropped out. The house rules may limit the number of raises allowed. However, if only two players are in the pot they can keep raising each other indefinitely.

The sequence of dealing cards and having a round of betting continues according to the rules of the specific game. At the end of the last betting round, all players who are left in the hand have a *showdown* in which the player with the best hand is awarded the pot. It is the obligation of the player who made the last bet or raise (not call) to show her hand first in the showdown. The other remaining players then show their hands in a clockwise fashion. However, the other players do not have to show their hands; if they know they are beaten, they can just concede the pot. Remember that not all hands will reach the showdown stage; very often, a player will win the pot because all other players have folded their cards.

RANKING THE HANDS

You need to know the hand rankings in order to play poker competently. Ask during a game, "Does a straight beat a flush or the other way around?" and you declare yourself a rank amateur (forgive the pun). More important than your table rep is the fact that such ignorance will cost you money—you'll stay in hands that you shouldn't and vice versa.

Study the chart on page 183 and make sure you know the hands down pat. It's not tricky.

Ranking of Poker Hands

Royal flush	Ace, king, queen, jack, and 10 all of the same suit. The highest possible straight flush. All royal flushes are equal.	A♥ K♥ Q♥ J♥ 10♥
Straight flush	Five cards of the same suit in sequence. Straight flush headed by the highest card wins.	10♣ 9♣ 8♣ 7♣ 6♣ beats 9♣ 8♣ 7♣ 6♣ 5♣
Four of a kind	Four cards of the same rank and any other card. Highest-ranking four of a kind wins.	8♥ 8♣ 8♦ 8♠ 2♥ beats 7♥ 7♣ 7♦ 7♠ A♣
Full house	Three cards of one rank and two cards of another rank. Highest-ranking three of a kind wins.	J♠ J♦ J♥ 2♣ 2♦ beats 10♣ 10♥ 10♦ K♦ K♠
Flush	Any five cards of the same suit. Between two or more flushes, the one with the highest card wins. If the highest cards are the same rank, then the next-highest card determines the winner, and so on.	K♥ 5♥ 4♥ 3♥ 2♥ beats Q♠ J♠ 10♠ 8♠ 7♠ A♣ 10♣ 9♣ 7♣ 2♣ beats A♥ 10♥ 9♥ 6♥ 5♥
Straight	Any five cards in sequence (of two or more suits—otherwise, it would be a straight flush). The straight headed by the highest card wins.	J♣ 10♦ 9♥ 8♦ 7♠ beats 10♥ 9♥ 8♣ 7♣ 6♦
Three of a kind	Three cards of same rank and two unmatched cards. The higher-ranking three of a kind wins.	9♣ 9♠ 9♥ 5♦ 3♣ beats 8♠ 8♣ 8♥ A♠ Q♥
Two pair	Two cards of one rank, two cards of second rank, and an unmatched fifth card. Between two or more two-pair hands, the higher pair wins. If the high pairs are tied, the second pair determines the winner. If those are tied, the highest unmatched card wins.	K♦ K♥ 5♣ 5♥ 8♦ beats Q♣ Q♥ J♠ J♣ A♥ 9♥ 9♠ 7♦ 7♣ J♥ beats 9♦ 9♣ 6♣ 6♠ K♥ A♠ A♣ 5♦ 5♠ 9♦ beats A♦ A♥ 5♥ 5♣ 8♥
One pair	Two cards of same rank and three unmatched cards. Highest-ranking pair wins. If the pairs are the same rank, the highest unmatched card determines the winner. If tied, the next highest, and so on.	9♣ 9♦ 6♥ 4♥ 2♥ beats 8♣ 8♠ A♦ K♠ Q♠ K♣ K♠ 9♥ 7♠ 3♣ beats K♦ K♥ 9♠ 6♦ 5♦
High card	All five cards different ranks and two or more suits. The highest card wins. If the highest cards are the same rank, the next-highest card determines the winner. If still tied, the next highest, etc.	Q♥ 9♥ 7♣ 5♣ 4♦ beats Q♠ 9♣ 6♥ 4♥ 3♥

The chart above shows the ranking of hands from highest to lowest. It also shows how the winner is determined when more than one hand has the same general ranking.

As the chart indicates, a poker hand is always based on only five cards. If two hands are tied after all five cards have been compared, the pot is split between the holders of the equal hands. Even in games where you can use more than five cards to construct your best hand, the cards that aren't used for your final five-card hand have no relevance. For instance, in seven-card stud, a sixth (or seventh) card would never be used to determine the winner between two equal five-card hands. Also, suits have no bearing on the determination of a winner—one suit is not "higher" than another.

Here's a quick way to test your prowess: Take a deck of cards and deal out a 7 × 7 box. You'll have 16 "hands" of seven cards (seven horizontal, seven vertical, and two diagonal). Within each seven-card hand make the best five-card hand possible. Then rank all 16 five-card hands from best to worst. Check your results against the chart. This exercise will quickly give you confidence about hand ranking. As a bonus, you'll gain familiarity with using seven cards to make a hand, which is the common way casino poker games are played.

In *low poker*, the rankings are reversed. That means the lower your hand the better. It's important to note that straights and flushes are ignored in most casino forms of low poker.

THE CASINO POKER ROOM

Okay, so you're comfortable with poker and you want to try out the casino game. It's still basically the same game you enjoy at the kitchen table, but there are differences in environment and protocol that you need to know.

- The players do not deal. Each table has a dealer who is a casino employee and who is not a player in the game.
- There's a limited variety of games. Seven-card stud and Texas hold'em are the two pillars of casino poker. Bigger rooms will offer a few other variations such as Omaha and lowball. But old-time staples such as draw poker and five-card stud are rarities in the casino (and in neighborhood games) these days.
- Don't look for any "dealer's choice" variations. You won't see any wild deuces or one-eyed jacks or cards on players' foreheads. If you're gearing up to play in a card room, you needn't worry about the wild, and often ludicrous, permutations of living-room poker games.
- Each specific table has only one kind of game and stakes.
- Casino poker tables seat more players than a neighborhood game table.

- Even though you're not playing against the house, that doesn't mean the casino doesn't get its due. You pay for the privilege of having the casino host and regulate the game. This is done either with a *rake* or *taking time*. The rake is a percentage of each hand's pot that is removed by the dealer; a typical rake is 10% of the pot up to $3 or $4. When a poker room takes time, a flat table charge is typically collected every half-hour (which is how often the table changes dealers). Time payments are usually used in higher-stakes games.
- Many games don't have players throw in a typical ante before each hand. There are different methods of seeding the pot for different games and different stakes. These will be discussed in the individual games.

SETTLING IN

If it's your first time (heck, even second or third) in a poker room, you don't have to act like you've played in every room throughout the country. Feel free to ask the staff for assistance and explanations on any of the games or procedures.

Poker rooms also have sheets or booklets that explain the house rules and procedures. For the most part, these poker guides will reflect the information in this chapter, but will go into more detail about protocol, misdeals, and the handling of disputes. The guides are worth a glance to clarify specific procedures that may vary from casino to casino; for example, the number of raises allowed in a round.

So now you're ready to get into a game. What do you do? Head on over to the poker room's front podium or counter and speak to the poker room host. This employee is known as a *brush* and her job is to seat players, maintain the list of games, and provide general assistance. The brush will let you know which games are currently available and which ones will start soon (most rooms will also have a board posting this info). She then will ask your name (or initials) and what game you want to play. If a seat is available at a game you wish to play, you'll be seated immediately. If there are no openings in your game, your name will go on the waiting list and you'll be called when a seat is available. (You can put your name on the list for multiple games; whichever has an opening first is the one you'll play.) Some casinos can page you throughout the casino so you're free to go eat or gamble elsewhere while waiting.

Every poker room also has a manager. The size of the room usually determines how visible the manager is. In large rooms, the manager may stay mostly behind the scenes, working on administrative matters. In smaller rooms, the manager may work as a brush and provide more hands-on service.

Once you're seated at a table, you'll need to buy chips. In smaller poker rooms, the dealer may sell you the chips. In larger rooms, either the brush or an official chip runner will sell you your chips. Now you can be dealt into the next hand. Be aware of the all-important dealer; he'll handle the cards, the rake, and the patrons, determine the winner of the hand, and make sure the game runs smoothly.

Let your dealer know that you're a rookie—he'll help you with the mechanics of the game. Most players will cut you some slack if you're new to casino play. In fact, they may be overly solicitous since they'll also assume that your lack of familiarity with card room procedures means you lack poker skills as well. Of course, it's wise to cut your teeth in a way that won't bring too much financial or social distress—pick a low-stakes table at an off-peak hour. After a few playing sessions—maybe even a few hands—everything will seem like second nature.

BETTING STRUCTURE AND BUY-IN

As with any casino game, you must be aware of the table requirements as well as the rules of the game when you sit down to play poker. Although you'll probably see only two types of poker games in a casino, you will see considerable variety in betting limits.

In a *fixed-limit* game, you'll usually find a two-tiered betting structure, with one number specifying the amount you can bet or raise in early rounds of the game and a second number the amount that you can bet or raise in later rounds. Some common fixed limits are $1–$4 and $5–$10. You may even encounter $100–$200. Usually the higher limit is twice the lower limit, but as you can see with $1–$4 that is not always the case. The amount is both

a minimum and a maximum in a fixed-limit game; that means in the $5–$10 game, you can bet only in increments of $5 in the early rounds and only in increments of $10 in the later rounds.

In a *spread-limit* game, a player may bet any amount in a specified range during each round of a hand. $1–$4/$8/$8 is typical shorthand for the betting limits of a spread-limit hold'em game. This means that in the first two rounds players may bet anywhere from $1 to $4. In the third round, they may bet $1 to $8. In the fourth round, they may also bet $1 to $8. (What constitutes a round will become clear in the game descriptions.) However, any raise must be at least as large as any bet or raise that was made earlier in the round. So if a player opens a round with a $3 bet, the next player cannot raise it by $1; the raise must be at least $3.

Each game has a minimum buy-in, which indicates the smallest amount of chips you must purchase. You should ask what the buy-in is when you're finding out the stakes for the game. In most cases, the minimum buy-in is five times the maximum bet. So for a $5–$10 Texas hold'em game, the minimum buy-in would be $50.

All casino poker games are played *table stakes*. This means you can bet only with money you have on the table during a hand—this includes cash you have on the table as well as chips. You cannot reach into your pocket for money or "go shy," as you might in a home game. If you use all your remaining chips to call or bet, you are *all-in*, meaning all subsequent wagers by other players go into a side pot in which you have no interest. You are only contesting the pot to which you contributed chips. At the end of the hand, you cannot win the side pot—even if you have the best hand—because you invested no money in it. But you can win the main pot. Obviously, an all-in player who loses the hand must buy more chips or leave the game. Between hands, you are free to buy more chips or put cash on the table.

Two betting structures that you are unlikely to encounter unless you're getting very serious about poker are *pot limit* and *no-limit*. In pot limit, a player may bet any amount up to or equal to the amount of chips in the pot. In

POKER PATOIS

If you hang around poker rooms long enough, you may not become rich, but you sure will pick up some snappy patter. Here's some of poker's specialized, colorful vocabulary that you can try out on your Thursday night poker buddies. Normally, the acquisition of this lingo will cost you your shirt. Here it is for free.

Bad beat: Losing with a hand that by all rights—statistically and logically—should have won.

Boat: A full house.

Bullets: A pair of aces.

Bump: Raise.

Calling station: A weak player who stays in most hands, but only by calling.

Catching perfect-perfect: Having the last two cards in a game complete a straight or flush. (Often said with a fair amount of resentment by opponents, especially when the person who catches perfect-perfect shouldn't have remained in the hand.) Also known as "making runner-runner" or a "backdoor" hand.

Door card: Each player's first face-up card.

Gutshot straight: Inside straight. For example, if you are dealt 10♦ 3♦ J♦ in seven-card stud, and then 8♥ 7♣ 2♠, you'll need a 9 on the last card to fill your gutshot straight.

Heads up: Playing against a single opponent.

Nuts: The best possible hand, given a particular set of community cards.

On tilt: Playing recklessly and emotionally, usually to make up losses.

Pocket: Downcards or hole cards.

Quads: Four of a kind.

Rainbow: In flop games, a flop that has three different suits (thus making flush possibilities more remote).

Scare cards: Upcards that suggest a strong hand.

Set: Three of a kind. Also called "trips."

no-limit, a player may bet any amount of chips up to or equal to the amount of chips in front of him. Both of these versions involve a lot of posturing, bluffing, and intimidation. Particularly in no-limit, players can be bumped out of the game in the blink of an eye. Not surprisingly, no-limit is the format used for the World Series of Poker, the game's premier high-stakes tournament.

SEVEN-CARD STUD

It's safe to say that seven-card stud is the most popular form of poker in the United States. It's the core component of many a home game and it's certainly available in every casino poker room. Because of its familiarity, the game attracts more casual players than Texas hold'em, a game that always threatens to eclipse seven-

card stud in the poker room, but has yet to do so.

For our walk-through of seven-card stud, we'll assume the conditions of a very common low-stakes game: a $1 to $4 betting spread and no required ante. Okay, so we buy in and are seated as one of eight at the table. Let's start the hand.

Each player at the table is dealt three cards to begin the hand—two face-down (known as *hole cards*) and one face-up. The player with the lowest-ranked upcard must make a bet called the *bring-in*. This is not optional—it's a forced bet to get the action started. The amount of the bring-in varies based on the table limits, but it is generally lower than the minimum bet. In this instance, the bring-in at our $1–$4 table is 50¢. When two or more cards are tied as lowest (aces only count high in this situation), the card suits are used to break the tie. This is the only instance where card suits have ranking significance in poker. Suits are ranked alphabetically from lowest to highest, as in bridge: clubs, diamonds, hearts, spades. Thus, if the 2♣ is your first upcard, you are guaranteed to make the bring-in bet.

Betting always moves around the table in a clockwise fashion. Let's say Allen made the bring-in bet. Now Betty (sitting to the left of Allen) has three options: call, raise, or fold. If she folds, she turns her face-up card face-down and lets the dealer collect her cards. If she calls, she must put in the 50¢ that was bet originally by Allen. If she raises, she must raise in whole-dollar increments—meaning she bets $1, $2, $3, or $4. (To be precise, the raises involve a half-dollar from the perspective of the first bettor. If Betty says, "Make it $2" the raise is really $1.50. However, all the other players will have to bet $2 in order to stay in—only Allen, the first player, has to deal with the awkward half-dollar amount.)

So if Betty folds or calls, the player to her left, Carl, has the same options: fold, call, or raise. If Betty raises, Carl must either fold, call, or reraise. Remember, any reraise must be at least equal to the current bet. So if Betty bet $2, Carl can raise $2, $3, or $4. The betting continues clockwise as every player makes a decision based on the preceding betting action.

Let's say Betty raises to $3. Three other players stay in by putting in $3 and three fold. Now the betting comes back to Allen. Originally compelled to make the bring-in bet, Allen can now assert his free will. He can call by putting in $2.50 (remember he bet the original 50¢), reraise, or fold.

After the first round of betting is complete, the remaining players are each dealt another face-up card and move on to *fourth street*. (Street is the term used for the round of betting after a certain card has been dealt. Fourth street is the round after the fourth card has been dealt). As opposed to *third street* (the first round of play), here the player with the highest hand showing acts first. If two hands have the same value, the one closest to dealer's left acts first. (Partial straights and flushes don't mean anything.) This player can either check or bet. A check, indicated by knocking one's knuckles on the table and/or saying "check," means a

player chooses not to bet and is passing that option to the next active player clockwise. A player who checks retains the option to call or raise if the betting comes back around. If everyone at the table checks, the round is over and the next card is dealt. If any player bets, all players must respond as we have already outlined: fold, call, raise, or perhaps reraise.

This process is repeated for two more face-up cards (*fifth street* and *sixth street*, respectively) and one final face-down card (*seventh street* or the *river*). There is a round of betting after each card is dealt and the player with the high hand showing ("on board") always acts first. Assuming that the hand reaches the seventh card, there will be five rounds of betting in total. Remember that the hand can end sooner if, during any round of betting, a player makes a bet that no other player chooses to call.

In the end, each remaining player will have three face-down cards and four face-up cards. After the final betting round, you have the showdown: The last person to raise reveals his hand and then the remaining players, in a clockwise order, turn up their hands (unless they want to concede the pot) and the dealer determines the winning hand. Remember, it's the player who can make the best five-card hand from his seven cards who wins the pot. The dealer pushes the pot to the winner and then deals the next hand.

BETTING VARIATIONS
The actual play of seven-card stud will not vary, but its betting structure will. You can always ask a poker room staff member to explain the betting at a particular table. As shown in the example above, lower-limit games often have no ante and are spread-limit (our sample game allowed a range of $1–$4 to be bet in any round). In higher-stakes stud games, you'll often find a fixed structure. Each bet and raise is a predetermined amount—usually at the lower level for third and fourth street, and then the higher level for the following rounds. There will generally be an ante posted by every player before each hand. For example, one might see a $10–$20 stud game where each player antes $1 and the bring-in is $3. Players may call that bring-in or "complete" it to the requisite $10 (no more, no less). All

bets and raises must be $10 for the first two rounds. Starting on fifth street, all bets and raises are made in $20 increments. One exception to note: If a player has a pair showing on fourth street (which means his two upcards match), he has the option to make the higher bet ($20 in this case) a round earlier than normal.

SEVEN-CARD STUD STRATEGY AND SMARTS

Seven-card stud is considered one of the most difficult poker games to master. The number of cards out on the table and ever-evolving permutations can stress the most agile mind. That being said, it's also a very accessible and fascinating game. I cannot do justice to the complexity of this game here, but I can give you a taste of some of the reasoning that is used by successful players.

- You must be able to distinguish between a "live" and "dead" hand. Live hands are those that have a good chance to improve; dead hands are those that are unlikely to improve. You make this evaluation based on the open cards on the table. For example, if you have a pair and the other two cards in that rank are showing, you know you're not going to improve.
- Get a kick from your kickers—those side cards apart from your main pair. High cards can be very powerful. If you and your opponent both have middling pairs, the fact that you have high cards that might pair up can win you the pot.
- Starting hands are crucial in seven-card stud. You must decide whether to pursue your hand at all by the time the third card is dealt. It takes patience and discipline to play only good starting hands. Here's a simplified breakdown of how to evaluate your starting hand:
  → *Three of a kind.* Obviously a great start, but you won't see it too often. On average, it shows up once in every 425 hands.
  → *High pairs (pair of 10s or better).* You'll probably see this through to the end, unless your opponent seems to have paired up an even higher pair.
  → *Small and medium pairs.* Can be dangerous to play—it depends on the size of your

kicker (the third card you have) and whether your pair is live.
  → *Drawing hands.* These are hands that need improvement through additional cards to be powerful enough to take the pot. A three-card open-ended straight or a three-card flush in the first three cards constitutes a drawing hand. But remember, you must first determine if it's a live or dead hand. Check to see if the cards you need to fill that straight or flush are showing on the table.
  → *Don't be foolish.* Throw in your other starting hands. Don't expect something miraculous to unfold in the next four cards.

STARTING HAND ODDS

Three of a kind	424–1
Pair of aces (any specific pair)	76–1
Three to a flush	18–1
Three to a straight	30–1
Any pair	5–1

- Drawing hands play better when you are up against a full table of opponents. Because you're more likely to miss the mark on a drawing hand than make it, you need many opponents so that the pot gets built up. When you do pull off the hand, you'll get a big payoff that justifies your risk. (See the expectation discussion in the sidebar on page 193.)
- By the same token, high pairs play better against fewer opponents. You should seek to drive out other players early on—you don't want to make it easy for someone to stick around and improve his hand. Be aggressive—don't encourage others to give chase.
- Once you're in past fifth street, you'll usually want to stay till the end unless it's clear an opponent has you beat.

TEXAS HOLD'EM

While seven-card stud still holds the title as the popular choice of casino poker, it does so by a scant margin over Texas hold'em. In many poker rooms, hold'em (as Texas hold'em is commonly called) is the dominant game. Many players feel that hold'em is intrinsically more exciting and sophisticated than old-fashioned stud—that it's the game that stud players should graduate to. (Of course, stud devotees would heartily disagree.) Hold'em does deliver a lot of poker action: It can accommodate 9 to 11 players and it plays incredibly fast. No wonder hold'em is the game used for the World Series of Poker tournament.

Here's how hold'em plays out. Players receive two personal face-down cards and share five face-up community cards with all other players. The winner of a hand will either be the player with the best five-card hand made from the seven cards or the last remaining player in the hand.

The first thing you may notice—and that may confuse you—when you check out a game of hold'em is that one player will have a white disk labeled DEALER in front of him. This *button* only indicates that the person is the designated dealer. Obviously, all the functions and responsibilities of dealing still fall to the house dealer. Unlike stud, there aren't any face-up player cards to determine who acts first in each round. By having a designated dealer (this player is often referred to as "the button"), we know that the cards should be dealt to her left and that the first player to her left still in the game acts first on each round of betting. This leaves the button to act last on each betting round—except the first, as will be explained shortly. After a hand is completed, the dealer button moves around the table one position clockwise.

Hold'em games very rarely use antes to seed the pot. Instead, the pot is initially built through the use of forced bets known as *blinds*. The blind bets are posted before any cards are dealt—that's why they are "blind." The two players to the left of the button (also called "in front of" the button) make the blind bets. The first player posts a small blind, which is usually a fraction of the minimum bet. The second player posts a big blind, which is usually equal to the minimum bet. For example, in a $3–$6 hold'em game, the small blind would normally be $1 and the big blind $3.

After the blinds are posted, the dealer gives two face-down cards to each player, starting with the small blind. (That makes sense because this player is to the immediate left of the "designated dealer"—the player who has the button.) The player to the left of the big blind is the first to act, because the small and big blinds have already, in compulsory fashion, started the betting. This player has three options: fold, match the amount of the big blind (call it), or raise. Play then moves clockwise around the table with all players getting a turn to act.

When the betting returns to the players who posted the blinds, they have the same options as the other players: fold, call, raise. However, since they already have a partial bet (the small blind) or full bet (the big blind) in the pot, they only have to make up the difference of the current bet. For instance, if it's a $3–$6 game and there have been two raises of the big blind, the current total bet would be $9. That means the small blind, having already put in $1, would have to add $8 to stay in the hand. The big blind, having put in $3, would have to add $6. Otherwise the blinds can fold or raise.

One last note about the blinds: In most games they are considered "live blinds." This means that they can raise when the betting comes around to them even if no other player has raised. Since the blind bets were forced, these players can raise their own bets. For example, three players call the big blind (including the small blind, who "completed" his $1 forced bet with a voluntary $2 bet). The big blind can end the round by doing nothing—essentially "calling"—or he can raise his own initial bet.

Once the first round of betting on the two face-down cards is completed, we are ready for the next round. First, the dealer *burns* the top card of the deck (puts it out of play face-down) and then deals out three face-up cards in the center of the table. These three cards are known as the *flop* and they are community cards shared by all the players. On this, and all subsequent betting rounds, the first active player to the left of the button is the first to act (there are no more blinds to deal with).

Once this betting round is completed, the dealer burns another card and deals the fourth community card (known as the *turn* or fourth street). After another betting round, the dealer burns another card and deals the fifth and final community card (known as the river or fifth street). The fourth and final round of betting ensues. If more than one player remains, there is a showdown. Each player tries to make the best possible hand from the five community cards (known as the *board*) and her two hole cards. A player can use two, one, or none of her hole cards to make her best hand. If she uses none, she is taking the five community cards as her hand (called "playing the board") and the best she can hope to do is tie. The dealer will determine the winner and push the pot to that player. In hold'em, players often have the same hands; in the case of a tie, the players split the pot. At the completion of the hand, the dealer moves the button one spot clockwise and then deals the next hand.

BETTING VARIATIONS

Hold'em is typically played as a structured game where there's a fixed amount that a player can bet or raise in a particular betting round. The bet is usually at the lower level for the first two rounds of betting and then twice that amount for the last two rounds. So, in a $3–$6, you can bet in increments of $3 before and after the flop, and then bet in $6 increments on the turn and river. You may see some games that have a fixed structure where the limit is raised for the last round, such as $3–$6–$12.

There are also spread limit games for hold'em. A typical game may be $1–$4–$8, where you can bet anywhere from $1 to $4 on the first three rounds, and then from $1 to $8 on the last round (the river). Of course, any raise must be equal to or larger than the largest bet made thus far in the round.

When joining a hold'em game, the dealer will let you know if you have to post a bet in order to be dealt in—remember, that the obligation to post blind bets has been moving around the table and it wouldn't be fair for you to play without having met that obligation. However, if you must post a bet, you may want to wait for the button to pass you before being dealt to. Otherwise you'll pay the "entry fee" (the bet required in order to be dealt in) and then get hit shortly after by your normal blind bets. You will probably be able to just sit and watch—which always helps in an unfamiliar poker game—until the button passes you.

TEXAS HOLD'EM STRATEGY AND SMARTS

Many beginners think that hold'em is essentially the same as seven-card stud with just a different style of working with seven cards. This isn't accurate. Hold'em is a very different game that demands different strategies.

Even though part of the game's lure is its simplicity, it's a lot more intricate than you may think. While it's hard to see the challenge in a game where you work with only two cards and everyone shares the other five, it's the paucity of information that makes the game challenging. You must master hand evaluation, analyze other players, calculate scenarios, etc. We don't have the space to fully explore what makes this game so rich and challenging—here's just a taste of the strategy and analysis that goes into hold'em success:

• The first thing to do with hold'em is to reign yourself in. It is a faster-paced game than stud, so you must be even more watchful. Your discipline will pay off since your best hands will stand up to the competition more often here than at the stud table.

• Betting position is a key element of hold'em. The order in which players act doesn't change throughout a hand (as opposed to stud, where the high hand leads off the betting). The later you act, the more information you have, and that gives you an advantage. Conversely, you should be more selective of the hands you play when you bet from an early position, because you don't know how other players will bet.

• You must be able to identify the *nuts*. This rather colorful term refers to the best possible hand that can be made using the five community cards. For example, let's say the board shows: A♠ J♥ 9♣ 6♦ 4♦. If someone holds two aces, he has the hand won with three aces. No other cards could make a better hand. However, if the 9 of clubs were a 10 of any suit, the nuts would change. Now the best possible hand would be a straight running from 10 to ace. Anyone who held a queen and king would have the nuts. One more variation: Let's change the 9 of clubs to a 9 of diamonds. See what happens? Now the nuts is an ace-high diamond flush. Here's another example: K♦ K♣ Q♠ 3♣ J♥. What's the nuts? The best possible hand would be four kings if someone were holding a pair of kings. Let's say that you're holding one king and one jack. You have a full house, but you don't have the best possible full house. A player holding the other king and a queen could beat you—not necessarily likely, but something to be aware of. One last example: 8♣ J♠ Q♠ 2♣ 3♣. Suppose you hold a 9 and 10. You have a straight. Not bad. But those three clubs are trouble—a flush might be lurking out there to sink your straight. The nuts? If someone holds the ace of clubs and another club, she is guaranteed to take the pot.

- I don't mean to make you nuts about nuts, but it's an important concept. If you think you have the best possible hand and you don't, you're likely to throw away money. If you do have the best hand and don't realize it, you're likely to throw away earnings. Other players' betting behavior will clue you in to how close they are to having the nuts. Not because someone will have the perfect hand every time (although they sometimes will), but because you can construct an idea of what other players hold and what they aspire to, based on their betting and what's on the board. Of course, the greater the number of players who stay in a hand, the more likely it is that one of them has the nuts.
- As in seven-card stud and most forms of poker, strong hands want the weaker hands out of the hand. Drawing hands want more people in the pot.
- Starting hand decisions in hold'em are important, although they are not as critical as they are in seven-card stud. The betting can get hot and heavy before the flop, and it can cost you serious money to stay in and see what turns up. You need to play strong hands, the definition of which is complex. On average, strong players see the flop about one in three hands. Here are some guidelines:
  - → *High pairs (10s or better) are always a delight.* Even if they don't improve on the board, they have a good chance to win. Bet them aggressively. You can scare off your opponents and have fewer reasons for concern.
  - → *Beware of small pairs.* They are drawing hands—that means you need more money

in the pot (which means more opponents in the hand) to make them worth pursuing. The odds of improving a pair to three of a kind on the flop is nearly 8-1 against. If you don't improve on the flop, be prepared to fold the hand.

- → *Don't fall in love with cards of the same suit.* Unless the suited cards are of high rank or "connected" (meaning in sequence; for example, 8-9), you should most often fold the hand.
- Novices wrongly assume that any two cards can win. Since five cards are shared, they believe they don't have to worry about building a hand and they just might sneak in with a good fit. It's true that any two cards could win, but pursuing that philosophy will leave you broke. Some hold'em players will stay in for the flop no matter what two cards they have. They're playing too recklessly and you can take advantage of them if you don't do the same.
- On the other hand, don't get scared out of a hand before the flop. Once you know how to evaluate playable hands, you should give yourself a chance to see the three cards.
- Accept the fact that your hand often becomes a flop on the flop. Even the strongest hand can become neutered after those three community cards show. Let's say you hold a pair of kings (K♦ K♥) and the flop comes up 6♣ 7♣ 8♣, which promises straights and flushes. If the betting is heavy before it reaches you, the smart thing to do is bail out.
- Prepare for some frustration. You can play patiently and wisely, staying in hands only when you have quality starting cards, and then get burned on the community cards over and over again.

OTHER GAMES

Here's a quick look at a few other games you may encounter in your poker room travels.

OMAHA

Omaha is gaining in popularity, but it's not a game for novices. The game is very similar to hold'em, but instead of two face-down cards, players receive four face-down cards. There are still five community cards. Players must use two of their personal cards and three community cards to make the best possible hand. The added downcards make for even more tantalizing possibilities and wilder betting. Every hand seems to have potential before the flop. The number of possible five-card hands increases dramatically as the number of cards increases.

Number of Cards	Number of Hands
5	1
7	21
9	126

As such, good players typically see the flop on half the hands (compared to one-third for hold'em). Strong flushes or full houses usually claim the pot. Omaha is fun, but dangerous. It's best to hone your skills in hold'em before entering these waters.

HIGH-LOW SPLIT

You will often find that Omaha and seven-card stud are played *high-low split*. In that format, the pot is divided equally between the players with the highest hand and the lowest hand. Remember that aces are both high and low. A low hand is evaluated by simply reversing the poker hand hierarchy—the lower the better. In most games, however, straights and flushes do not count when assessing your low hand. That means that A-2-3-4-5 (known as the "wheel") is the best possible low hand and that A-2-3-4-6 is the second-best low hand.

It's very important to note that most high-low games are played with an 8 or better (meaning 8 or lower) qualification for the low hand. That means your low hand must consist of five unpaired cards with none being higher than an 8 in order to compete for the low half of the pot. A hand of 4-5-6-7-8 qualifies (in fact, it's the highest possible qualifier), but A-2-3-4-9 and 2-2-3-4-6 do not. There will often be times when the pot goes only to the high hand since no one qualifies for the low. In Omaha, if the board doesn't contain three unpaired cards of eight or lower, then no low hand is possible. (Remember that you must use two cards from your hand and three from the board.)

Realize that you can win both halves of the pot in these high-low split games. You can make two different sets of five-card hands from your cards. Since flushes and straights rarely count when used low, some hands—like the wheel (A-2-3-4-5)—can qualify for both low and high.

A quick example will give you a sense of the intrigue and occasional confusion these games invite. You're playing Omaha and you are holding A♥ 2♠ 4♥ Q♠. The board shows the following: A♠ 4♦ 6♠ 7♣ J♠. So what do you have going for you? A low hand of A-2-4-6-7 and a high hand of a spade flush. Not bad, but you don't have the nuts. Someone holding a 2 and 3 would have the best low hand (A-2-3-4-6), and someone holding the K♠ along with another spade would have the best high. Remember, everyone shares the A♠, so the next highest card in the flush is key—you have the Q♠, but what if someone has the K♠? Will you manage to win at least half the pot? Maybe …

Make sure that you ask about the specific rules when you sit down to play a high-low split game. As you can see, there's enough to think about without having to wonder whether you need 8 or better to qualify low. It's also worth noting that in seven-card stud high-low, the player with the *highest* upcard makes the bring-in bet in the first round of betting (in normal stud, it's the lowest card). For lack of a better explanation, I will say that this is done to further confuse poker room newcomers who finally think they know what's going on.

GENERAL POKER STRATEGY AND SMARTS

Poker is complex. It's complex, not because of its rules, but because of its variables: human behavior and ever-changing odds. There's no doubt that luck plays a major role in short-term poker success, but over the long run poker is certainly a game of skill. Like any classic game of skill, poker demands study and practice from those who want to achieve mastery.

If you enjoy poker, it's rather fascinating to commit yourself to being a student for life. You can prepare as if you want to play in the high-stakes games, and then, if you don't want to follow through, you can at least stomp on the players in your home game. As hard as it may be to believe (especially if you generally wallop

INSIDE THE NUMBERS

Expectation, as discussed in Chapter 2 and throughout the book, is the amount that you expect to gain or lose when making a particular decision. In poker, your expectation will change with each hand since it is based on the cards that are known to you and the amount in the pot. For example, you're in a hold'em hand and, after the flop and the turn, you have four cards to a diamond flush. You've seen six cards—the two in your hand and the four on the board—and you haven't seen the 46 other cards in the deck. There are nine diamonds that will complete your flush and 37 cards that won't. Right now, the odds are 37–9 against getting your flush.

Let's assume you win every time you make the flush and lose every time you don't. There's $60 in the pot and it will cost you $12 to call the bets and stay in the hand. What's your expectation? Let's look:

$$E = [^{37}/_{46} \times (-12)] + [^{9}/_{46} \times (+60)] = ^{96}/_{46} = \$2.09$$

With an expectation of $2.09, it looks like a good play to make. Remember, you'll lose about four out of five times, but the one win will offset those losses and make a profit. The situation would be different if there were $40 in the pot:

$$E = [^{37}/_{46} \times (-12)] + [^{9}/_{46} \times (+40)] = -^{84}/_{46} = -\$1.83$$

Here the expectation is negative and therefore a losing proposition in the long run.

your poker cronies at home), you need the scholarship obtained through experience and study to play well. It takes work to acquire the discipline, patience, and card smarts of a consistent winner.

Why do you need to study books? Because you need to learn the standards for play in the game of your choice. Then you have to learn how these standards shift, based on whom you're playing against, where you're sitting, and the mood of the game. Here are some of the basic building blocks of a poker education:

• Successful poker players have a conscious or unconscious understanding of odds and expectation. Of course, these numbers are not often as clear-cut as in other casino games. It's likely that you would have to work with the numbers mechanically before they became second nature to you.

• The concept of pot odds is just another way of looking at expectation. It compares the amount of money in the pot to the amount of money you would have to put in to continue playing. It helps answer the eternal question: "Is it worth it to continue in this hand?" To answer that, you also have to have a sense of card odds. Let's say the pot contains $100 and

you need to put in $10 to continue playing. The pot odds are 10–1. If you have a better chance of winning than that, it's worth calling. When the card odds are larger than the pot odds, you should get out. Have a 25–1 chance of getting that inside straight? Time to fold. Does every formidable poker player crunch numbers with the greatest ease and have fractions and decimals dancing in his head? Probably not all, but many do—and those who don't most likely have an intuitive grasp of the probabilities from their many years at the tables. Put as simply as possible, if the pot odds of winning are equal to or larger than the true odds, winning players will want to see it through.

• Most players play way too many hands. You will win more by folding more often. This sort of discipline is difficult for the recreational player. If you read the experts' books, you'll see how they preach patience and discipline, and you'll be shocked by how many hands they say to throw away. Particularly in casinos, you have to play tight—there are more players at the tables and thus there's less of a chance that you'll have the best hand. Learn the guidelines for what hands to play. You'll immediately have an edge on most of the low-limit competition. If you opt for action over the guidelines, just realize the cost of your looser play.

• Be observant of the players at your table. You'll be surprised at how often you'll be able to read their hands. I'm not talking about overt *tells* like a nervous cough when bluffing or fiddling with chips when in possession of a killer hand—these tip-offs exist but they aren't as common or reliable as poker-based movies would have you believe. More successful "reading" comes through scrutiny and deduction as you develop a profile of a player's psychology and his patterns of play and behavior. Just because you're not sitting with Speed, Vinnie, and Roy from the home game doesn't mean you can't get a bead on your competition.

• The bluff is not as key an element of the game as you may think. Clever deception has its manifold pleasures, but it shouldn't be done indiscriminately. You can use the concept of pot odds to guide your bluffing. For example, let's say you estimate that your $10 bluff will succeed one in four times against a certain player. That means there must be at least $30 in the pot for your bluff to be an even proposition. Three out of four times you'll lose $10 for a total loss of $30. One out of four times, your bluff will succeed and you'll get $30. That sounds sensible, but it's not easy to execute. First of all, it's hard to quantify how often a bluff will succeed. Second, some players never fold, particularly in low-limit games. (So the pot odds can never favor you.) Also, casino games have many players, and the more players there are, the more likely it is someone will see you through to the end. Then again, against one player, a bluff can be the whole game. In a high-stakes game, a bluff is more likely to succeed, but pro players don't consider a pure bluff a major weapon in their arsenals. Still, an occasional, not-too-costly "discovered bluff" (one that doesn't work) might help you win bigger pots in later hands. Players may think you are a "bluffer" and stay in when you actually do have a good hand.

• For the player seeking a profit, a good poker game is not one where titans of equal strength square off against each other. If all else were equal, the money would just be redistributed around the table based on chance; that would mean everyone would end up 10% poorer because of the house rake. The law of the jungle rules the poker table. The secret of winning money consistently is to find games with players who play worse than you do. Successful players need weak players who obliviously allow their money to be siphoned away by strong players. Guilt does not pay in poker, guile does.

• No matter how accomplished you get in your own playing, you will always be reminded that bad players do get lucky. Of course, luck will equal out in the long run and skilled players will be way ahead. However, awareness of skill can also turn poker into a dangerous game. Many players are overconfident in their "skill" and compound their bad streaks by playing recklessly against opponents whom they consider "lucky."

• In the long run, you do have control of your poker fate. But in the short run, luck and chance will have their way with you. Don't let the illusion of control lead to loss of control. Poker players—good and bad alike—are notorious for going *on tilt*, which means to play wildly and desperately in order to regain lost money, repair a bruised ego, prove competence, get payback, etc. This foolish and self-destructive behavior is also called *steaming* and must be avoided at all costs. Of course, players who are on tilt are welcomed with open arms by other poker players who hope to capitalize on their irrational play. When you feel desperate, it's time to leave the poker tables.

CASINO POKER VS. KITCHEN POKER

Playing poker at a casino can seem very intimidating, particularly for players whose experience has been limited to penny wagering at family get-togethers. Even competent and experienced home players envision entering a poker room as the equivalent of wading into a pool of sharks—sharks who will quickly and efficiently gobble every last bit of their money and self-esteem. In our collective pop culture consciousness, we carry the Western movie images of the card hustler who deals from the bottom of the deck and carries an ace up one sleeve and a derringer up the other.

So is it wise to shy away from casino poker rooms? Not necessarily. Some anxiety is healthy—it will keep you focused on becoming a better player and will hopefully keep you from playing beyond your means. Overconfidence will hurt you; you will get shot down by better players. However, an experienced poker player who plays in an informed and prudent manner can survive, even occasionally thrive, in the poker rooms. I win more often than not in low-stakes games and I have never been confused with Amarillo Slim or the Cincinnati Kid. I didn't cut my teeth playing thousands of hands in back rooms and smoke-filled poker parlors; I got my poker experience in the same manner as the majority of recreational players—playing in a weekly game with my pals.

The poker room would make Darwin proud—it's a survival-of-the-fittest world where everyone is looking to chomp on someone lower on the food chain. The professional poker players make their living feeding off the players who are weak, inept, impulsive, reckless, stupid, and/or drunk; these poor souls are referred to as "pigeons." Too often, they're more easily identified as "tourists." Okay, so you're willing to be a tourist (that can't be avoided if you're not a local), but you'd rather avoid the pigeon label. That's an obtainable goal.

There's an oft-quoted maxim in the world of poker: If you can't spot the sucker at the table within your first half-hour of playing, then *you* are the sucker. The good news is that there are plenty—an inexhaustible supply—of lousy poker players sitting at poker room tables. The better news is that you don't have to be among their ranks. If you sit down at a low-stakes game, you will soon discover the spectrum of competence and incompetence among players. Don't assume that you are the sucker—even if you are, you can counter that. Sit back and only play your best hands. Be conservative and observe. The more you watch and learn, the less of a chance there is that you will be a vulnerable player.

Who will you find at the tables? If you're getting your feet wet at low-limit tables, you're not going to run into any World Series of Poker competitors. There will be casual players, such as yourself, who are tourists or infrequent visitors. Many of them just to want to drink, get some action, and throw around money—those are the ones you want to play with. (If they're too irritating, you'll have to weigh their money against your sanity.)

Then there are regulars—retirees, students, off-shift dealers—who probably aren't as good as they think they are. However, they may be better than you, just by virtue of the fact that they play regularly. Downtown Las Vegas is notorious for its poker rooms inhabited by local poker players who will grind you down with their solid, if unexciting, play. When you play with the locals, you are at a disadvantage because they know how the regular players play. They know who bluffs after losing a few big hands, who bets recklessly, who raises only when he has a killer hand. They know who the rocks are—players who only play the best hands. The more chummy the players are with each other, the worse shape you may be in.

Two other inhabitants of the poker room are *shills* and *proposition players* (or *props*). Shills are casino employees who are used to fill out tables so that the minimum number of players needed for a game are present. A proposition player uses his own money, but is paid an hourly wage by the casino to help start games or fill out short-handed games. These players aren't necessarily very skilled and the casino doesn't care whether they win or lose; they just use them as live bodies to keep the games going.

There are certainly professionals lurking in the poker rooms, but it's unlikely that you'll see them in your low-limit game. They usually play in at least $10–$20 games. They won't be slumming unless they've been hit hard and are trying to build up a bankroll or they want a distraction while waiting for a big game to start. There's no need to be afraid of a pro being in your game. He'll probably just play a steady, sane, and effective game. (You might even learn something.) Ironically, it's the wild players who may hurt you more in the short-term, because they may beat you in hands that they have no business being in.

The difference between casino poker and the poker you played at your Aunt Millie's house is the skill level of the players. That doesn't mean the poker games in casinos are played only by humorless automatons who check and raise while coldly and inhumanly scrutinizing their opponents. Quite the contrary. Many players, particularly in lower-stakes games, will joke, chat, and act very congenial, but in a less time-consuming and digressive way than your typical home game. (After all, the game must keep moving!) Of course, just because people are pleasant doesn't mean they don't want to drain you dry—heck, that's what poker's all about. You, as a self-respecting poker vulture, have the same cruel designs on the bankrolls of your table comrades.

POKER ROOM PROTOCOL AND ETIQUETTE

While you should have fun playing casino poker, you'll also have to accept that it's not your informal home game. The house rules are interpreted strictly and applied consistently. Your fellow players and the dealer will expect you to adhere to certain standards that prevent confusion, cheating, and slowing down of the game. Most of the folks you'll encounter at the poker table will be pretty pleasant, but, as we know, whenever money and ego are involved, people can be rude and short-tempered. Learn the protocol and you'll save yourself aggravation and embarrassment—maybe even some money. You'll even have a good time, albeit without anyone asking you if want something from the fridge or what topping you want on your pizza.

Here's some basic etiquette that you should follow in the casino poker room:

- Games move efficiently and quickly in a poker room. Not at light speed, mind you, but faster than when friends intersperse playing decisions with complaints about their jobs or critiques of the latest movies. Particularly in games with a time collection, players and dealers try to move the game along quickly because the money will be paid for a half-hour's play regardless of how many hands are dealt. So be prepared when it's your turn.
- On the other hand, don't throw away money just to avoid the glares of the other players. If you have a question or a doubt about what's happening when it's your turn (that "did I miss something?" feeling), you can ask for extra time simply by saying, "Time." Then ask your question and make your decision. Just don't abuse this option—try to keep your head in the game.
- Always make your intentions clear. The best way to do this is to state your action verbally. If you put down a $5 chip when the bet is $1,

it isn't clear whether you want to raise or only wish to call the $1 bet but need the dealer to make change.

- If it's your turn to act, any verbal statement you make is binding, assuming that it is within the rules of the game. If you say "fold," "check," "call," "raise," or a specific money amount, you must stick with that action.
- Pay attention to the action so you don't blunder and act out of turn. If you give away information about your intention to call, fold, raise, or check, you put other players at an advantage (or disadvantage). They may voice their displeasure.
- Similarly, you shouldn't fold when the betting has been checked to you, even if you have the world's most godawful hand. Only fold when you have to fold due to someone else's bet; otherwise, players who act after you get an unfair advantage.
- You aren't allowed to rearrange your upcards in stud poker. The sequence of the cards gives information to your opponents and shouldn't be tampered with.
- A great source of whining and bellyaching in poker is the use of the *check-raise*, also known as *sandbagging*. This tactic is executed by checking initially in a round, but then raising later in the same round when someone after you bets. In many home games, this maneuver is considered devious and underhanded and may actually be banned. However, the check-raise is perfectly legal to use in the casino, although it may raise the ire of some unsophisticated opponents. They should get over it. (A few casinos offer "beginner" games where the check-raise is not allowed.)
- Be careful that you don't pull a *string raise*—whether intentional or not—because you'll certainly be nailed on it. A string raise entails calling a bet by putting your chips down and then reaching back for more chips to make a raise. This is not permitted. Why? Because an unscrupulous player can put in some chips as if only to call, evaluate the reactions of the opponents, and then use that info in deciding to raise. If a player or the dealer notices the string raise, the culprit has to take back the raise and just call. Make sure you use one motion to bet all the chips you want to bet. Better yet, verbally declare "raise" and then

take your time counting out the chips you want to bet.

- Don't put your chips directly into the pot. Tossing your chips into the pot at the center of the table is called "splashing" the pot and it's a no-no. You'll have to sacrifice this bit of casual flamboyance because it makes it difficult for the dealer and other players to keep track of the round's betting and the accuracy of your bet. Put your chips in a neat stack in front of you and the dealer will pull them into the pot when all the betting has been completed for that round.

- You are always responsible for your hand's protection. It is not unheard of for wandering cards to be inadvertently picked up by the dealer and placed in the *muck* (the discards maintained by the dealer). Also, your hand can be *fouled* (ruled invalid) if someone else's cards end up mysteriously intermingled with yours. It's a good idea to always keep a hand on your cards or place a chip on them. Obviously, just like everywhere else in the casino, your cards must be kept on or above the table at all times.

- The cards "speak" in all casino poker games. That means you don't have to name the value of a hand during a showdown. The dealer will read your hand for you. Therefore, if you have any doubt that you may have the winning hand at the showdown, turn your cards face-up and let the dealer determine the winner. Of course, dealers can make mistakes. If you think you have the best hand, bring it to the dealer's attention before he collects the cards.

- Don't trust other players' declarations in a showdown. Put less cynically, anyone can make a mistake—so you shouldn't concede the hand just because someone *says* he has a better hand than you.

- Of course, you can discard your hand at the showdown. You may very well do this when you know you have a losing hand and you don't want other players to know the nature of the losing hand. Interestingly, the casino can require the hand's disclosure—as a safeguard against collusion or cheating—but this very rarely happens.

- It is customary for the winner of a pot to give the dealer a toke (a tip). Fifty cents or a dollar is usually appropriate. Huge wins may make you feel more generous. Some players—including "pros"—won't tip because the expense cuts into their hourly earnings. That decision may make financial sense, but it's morally dubious—dealers provide a service and rely on tips for most of their income. Get them miffed and they just might start dealing from the bottom of the deck on you. (Just kidding … I think.)

- Poker rooms, and casinos in general, are not geared toward the smoke-sensitive. However, larger poker rooms usually provide a few non-smoking tables for lower-limit games. For those who like to puff away, be aware that the two seats immediately to the right and left of the dealer are often nonsmoking seats.

- You are not chained to your seat. It's perfectly fine to get a bite to eat, answer nature's call, or just take a walk to get your blood flowing. Ask the dealer how long you can vacate your seat—it's usually about an hour. When you take your break, the dealer will place a marker on your spot to reserve it for you and you can leave your chips. If you overstay your absence, your seat can be given away. No, your chips won't be given away—the room will hold them for you.

WHY PLAY CASINO POKER?

As stated throughout this chapter, casino poker is a tough game. It sets up some substantial hurdles for the casual player. In general, the game moves faster than a home game and you're playing against experienced, unfamiliar competition. Also, you're fighting the house rake that comes out of every pot.

However, there are many reasons why you would want to leave the friendly confines of your home to play casino poker. Don't forget that poker is a game where you can control your losses while still being "in the game." You could play $1–$4 seven-card stud all night, drop out of every hand, and the only cost would be the occasional 50¢ bring-in. (This is not a fun, smart, or advisable way to play, but it shows that it is easily in your power to spend a night taking in the sights and sounds of the poker room without losing your shirt.)

Some casinos throw in a few other inducements to keep you coming back for their card action. Casinos that pride themselves on their poker rooms do provide comps for their players. If you're a low-limit player, it won't add up to much, but a night of play could get you a buffet meal. Many poker rooms feature jackpots for certain hands such as four of a kind or better. You may also see a bad beat jackpot which is awarded to a player who loses a hand while holding a powerful hand such as four of a kind or better. Generally, percentages of these jackpots are shared among all the players.

Perhaps most of all, convenience and availability may lead you to the casino poker room. Your home may not have a game going, but you can always find a casino where a game is available at a betting level you're comfortable with. If you accept the house's rake as a "hosting fee," you're ready to take on opponents on a level playing field. (Of course, your skills will determine how truly "level" the field is.) Also, if you have a casino that you can visit regularly, you'll get to know the personalities and characters around the poker room. It won't be long before you're comparing bad beat sob stories with other poker folk.

TOURNAMENTS

One sign of poker's explosive growth and popularity is the huge increase in poker tournaments. Nearly every casino poker room offers tournaments. In order to participate in a tournament, players put up entry fees, which are considered their buy-ins. There are many different levels of games and buy-ins/entry fees. Some tournaments are "satellite" events where the winner qualifies for a bigger event. The buy-in can be under $20 for some tournaments; you may want to wait a bit before you fork over the $10,000 buy-in for the World Series of Poker.

After buying-in, players receive tournament chips that aren't redeemable for money like ordinary casino chips. The format is knockout elimination—you play until you lose all your chips or you force everyone else to lose all their chips. A few tournaments are winner-take-all, but most give different percentage payoffs to the top finishers. So if 30 players put up $100, there will be $3,000 in prizes (or less if the casino takes a cut). First place might get 50% of the prize money, second place 30%, third place 15%, and fourth place 5%. For larger tournaments, the structure might be 40% for first, 20% for second, and then smaller payouts down to maybe eighth or ninth place.

Tournaments give you a chance to get big winnings for a small investment. While it's hard to end up in the money, the buy-in lets you know how much you're committing to the action. Whole books have been devoted to the strategy changes required in tournament play. Your style of play varies: Sometimes you play tighter than you normally would, other times you play looser. Your tactics revolve around the need to survive to the end, so you don't always make decisions that would help you in the long haul. Also, as you progress in a tournament the stakes, antes, and required bets increase. You can't just watch and wait.

THE ESSENTIALS FOR PLAYING POKER LIKE A GENIUS

- The two most popular games in the casino poker room are seven-card stud and Texas hold'em.
- Play a game with which you're familiar. This will give you a chance to acclimate to casino poker without feeling at sea.
- For most recreational players, seven-card stud will be the game of choice, because it's more commonly played at home than hold'em. (That also means that you'll find more stud players in the casino who don't play very well.)
- Understand the differences between playing at the casino and playing at home. At the casino, you'll have to play more wisely against more skilled competition.
- Play in games you can afford. Don't think about winning a couple of big hands because of your superior skills. Go into a game at a level and with a stake where you feel you could play for three or four hours. If you feel outmatched or uncomfortable, leave.
- For a $1–$4 spread-limit game, a $100 bankroll should be okay. For a $3–$6 fixed-limit game, you'd want more like $300.
- If you're having a bad time at the tables, take a break. In fact, take breaks anyway just to keep yourself fresh and fed.
- Like everywhere else in the casino, beverage service is provided free of charge while you're playing. But indulging in some potent potables will hurt your bottom line. Poker is not a game where you want your senses dulled.
- Always keep your cards secure. Information is the hottest commodity at a poker table; don't give any away for free.
- It's hard enough to beat the other players. You also have to consider the casino's rake and tips for the dealer. All things being equal, you will lose money.
- The best way to improve your game is by study (see Appendix D) and by practicing your skills in low-stakes games.
- You can't expect to win every session you play. Realize that every session is part of your career session.
- Once you head into the card room, don't be intimidated. Play steady, and have fun.

13
SPORTS BETTING

Where sports go, the money follows. Does two million dollars for a 30-second commercial during the Super Bowl sound outrageous? How about an estimated $300 billion in sports bets made annually by Americans? Of that amount, Nevada, the only state where sports gambling is actually legal, contributes a mere $2.5 billion in bets.

Sports betting adds extra excitement to contests that are already exciting. How often do people say, "Care to make this a bit more interesting?" A very dull contest can become very riveting when a few points here or there will win or lose some cash. You have your Super Bowl pool at the office or the NCAA basketball bracket that you fill out or the friendly wager with your best friend—all ways to spice up the games a bit. From the workplace to the living room to the local bar, people like to add some "action" to their sports action.

The sports leagues and their officials will cry to the heavens about their opposition to gambling, but the sound is hollow. Like it or not, sports gain much of their attention and rooting interests from gamblers. It's not just the true-blue fans who scour the newspapers looking for inside information on teams and player injuries. Also, why does nearly every newspaper in the country carry the betting lines if gambling is allowed in Nevada only? No need to put Holmes on the case.

While Nevada may account for only a fraction of sports bets, it's the place to go for betting variety, high-tech amenities, and, if you care, legality. (You won't have to worry about your kneecaps.) No matter your sport—football, basketball, baseball, hockey, golf, boxing—

you can find a place to bet on it. Most every major casino in Las Vegas contains a *sports book*—an area set aside for sports and race wagering. The variety of bets available in the over 100 established Nevada sports books boggle the mind: Wager a few bucks on your hometown baseball team, take a long-term shot on who will win the Super Bowl, back your support of Ernie Els at the U.S. Open, pick a horse at Saratoga (see page 212 for the lowdown on horse racing). The list is endless.

In order to successfully bet on sports, you have to know much more than how to read sports lines and odds. This chapter will give you an introduction to the mechanics of how sports betting works, but there are no magic tricks to becoming a good handicapper. To really be successful as a sports bettor, you have to live, eat, and breathe sports—and still get a little lucky.

HOW SPORTS BETTING WORKS

While it pales in monetary comparison to the only-slightly-underground world of illegal betting, legal sports betting has experienced a makeover in the last 10 years. Race and sports books used to be considered Nevada gambling's poor and seedy relation. Now they are attractive, comfortable, state-of-the-art electronic marvels with gigantic television screens that show major sporting events and horse racing from around the country.

THE SCENE
Nevada sports books have now become integral parts of the ritzy casinos and mega-resorts. They vary in size, style, and extravagance: Some are

functional parlors, others are restaurant lounges, and others are huge, high-tech auditoriums. A good sports book offers quality seating and large-screen televisions in addition to private viewing stations, food, and complimentary drinks for its patrons. Many have satellite systems and the better ones will allow you to see virtually every televised sporting event available. You'll also get constant updates on non-televised events. Even if you don't spend a dime, it's a sports fan's nirvana—especially on weekends.

Watching a game at a Las Vegas casino can be relaxing and thrilling. You can just hang out and cheer the multitude of events being screened. You get to see two worlds collide: the real game and the bettor's game. While Lakers fans are celebrating a win, some bettors are bemoaning a meaningless free throw that rolled in and out and kept the Lakers from covering the line.

The gigantic screens and betting boards of the bigger books can be intimidating for the first-timer. All the numbers and activity may make you think you're at Mission Control at NASA rather than your favorite sports bar. But once we decipher what's going on, the electricity is apparent. There's nothing quite like watching a full slate of Sunday football games at a sports book with all the highs, lows, and adrenaline running through the air. Once you get over the initial strangeness, you'll discover that sports betting is pretty straightforward. In the following sections, we'll cover all the bets available.

THE ACTION

To place a bet you walk up to a sports book writer who may be at a window or behind a counter. You tell the writer what bet you are making (using a specific number as we'll see below) and for how much. After you give him your money, the writer will give you a ticket with your bet printed on it.

If you lose your bet, you can trash your ticket. If you win your bet, take the ticket to a cashier window at the sports book to collect your winnings. You'll get your winnings plus your original bet. If the sports book is closed, you may be able to cash your ticket at the normal casino cage.

Make sure to check the ticket for accuracy and to keep it secure. If you lose the ticket and

it's a winner, anyone who finds it can cash it in. Read the back of the ticket to know how long you have to cash a winner before it becomes void. The standard is 60 days, but it could be more or less. If you're leaving town before your game is played, don't worry. Winning tickets can be redeemed by mail—just make sure you know the time restrictions on that as well.

Minimum bets vary depending on the casino—usually it's $5 or $10. The maximum limit in a sports book will generally be higher for sports with the smallest percentage of knowledgeable bettors. This means that the Super Bowl, which draws in the largest number of casual fans, will have a higher betting limit than the Stanley Cup championships in hockey, which attracts fewer but more informed fans. A pro football game may have a maximum limit of $5,000; a college football game, $2,000; pro and college basketball, $1,000; hockey, $500.

When a sporting event is circled at a sports book, it indicates the book is not willing to take much risk on it; perhaps a key player's status is unknown due to injury. This means that the book will not let you bet the normal maximum on the game. So you may be able to wager only $2,000 instead of $5,000 on a pro football game.

If you're just getting your feet wet in sports betting, try to get to the book early on heavy betting days such as Saturdays and Sundays during football and basketball season. By going at a non-peak time, you'll get better attention, your questions can be answered, and you can absorb the betting options without too much chaotic activity around you.

Unlike everything else in the clockless casino world, sports books don't run 24 hours a day. They often close after the last telecast sporting event of the evening is finished and then open again in the morning. Since sports books aren't big money makers, it probably isn't worth it to the casino to keep them open to satisfy the urges of 3 A.M. bettors.

THE WIDE WORLD OF SPORTS BETS

Let's say there was a showdown between your high school basketball squad and the San Antonio Spurs. Think anyone would have a

THE CASINO'S "JUICE" ON THE POINT SPREAD

When you bet on a game, you're not betting against the casino. Unlike casino games, the house doesn't have a built-in mathematical advantage in a sports contest. How could it? Sports are independent events and not ruled by probability theory. Instead, the sports book acts as a broker and gains a commission on losing bets. This commission is known as the *vigorish* or vig or *juice*. The vig on all bets using the point spread is 10% of your wager. In other words, the casino pays 10 to 11 on your bet. Sometimes you'll see –110 actually posted next to a team; that's just another way of expressing the 10 to 11 odds. You have to bet $110 up front for the chance to win $100. Of course, you would get back $210 if you win (your $110 bet plus your $100 winnings). Realize you don't have to actually bet $110—you merely have to bet in multiples of $1.10.

It's easy to see how the house makes its money. Let's say you decided to cover both the favorite and the underdog. You place $110 on both and are thus assured of winning one of your bets (assuming there is no tie). The bet you win will pay you back $110 (the amount you bet) plus $100 (the amount you won). That's $210 back in your pocket, but you bet $220 total. The house holds on to the extra $10 from your losing bet.

The casino doesn't care whether Team A or Team B covers the spread. They only want a nearly equal amount of money to be wagered on both sides because that guarantees them a profit. Let's see how this works: Imagine the Miami Dolphins are 6-point favorites over the Philadelphia Eagles. The oddsmaker peered into the mind of the general public and created a perfect split in the betting: $11,000 on the Dolphins and $11,000 on the Eagles. If the Dolphins win by greater than 6 points, the casino pays out $10,000 to Dolphins bettors from $11,000 bet by Eagles bettors. That provides a $1,000 profit. If the Eagles win or lose by less than 6 points, then Eagles bettors are paid $10,000 from the $11,000 bet by Dolphins bettors. Again, the casino makes its $1,000.

We can easily determine the house edge in betting against the point spread. Unless you're an expert handicapper (a rare breed), there's a 50–50 chance of picking the right team with the spread. Using an $11 bet as our base, here's the house edge.

Expected outcome = $[0.5 \times (+10)] + [0.5 \times (-11)] = -0.5$

Expected outcome per dollar bet = $^{-0.5}/_{11} = -0.045$

House edge = 4.5%

That's not an insignificant house edge to buck if you're betting blind. Just how good would you have to be to overcome the house edge? That's also simple enough to calculate. Since you risk $11 for every $10 you win, you would have to win 11 times for every 10 loses.

$[10 \times (-11)] + [11 \times (+10)] = 0$, which means you're even.

So you have to win 11 out of every 21 bets = $^{11}/_{21} = 0.5238 = 52.4\%$.

Does 52.4% sound like an easy way to make a living off being an ESPN junkie? It isn't—as any sports bettor will surely let you know.

Nonetheless, based on cost-per-hour, a sports bet can be one of the best bets in the casino. Let's say you're content to make a small $11 wager to add some extra oomph to your rooting interest in a football game. The expected loss for that wager over the long term is about 50¢ ($11 × 4.5%). Watch the game for three hours and you're looking at an expected loss of about 17¢ per hour ($^{50}/_3$). That's a steal in the world of the casino.

problem picking the winner? Unlikely. But what if you could pick your alma mater and add 100 points to their score? That might make things more interesting. Sports *oddsmakers* look to make all contests more interesting—and generate a decent profit for legal and illegal bookies throughout the world. The various sports bets reflect the manner in which sports books level the playing field between competitors.

FOOTBALL: THE FOUNDATION

College and pro football are the most popular bets in Nevada sports books (followed by college and pro basketball). So we'll use football as an example to guide us through the various types of sports bets that can be made. If you walked into a sports book in autumn, you would likely see a multitude of games posted on the sports book walls and printed up on sheets. Here's an example of how the bets are presented for a football game:

Bet #	Team	Line	Total	Money Line
159	Vikings		42	+150
160	Packers	−4		−170

Let's break this down element by element.

Bet Number

You use this number to make the bet with the ticket writer. The number is merely a shorthand code for the team you want to bet on. For example, if you said, "Number 159 for $11" it would mean you want to bet $11 on the Vikings.

Team

The home team is always listed underneath the visiting team.

Line

The *line* or *point spread* is the bread-and-butter wager of sports betting. You see it all the time in the newspapers, where it would typically look like this:

Favorite	Points	Underdog
PACKERS	4	Vikings

(In newspapers, the home team is often indicated by all capital letters.)

The way the line works is very straightforward. In our example, the Green Bay Packers are a 4-point *favorite* over the Minnesota Vikings. Another way of saying this is that the Packers are "laying" four points. If you bet on the Packers, in order for them to *cover the spread* they must win by more than 4 points. You have to subtract 4 points from their final score at the end of the game and then see who won. Thus, at the casino, you have −4 next to the Packers (sometimes the minus isn't indicated, but it's understood anyway). Conversely, if you bet on the Vikings, the team must either win the game outright or be fewer than 4 points short of the Packers' score in order to win your bet. Most often there will be no number after the *underdog* (no +4 as you might expect), but it's understood that the underdog gets the points added that the favorite has subtracted.

Think of it this way: Before the game is even played, the Vikings are ahead 4–0. So if the final score of the game is Packers 30, Vikings 24, those bettors who took the Packers would win their bet because the Packers won by more than 4 points. If the final score were Packers 30, Vikings 27, the Vikings bettors would win because the Vikings came within 4 points. Even though they lost the "real" game, they won the betting game by an adjusted score of Vikings 31 (27 + 4), Packers 30. In this case, the Packers did not cover the 4-point spread. If the game's final score were Packers 27, Vikings 23, the game would end as a tie or push because the adjusted score would be Packers 27, Vikings 27 (or looking at it from the minus view, Packers 23, Vikings 23). All money would be refunded to bettors on the push.

If you see "PK" in place of a number on the line, that means that neither team is a favorite and the game is classified as a *pick* or *pick 'em*. The team you bet has to win outright (straight up) in this case—no points will be added or subtracted from its score.

Don't be confused by lines that have half-points. A half-point simply has the effect of preventing ties. So if, in our example, the Packers were 4½ point favorites rather than 4, they would lose, rather than tie, a game with a final score of Packers 27, Vikings 23. Thanks to the half-point, the point-spread adjusted final score would be Vikings 27½, Packers 27. An equivalent way of looking at the adjusted score would be Vikings 23, Packers 22½.

Point spreads often change from the time that they're initially posted to the time of the game. A football spread may shift a point or two during the week. The listed spread at the time you make your bet is your spread, and it will be recorded on your ticket. It doesn't matter if the spread changes afterward, you are locked in at the spread that existed at the time you made your bet.

Totals

After the use of the point spread, the next most common bet is betting on *totals* or the *over-under*. This is a separate bet on whether the combined points scored by both teams will be more or less than the posted number. If the final score of our Packers-Vikings game were 30–17, bettors who wagered on the "over" would win because the point total of 47 is greater than the 42 listed. Those who bet "under" would lose. It doesn't matter who actually wins the game and the point spread has no bearing on this bet. If the final score of the game were 27–15, the bet would be a push and all money wagered would be refunded. Remember, it's the combined total of the final score that matters; all points scored in the contest, including overtime (or extra innings in baseball), count. (If you're betting football, you don't always have to make the beginning of the game to get a wager in. Almost all books offer half time opportunities to make bets on the point spread or the total.)

Very often the total bet and the line bet aren't posted in separate columns, but are placed next to the teams as follows (total next to the underdog and line next to the favorite):

Vikings 42
Packers −4

Don't be confused by this. It simply compresses the information and saves space. We know that the Packers can be taken at −4, the Vikings at +4, and the over-under number is 42. If you bet a total, give the ticket writer the bet number of either team (in our example, 159 or 160) and specify either "over" or "under" the total. As with point-spread bets, the payout for totals is figured at odds of 10 to 11, which may be shown as −110.

Money Line

The money line is a bet on which team will win outright without factoring in a point spread. This wager is standard for baseball, hockey, and boxing (as we'll see below), but many sports books offer it for football and basketball as well.

The money line is not as easy to grasp intuitively as the point spread, but it's not really complicated once you're familiar with it. Let's continue with our football example:

Vikings +150
Packers −170

In money line betting, you don't put up $11 to win $10 as you do in point spreads or totals. The money line bet is composed of two odds— one for the favorite and one for the underdog. The favorite gets a minus sign before its number while the underdog gets a plus sign. To put it simply, the *minus* number tells you how many dollars—just add a decimal point two places from the right—you would have to *wager* to win $1. In our example, a $1.70 bet on the Packers will win $1. A *plus* tells you how much you will *win*—again add a decimal point two places from the right—if you bet $1. Viking bettors can put up $1 to win $1.50. Three important things to note:

1) When you win, you get your original bet back plus your winnings.

2) Bets should be in multiples of what you have to put up (in this case, multiples of $1.70 for the Packers and multiples of $1 for the Vikings).

3) You have to meet the minimum bet requirement of the book ($5 or $10), which means you couldn't actually bet only $1.70 or $1.

Remember that this is not a playing field leveled by the point spread. Risking less to win more may draw you to the underdog, but keep in mind that the underdog has to actually win the game in order for you to win money. Since the underdog is not expected to win, you get paid more on the off chance it does.

The House and the Money Line

Money lines are described in terms of the discrepancy between the two odds. At the very least the underdog will be a value of 10 less than the favorite. This is called a "dime line" or "10-cent line," because everything is based on a one-dollar wager. In our Packers-Vikings example, the difference is 20 and therefore is known as a 20-cent line. If the money line were Packers −170, Vikings +140, it would be a 30-cent line.

The house makes its money when the underdog wins. It's easy to see how this works. Imagine one bet is made on each side in a game where the favorite is −130 and the underdog is +120. With both bets, the house has $23 before the game starts: $13 from the favorite bet and $10 from the underdog bet. (We're assuming a $10 minimum.) If the favorite wins, the house pays out $23 (the $13 original bet and $10 in winnings) and doesn't earn anything. However, if the underdog wins, the house pays out $22 (the $10 original bet and $12 in winnings) and therefore makes a profit of $1. On the "dime line," the house edge is usually around 2%. The larger the difference in the odds, the more the casino's edge goes up.

BASEBALL: BAT BETS

In baseball, you will always see a money line. The money line posting might look like this:

| 901 | Atlanta Braves | Hampton | −130 |
| 902 | Colorado Rockies | Jennings | +120 |

To review what we've already covered in discussing football: the number preceding the team name is used to make the bet; the Rockies, being listed on the bottom, are the home team; they also happen to be the underdog because of the plus sign; the Braves are the favorite because of the minus sign. The Braves' odds are −130, meaning a $13 bet would win $10, for a return of $23. The Rockies' odds are +120, meaning a $10 bet would win $12, for a return of $22.

Since pitching is such a crucial element of baseball, each team's starting pitcher is listed. When making a baseball bet, unless you specify otherwise, you are betting team vs. team. You can specify that either or both listed pitch-

ers must start the game in order for your bet to stand. Since baseball odds rely on starting pitchers, any late pitching changes will change the odds and subsequently increase or decrease the payout on a winning ticket. However, if a pitcher that you listed didn't start, then the bet is refunded.

You can also bet total runs in baseball. Very often this will use the typical −110 odds that we saw in football, meaning an $11 bet wins $10. However, you'll also see instances where the odds differ for over and under. For example, in a game between the Yankees and Red Sox, the run total may be 9. Taking the over may be −120, but taking the under pays even money. So a $12 bet on the over earns you $10, while a $10 bet on the under earns you $10. When betting a baseball total, the game must go the full nine innings (or 8½ if the home team wins) and both listed pitchers must start the game. If either thing doesn't happen, all bets are refunded. All extra inning scores also count toward the total.

Some books also offer baseball run line bets that combine a point spread with a money line. For example:

| San Francisco Giants | Rueter | +1½ −160 |
| Arizona Diamondbacks | Johnson | −1½ +140 |

In order to make this wager, you choose a team and you get the listed number of runs added (or subtracted) from their score. But unlike football, this isn't a straight 110 wager for both sides. You have to put up a different amount depending on the team you wager on. If you want the underdog Giants with 1½ runs added to their score, you must put up $16 to win $10. If you want the favorite Diamondbacks with 1½ runs subtracted from their final score, you must put up $10 to win $14. You won't see this kind of line in isolation; it will always be offered with the standard, straight-up money line. When you add all the baseball bets together, the sports book posting can look daunting, so familiarize yourself with it before you bat your money away (see below).

Bet #	Team	Pitcher	Odds	Total	Run Line
1201	Cardinals	Morris	−120	9 +115	−1½ +140
1202	Pirates	Wells	+105	−135	+1½ −160

HOCKEY: THE PUCK LINE

Hockey games are wagered on in one of two ways. One method uses the straightforward money line as is typical in baseball. For example:

Islanders   +120
Red Wings   −140

If the Red Wings win, a $14 bet would win $10 and return $24 to the bettor. If the Islanders win, a $10 bet would win $12 and return $22 to the bettor.

The other method is like the run line discussed in baseball in which the game has both a point spread and a money line. Because of the frequency of ties in hockey, this method has become more common. It prevents the house from having to return all the money and it keeps bettors more interested.

Senators   −1½   −170
Capitals   +1½   +150

If the Senators win by at least two goals, a $17 bet would win $10 and return $27. If the Capitals lose by one goal, win, or tie, a $10 bet would win $15 and return $25. In other words, the betting outcomes are determined by the final score as adjusted by the point spread and the payoffs are determined by the money line. Why not just a point spread? Since hockey games are very close-scoring, a half-goal can make a big difference and therefore require a money line adjustment.

BASKETBALL: POINT SPREADS AND TOTALS

Basketball uses a point spread and totals in the same manner that football does. So you'll see a line like the following:

Utah Jazz   −3½   198
New York Knicks

The Jazz are 3½-point favorites, and bettors can take either the Jazz at −3½ or the Knicks at +3½. As usual, the bettor must put up 11 to win 10. There will be no ties because this is a half-point line. The total of 198 can be bet over or under at the typical 11 to 10 odds (our pal, −110).

OTHER SPORTS

Betting on boxing is done using a money line in which you lay or take odds. In the example that follows, a bettor would lay $200 to win

$100 on Holyfield or a bettor would take $100 to win $180 on Lewis.

Bet Number	Boxer	Odds
2001	Lennox Lewis	+180
2002	Evander Holyfield	−200

Boxing matches will often give money line proposition bets on the possibility of a knock-out or number of rounds.

You can also bet on major golf tournaments. This is typically done by betting one golfer against another using a money line. The winner between the two players is the one with the highest tournament finish.

Many casinos will give you odds on NASCAR races, as well as take bets on which drivers will win their respective championships. You'll even find opportunities to wager on tennis and world soccer. It depends on the expertise of the book. Most of these bets use the money line, with which you are now familiar. You can decipher any bets that are posted—but that doesn't mean you know if they're good bets or not. For that, you must rely on your sports sense and handicapping skills.

THE EXOTIC BETS
Parlays

A *parlay* is a popular betting option in which several bets—usually two to seven—are combined into a single wager. The parlay bet generally includes any combination of team bets ("sides") or totals and can usually cross different sports. The more bets you combine, the greater the payoff if you win. Of course, you have to win all the bets in order to win the parlay.

Let's say you like the Giants, Bears, and Buccaneers to win with the point spread and the over bet in the Chiefs-Seahawks game. You can turn all four bets into a four-team parlay, but if any one of the bets loses, you lose the parlay. Any entry that results in a tie reduces the parlay one team. For example, your four-bet parlay would become a three-bet parlay with the new odds applying to the wager that was originally made.

The appeal of parlays is the potential for a big payoff on a small wager. However, you pay for the excitement of a big return with a heavy house edge. Look at the table on the next page for an example of typical parlay payoffs and the

House Edges on Parlays

Parlayed Wagers	Typical Casino Payoff	Probability of Winning Parlay	True Odds	House Edge
2 for 2	13–5	$1/4$	3–1	10.0%
3 for 3	6–1	$1/8$	7–1	12.5%
4 for 4	11–1	$1/16$	15–1	25.0%
5 for 5	22–1	$1/32$	31–1	28.1%
6 for 6	44–1	$1/64$	63–1	29.7%
7 for 7	90–1	$1/128$	127–1	28.9%

house edge associated with them. Then check out the sidebar on page 208 to see how these numbers were calculated.

Teasers

Teasers are parlays in which you're allowed to adjust the line a certain number of points to your advantage. This means you can add points to the underdog or subtract points from the favorite. Typically, Las Vegas sports books offer 6-, 6½-, or 7-point teasers.

Suppose the 49ers are 7-point favorites over the Jets. You can "tease" this line by adding 6 points to the line for the Jets and make them get 13 points. Or you can tease the line by subtracting 6 points from the points the 49ers are giving and thus make them give only 1 point. In another line, a four-point favorite can be turned into a two-point underdog. You must play at least two teams when you create your own teaser parlay.

While your probability of winning a game is increased, the payoff odds are lessened compared to a regular parlay. A two-team, 6-point teaser could typically pay 10–11. Preprinted teaser cards usually require at least three bets. Then there's the "super teaser" in which you can move a line by 10 points … sheesh!

Most sports books print up their own parlay and teaser cards that are simple to fill out and are very enticing. Make sure you read the instructions carefully; you are committed to the spreads and totals printed on the card if you make the bet. Generally the minimum wager is $2 on a parlay. Also, there are no ties on preprinted parlay and teaser cards because all the spreads and totals have half points. You may find some cards in which ties win, but the payoff odds will be reduced to compensate for that boon. Also, the preprinted parlay card odds usu-

ally have higher paybacks than a parlay you create on your own—that's because no ties can occur and you're giving up the flexibility of seeing if the lines move and creating your own opportunities.

Parlay and teaser cards are part of the party atmosphere of the sports books, where buddies drink beers and go for the gusto. That's fine if you only pay a small amount for that kind of fun. Sometimes casinos will promote $20 parlay cards with T-shirts and free beers, but if you look at the odds you'll quickly realize who's paying for the "freebies." Parlay and teaser odds will vary from casino to casino and if you're drawn to this type of atmosphere and action you may as well get the best deal, but you can't really get a *good* deal.

Futures

Futures are bets on who will win a future event such as the Super Bowl, the World Series, or the NHL Stanley Cup. Payoff odds are provided for every team. For instance, just minutes after this year's Super Bowl, the casino oddsmakers posted betting lines for next year's gridiron championship. The house builds in a large edge to these far-flung wagers, but these bets can provide you up to a year's entertainment for a small investment, if you are willing to have the house hold your money for a long time. The payoff odds will change for future bets based on team performances, but you lock in at the odds that existed when you made the bet.

Propositions

Proposition bets ("props") are unique bets that are developed for specific events. The center of the proposition bet universe is the Super Bowl. A small sampling of possible Super Bowl bets:

INSIDE THE NUMBERS

Assuming that each wager has a 50–50 chance of succeeding, the probability of picking one wager correctly is ½. To calculate the probability of picking multiple wagers correctly we multiply. So the chance of correctly parlaying two wagers would be ½ × ½ = ¼. Over the long haul, we'll lose the wager three times for every one time we win it. (Thus the fair odds of 3–1.) Knowing this, we can calculate the house edge based on a $5 wager. We'll use $5 since we're using a casino payoff of 13–5. Here's how the edge is calculated:

$$\text{Expectation} = [¼ × (+13)] + [¾ × (-5)] = -\tfrac{2}{4} = -0.5$$
$$\text{E per \$1 bet} = \tfrac{-0.5}{5} = -0.10$$
$$\text{House edge} = 10\%$$

Let's look at the six-team parlay. The true probability of hitting this is ½ × ½ × ½ × ½ × ½ × ½ = ¹⁄₆₄. We'll lose 63 times for every one time we win. Based on a casino payoff of 44–1, the house edge for a $1 bet is figured as follows:

$$E = [\tfrac{1}{64} × (+44)] + [\tfrac{63}{64} × (-1)] = -\tfrac{19}{64} = -0.297$$
$$\text{House edge} = 29.7\%$$

The more bets you parlay, the more you can win, but, naturally, the steeper the house advantage.

Who will score the first touchdown? Who will kick the longest field goal? How many catches will Joe Receiver have? Will Halfback X or Halfback Y have more rushing yards? Et cetera, et cetera, ad nauseum.

The sports book will display odds or money line bets for all the various propositions they offer; some sports books are more exhaustive in their offerings than others. You generally don't receive the odds you should on these bets, and they are often posted to draw in the gullible tourists—a group you'd rather not be associated with.

....
SPORTS BETTING STRATEGY AND SMARTS

UNDERSTANDING THE LINE
The line for a football or basketball game is created by professional oddsmakers or *linemakers*. Despite what rookie bettors may believe, the point spread is not an oddsmaker's prediction of how much the favorite will win by. It reflects the comparative value of the two teams and—just as important—the public's perception of the value of the teams. The oddsmakers have plenty of analysis tools at their disposal including sophisticated computer-generated power rankings. They also factor in injuries,

weather, scheduling, and many other variables.

If you compare final results to the line, you'll see that many fall close to the predicted spread, but very often there are gigantic differences. What's more amazing than the linemakers' ability to nail a game's final score within a few points is the ability of linemakers to gauge the public's perceptions so well that the line becomes a 50–50 proposition for the consumer.

Accuracy is not a badge of honor for bookmakers; balanced action is their goal. If a line is 5 points and the favorite loses by 10, it doesn't mean that the line was a failure. The only measure of success for a line is whether or not it divides the public's betting action. The linemakers want to create a situation where bettors can equally justify betting on either side.

A casino wants to have an equal amount of money wagered on each side of a sporting event. As shown in the discussion of the vig in the sidebar on page 202, the house profits by equal action on both sides. They pay out the winners, keep the losing wagers, and hold on to the vig.

When a line moves up or down by a few points or by a half-point, it's not because the bookmakers had a sudden insight into how the final score will look (except perhaps in response to an injury). The line moves are based on the action (the betting) on the game and the casino's attempt to maintain equilibrium on both sides. When a line moves, it's money that nudges it. If $4,000 is wagered on Team X and $2,000 on Team Y, it's time to change the line. So, strangely, the line doesn't necessarily have anything to do with the skills of the teams involved. The betting population votes on the line with their money—whether they're right or wrong is immaterial as long as half the population disagrees with the other half.

An opportunity that savvy bettors often seek is called *middling*. The object of middling is to find lines at different casinos that differ by at least 1½ points. You bet both sides of the contest in the hope that the final score or final total is in between the different lines you bet. In that way, you win both bets even though they were on opposite sides. Here's an example of this rare but nifty maneuver. At one casino, you take the favorite Pittsburgh Steelers (–5½) against the Cleveland Browns. Then at another casino you find the Browns are getting 7 points. At that sports book, you take the Browns (+7). Let's say you bet $110 on each game. You may win just one bet, in which case you're down $10. If Cleveland loses by exactly seven points, you win $100. But the fruition of this middling opportunity is when the game has exactly a six point difference: You win both bets and end up ahead $200. Particularly in basketball you may have the luck to find a point total situation where the difference gives you a 2-point zone of winning both bets.

You don't always have to find two different casinos for a middling opportunity to arise. If you wager early in the week, the line may move up or down later in the week and you can place another bet at the same casino with a different line. Of course, you wouldn't know for sure that the line was going to move when you make your first wager. Middles are attractive because of the low risk/high return nature, but the middle isn't necessarily going to be hit just because it exists. It's also hard to middle these days, because sports books are more sophisticated and more uniform in their offerings.

THE CASUAL BETTOR VS. THE SERIOUS HANDICAPPER

What makes sports betting so inviting and intriguing is that each bet has its own personal-ity—you're not a slave to the preset rules of chance that determine other casino games. From a multitude of bets, you can select the one that seems right to you.

A very small bet can transform a meaningless game into a titanic struggle that will hold you riveted. If you get three hours of gambling excitement from a $10 bet, then that's very good value. It's certainly fun to put a little action on your favorite team, one that you root for anyway. That's one perfectly legitimate mind-set for the casual sports bettor. If it's an occasional and frugal recreational lark, then that's fine. However, the mind-set where you have to bet on a game—or will bet on *any* game—in order to make it "interesting" can be dangerous.

If you're betting serious money, you better get serious about your game selection and money management. Successful sports bettors who make money never bet on a game just for the hell of it.

Pros relentlessly pursue their own handicapping and have no loyalty. Good sports bettors have access to all the info, have some aptitude for number play (as you may have noticed from the rundown of the bets), and put in the time as if it were a job. They try to find the weak spots and the one or two key opportunities on a weekend where there may be 100 games being played. To gain the edge, sports betting pros do research and specialize. From injury updates and game-day weather reports to detailed analysis of trends, the Internet has been the handicapper's best friend. The linemaker uses handicapping to gauge a way in which to have the public bet evenly; the handicapper/bettor wants to perfectly gauge the outcome of a game, because he knows that when there's a discrepancy between the two, that's when he might have a good bet on his hands.

Be aware that most of the available information, particularly on popular teams, is already reflected in the line. It's similar to the stock market: Once you read the hot info in the newspaper, the market has probably already incorporated it into the stock's price. A winning sports bettor bets only the games that he thinks he has an advantage on through insight or knowledge. No sentimentality, no need for a "bet buzz," or any other flimsy approaches.

BETTING STRATEGY

Unfortunately, there are no cut-and-dried strategic tips that will improve your odds as a sports bettor. Unlike all other casino games (except poker), outcomes in sporting events are not ruled by mathematical certainties. Sports are fluid, dynamic, and unpredictable—a mix of skill, chemistry, psychology, and luck. So the only way to really succeed at sports betting is to know your sport very well and know when to bet. It's beyond the scope of this book to expound on how to achieve that state of expertise. But here are some strategies the casual bettor might want to consider.

- You don't have to play every game. In fact, you shouldn't want to play the majority of them. You should be able to justify why you think your team will win or cover.
- Be aware of key injuries, weather conditions, long road trips, and other variables. Yes, be aware, but also realize that these factors are almost always reflected in the line.
- Public perception and betting dollars can create lines that work to the handicapper's advantage. Point spreads tend to favor underdog bettors, since most people like to bet on favorites. Also, very often a popular or successful team, such as the Green Bay Packers or the Chicago Bulls (in the Jordan days), will have its high expectations translate into an overinflated line.
- Most of the pundits—the newspaper writers, the radio and television personalities, the pregame analysts—are not to be relied on for handicapping. Many just follow their hearts and the ones who don't are offering information that most assuredly has already been incorporated into the betting lines. Don't be razzle-dazzled by historical trends. It's not difficult to generate esoteric statistics to validate any pick: "Team X is 8–2–2 against the spread on Monday games played on artificial turf after two consecutive home victories." If you don't have a feel for the teams involved, don't be impressed by number-crunching.
- Specialize as much as you can. Being an all-around sports trivia buff is great, but if you want success as a serious bettor, you have to go deeper. Successful bettors may know one college football or basketball conference like their own families. The more specialized and less mainstream your focus, the more likely you'll find instances where you know more than the betting public and perhaps even the linemaker. For instance, in college basketball you may get an edge when American University is playing North Carolina Wilmington rather than when Duke plays Kentucky.

- Even the best sports gamblers lose very often. Sports are unpredictable and you can't know every factor or random variable. The serious gambler just needs to be slightly over 50 percent. He isn't attempting to turn into Nostradamus—he's looking to cash in on spreads or odds that seem inaccurate, seizing on oddsmaker errors or the ignorance of the general public.
- Don't chase your losing bets. This is very common in sports betting because you want to make up for picks that you thought were locks but that didn't go your way. You lost some money on college football games on Saturday and now you're chasing pro games. This is a sure way to turn little losses into big losses.
- Stay away from the exotic bets: the parlays, the teasers, the futures. Handicappers stick to the "straight" bets, which are the ones made on a team (using the point spread or the money line) or on a total. There are no sure things in sports and it's hard enough to win one game without having to worry about linking a few together.
- Don't believe the tip sheets and 900-numbers. First of all, you need up-to-date information; don't buy books and tout sheets printed months in advance. Second, while a few are honest, many just flat-out lie. If they really had the winning percentages they publish, they wouldn't be selling their advice. They'd be watching telecasts of sporting events on the 20 jumbo TV screens in their mansions. The only way they're making money is off you. Gambling writer and radio personality Larry Grossman has a standing offer where he'll pay 2 to 1 (up to a million dollars) on money put up by someone who can actually go 75 percent or better on 100 games over a football season. No one has taken him up on it. Mort Olshan, founder and publisher of the *Gold Sheet* (a sports tout sheet since 1957), has never heard of anyone

ever hitting over 70 percent for a full season for all his time in the business.

• Go line shopping. That is, compare sports books and find the one that has the best line on the game you wish to bet. Lines have become very stable in this modern computer and communications age, but you can still find some variation. It's worth checking out—use the phone or Internet if you can. If you want to bet on the Knicks and one book has them at −3 while another has them at −4, it doesn't take Jimmy the Greek to figure out where you want to make the bet. If you don't like the facilities at the casino that has the best line, you can place your bet there and go watch the game somewhere more cushy. (But don't forget to return to the original book to cash in your winnings!)

• Lines are different throughout the country. For example, Denver fans may face an inflated point line on their Broncos because the bookies know that fans bet with their hearts. Of course, this would matter only if you made illegal bets with a bookie outside Nevada and we know only millions of Americans perpetrate such a heinous crime.

THE ESSENTIALS FOR BETTING SPORTS LIKE A GENIUS

• Learn the various basic bets: the point spread, totals, the money line.
• The house has a 4.5% advantage on a standard point-spread bet.
• You must win 52.4% of your point-spread bets in order to come out ahead.
• Don't lose your betting ticket! If you can't find it, you can't collect on it.
• A sensible sports wager can give the casual bettor good gambling value over the course of a sporting event.
• If you want to become a serious sports handicapper, prepare to become a full-time junkie hooked on sports data, gossip, and analysis. In fact, if you had the temperament to be a serious sports bettor, you wouldn't be reading this right now, you'd be watching the game—any game.
• Don't rely on 900-numbers for your sports betting tips. You're more likely to come out ahead by putting that money toward your own hunches.
• Sports betting can be a fun recreation, a tough business, and a lousy addiction.

OFF TO THE RACES

The racetrack used to be the nexus of activity for inveterate gamblers and sharp handicappers. Nowadays horse racing has lost much of its drawing power with a younger generation turning toward lotteries, casinos, and sports betting for their thrills. In fact, some racing facilities have had to close their doors and others have been able to stay open only by augmenting income with—ironically enough—slot machines. These racetracks now have to suffer the ignominy of being referred to as "racinos."

Despite the general air of doom and gloom about horse racing, there's still plenty of money being placed on the ponies. Most Nevada casinos have combination race and sports books (or a separate race book) where you can wager on the sport of kings. They feature simulcast coverage of racetracks across America and all the wagering options of an OTB (Off-Track Betting) parlor. Casinos outside Nevada, particularly in Atlantic City and Connecticut, offer race books without sports betting (since it isn't legal). Many of these books feature comfortable seating, large-screen TVs, personal wagering terminals, and other amenities. If you've been to the racetrack or to the OTB parlor, you'll feel right at home at most any race book.

For those with no knowledge of horse racing, I can only provide the briefest flirtation with its basic workings and its many complexities. I will not attempt to do justice to its full vocabulary or nuances. You'll have to decide if you want to go further. If you're intrigued, check out Appendix D for more on the basics of horse racing and the sublime science of handicapping.

A BRIEF PRIMER ON HORSE RACING

When you picture a jockey riding astride a galloping horse, you're picturing him on a *thoroughbred*. Thoroughbreds are bred for speed and endurance. Those are the horses that run the famous Triple Crown races: the Kentucky Derby, Preakness, and Belmont Stakes. The sport of harness racing is very different from thoroughbred racing. In harness racing, a *standardbred*, bred for strength and gait, pulls a driver in a light, two-wheeled cart called a *sulky*. Since thoroughbred racing is much more popular than harness racing in America, it will be the focus of our discussion.

Most tracks are one-mile ovals on which the furlong (one-eighth of a mile) is the basic unit of measurement. Most races are six furlongs long. There are usually nine races a day at a thoroughbred racetrack. Each race has certain conditions—sex, age, winnings, etc.—that a horse must meet to qualify for the race. In order to acquaint yourself with the horses and the race conditions, you need to get the *Daily Racing Form* or an official program from the track. The *Daily Racing Form*, a newspaper that is considered horse racing's bible, is released regionally and offers endless info on the races being run and each horse's performance history.

WAGERING: "I'VE GOT THE HORSE RIGHT HERE"

Once you have a racing form in your hand, you may want to rush up to a window and place a bet. Maybe you like a horse's adorable name or the colors that the jockey is wearing. I wouldn't recommend using those as your criteria, but serious money has been squandered on less. To place a bet, the least you need to know is: the track name, the race number, the dollar amount, the type of bet, and the program number of the horse you want (that's easier than the horse's name).

For example: "I'd like $2 on number 4 to place in the seventh at Santa Anita." The clerk will punch out the ticket and (in this example) you pay $2. Be sure to check your ticket. Once you leave the counter, your bet cannot be changed.

Most race books and simulcast centers have multiple TV monitors where you can watch the race you bet on. Also, all the results are usually displayed on tote boards. Make sure to keep your ticket until the race results have been declared official. If you win, take the ticket to a teller, who will give you your winnings.

Here's a rundown of some of the betting possibilities (the most common bets, called straight wagers, are win, place, and show):
• Win: You win only if your horse finishes first.
• Place: You win if your horse finishes first or second.
• Show: You win if your horse finishes first, second, or third.
• Daily double: You win if you select the winning horses in two consecutive designated races (usually the first and second races or the fifth and sixth).
• Exacta or perfecta: You win if you select a race's first two finishers in *exact* order.
• Quinella: You win if you select a race's first two finishers in *any* order.
• Trifecta: You win if you select a race's first three finishers in *exact* order.
• Superfecta: You win if you select a race's first four finishers in *exact* order.
• Pick 6 or pick 9: You win if you select the winners of six or nine designated races. (Sure, no problem!)

THE ODDS, PAYOFFS, AND THE WAGERING SYSTEM

When you're betting at a race book, your winning wagers are paid off on the odds that are posted at the track your race is being run at. You are part of the betting pool at that track and paid off according to its odds. Even though the minimum bet is usually $2, the odds quoted are based on a $1 bet. Let's say that the odds for Horse #4 are 10–1; if the horse wins you receive $10 for every $1 bet. The final payoff is posted after the race and is based on a $2 bet. Below is an example of posted payoffs.

	Horse #	Win	Place	Show
1st place	3	5.60	3.80	3.00
2nd place	7		9.20	5.40
3rd place	1			2.60

These payoffs include the initial $2 wager. You can calculate your winnings if you bet more than $2. For example, if you bet $8 on Horse #7 to place, you would multiply the result by 4 (since $2 × 4 = $8) and get $36.80 ($9.20 × 4).

The system used for betting at racetracks worldwide is known as *pari-mutuel betting*. The racetrack places the same kind of bets into specific accounts or pools; for example, win, place, or show. The money in the win pool is paid only to those people with a successful win ticket. Similarly, the money in the place pool will be divided between two groups of successful ticket holders—those who made place bets on either of the two horses that came in first and second.

You aren't betting against the track or "house"; you are betting against the other bettors. The odds are determined by the amount of money bet on each horse and not by the racetrack. When you make a wager in racing, you affect the odds. The more money bet on a horse, the lower that horse's odds become. But how are those odds arrived at before the betting action kicks in? The morning-line maker sets the odds for all the day's starters based on their class, the projected pace, and how well they fit the conditions of the race.

Unlike lotteries, most table games, and slot machines, racing has no preconceived set of odds or built-in mathematical advantage that make long-term winning an impossibility. In pari-mutuel wagering the player is pitted against his fellow player. Simply put, if you can beat the guys next to you, you win. The thrill of betting the horses is outsmarting the rest of the betting public. In this way, a gifted handicapper feels like he might come out ahead.

Yet, the bettor doesn't just have to stay ahead of his fellow bettors—he must overcome a nearly insurmountable house edge of 18 to 22 percent. Like sports betting, horse racing does not rely on random events to determine a winner. So where does this outrageous disadvantage come from? Thanks to the pari-mutuel system of betting, it gets skimmed right off the top. The "house/track" takes its cut for providing its services. Racetracks are allowed by the state in which they operate to take a certain percentage of every dollar wagered before paying winning bets. The percentage taken varies from bet to bet and is often higher for exotic bets. The track uses the money for operating expenses and purses rewarding the owners and jockeys of the winning horses. Bettors also lose money on the rounding down of payoffs to the nearest 10¢, a practice known as "breakage." It can be an exercise in futility to buck the track edge.

In the past, Nevada race books weren't part of the pari-mutuel system and accepted bets under their own bookmaking. The money didn't become part of a pari-mutuel pool, but did pay what the horses paid at the track. This led to opportunities for big wins and losses by the betting public and the casino. Unfortunately, almost all race books are now part of the pari-mutuel system and are therefore agents of the 20% grind.

HANDICAPPING

The mission in horse betting is simple: Bet on horses whose actual chances of winning (determined through your own handicapping judgment) are higher than the odds reflected on the tote board. These essential finds are called "overlays." For example, if your handicapping says that a horse has roughly a one in five (20 percent) chance of winning, and the tote board reveals that your hero is being offered at 8–1 (12.5 percent), a wager is in order. Value can be anywhere; it can come in the form of 6–5 or 20–1. It's all based on the probability of your horse winning in relation to the corresponding odds offered by the tote board. After all, wouldn't you take a 6–5 return on a coin flip (which is an even-money proposition)? You wouldn't win every event, but long-term profits would ensue.

Although the objective of finding overlays is clear-cut, its execution is no easy matter. The art and science of horse race wagering is in the handicapping of the races. This entails interpreting racehorses' past performances, or *form*, in order to predict the outcome of the race. It is a challenging, intriguing pursuit—much like solving a puzzle. You can analyze and ponder a horse's overall form or be selective and focus on key elements. Just a brief list of factors: the horse's trainer, the jockey, the class, the pace of the course, and standardized speed figures. Because horse race betting is not a game of chance, the more you know, the better chance you have of making money.

Despite the bleak prospects for being a long-term winner, many souls dedicate their minds, spirits, and dollars to mastering the ponies. Handicappers constantly work to assign their own probabilities to a horse's chances. The material that must be absorbed is formidable: knowing if a horse is a good sprinter or better at long distances, if it runs well on dirt or grass, its breeding, conditioning, speed ratings, and more. Handicappers visualize how the race will develop, conjuring up the distinct style and habits of each entrant.

Horse betting can become quite a passion, but being a consistent winner is a quixotic pursuit. There are racetrack sages who know the genealogy of seemingly every equine on earth, who can quote the *Daily Racing Form* chapter and verse, and who can describe the most minute specifications of every racetrack on the continent. Yet nary a one of them can come up with a way to vanquish the 20% bite taken out of their winnings.

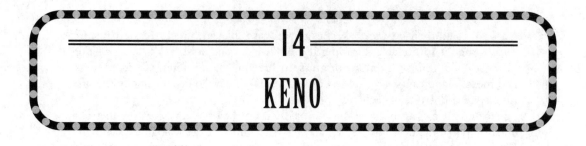

14

KENO

Keno, like the lottery, is a game of pure luck. If you're familiar with state lotteries, you already have most of the information you need to play keno. In both cases you pick numbers and hope that those numbers will be picked in a drawing. In both cases probability says you won't win—at least not a really big payoff, at least not in this lifetime. One important difference between the two is that keno pays more prizes than the lottery and you have more choices in how to play, so keno is perhaps the wiser of two unwise temptations.

Like many other easy games of luck, keno gives the casino an enormous house advantage. So even if you do win in keno, the casino makes sure you won't be paid in proportion to the risk taken; the house edge runs from 25 to 40 percent. (Casinos justify this outrageous advantage by claiming that the overhead for keno is the highest for any casino game. This may be just a case of the casino getting away with whatever it can.) If you want to make the house fight for your money this is probably not the game to play. It might be said that "keno" stands for Know Enough Not to bet this One. Now that may be a slight exaggeration—you may actually have good reason to choose to play this game.

Keno does hold a certain appeal in some situations. The pace of the game is very slow—each game takes about five to ten minutes. (Compare this to slot machines, where bets are made every 6 seconds or leisurely roulette, where wagers are made every two minutes.) So you can play a few games while you relax over your (hopefully complimentary) breakfast, lunch, or dinner. Keno is also fairly inexpensive to play. The minimum bet is usually $1 or $2;

most other games have $5 minimums. More than anything else, the appeal of keno is the fantasy of the big payoff for a relatively small investment.

Another perk is that keno has its own special lounge area where you can lean back and enjoy the complimentary drinks as you watch the monitor for the winning numbers. Most casinos will let you play up to 999 games in advance if you really want to—so you can be in the action even when you are asleep. So who's the wiser gambler: the savvy craps player who whittles the house edge down to less than 1%, but has a rough day and loses $600 in 4 hours; or the keno player who throws away $25 for a day's amusement?

Basically, keno is a paradox. Its steep house edge makes it one of the biggest "sucker" bets in the casino. Yet with moderate play, you can get a lot of entertainment from keno without losing big.

HOW KENO IS PLAYED

THE SCENE

Keno is unique in that you can play almost anywhere. Most casinos even broadcast the games on the televisions in their hotel rooms. In the keno lounge, at most dining facilities, and at various other places in the casino, you'll find a stash of keno tickets and the requisite crayons with which to mark them. In close proximity, there should be keno brochures, outlining the specific payouts and any specials the casinos may have. Keno *boards* (television monitors) are also located throughout the casino. You can keep track of the winning numbers in your games from just about wherever you happen to be, even if it's at a gaming table or slot machine. The casino will usually provide *keno runners*, who make playing the game even less taxing. These employees will take your ticket and money and make your bets for you while you eat, play another game, or just sit back and relax. A few caveats though: There is no guarantee that the runners will be at the keno window in time for you to be in a specific game (keno runners are usually taken last at the window) or that they will register your ticket exactly as you have indicated. And, of course, if you avail yourself of their services, you should tip them, even when you lose.

THE ACTION

A keno ticket, called a *blank*, has 80 numbers separated into two halves—the top half has numbers 1–40 and the bottom has 41–80. Let's see what to do with them.

The basic game is extraordinarily simple: The computer randomly picks 20 numbers from 1 to 80. (Some keno lounges still use numbered ping-pong balls blown around in a hopper. Air forces one ball at a time up a goose neck, and a casino employee announces each arrival. These casinos will still display the winning numbers on monitors throughout the property, so there is not much practical difference for the player.) You, as the player, try to guess what some of those numbers—also called *spots*—will be. You win varying amounts of money based on how many of your numbers appear among the 20 drawn.

The most basic keno game is a *straight* ticket, in which you select one to fifteen numbers. The payoff schedule for the number of spots you play will be listed in the keno brochure. The more numbers you mark on your keno ticket, the more numbers you have to *catch* to win anything, although you don't need to catch them all to win some money. For example, on a 6-spot (a ticket where you are trying to catch six numbers) you need to catch three numbers to break even. On a 15-spot you usually need six numbers to win money. Most casinos offer a special 20-spot game. With its "odd" payoff schedule the 20-spot gives you an opportunity to win if you catch no numbers, and win more money if just one of your numbers comes up

than if six of them do. (Of course, this is not odd at all, since it's all based on probability rules, but more on that a little later.)

Don't be fooled: The myriad variations offered by the casino—*way* tickets, *combination* tickets, *king* numbers—are just different ways to play more games on one ticket. They present no advantage (or disadvantage) to the player, except that, as is explained shortly, you may be able to play each game for less money.

Let's go through a few examples that illustrate what we're discussing.

Straight Tickets

Assume you want to choose six numbers to play; let's say 4, 5, 8, 25, 26, and 45. On the keno ticket, indicate the numbers you want by marking an "X" over them with your crayon. On the top right of the ticket there will be space to write the number of games in which you want to play these numbers, how much money you want to play on each set of numbers or *way*, and the total price of the ticket. On a straight ticket, you should also write the number of spots you're playing in the space that says "mark the ways played" or similar instruction. In our example here, you would write "6." (See ticket #1 on page 220.)

A typical casino payout for a 6-spot (found in the keno brochure) might say something like this:

MARK AN "X" OVER ANY SIX NUMBERS

CATCH	BET $1.00	BET $2.00
3	$1.00	$2.00
4	$5.00	$10.00
5	$75.00	$150.00
6	$2,000.00	$4,000.00

You'll notice there is no mathematical advantage to wagering more than the $1 minimum. In most cases, you are just getting paid double the $1 payout for risking twice as much money (or triple the payout if you bet $3, etc.). However, if you were to play (and in the unlikely event, catch) 14 or 15 spots, the jackpot payouts will probably not be double—they very well might be the same for a wager of $1 as for $2. It works out this way because the house usually has an upper limit of how much it will pay per game to all players regardless of

INSIDE THE NUMBERS

While you may just be hoping your children's birthdays pop up on the keno boards, actually figuring out if they will is not child's play. Probabilities for keno games are figured out using combinatorics—the branch of mathematics that deals with calculating combinations. I won't go into all the details here, but the gist of the calculations has to do with the number of different ways you can arrange a portion of a larger group of items.

Let's say you are having a dinner party with 12 guests and you want to know how to seat them. First you need to figure out how many people you want at each table (3 tables of 4, 4 of 3, 2 of 6, 6 of 2, or 1 of 12). Then you would decide whom you want at each table. Combinatorics would be used to figure out all the possibilities of table arrangements just as it is used to figure out the odds of keno, given the numbers you want to catch.

Once combinatorics has been used to figure the probabilities, the next thing to look at is the expected return (ER). The ER is calculated as follows:

ER = payoff × probability

Now that we have the ER, we can use it to find the numbers we are really interested in—the expectation (E). Expectation tells us how much we can expect to win or lose over the long run with a given bet. We can get the house edge from the E.

Let's see how the numbers shake out for a one-dollar 5-spot bet.

Winning Spots	Payoff	Probability	Expected Return
3	$1	0.0839	0.0839
4	$11	0.0121	0.1331
5	$750	0.000645	0.4838
		Total ER:	0.7008

E = Total ER – amount bet: 0.7008 – 1 = –0.2992
House edge = 29.92%

This boils down to an expected loss of nearly 30¢ for each dollar you bet on this ticket. On average, you would have to play 1,550 games (1/0.000645, where 0.000645 is the probability of catching 5 spots) in order to get the "big" prize here—$750. At a dollar a ticket you'll be spending $1,550 to finally snag $750.

Kind of makes you want to put the emphasis on the last part of the word: keNO.

the amount wagered. The *aggregate limit* may range from $100,000 to $1 million. Always check the casino's specific keno brochure carefully before wagering. If you are playing for the impossible payout (and who isn't?) you shouldn't shortchange yourself by betting an amount that can't be paid out in full. The house does enough shortchanging in keno—no need to help them along.

One more thing to keep in mind about payout listings: This is an A *for* B scenario (not A *to* B). Let's say you catch four of your six numbers. You paid your one dollar when you brought the ticket to the keno window, and now you are back to collect. The cashier at the window will give you $5 (not $6)—in reality you are winning just four dollars.

Now I know $2,000 seems like a lot of money for risking just $1 and guessing 6 out of 20 numbers. But as we'll see in the Strategy and Smarts section, the chances of this happening are not only slim, the payout is not proportionate to the true odds. The house advantage here is nearly 30 percent, one of the highest you'll find at a casino.

Back to our 6-spot. After checking the payout schedule and marking your ticket, take the ticket to the keno window (or flag down a runner to do it for you). A *keno writer* will register your wagers, make a computerized copy, and give you a receipt. Now all you have to do is sit back and check out the monitors for your lucky numbers to appear. In most casinos, games run continuously, so watch the monitor for the number of your game—the ticket you get back from the window will have the game number on it. Hold on to your receipt and don't space out too much, because in many casinos you'll need to cash in your tickets right away. (This may not apply if you're playing multiple games in advance. Check the rules where you play.) You can also use that receipt (or *duplicate* ticket) as an original in the next game if you want. Just take it up to the window or give it to a runner like you did with the first ticket you marked up.

Variations on the Straight Ticket: Ways, Combinations, and Kings

The purpose of all the ticket variations is simply to make it easier (theoretically) and more exciting (theoretically) for you to wager more money on more numbers. You would have the same odds, the same chance to win, and the same payouts if you played one 4-way ticket as if you picked the same numbers on four 1-way (straight) tickets. The different types of tickets are merely terminology to denote different options for making more than one bet on one ticket. In fact, a "way ticket" at one casino might be called a "combination ticket" at another. It really doesn't matter as long as you know you are betting the way (!) you want to.

Ways: You are playing a way ticket if you use one ticket to mark two or more sets of numbers you want to wager on. Let's say you wanted to play three 3-spot tickets. One group: 4, 5, and 8; a second group: 25, 26, and 45; and a third group: 12, 13, 17. On a single ticket, you would "X" out those numbers individually and then circle each of the three groups of three. To mark the number of ways played, you would write "3/3," meaning you are betting on three sets of three numbers each, or, in keno lingo— "3-way-3"—three ways to make a 3-spot. (See ticket #2 on page 220.)

In many casinos, when you are playing three or more ways you can get a discount on the price per "way"; you may be able to play for 50¢ or 25¢ per bet rather than $1. Of course, your winnings will be half or a quarter of those listed on the payout schedule for $1 bets.

Combinations: Combinations are just that. You are playing a combination ticket when you combine the groups that were previously treated separately on a way ticket. Building on the example from the way ticket, you could place seven bets on that ticket simply by including the additional notations "3/6" and "1/9." This indicates that in addition to the three original 3-spot bets, you are combining the groups in all possible ways to make three different 6-spot bets and one 9-spot bet. This ticket will cost $7 at the $1/way rate (see ticket #3 on page 220).

The individual groups do not all have to have the same amount of numbers in them as this example does. Be aware that if you were to mark one ticket with a group of four numbers and a group of five numbers and you played them only separately (1/4 and 1/5, *not* 1/9) and you miraculously caught all nine numbers, you would be paid off only at the 4-spot and 5-spot rates, not the 9-spot rate, and you would definitely be, er, … seeing spots. (Such regret is very unlikely—the chance of catching all nine is about 1 in 1.38 million.)

Kings: King numbers are single numbers (or "groups" of one) that are used in combination with other groupings. Using the same numbers from previous examples, let's "X" out and then circle 52 as our king number. That can now combine with every other combination we have already created. So in the proper location we would write: "3/4, 3/7, 1/10" and we would have to hand over $7 to play this ticket. You could also play "3/6" and "1/9" on this same ticket, which would then cost an additional $4. Play the ticket five times in a row and you are shelling out $55. (See ticket #4 on page 220.) Keno stops being a cheap diversion.

Things start to get really dizzying when you employ more than one king number. There are still other silly/fun ways to play keno including "top or bottom" (choose either the top 40 numbers or the bottom 40; if 13 of the 20 numbers chosen fall on your half, you win); "left or right" (same concept, different divisions); and "edges" (all the numbers around the edge of the ticket are marked, the amount you have to

SAMPLE KENO TICKETS

Ticket #1

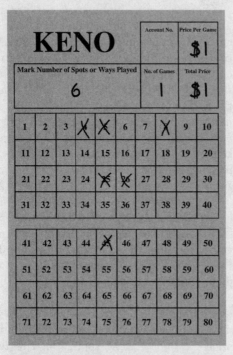

Ticket #2

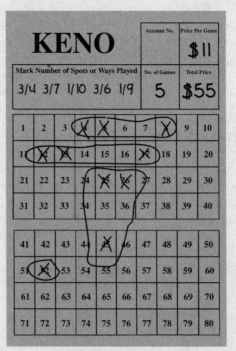

Ticket #3

Ticket #4

Ticket #5

KENO	Account No.	Price Per Game $5
Mark Number of Spots or Ways Played Top/Bottom	No. of Games 1	Total Price $5

1	2	3	4	5	6	7	8	9	10
11	12	13	14	15	16	17	18	19	20
21	22	23	24	25	26	27	28	29	30
31	32	33	34	35	36	37	38	39	40
41	42	43	44	45	46	47	48	49	50
51	52	53	54	55	56	57	58	59	60
61	62	63	64	65	66	67	68	69	70
71	72	73	74	75	76	77	78	79	80

Ticket #6

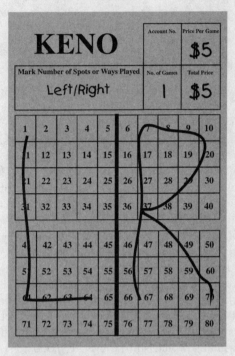

KENO	Account No.	Price Per Game $5
Mark Number of Spots or Ways Played Left/Right	No. of Games 1	Total Price $5

1	2	3	4	5	6	7	8	9	10
11	12	13	14	15	16	17	18	19	20
21	22	23	24	25	26	27	28	29	30
31	32	33	34	35	36	37	38	39	40
41	42	43	44	45	46	47	48	49	50
51	52	53	54	55	56	57	58	59	60
61	62	63	64	65	66	67	68	69	70
71	72	73	74	75	76	77	78	79	80

Ticket #7

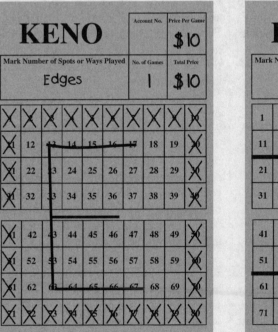

KENO	Account No.	Price Per Game $10
Mark Number of Spots or Ways Played Edges	No. of Games 1	Total Price $10

Ticket #8

KENO	Account No.	Price Per Game $19
Mark Number of Spots or Ways Played 190/8	No. of Games 1	Total Price $19

1	2	3	4	5	6	7	8	9	10
11	12	13	14	15	16	17	18	19	20
21	22	23	24	25	26	27	28	29	30
31	32	33	34	35	36	37	38	39	40
41	42	43	44	45	46	47	48	49	50
51	52	53	54	55	56	57	58	59	60
61	62	63	64	65	66	67	68	69	70
71	72	73	74	75	76	77	78	79	80

catch to win this "32-spot" varies). (See tickets #5, #6, and #7 on page 221.) If you choose to play any of these combination tickets be careful filling out your keno slip (the keno writer can always help) and make sure you know how much you are really playing—and paying.

....

KENO STRATEGY AND SMARTS

Now that you know how to play, let's find out if you still want to play. First of all, there are 3,535,316,142,212,172,000 different ways for 20 numbers to be chosen from 80 numbers. (By the way, that's more than three billion billion, if you're grasping for a description.) I think we can all agree that the possibility of hitting all 20 numbers in any given game is fairly unlikely. How should we define fairly unlikely? Let's try this. Even if your family— we're talking about your children, your grandchildren, your great-grandchildren, *their* children, grandchildren, and great-grandchildren, and on and on—made an absolute commitment that someone would play one keno game per second for the next *million* years, the likelihood of winning would still be over 100,000 to 1. Your bloodline has a better chance of evolving than catching 20 out of 20.

So let's assume you aren't going to play the 20-spot ticket. What are the odds on something more reasonable like the 6-spot ticket? Here's how the numbers break down.

CATCH	PAYOUT ON $1 BET	PROB-ABILITY	ODDS
0	——	0.16602	1 in 6
1	——	0.36349	1 in 2.75
2	——	0.30832	1 in 3.25
3	$1	0.12982	1 in 7.7
4	$5	0.02854	1 in 35
5	$75	0.00310	1 in 322.5
6	$2,000	0.00013	1 in 7,962

These numbers get depressing when we add up the probabilities for catching 0, 1, or 2 numbers—outcomes where you lose money on this bet. We wind up with 0.83783; that means 83.78% of the time you lose. Yes, out of 100 6-spot tickets played, you're likely to lose about 84. Worse yet, 13% of the time you only come out even, winning your $1 back. So you can expect to actually win money on only 3 out of 100 tickets.

STRATEGY

The most important thing to know about keno strategy is that there is no strategy. The best thing you can do is shop around to see what casinos offer the best payouts on the kinds of tickets you like to play. Crunching the numbers, though complicated, is not mysterious and will always give you the same basic answer: The hefty house edge is going to make keno a pretty big losing proposition. One thing that I do like about both regular and video keno—at least in an academic sense—is that you can calculate the expected return. By knowing the payouts and the outcome probabilities (those can be found on the Web—see Appendix D for addresses), you can use the calculation explained in the sidebar on page 218 to know exactly what to expect. Then again, most people who would bother with the number-crunching wouldn't bother with keno. Whether you calculate it or not, the best strategy is to take advantage of keno's slow play. Just bet small, dream big, drag out the time, and relax.

CLOSING RE-MARKS

Many casinos have special ways to play keno and special "deals" that go along with them. Because you won't be able to figure out each new deal you come across, it's best to stick to the old rule: If it seems too good to be true, in keno it definitely is.

Almost every casino will offer a special deal on the "190-way-8" ticket (see ticket #8 on page 221). Here, the entire ticket is in play by dividing it into 20 groups of four numbers; if any two complete groups (an 8-spot) hit, you win. You can play each way for only 10¢ so the game costs you $19 instead of $190. But don't be fooled into thinking the way the casino wants you to. Just because every number is in play does not mean that you have a sure winner.

Let's look at this "deal" more closely. First of all, you are betting that one of your 190 groupings of eight numbers will come up. It may seem like you are allowing for a large number of possibilities: After all, you have 190 ways (instead of the more usual 2 or 3) to make your catch. Just to put things in perspective, there are still 229,906 ways to make that 8-spot that you are *not* playing.

Second, while the house edge determines that you'll be losing $5.70 on each ticket, probability dictates that you would hit your 8-spot once every 1,211 games. On average, to win the top prize of $2,500 you would need to put up $6,902.70 ($5.70 × 1,211). You might indeed win something, if, for example you catch five numbers—which is fun, until you realize that you've won only 80¢ and paid $19 for the privilege. (Granted, you'll usually hit more than that, but you'll still lose a good chunk of your $19.)

VIDEO KENO

Another option for number-guessing aficionados is video keno. This version of keno is played on machines that can be found in the slot machine areas. You make a bet (usually 1 to 10 coins), pick some numbers (usually 3 to 10), hit PLAY, and the machine draws 20 numbers. If you hit a certain minimum amount or more, you win. Remember that a keno machine is actually many machines in one because you'll get different payouts based on how many numbers you pick. When you play a 3-spot ticket, it'll return one percentage and when you play a 10-spot ticket, it will return a different percentage. Just choose your numbers on the screen and you can play as many rapid-fire sessions as you like. You can't get fancy with combos or multi-ways, but you can crank out the games.

There's also this bit of seemingly good news: The house edge on the video version is much lower than what you suffer at the live game. At 8–12%, the house edge on the video version runs about one-third of the live version's edge. That might sound good—instant gratification and an improved house edge (though still lousy compared to other bets available in the casino). But it's actually quite bad. The improvement in house edge is more than negated by the increased speed of play.

Let's take a look at this in terms of cost-per-hour. You can play live keno, relax, kick back, and squeeze in 10 games an hour for $1 each. Let's pick 30% as our breathtaking disadvantage. So your cost-per-hour is as follows:

Cost for live game = $1 bet × 10 games per
hour × 30% house edge = $3 per hour

Now, what if you head over to a machine instead? The quarter machines offer the best payback and you decide to play four coins a game. So that's $1 per play. Your reward is a house edge of only 8%. At the machine, you can breeze through 300 games in an hour. So your cost-per-hour is:

Cost for video game = $1 bet × 300 games
per hour × 8% house edge = $24 per hour

So you saved yourself 22% in house edge, but cost yourself an extra $21 per hour ($24 – $3) over the long term. That's why we always have to consider how much of our bankroll we're exposing to a negative expectation. I set up this scenario to make the argument convincing, but there isn't much you can do to alter it. Sure, if you normally write out 300 combos in live keno, then you're better off playing video keno one game at a time. Or if you can just stop by the machine 10 times in an hour for one game you're better off playing video. But real people don't play like that. In other words, beware the drain of video keno.

As with live keno, you can calculate the expected return of a keno machine, if you really want to. This is an attribute also available for video poker machines, but missing from slot machines. Video keno payouts do vary widely, but unfortunately no machine that I'm aware of returns better than 7% on any of the games. At the very least you should comparison shop by eyeballing. If two 8-spot pay tables are exactly the same except one pays more for catching five spots than the other does, I don't think you need me to tell you which to choose.

Be aware that there's no incentive to play maximum coin—the advice that you'll often hear for slot machines and video poker because it can increase the payback on those games. So don't play many coins when you're happy playing just one; you don't get an added advantage.

If you like video keno, join a slot club so you get something in return for your action. Better yet, if you gravitate toward the machines, try video poker or slot machines with high certified returns.

THE ESSENTIALS FOR PLAYING KENO LIKE A GENIUS

- Keno has a reputation as king of the sucker bets. And the rep is earned. The typical house edge is so exceptionally high—25% to 40%—that it causes vertigo in smart gamblers.
- If you like keno, just use it as a leisurely long (very long) shot. Try to keep your bets low and use them to extend your play and enjoyment of your casino stay without much risk to your bankroll.
- There is no system that will beat keno. It is a game of pure chance.
- As in roulette, the numbers are completely random. It doesn't matter what happened in the previous game (or the previous 10,000 games). There's no such thing as numbers being "hot" or "due."
- The printed ticket is your official ticket for the game. Make sure it matches the ticket you marked up.
- Always find out how much time you have to redeem a winning ticket. It varies from casino to casino.
- Be wary of special deals. Casinos have no shame in advertising a big payout that will a) never occur and b) doesn't pay you nearly what you deserve if it did happen.
- Video keno has a lower house edge (typically 8% to 12%) than "live" keno, but the speed of play prevents it from being a preferable game. If you churn away at a video keno machine, you stand to lose significantly more than if you lounge around waiting for live numbers to pop up.

15

OTHER CASINO GAMES

The vast majority of table games that you will encounter in a casino have been covered in the other chapters. But there are still a few stragglers that you may find yourself bumping into as you wander the casino floor. These odds and ends are comprised of long-standing sucker bets that have managed to stick around (big six, sic bo) and feisty newcomers that hope to turn into mainstays (Three Card Poker, Casino War).

One thing that is pretty much universal about most "new" casino table games is that they rarely get old—because they don't stay at the casino for very long. With traditional table games holding their own as proven winners (for the casino, of course), and slot machines taking the lion's share of valuable floor space, there is a reluctance to give up any space to newer games that might not draw in customers. While some new games might initially cause excitement and curiosity, casino owners are looking for repeat business—games that will continue to have players pouring in to play.

To succeed, a new game must do two things: please the player and please the casino. This leads to an inherent conflict. The traditional table games work for the casino because they have a house edge that serious players can live with. If the buzz on a new game is that it stings players, most people will go elsewhere. So we have a Catch-22 (no, that's not a new Keno variation): New games might have a chance to stick around if they offered players a reasonable chance to win, but a new game won't be added by the casino unless it has a house advantage higher than the game it replaces.

Nonetheless, newer games like Caribbean Stud and Let It Ride have gained widespread popularity despite less-than-attractive house edges. Their success can be attributed to their relatively simple rules, clearly defined pay tables, and slots-like progressive jackpots. Some see these games as a bridge between non-intimidating slots and traditional table games.

So how do you know if a new game you come across is worth playing? A cynical but sensible rule of thumb would be to avoid it. What you don't play can't hurt you. This advice applies only if you want to feel in control of your gambling experience—which, since you're reading this book, you probably do. Analyze the game yourself if you can. Read the latest magazines. Or hop on the Internet and try to track down reliable information on the game. Be especially wary if the game involves the possibility of winning a huge jackpot for a very small wager. Of course if you want to spend a few extra bucks trying for a monumental sum, go for it. Just make sure you understand the monumental chances of losing that generally go along with a wager of that kind.

That being said, there are some peripheral, nontraditional games that have redeeming value, such as Three Card Poker, bingo, and Casino War. But then you have perennials like big six and sic bo, whose very betting structures and larcenous house edges remind you how content the casino is to suck unwary bettors dry. They should be avoided like the plague.

THREE CARD POKER

Most of the newer games are really just twists on older games. Poker variations in particular abound. Some take hold such as Caribbean

Stud and Let It Ride, but most others disappear from casino floors shortly after appearing. While the point of these games is to remind you of poker by using the same words and conventions, most also give a sizable advantage to the house. Three Card Poker is a poker-based concoction that may stick around, because of its fast action, simple play, and house edge in the 2–4% range.

Three Card Poker is really two games in one: Pair Plus and Ante/Play. It draws on its poker roots in the ranking of hands (straight flush, three of a kind, straight, flush, pair, high card) but with the notable exceptions that a straight ranks higher than a flush and a three of a kind beats them both. You can either take the noncompetitive "slots" approach by making the Pair Plus bet (similar to Let It Ride) or you can face-off against the dealer by making the Ante/Play bets (similar to Caribbean Stud). If you choose to play both Pair Plus and Ante/Play, you don't need to bet the same amount on each wager.

The Pair Plus game is pure simplicity. It's not played against the dealer or other players—it's just your three cards and you, hoping to get a pair or better. The bets are paid according to the table below.

PAIR PLUS HAND	PAYOUT
Straight flush	40 to 1
Three of a kind	30 to 1
Straight	6 to 1
Flush	4 to 1
Pair	1 to 1

In Ante/Play you are pitting your cards against the dealer's. After you look at your cards, you can choose to place the additional Play bet equal to the Ante or you can fold and lose the initial Ante wager.

As a procedural point, be aware that when you choose to play both Ante/Play and Pair Plus, if you fold your Ante bet (by not placing the Play bet), you are simultaneously folding your Pair Plus bet. Realistically, you would never fold a hand that qualifies for a Pair Plus payout, so don't worry about it.

Once all the Ante/Play players have decided whether to make the Play bet or fold, the dealer turns over her three cards. The dealer must

have a hand of queen high or better in order to qualify. If the dealer doesn't qualify, all Ante bets are paid even money, Play bets are returned, and the next hand is dealt. If the dealer does qualify, her hand is compared to each player's hand. If the player's hand is higher than the dealer's, both the Ante and Play bets are paid off 1 to 1. If the dealer's hand beats the player's, both bets are lost. If dealer and player tie, both bets push.

Additionally, bonus payouts are given for some premium hands. These bonuses are made only in relation to the Ante bet, not the total of the Ante and Play bets. The bonuses are always paid, even if the dealer doesn't qualify or beats your hand. The bonus schedule is as follows:

HAND	BONUS PAYOUT
Straight flush	5 to 1
Three of a kind	4 to 1
Straight	1 to 1
Flush	None
Pair	None

Let's say you make a $5 Ante bet and receive a hand of J♦ J♠ J♣. You merrily place the Play bet. Unfortunately, the dealer beats you with a straight flush of 3♥, 4♥, 5♥. You don't lose $10 (your $5 Ante bet and $5 Play bet). You lose the $5 Play bet, but your three of a kind gets you a bonus payout of $20 (4 to 1) on your Ante. You end up ahead $15.

Assume that you only bet $5 on Pair Plus in the previous hand. The dealer's hand is immaterial; you get paid according to the Pair Plus payout table. That translates into a win of $150 for your three of a kind (30 to 1). If you made both bets, you would be up $165. Of course, if you made both bets and had a hand of J♦ J♠ A♣, you would be down $5 (losing $10 to the dealer's straight flush on Ante/Play and winning $5 on the Pair Plus payout for the pair).

THREE CARD POKER STRATEGY AND SMARTS

Three Card Poker demands very little from the player in terms of strategy. It's primarily a game of luck rather than skill, not to be confused with table poker in any way. (And that may be part of its appeal.) You're playing against the built-in house edge—the pure and simple mathematics of the game—rather than against skilled players.

How do your opponents stack up? According to mathematician and gambling expert Michael Shackleford (see Appendix D for information about "The Wizard of Odds," Shackleford's highly informative Web site), the house edge on the Ante wager can be lowered to a somewhat hefty 3.37%. This can be accomplished by adhering to one simple strategy: fold with any hand less than Q-6-4. That's it.

Yes, the house edge takes into account all the possible outcomes of a hand: folding after the Ante, winning the Ante but pushing the Play when the dealer doesn't qualify, winning the Ante and the Play, and winning the Ante bonus for a premium hand. If you want to rationalize a bit, the house edge on your total average wager (thus including the money you risk when you make the Play bet using the best strategy) is 2.02%. But realize that you're always locked into the Ante, because it's your base bet. I would consider the house edge to be the larger number: 3.37%. It's your tax on every Ante.

Oddly, the Ante/Play neither teases the player with super payouts nor rewards him with a quality house edge. This light diversion comes at a pretty heavy price. Its cousin, Pair Plus, is a superior choice with its somewhat less surly 2.32% house advantage. Pair Plus strategy is really simple: You just sit there and make the bet.

Three Card Poker doesn't rank anywhere near the best bets in the casino. But that's compared to its elders; compared to some of its peers, it's not bad. It asks even less from the player than Caribbean Stud and Let It Ride, yet it has a lower house edge than both those games. Plus, it's fast and fun to play—for some players that's enough to take the "edge" off this interesting newcomer.

....
BINGO

Classifying bingo as an "other" game may come as a shock to the legions of dedicated players who wagered over $6 billion on the game in 2003, though only a small percentage of that wagering took place in casinos. Surprisingly, the casino can be the best place to play bingo—it is often operated at a loss to the house. Casinos do this with an eye on the big financial picture. Games are generally held intermittently throughout the day, so players need to find something else to do in between. The casino is there to help—with their slot machines and keno games.

Not every casino offers bingo; you'll be more likely to find it if you wander into a local Las Vegas casino than one on the Strip. Once there, you can start to play by putting down as little as $1 to purchase a card like the one below. You can play as many cards as you like, just be sure you can keep track of all of them.

B	I	N	G	O
5	18	37	51	67
3	23	41	54	72
13	22	FREE	49	70
8	16	32	46	65
2	29	44	60	66

The card is a five-by-five grid of numbers, with the name of the game across the top. Each column defined by the letters B-I-N-G-O has a certain range of numbers associated with it. In the B column are numbers 1-15, I has numbers 16-30, N 31-45 (along with the "free spot" in the center of the card), G 46-60, and O has numbers 61-75.

Once you have your card and the game is closed, the caller will draw letter-number combinations either electronically or by hand out of a big hoop cage, and call them out ("B-3"). Mark the preprinted numbers on your card as you hear them called. If the marked numbers complete the required pattern, shout "bingo!"

If you choose, you can go for a bigger payout by playing in special games like "four corners" (the winning card has all four corners marked), "coverall" (numbers are called until an entire card is covered), or "no-number" (numbers are called until one card remains completely unmarked). In every game the caller announces the particular pattern being sought and an attendant verifies the winning card.

BINGO STRATEGY AND SMARTS
The first rule of thumb with bingo is to play only in Nevada; the payouts and the odds

everywhere else aren't worth it. In a local Vegas casino away from the Strip you'll find bingo to be very competitive with a house edge of only 1 to 3 percent. Some casinos even advertise and offer free sessions (which helps answer the question of why the rooms often operate at a loss).

Another strategy to bear in mind is to try to play with the fewest competitors as possible. Ask casino personnel when the slow times are and try to fit in a game then.

You can buy multiple game cards if you like a lot of action. Just make sure you can coordinate marking up all your cards as the numbers are called. Multiple cards will increase your chances of winnings, but won't improve the payback percentage on your overall outlay. Most often you'll just be investing more in the game—both financially and emotionally.

The payouts vary, but a minimum payoff of $1,000 on a coverall game is fairly universal, with some casinos paying as much as $25,000. (These payouts go down considerably if no winner is made with 48 numbers drawn. The game goes on with the payouts decreasing with every additional number called.) Other casinos run promotions where the prize might be a new car or vacation package. Of course while this sounds very appealing, the odds of winning a coverall (with the standard 48 numbers drawn) are about 800,000 to 1.

Even if you don't get to say the word out loud to the whole room, bingo has other advantages. It is obviously a slower game than most anything else you might play, so at the very least, it's good for a change of pace if you want to slow your losses elsewhere.

CASINO WAR

Casino War hopes to lure in players because it is familiar to them as a game they played as kids. This doesn't make it a smart game to play now as adults. Perhaps some people are attracted to the simplicity of play, but you can get a significantly lower house edge and the same mindless play from baccarat, or even the Pair Plus bet in Three Card Poker.

The dealer deals one card to each player and to himself, all face-up. If the dealer's card is higher than yours, you lose; if it's lower, you win even money. Isn't that scintillating? If the dealer's card matches your card, you have two choices: surrender (lose half the original bet) or go to war (bet an amount equal to the original wager). If war is waged, the dealer burns three cards and then deals one card to you and one card to himself. If the dealer's second card beats your second card, you lose both the original and additional bets. However, if your card beats or ties the dealer's, *only* the original bet is paid off.

Players eager for a bloodbath can place a side wager that their original card will tie the dealer's. The payout on this bet is 10 to 1, which is our first warning that the edge is probably astronomical—and the casino doesn't disappoint, giving itself an advantage of 18.65%.

CASINO WAR STRATEGY AND SMARTS

Did you catch that little bomb in the rules? That's right, the additional bet when you go to war forces you to risk twice your bet for only a single payoff if you win. You must expose yourself to odds of 1–2 ($1 paid for every $2 you risk) just to stay in the running.

If you decide to play Casino War anyway, doing battle with the dealer in the event of a tie is the only way to go. It may seem counterintuitive, but it's better to risk two units in order to win one as opposed to sacrificing just half of one. The house edge for a strategy that involves always going to war after a tie is 2.88% compared to 3.70% for a strategy of surrendering. Of course, you should never bet on the tie even though the payout is appealing. Your wagers will line the casino's coffers quickly enough since Casino War tends to play rather fast. Helping the casinos further by letting them take 18.65% is obviously not a good tactical maneuver.

While the 2.88% edge is not horrendous, you can certainly do better elsewhere. Add that to the fact that Casino War is not that involving or interesting as a game; once you've sat at the table for a while you may soon hear yourself humming, "War, war what is it good for? Absolutely nothing."

SUCKER GAMES

BIG SIX

I can tell you why it is called the big six—there are six big bad bets available. Unfortunately, I can't offer up a good reason, other than pure sentimentality, for why it is still around. It's roulette with much, much worse odds and with a complete lack of charm or elegance.

Suckers—uh, er, I mean players—place chips (or, in Nevada, money) on symbols on the table layout in front of the wheel corresponding to the six possible bets on the wheel: an image of a $1 bill, $5 bill, $10 bill, $20 bill, a joker, and a casino logo (see below). The dealer spins the five-foot wheel and the leather or plastic flap at the top begins to make its characteristic noise as it hits each peg separating the 54 spaces on the wheel. When the wheel stops, players who have chosen that symbol are paid off at the rates listed in the chart on page 230. Be aware that the joker and the casino logo have the same payouts and odds, but they are separate bets and only one can win at a time.

The only potential advantage of this game is its low stakes. The minimum bet is $1 compared to roulette where the minimum is usually at least $5. Even so, you'd almost make better use of that one dollar throwing it into a wishing well.

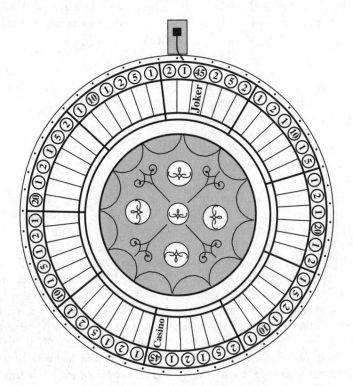

Joker			Casino	
45 to 1			45 to 1	
$10	**$20**	**$10**	**$20**	**$10**
10 to 1	20 to 1	10 to 1	20 to 1	10 to 1
$5	**$5**	**$5**	**$5**	**$5**
5 to 1	5 to 1	5 to 1	5 to 1	5 to 1
$2	**$2**	**$2**	**$2**	**$2**
2 to 1	2 to 1	2 to 1	2 to 1	2 to 1
$1	**$1**	**$1**	**$1**	**$1**
1 to 1	1 to 1	1 to 1	1 to 1	1 to 1

Big Six Bets

Symbol	# of Times on Wheel	Payout	House Edge
$1	24 (23 in A.C.)	1 to 1	11.1% (14.8% in A.C.)
$2	15	2 to 1	16.7%
$5	7 (8 in A.C.)	5 to 1	22.2 % (11.1% in A.C.)
$10	4	10 to 1	18.5%
$20	2	20 to 1	22.2%
Joker	1	40 to 1 (45 to 1 in A.C.)	24.1% (14.8% in A.C.)
Casino logo	1	40 to 1 (45 to 1 in A.C.)	24.1% (14.8% in A.C.)

Big Six Strategy and Smarts

Are you kidding? The above headline may be the funniest thing you'll read until "Sic Bo Strategy and Smarts" on page 232. Roulette is definitely worth a spin over this wheel. Look at the chart above. Go play another game.

RED DOG

Red dog seems to have been put to sleep at most American casinos. It's rarely encountered anymore. Yet the game remains frisky in Canadian casinos and in cyberspace. The fact that red dog is such a popular offering at Internet casinos is just one more reason to be wary of on-line gambling.

Red dog may already be familiar to you as "acey-deucy." The object is to guess if the value of a card will fall in the range between a second and third card. Suits are irrelevant and aces are high. Play begins by placing a wager in the "bet" circle on the table. The dealer then draws two community cards from the shoe. These cards can fall into three categories—matching, consecutive, nonconsecutive—that each dictate different outcomes.

Matching: A third card is drawn. In the unlikely event that a third card of the same rank has been drawn, players are paid off at 11 to 1. (This may seem like a lot, but the true odds on getting a matching third card with eight decks is 12.8 to 1, so even this payoff is far from ideal.) If the third card following two matched cards does not match, the hand is a push.

Consecutive: The hand is a push.

Nonconsecutive: The dealer announces to the table the spread between the numbers and gives the players the option to place a Raise bet equal to their Bet bet. Once the additional bets are placed, the dealer draws a third card. If the third

card is within the range, the players win; if the third card is equal to either the first or second card or falls outside the range, the players lose. There is never a push hand at this point.

Payouts are summarized below:

SPREAD	PAYOUT
Pair	11–1 (if 3rd card matches)
Pair	push (if 3rd card doesn't match)
0 (consecutive cards)	push
1	5–1
2	4–1
3	2–1
4 to 11	1–1

For example, if the dealer draws a 5 and then a queen, he announces a spread of six—6, 7, 8, 9, 10, jack. If he then draws an 8, each player is paid even money.

Red Dog Strategy and Smarts

Red dog does present the player with some decisions to make. The first one is whether or not to play. When you finish reading this section I think you'll agree with me that the answer to that query should be "No." If you decide "Yes," then you'll want to know how to go about the next decision, which is whether or not to Raise.

First of all, remember that the payouts are not indicative of the true odds, so don't be tempted to Raise by the promise of a high payout when the spread is small. Take a look at the chart on page 231 and you'll see that on any single wager, the player has the advantage (a greater than 50% chance of winning) only when the spread is seven or more. This is the only time you should Raise.

The problem with red dog becomes clearer when you remember that you are not in control of whether you will get a spread of seven or

Red Dog (Six Decks)

Spread	Payout	Chance of Winning	Player's Edge
1	5 to 1	7.7%	−53.5%
2	4 to 1	15.5%	−22.6%
3	2 to 1	23.2%	−30.3%
4	1 to 1	31.0%	−38.1%
5	1 to 1	38.7%	−22.6%
6	1 to 1	46.5%	−7.1%
7	1 to 1	54.2%	8.4%
8	1 to 1	61.9%	23.9%
9	1 to 1	69.7%	39.4%
10	1 to 1	77.4%	54.8%
11	1 to 1	85.2%	70.3%

more. The reality is that you don't have the justification to make that Raise often enough, considering the other possible outcomes of a hand—matching or consecutive community cards or spreads of one to six. The overall house advantage for this game is a real dog—3.49% with 8 decks to 3.95% with one deck.

SIC BO

Based on an ancient Chinese gambling game, sic bo should have been lost to antiquity. You won't find this game in many casinos, but if you do, run—don't walk—away. Wagers on combinations of three dice are exposed to a house edge ranging from 2.78% to a jaw-breaking

18.98%. In its design—an intricate table layout equipped with flashing lights—sic bo appears like a game with a great variety of exciting options. But when you know the truth about the odds, it makes sense to just stay away altogether.

If you must know how it works, here goes: Players place chips on the table layout (see below) according to the combinations they think will appear on the dice. More than 50 lousy bets can be made. The dealer then spins a small cage containing the dice, the table lights up under the winning combinations, and the dealer clears the bets that don't match and pays the ones that do.

Sic Bo Bets

Wager	House Payout	Edge
Single-die wager		
One of a kind	1–1 when number is on one die	7.87%
	2–1 when number is on two dice	
	3–1 when number is on three dice	
Two-dice wagers		
Two of a kind	10–1	18.52%
Two-dice combination	5–1	16.67%
Three-dice wagers		
Three of a kind	180–1	16.20%
Any three of a kind	30–1	13.89%
Total value = 4 or 17	60–1	15.28%
Total value = 5 or 16	30–1	13.89%
Total value = 6 or 15	17–1	16.67%
Total value = 7 or 14	12–1	9.72%
Total value = 8 or 13	8–1	12.50%
Total value = 9 or 12	6–1	18.98%
Total value = 10 or 11	6–1	12.50%
Small (or low)	1–1	2.78%
Big (or high)	1–1	2.78%

Sic Bo Strategy and Smarts

So many bets are available and tempting, yet all but two put the player at a 7% to 19% disadvantage. The two bets that are at all reasonable (and that's just relative in this game) are the Small and Big bets with their 2.78% disadvantage. True, those two bets have a lower house edge than some of the games that I've treated with more "respect" (like Let It Ride and Caribbean Stud), but sic bo surrounds these two mildly offensive bets with a sea of outrageously insulting ones. And all of these bets are "sucker" magnets because they offer seemingly high payouts. Does 180 to 1 on a triple seem juicy? Well, the true odds would have it paying 215 to 1, so you end up with a negative expectation of 16.20 percent! Also note that many casinos pay even worse odds than the ones shown in the diagram.

So your best bet is just to play a different game. (If you are drawn in by the clicking of the dice, give craps a whirl.) If you stay at sic bo, you and your bankroll may soon be feeling quite sic.

THE ESSENTIALS FOR PLAYING OTHER CASINO GAMES LIKE A GENIUS

- Be wary of new and obscure games; they often come with an outrageous house edge.
- Do research on any new game you think you'd be interested in playing.
- Check out the Resources section of this book for magazines and Internet sources that will be useful.

BECOMING A SMART PLAYER—PART II

16

YOU AND YOUR MONEY

The purpose of this chapter is to give you the best chance to maximize your enjoyment at the casino. There are no secret hints or surefire formulas, just the essential commonsense advice that the vast majority of gamblers ignore. Don't knock common sense—it's a very easy thing to lose while in the intoxicating environs of the casino.

Even if much of the information included here seems intuitive or obvious, take it to heart. Trust me, it will save you grief. To have a fighting chance in the casino, you need to know the rules of the games you're playing and the best bets. That's what the other chapters were for. To get the maximum pleasure out of gambling and avoid its woes, you have to win the battle with yourself. You must understand not only where your money is going but where your head is at as well. At the end of the chapter, you'll get essential advice on how to get the most value on your gambling trips through casino incentives and comps. It may take a little effort to be a smart, value-conscious gambler, but once you've digested this material, you'll be able to go to any casino and stand with the steadiest legs and see with the clearest eyes.

DOLLARS AND SENSE

Much of this chapter will address the merits of seeing gambling as an entertainment and recreation. But the fuel for our excitement, the measurement of our risk, is always money, money, money. Money isn't just a scoring system; it isn't just a means to the thrills and chills of the casino wonderland. Money is hard-earned and precious. That's very obvious as you read it now, but it's not so obvious when you're playing at the casino. Money can easily lose meaning—it just becomes a means to keep the action going. But we can't forget that despite all the ringing bells and suspenseful games, money can be lost in massive and miserable quantities.

Does it seem unlikely that people would be cavalier about their money? Well, then you'd be surprised and amazed by how many don't know the rules of the games they play or the odds against them. People who are intelligent and money-conscious in their everyday lives don't even think to read a reliable book on gambling (preferably this book, I say out of pure self-interest) and learn how to get the best value. Why scrutinize supermarket prices and bank interest rates, but have absolutely no clue what you're getting into at the casino? The smart thing to do is decide what you're going to do with your money before the fact rather than lament its disappearance afterward.

GOOD BETS VS. BAD BETS

It's difficult to define what a good bet is or what a bad bet is. People possessed of pure logic—probably not your average casino visitors—would say that any bet that has a negative expectation is a bad bet. Well, that just about eliminates every bet in the casino. I think we have to give ourselves more latitude than that.

The most important way to define a good or bad bet is to compare its expected cost to the value you derive from it. And you'd better contemplate what you get out of it other than a "big win," because that's hardly a sure thing. Factors to consider: entertainment, thrill, test of skill, chasing the jackpot, social interaction, and any other intangible you consider important. Your job as an intelligent and informed player is to compare the value of your money to the value you place on these factors.

Personally, I think most any bet that carries more than a 1.5% house edge has too big a price tag. With rare exceptions (some sports betting and poker), just *knowing* that the casino is taxing my play by more than 1.5% detracts from the entertainment value of the game. (The more you're acquainted with gambling, the more you may gravitate toward this way of thinking as well.) Using this criterion, I mostly stick to the best bets and strategies in blackjack, video poker, craps, and baccarat.

WHAT IT REALLY COSTS TO PLAY

The house edge is an important guide to how fair or unfair a bet is. An even more meaningful assessment of your prospects is your theoretical win or loss per hour. The result-per-hour formula incorporates the house edge along with the number of bets per hour and the size of the bets. Here's how it breaks down:

Theoretical result per hour = average bet × number of bets per hour × house edge

Casinos rely on this formula when rating players in order to see what they can expect to win from the players (and therefore what they can return in comps). You should use this to evaluate the cost of your entertainment. The speed of the game (how many bets made per hour) and the average bet are nearly as critical to the equation as the house edge. It's a perfect tool for putting a price on your betting choices. And it will be accurate in the long run. Let's say you're a craps player and you only make the standard pass line bet, which has a house edge of 1.41%. You bet $5 and you can expect to make about 30 of these bets an hour. Here's your cost per hour:

$5 × 30 × 1.41% = $2.12

If you play for eight hours over a weekend, you can expect to spend, on average, almost $17. (Remember, like the house edge it is based on, cost per hour is a theoretical value. It tells you what the most likely outcome is based on probability. You might lose more than this amount, you might win big.)

Appendix B contains a chart that lists the expected cost per hour for various bets. This is a very powerful tool and enables you to smartly compare your gambling options.

It's easy to see what *really* bad bets are: those with huge house edges such as keno and the big six wheel. But, at least in the case of keno, an argument could be made for it based on the cost per hour since it is a relatively slow game.

Similarly, sports betting may have you at a 4.5% disadvantage—not the best you can do—but it allows you to plunk down one wager for hours of entertainment. On a three-hour football game, an $11 bet with its theoretical loss of 50 cents, turns into 17 cents per hour. Not a bad deal to add some spice to a sporting event you were interested in anyway. (You might get a comfy seat, free drinks, and a T-shirt to boot.)

BUT WHAT ARE YOU BUYING?

Cost per hour clarifies much of our evaluation, but also clouds what seem to be clear-cut choices. Let's say you have this choice: You can play a five-coin $1 video poker machine that has 99% payback (1% house edge) or you can play a five-coin nickel slot machine with a 90% payback (10% house edge). What kind of choice is that? Haven't I been listening to anything I've been writing?!

Our choice would seem clear-cut based on our prime directive: Always try to cut down the house's edge. But the picture is a bit different if you look at the choice on a cost-per-hour basis. Let's assume both games would be played at the same speed and at maximum coin, which means $5 on each play for the video poker game and 25¢ per play for the slot machine. Here's how it looks:

Video poker cost per hour =
    $5 × 500 plays × 1% = $25
Slot machine cost per hour =
    $0.25 × 500 plays × 10% = $12.50

It's cheaper to play cheaper. This is something to consider when looking at the cost-per-hour chart in Appendix B. All things being equal, it's best to make the bet that has the lowest house edge. But all things being equal means taking into account how much time and money you plan to commit. If you knew that you were planning to gamble $2,500 and *only* $2,500 (the amount you run through in an hour of video poker in the example above), then you should risk it on the game that has the smallest edge. In other words, if you were to put the same $2,500 in the nickel slots, then that would be a bad choice. But if you just wanted to extend your playing time and get the most hours out of your bankroll, then the nickel slots would be a reasonable choice.

You can make your decision based on the amount of time you want to spend playing or on the amount of money you want to spend playing.

To get a sense of the cost of a game over the course of a casino visit, we can use the calculation again, but with the "per-hour" part removed. Here we're looking at the cost for all our playing time and therefore include the total number of hours played:

Cost to play = average bet × number of bets per hour × hours played × house edge

Also, you should always comparison shop. If you're a roulette lover, you buck a hefty edge of 5.26%, but if you find a single-zero wheel (not easy to do), you cut the edge to 2.70%. If you know that roulette is your game, that's a great bet in my opinion. If you're devoted to the slots, find machines that have certified higher payouts. If you're committed to a game, always check out what the best options and bet opportunities are in that game.

CHOOSING THE RIGHT GAME FOR YOU

To choose the best game, you need to know the facts. But the facts aren't only about dollars and cents—unless that's all you're interested in. If you want to go solely by the numbers, there's not much to dispute. All the information is laid out for you in the charts in the Appendices.

But don't denigrate your entertainment preferences. As someone who takes gambling seriously and advocates that people play smart, it would seem to be my duty to tell you that you're a fool to play keno or slots. Many gam-

bling experts agree, and, while some are motivated by arrogance and a savvier-than-thou attitude, most genuinely have the players' interest at heart. They don't want to see people throw their money away when there are better bets in the casino. Nor do I.

However, I don't know if every long-shot chaser is throwing his money away. I don't know the value he puts on that entertainment. What I do know—and can tell you—is the expected cost of that entertainment and the best ways to reduce that cost. Then you can go do whatever floats your boat, and I have a clear conscience because you have become that most rare and precious thing—an informed gambler. If you know the odds against you, the amount of money you're risking, the amount of money you can stand to risk, and the pleasure you're receiving in return for your money and your effort, then you're a genius in my book.

I merely accentuate that it's essential to fill out the ledger sheet in your head (or, better yet, on a piece of paper) with all the factors. In that way, you're making an informed choice and not just bouncing around the casino getting sucked in and, most likely, sucked dry.

Your choice of games and wagers will also be contingent on your circumstances and bankroll. Personally, if I were given only $10 to gamble with, I'd probably go over to the Megabucks slot machine and give it a few spins for the million-dollar payout. However, if I were given $1 million to gamble with and only gamble with (the stock market doesn't count), I would make a long-term positive expectation move like counting cards in blackjack or playing the right video poker machines.

The game chapters went into all the necessary detail to allow you to decide what games are your cup of tea. But the chart on the next page can be used as a quick reference guide to some of the important factors that drive players toward (or away from) certain games. Think of these as brief character profiles to see what appeals to you.

MONEY MANAGEMENT: MYTH OR REALITY?

This whole chapter is, in essence, devoted to how you choose to manage your money in the

Casino Game Profiles

Game	Com-plexity	Skill Needed	Social	Variety of Bets	Potential for Big Payoffs	Highest House Edge	Lowest House Edge
Baccarat	Low	Low	High	Low	Low	14.4%	1%
Blackjack	Medium	High	Medium	Low	Low	3.5%	−1%
Craps	High	Low	High	High	Medium	16.7%	0.01%
Caribbean Stud	Low	Medium	High	Low	High	6.5%	5.3%
Keno	Low/Medium	Low	Low	High	High	40%	25%
Let It Ride	Medium	Medium	Medium	Low	High	5%	3.5%
Pai gow poker	Medium	Medium	Medium	Low	Medium	3%	1%
Poker	High	High	High	Medium	Low	N/A	N/A
Roulette	Low	Low	Medium	High	High	7.9%	2.63%
Slot machines	Low	Low	Low	Medium	High	25%	1%
Sports betting	High	High	High	High	Medium	30%	N/A
Video poker	Medium	High	Low	High	High	15%	−1%

casino. Almost every gambling book and gambling pundit runs on at length about the necessity of "money management." To judge by its treatment, it's gambling's most hallowed and sacred concept.

And it is an important concept, but only when it's not burdened by tricks or window dressing; many gambling sources treat money management as a system or a process by which you can come out ahead at the casino. This does gamblers a great disservice. No money management technique will help you win; no special method or magic formula will turn a negative expectation game into a positive one.

Most often, the intentions of the money management proponents are very honorable. They want to increase a player's playing time or give him an awareness that he can walk away a winner. The only problem I have is that certain money management "systems" can be very convoluted and, in their betting manipulations, may confuse players into believing that their chances of winning have improved.

As long as they don't lead to delusions of invincibility, money management systems will usually do no harm. At worst, they give you an amusing way to tinker with your betting patterns. At best, they'll remind you to gauge how you feel about your wins and losses.

Just make this distinction: Money management is an essential *psychological* construct, but

it is not a *mathematical* reality. You have to choose an approach to your money that seems sensible and emotionally satisfying to you. Here are some ways of handling your money that seem very sensible to me and many other gamblers. Just remember: Nothing in this list will change your overall mathematical chances! But these tips can improve your enjoyment and durability in the casino.

Go in with a plan. No, not the "today I break the bank" plan. A real plan where you understand what you want to achieve and what you're willing to accept in terms of time, entertainment, and money. You will be in much greater control—of yourself—if you have realistic and predetermined notions of what might happen in the casino and how you will respond. Following a plan will bring you much joy ("Hey, I walked away with my winnings!") and save you grief ("At least I stopped when I reached my loss limit").

Set a loss limit. As much respect as I have for personal choice, I would say that setting a loss limit is just about mandatory for players who want to remain sane. Put aside an amount of money for your gambling excursion—whether it's an evening, a weekend, or a week—and don't go beyond that amount. Call it your entertainment budget. If you say you're willing to spend $500 on your casino gambling and you lose that $500, stop playing. Find other distractions. If you feel more comfortable setting a loss limit and then having an "emergency" reserve for desperate times, that's fine as long as you decide beforehand that the reserve money is still a comfortable amount to risk. It's a very slippery slope once you start to chase your losses with money you're not comfortable gambling—the destination can be stomach-churning regret, if not self-destruction.

Set a limit, determine your play, and stop in the unfortunate case that you reach that limit.

Set a win goal. If you're up a certain amount, you end your session, take your profits, and take a break. This seems quite appealing, because you will notice as a gambler that there's often a point in almost any game where you're "up" a little. So if you diligently follow this approach, you should be able to beat the casinos at their own game, right? If only it were so. Notice the phrase "if you're up" rather than "when you're up." A "take the money and run" approach is fine as a psychological boost, but it does not change the math.

If you were incredibly modest in your desires, wishing to profit only by the amount of your normal bet, you would often be able to leave with your meager profit. But eventually you would run into a losing streak that would leave you with your expected (negative) earnings.

A variation on this approach has you reaching a satisfactory (as judged by you) profit level and then pocketing a percentage of profit (perhaps half) and then continuing to play, but only with the profits. You don't go into your original stake because you want to make sure you leave with some profit. If profit play appeals to you, keep your goals modest—you're not likely to double your stake.

See how your money stacks up. Here's a neat and easy way of determining how much action you're generating at the table games. When you buy in for chips, place the chips in a stack to your left. Make all your bets from this pile. When you win bets, collect them and place them in separate pile on the right. After you've gone through all the chips on the left, you can see how you're doing by counting the chips on the right. For example, you buy in at blackjack for $100 and get twenty $5 chips, which you place on your left. After all the chips have been bet, you see that you have $125 worth of chips on your right. Now you can put $100 in chips

back on your left and pocket the $25. You play the left pile and end up with $80. You lost $20 this cycle, but you still have the $25 in profit from the first cycle set aside. So now you are up $5 after playing $200 worth of action. You can move the $80 pile on the right to the left and play through it. Or you could add $20 to it so you have another $100 cycle. (If that's within your budget.) Or you could do whatever manipulation strikes your fancy.

The fun and intriguing part of having the right and left piles is that you can track how much money you're really betting in total. A $100 investment may get you $500 or $1,000 worth of action. This also highlights how the house edge adds up: It's not only your initial $100 that's exposed to the house edge, it's the total amount of your bets, which can add up rather quickly.

This "money moving method" also gives you another option for money management: You can look to achieve a certain amount of action during a playing session and end that session once it's reached, no matter your wins or losses.

Break your play into smaller sessions. Take your total gambling stake and divide it among the number of playing sessions you wish to have. For instance, let's say you come to a casino for two days with a $400 stake. You could break each day into four playing sessions of $50 each (2 days × 4 sessions × $50 = $400). A playing session can be defined by either an amount of time you wish to play or by a profit you hope to achieve. If you lose the money for a session, you walk away and do something else. This is just an artificial way to extend your play and guarantee that your whole wad doesn't disappear in the first hour of your visit.

Take notes. If you really want to know how you're doing at the casino, write it down. (Do you really want to know?) After each playing session or after each game, jot down what you won or lost, your typical bet, and how long you played. This may be too anal retentive for some tastes, but it does allow you to see where you stand; that is, how you stand financially. In the short term, it won't tell which games are "right" for you or where you get "lucky." But after dozens of visits, the diary most likely will reveal a picture of which games are worth your while and which aren't, assuming you're using the proper playing strategies. One entry you never want to see: "Dear Diary: Mortgaged the house today."

SYSTEMS

Here's where "money management" really gets creepy. When you see the words "beat the casino" or "win" specifically attached to negative games of chance like roulette and craps, you should run—run fast and far away. The quick scoop on gambling systems: None of them work. You can't massage, manipulate, or trick the laws of probability and mathematics to turn negative expectation games into positive games. Yet the world of gambling is inundated with system sellers and advocates. Some systems have been around for centuries, but there are always enterprising hustlers who are happy to repackage them for the naive and desperate. Plenty of players who don't get a dime for pushing systems still do so. These foolish gamblers like to think they have an element of control where they can't and don't. No need to join their ranks. Here are some basic system scams and their inherent weaknesses.

THE MARTINGALE SYSTEM

This system is universally seductive at first and then universally scoffed at by those in the know. The "plan": You double your bet after every loss in an even-money game; whenever you win, you recover your losses and make the amount of your initial bet. Sounds not so bad, huh? The problem is you may lose more than you can make up for by the time you reach that pesky table limit. Although the casinos would love to take all the money you have on every bet, they put a cap on the amount of a single bet as a brick wall for Martingale system players. Let's look at how this would play out.

A Martingale player sits down at a roulette table with a $5 minimum bet and a $1,000 table limit (though we can be pretty sure he didn't take in that last bit of info). He likes to make the 50–50 bets like red and black. Eventually, the scenario described in the following chart will happen to this player. "Eventually" may be several playing sessions or it may be the first half-hour. But it will happen.

Spin #	Bet	Wins	Losses	Net
1	$5	$0	$5	–$5
2	$10	$0	$10	–$15
3	$20	$0	$20	–$35
4	$40	$0	$40	–$75
5	$80	$0	$80	–$155
6	$160	$0	$160	–$315
7	$320	$0	$320	–$635
8	$640	$0	$640	–$1,275

After eight quick spins this unlucky soul has lost $1,275, perhaps his entire bankroll for the weekend. He can no longer hope to make up these losses because his next bet, according to the Martingale doubling system, would have to be $1,280—$280 over the maximum allowed bet at this table. The real drawback to this type of progression betting system is that it gives the illusion that it is working. You will often win a series of 50–50 bets. But with Martingale, you'll be accumulating small wins by assuming a great amount of risk. Let's say in the example above that our roulette playing friend won the eighth spin. He would have put up $640 for a net win of only $5 ($640 – $635 net loss).

If you could guarantee a consistent win, even if it was small, that would be one thing. But with roulette, or any negative expectation game, you will—sooner or later—have a catastrophic loss. As much as you don't want to believe it when you are betting on red, eight blacks in a row will happen. This occasional unlucky sequence will likely wipe out any accumulated winnings.

So the best case scenario is that you risk a great deal to win very little. The probable scenario? Doubling your bet to recoup losses in order to win a pittance will eventually run you into the table limit or the limit of your bankroll. Ouch, that brick wall hurts.

CANCELLATION OR D'ALEMBERTO SYSTEM

This system used by rookies at roulette or on other even-money bets is a variation of the Martingale described above. It seems slightly more complex (if it's complicated it must be legitimate, right?) because you need pencil and paper to lose money this way. But the end result is the same. If you win, it will be a small amount compared to your risk and you very well could lose enough to hit either the table limit or your wallet's limit before winning anything.

Here are the mechanics: The player begins by writing down any 10 numbers that will represent the amount bet. She writes down

5 2 3 7 5 2 7 8 3 2

and then bets the total amount indicated by the first and last numbers in the series, in this case, $7. Let's say she wins her bet. She then crosses off the two numbers just used.

5̶ 2 3 7 ˙5 2 7 8 3 2̶

She then makes a second bet using the new first and last numbers as a total amount (2 + 3 = $5). Unfortunately, she loses this bet and now must add the amount lost ($5) onto the end of the series.

5̶ 2 3 7 5 2 7 8 3 2̶ 5

On the next bet she adds the new first and last numbers to get the amount to wager (2 + 5 = $7). The player continues to bet in this manner, crossing numbers out and writing down new numbers (which, by the way, are all amounts of money) until all the numbers are crossed out. When that happens, the player will have won an amount equal to the sum of the *original* 10 numbers (in our example $44). If she reaches the table limit before all the numbers are crossed off, she will have lost an amount equal to the sum of *all* the remaining numbers—which can easily total several times the potential win. No matter how you write it down, it still spells out the same message—roulette is a negative expectation game. You can play whatever games you want with your wagers, but, because of the 0 and 00 spaces on the wheel, you will still lose 38 dollars for each 36 won.

Over the long run, any player will lose at a negative expectation game and the danger is in thinking that you won't.

DETECTING STREAKS

The probability of an independent event happening in a game of chance has nothing to do with what happened before it. This important point applies to winning, losing, red, black, snake eyes, 7s, just about everything. Wheels and dice are neither hot nor cold, they are simply wheels and dice. If you have won several times and you are "up," that neither means that you are going to continue winning nor that you

are now going to start losing. All it means is that, in the past, you have won several hands in a row. There is no reliable way of predicting the future while you are in the casino. That's another reason to make a plan with your money before you go in. That way if you are up, in the present, you'll know when you want to leave so that you can perhaps keep some of those winnings into the future.

SYSTEM SOPHISTRY

System sellers will try to seduce you in ways that may seem convincing. For example, they'll tell you that it doesn't matter that no system holds up under computer trials simulating long-term play through millions of trials. The system pusher will say that in reality nobody plays millions of times, so the computer test doesn't apply to real life. (Bet that sounds kind of appealing to those of you sickened by my constant reference to the "long term.")

Well, computers are used in every aspect of our lives and we rely on their calculating speed to get us answers. If we devoted the manpower to manually test these gambling systems, the results would prove the systems are as flimsy as the computer printouts tell us. The millions of trials just give absolute precision to the truth. That truth doesn't change in real life. And if the system sellers fulfilled their impossible dreams and actually sold their useless methods to millions, we would have a live simulation of all their failings.

In any given gambling session, whether you are using a system, good common sense, the time-tested rules from a reliable book, or just your best hunch, you can lose despite a positive expectation and you can win despite a negative expectation. Over many, many, many, many gambling sessions the reverse is most likely. The thing to remember about any system is that no matter what it is doing, it isn't changing the laws of probability to make a negative expectation into a positive one.

....
THE ETERNAL QUESTIONS

What's the Right Bet Size for Me?

Okay, since this book isn't called *The Mensa Guide to Personal Finance and Planning Your Future*, we'll just have to assume that you're in touch with the financial realities of your life. That means you've thought about how much you can afford to lose and haven't assumed that you'll win a dime. Given that, you have two approaches. First, you should look at the cost-per-hour chart on page 253, which you can use to approximate the amount you can expect to spend on a game and to see roughly how many bets you'll make per hour. Second, you should go by your gut. Does the thought of winning or losing $10 on a single bet make you swoon? Does it make you bored? How about risking five $1 tokens on a round of video poker? Time to move down to the nickel machines or up to the $5 machines? Only you can tell what will keep your interest while keeping your sanity. Of course, you're not locked into a single bet size. You can always change if you want more or less of an adrenaline rush.

What's a Reasonable Bankroll?

You've found your comfortable bet size. Now you want to know what size bankroll you need to keep you in play for a while. This is a very difficult question to answer. Because there are so many fluctuations in gambling, it's never safe to say what a rational bankroll would be. If your goal is to elongate your playing time—which is the case for most gamblers—you definitely don't want your average bet to be too large a percentage of your bankroll. For example, you may feel comfortable with $25 bets, but a $100 bankroll won't get you far. If you want to invest only $100 in a playing session, you're better off with $5 bets at the table games or quarter bets at the slots. As a very general rule, you want to start off with 50 to 100 times your average bet in order to give yourself some room for extended play. Unfortunately, this information works at cross purposes with another fact covered before: If you want to win money in a negative expectation game, you should make the fewest and largest bets possible. That's because the longer you play, the more the house edge becomes a certainty. But the question is whether you want a five-minute casino visit or hours of play. Most people choose the latter.

What's a Sensible Loss Limit?

As with your bet size, only you, your close rela-

tions, and your accountant know the answer to this one for sure. If you're pretty rational about your money—and if you're not, the casino's not a good place for you to be—you'll know the right amount when you see it. Just think of what the maximum price is that you're willing to pay for your entertainment. I don't think it's reasonable to expect anyone to feel good if they reach their loss limit; therefore, I'm not talking about an amount that has you smiling widely and trumpeting that you still got a "good deal." (Although maybe that is the most sensible criterion.) I'm talking about an amount that is tolerable to lose because you only thought about it as your gambling money. Should you bottom out (and hopefully you won't), you should feel that you took a risk you were willing to take, and not feel cheated by fate and the casinos.

The maximum amount of money you're willing to lose—which is your loss limit—must be completely separate and apart from the money you need to make your life comfortable. It's a separate escrow account; it is not—and cannot be—money for the mortgage, college tuition, food, or any other part of your life that is essential to your physical and mental well-being (as well as your loved ones'). It has to be an amount you can cope with writing off and saying good-bye to. And, of course, you should take into account the number of casino visits you plan to make. Either come up with a reasonable limit on each trip or divide your annual gambling stake by the number of casino visits you're planning. This doesn't sound very spontaneous or "fun"; in fact, it sounds darn near ominous. The object is still to win, and if you make the right bets, there's a decent chance that will happen. So I'm not saying you are going to lose all your money, but you have to be prepared for where you say "whoa" given that eventuality.

MONEY AND PSYCHOLOGY

Unless a person is a professional gambler, the most reasonable way to approach gambling is as an entertainment and recreation. You pay for the sport of play—the excitement, the possibility of winning, the sights and sounds. The only problem with the entertainment model of casino gambling is that people aren't really sure of their financial and emotional commitment to it. You have a good sense of what you're spending and what you're expecting to get when you go to a movie or to the opera, dine in a fine restaurant, or take a week's vacation at a resort. In a casino, too many players (and, yes, this happens to all of us) get swept up in the psychological tempest of competition, superstition, and desperation. Players aren't guaranteed anything for their money, especially when they're chasing a big win. Simply put, to make gambling an excellent choice as entertainment, you have to know what you want to get out of it before you put anything into it. And that's not quite as easy to do as when you select a movie or restaurant. Let's look at the things to consider.

PSYCHOLOGICAL PITFALLS

Even when we know how to calculate our chances and apply skill to a game, we give ourselves over to notions of "luck" or "fate." I believe that making sensible choices increases the pleasures of the casino and keeps you sane while in these chance emporiums. Still, my intent is not to deprive gambling of its mystique or its fun factor. But the less you give in to voodoo or gut instincts or "the moment," the better chance you'll have to win. Some of the gambling errors I've listed below are just basic human nature and it's interesting to stand back for a moment and recognize our foibles.

Seeing patterns. As human beings, we have a natural tendency to impose order on chaos. We like to see patterns even in things that we know to be random. Thus, if we see a roulette wheel hit two black numbers, then two red numbers, then two black numbers, then two red, we think we're onto something. Or if the same worthless card appears twice when we're going for a royal flush in video poker, we think something is "fishy." But these are just chance occurrences that our human radar may pick up. They tell us nothing about the reality of our chances or our bets.

Selective perception. You sit down at a slot machine and the person next to you wins payout after payout while your money evaporates. You choose one of two available seats at a blackjack table; someone else takes the other

seat. You can't win a hand and the other fellow is getting blackjack after blackjack. You're sure that you're unlucky and destined to lose. But do you notice all the times you do these things and nothing unusual happens? Don't get steamed up because you latch on to negative "signs." The more flustered you get, the worse you will play.

Illusion of control. "If only I had chosen different dice, they wouldn't have come up snake eyes." "Had I been friendlier to that dealer, I would have had better cards." Of course it's hard not to be superstitious in a casino. But don't beat yourself up because you lost—and you're sure it's because you weren't wearing your lucky underwear. If you follow the advice in this book, you'll know that sometimes you lose simply because that is the mathematical reality of a trip to a casino.

"I shouldn't lose" syndrome. Most gamblers think that losing is something that is designated for all the other suckers in the casinos. Even veteran gamblers, who know about odds and the house edge, believe that they have some destiny to win. One problem with this thinking is that it assumes some element of control, even in games of pure chance. The other problem is that, when you expect to win and the losses pile up (as they will on occasion), you may be in danger of playing recklessly and self-destructively in order to catch up or get your due. This is called *steaming* or going *on tilt* by casino denizens and it's not a pretty place to be. It can be hazardous to your money and your health. Be humble and realistic in the casino. No one has the special favor of the gods. Prepare to win, expect to lose.

Table game anxiety. While blackjack, craps, and baccarat offer some of the best odds in the casino, many players cling to the slots because they're afraid to look "foolish" at the tables or because they don't know the rules. This book should help the interested-but-intimidated cure both those afflictions. I can't claim that you'll never run into a rude, loud-mouthed player at a table game—odds are you will (particularly in blackjack). But most folks are pretty nice and they're not looking to harp on your "mistakes." Plus, remember that everyone was a newcomer at some point. Here's an added incentive: After reading this book, you'll realize that 99.9% of the advice-givers you'll encounter at the tables really don't know what they're talking about. Sit down without fear and remind yourself that the ignorance of kibitzers can be very entertaining.

Greed? This story can be told by every gambler: "I was up so much money at the beginning and then I gave back all my winnings and more." Is this greed? I'm not so sure. Yes, it's true that the more we win, the more we want to win. It's human nature to always set the bar a little higher. But that's not the whole story. Simply put, casino-goers like to play. And playing means putting in hours at the games you like even after you win at them. But there's the rub: The more you play, the more likely you'll move back to the average, which in casinoville is a loss. If you win early, you're experiencing a positive fluctuation, and it's not unexpected to move back toward the norm. We are puppets of a natural process and the obstacle preventing us from walking away a winner is the casino dweller's belief that "the play's the thing."

Nonetheless, greed—or perhaps nearsightedness—may play a role in this drama. If you make a considerable profit, force yourself to take a step back and consider your good fortune. Maybe you should work to preserve that profit rather than turn it into a dream of world conquest. You could take a break—go for a walk or to eat. You could slow down your betting or decrease the amount of each bet. You could go try out a new game at a minimum wager. In other words, you can concoct strategies to keep your win in your pocket.

Having a plane to catch or someone dragging you away to go home while you're on a hot streak can be a great blessing. Then again, there are always players who want to trade quantity of playing time for their version of quality. This type of gambler comes to the casino looking to find a lucky streak and push it until it wheezes and dies (which will eventually happen). Assuming this behavior isn't self-destructive, no one can rightly cast a stone at this "greedy" yet satisfied player.

Playing with the casino's money. This tends to be the rallying cry for players who want to rationalize why they're throwing their money away. Wins come to be seen as play money that can be used to continue playing and to "really make a killing." Please, please realize that any money you win is no longer the casino's—it's yours. You own that money and you should remember that it's yours for the taking, not just for the giving back. Of course, you may want to use it to extend your playing or to try to increase the profits and that's legitimate as long as you acknowledge that it's part of your stake and not just play money. The worst result of this thinking is the tendency to make ill-considered or completely unthinking bets just because you are ahead. That's a guaranteed way to no longer be ahead.

NO HELP FROM THE CASINO

This may come as a shock, but the casino doesn't really have your best interests at heart when it comes to keeping you and your money together. Now that you've recovered from that revelation (pick yourself up off the floor), we can examine the subtle and less-than-subtle ways in which casinos help facilitate the transfer of funds from your wallet to their profit statement.

Free drinks. Almost all casinos keep free booze flowing to players who are in the action. Many gamblers see this as one of the perks of the casino life. The casino sees it as a lubricant for quicker money removal. Need I mention alcohol's effects on one's judgment and self-control? Nothing leads to the decline of controlled playing more than a good buzz. It's not about temperance; it's about your money. You'll end up paying for those free screwdrivers one way or another. Don't drink heavily when you're playing. Better yet, don't drink at all. Got that straight—no chaser?

Automatic teller machines. Money on tap is almost as bad as booze on tap at the casino. You've been diligent about setting limits and breaking your bankroll into small playing sessions. But the casino makes it so easy and so tempting to break into your bank. Stick to your guns.

Chips. Betcha can't lose just one. Sure, casino chips are easier to handle than paper money, but they serve another purpose for the casinos. It's hard to equate chips with real money—they're playthings. When we see a $25 chip, we don't see precious currency bearing the faces of Andrew Jackson and Abraham Lincoln; we see … a chip. It's a lot easier to part with plastic tokens than real greenbacks. Gamblers further devalue chips with their slang: a $5 chip is a "nickel" and a $25 chip is a "quarter."

When you accumulate many chips, the dealer is always happy to "color you up" giving you higher-denomination chips in place of your smaller ones. This may be for convenience, but looking at it more skeptically, it also could subliminally induce you to play at a higher level than you normally would. After all, a chip is a chip.

Also, you sometimes get in the mind-set that once your cash has been exchanged for chips, it's gone. Gamblers see their stack of chips dwindle and say, in a resigned way, "Might as well just play out these last few chips." Never forget that there's cash in them there chips and it can easily be extracted at the nearest cashier's cage.

The sights and sounds, oh my! The bells ringing, the hum of excitement, the sound of coins hitting metal. No windows, no clocks. Brisk air conditioning keeping you semi-alert through the wee hours of the night. It is all constructed for you to enter a separate self-enclosed world of fantasy. Take breathers. Go outside. Eat. Sleep.

Employee advice. Casino personnel often like to wax poetic about the gaming strategies that they've seen work or their own personal beliefs based on observation. It's not that they're trying to steer you wrong in order to boost casino profits—they just may not know what they're talking about.

CASINO FREEBIES

Although they are in the business of taking, casinos will give back as well. Of course that giving is done in the spirit of self-interest; casinos want to promote customer loyalty and retain players who play. In order to get the most out of your money and your entertainment, you should get the most out of what the casino is willing to provide. The bulk of casino incentives come in the form of comps, which is short for complimentaries.

COMPS

What exactly are comps and why do some players kill for them? (A slight exaggeration.) Comps are the freebies that casinos provide in return for a certain amount of play. They are intended to be a reflection of your gambling activity and therefore a reward for your play. The most common comps are free meals and discounted rooms (the "casino rate" comp is generally half the normal rate). Free drinks are the casino norm and can barely be considered comps. Perhaps the greatest comp perk is that with the comp slip in your hand you get to go right into the buffet or to a VIP check-in and don't have to stand on a giant line with mere mortals. High rollers who bet hundreds of dollars on a hand are sure to get *RFB* (free room, food, and beverage), and may get show tickets, limo service, and airfare included if they play long enough.

Player attitudes about comps frequently fall into either of two extremes. One is to believe that seeking comps is tantamount to begging or scrounging and is somehow undignified. The polar opposite is the thought that steady casino play will have you treated like royalty, with Dom Pérignon flowing at your request, a lavish suite with a gold-trimmed bathroom, and a private helicopter waiting to fly you to your backyard by dawn. Obviously, both extremes are wrong (although if you have a habit of making $10,000 bets, the second scenario isn't as off-base). You deserve comps because you pay for them with your play and the comps you get usually will be commensurate with your level of play. These aren't gifts from the casino—they are really discounts and rebates.

Put It On My Card

In most casinos, the fastest way to start getting comped is to become a member of the slot club or player's club. Always get a club card from every casino you play at; a card is usually issued on the spot and all it takes to apply is a driver's license. By using this card at slot and video machines and presenting it at the tables, your benefits and comps will be based on your play throughout the casino.

At the Slots

Slot club cards are the means by which casinos electronically track and reward a customer's slot play. To make sure the casino knows how much you are playing—and therefore how much they should reward you—insert the plastic slot club card into each slot machine you play. Casinos will often issue duplicate cards if you like to play more than one machine at a time or if you and a friend or spouse want to track your play together.

In terms of comps, sometimes slot players have it easier than table players. The slot clubs are very precisely worked out, while there are more gaps in the table systems. (This isn't a reason to play the slots if you don't already! It's not worth choking on a large house edge just to get some free food. But video poker can be a good deal with a low house advantage and reliable comps.)

At the Tables

In order to get comped for play at table games, you must let the casino know who you are and how much you are betting. This is referred to as a player's *rating*. At some casinos, you can make your presence known just by showing your slot club card, which acts as a player's card. Put it on the table (again, nothing must change hands directly with the dealers) and the dealer will give it to the floorperson. At casinos that don't use cards for table games, you need to let the floorperson know that you want to be rated. He will take some identification such as a driver's license. Depending on the casino's system, the floorperson will keep track of your play either on a rating slip or on a computer.

It's important to note that your play does not have to be continuous. You can play four one-hour sessions and receive the same benefits as if you played one four-hour session. If you do play shorter sessions, just make sure the pit personnel are tracking your play each time you sit down.

Sometimes your play won't be high enough to warrant getting rated. Some ritzy casinos won't rate you unless you play $25 a hand. Others will take you seriously at $5 a pop. If your action is high enough and you haven't already asked, the floorperson may ask you if you want to be rated.

Who will give you the comps? The dealer can't, so don't expect her too. But the dealer does talk to the floorperson so you want to be friendly. Usually the floorperson can give you a comp for a buffet or the coffee shop. If you warrant more than that, you'll likely talk to the pit boss or a *casino host*.

Getting What's Coming to You

Once you're on the casino's list (no, they won't call you up or use your information for nefarious purposes), you'll start to get offers in the mail about future promotions. These offers may include discounted rooms, two-for-one meals, show tickets, free stays, etc. Some offers can be quite generous—three free nights, free breakfast buffets, and show tickets—just for being a $25 blackjack player. The offers may fill up your mailbox, but if you fancy yourself a casino player, it always pays to know what deals are out there.

How Comps Are Calculated

Most casinos use a simple formula to determine what comps a player receives. This formula is similar to the expected cost-per-hour of playing that we discussed earlier in the chapter. From the casino's point of view, cost-per-hour becomes "expected win." In calculating the expected win (or your expected loss), the casino figures in the average bet, speed of play, hours played, and house edge. Sometimes the house edge is adjusted based on the player's ability. The formula looks like this:

Casino's expected win = average bet × bets per hour × total hours played × house edge

The casino will then return 20 to 40 percent of the expected win as comps. Let's look at an example. You're playing roulette, where the house edge is 5.26%, at a casino that generally gives back 30% of the expected win as comps. The game is not crowded and is moving along quickly, at about 50 spins per hour. (Most casinos require their floorpersons to take note of the specific speed of the games.) Your average bet is $10 and you play for three hours. Here's how much you "earn" in comps:

Comp = $10 (average bet) × 50 (bets per hour) × 3 (hours played) × 0.0526 (house edge) × 0.3 (comp percentage) = $23.67

So you earned about $24 in comps. Realize that this doesn't mean that someone from the casino is going to rush up and stick this money in your pocket. Nor does it mean that you are guaranteed 24 bucks, even if you scream to the rafters that it's what you deserve. Comps are part of a loyalty/reward system that has some fuzzy edges even with precise calculations. One casino might want to see more hours of play out of you before they give you anything. That's their prerogative—it's your prerogative to count it as a strike against the casino (I would). Another casino might give you a comp that's worth more than $24 because you seem like a player devoted to a high negative expectation game. The calculation is only a guideline and the casino does what it likes with it. Also, realize that while you're racking up your comp dollars, your expected loss for those three hours was $78.90. With that money you could pay for your own buffet and have plenty left over.

In the past, pit personnel had more flexibility in issuing comps. While casinos are focusing more on impersonal formulas, getting comps still has a lot to do with employee discretion. Personality and partiality have not been removed from the equation yet.

Can You Come Out Ahead with Comps?

Yes, it is possible. Let's see how it might occur at the table games. There are three factors that might make you earn more than the casino expects (although they may not translate into winnings if you are playing a game with an exorbitant house advantage):

1) *Miscalculating your average bet.* If they think you're betting $25 and you're betting only $10, that's a 250% increase in your comp value.

2) *Miscalculating the speed of the game.* If the dealer is slow or you take breaks, there is a chance that the floorperson is assuming a greater speed than is actually occurring.

3) *Assuming too high an edge.* Casinos are very sophisticated and this is not too common. But generally they assume 2% in blackjack, and having read Chapter 3 you'll be using basic strategy and have only a 0.5% loss.

Let's look at a happy comp situation for a blackjack player. Say you are using basic strategy, but the casino is still assuming its typical 2% edge. You're betting $10 on each hand at a rate of 100 hands per hour for 4 hours. The casino kicks back 30 percent in comps. The casino works out the following:

$$\text{Comp} = \$10 \times 100 \times 4 \times 0.02 \times 0.3 = \$24$$

However, your expected loss as a basic strategy player is this:

$$\text{Expected loss} = \$10 \times 100 \times 4 \times 0.005 = \$20$$

Hey, your expected loss is $20, but your comps are $24. Not bad—you're "up" $4. That's assuming that you truly value the comps you receive, meaning you get hungry and you like to eat at the casino or you're staying at the casino and you benefit from a reduced room rate. And it assumes that you receive the full value of your comp. In any case, you can see the benefit of two tenets of smart gambling: Reduce the house edge and take the comps you earn, especially when they have real value to you.

CASINO HOSTS

One of the most valuable allies you can have in your quest for comps and preferential treatment is the casino host. The host is the casino's goodwill ambassador and will generally try to do everything possible to make you happy. Casino hosts are often assigned to different areas—table games, slots, keno.

Request to meet a host at the casino host department, the reception desk, the promotions desk, or the VIP lounge. A good host will want your name and address in order to get you on the list for promotions and will want to know your gambling preferences and style. The hosts can pass out comps—food, room, whatever they believe is appropriate—but they may expect you to play at a certain level in order to receive these perks. Make sure you clarify this. Casino hosts are good people to ask the essential question "What level do I need to play at in order to get so-and-so?" Or, better yet, "I play at this level. What should I expect?" If you're a low roller, don't expect them to make your every fantasy come true. Take the hint if the host makes it clear that your level of play won't earn you much. (But, of course, the host shouldn't be rude.)

At the end of your trip, you should find your comps deducted from your hotel statement when you check out. If there is an error, ask to speak to a casino host—hopefully one you have a relationship with. When you're getting a series of comps—restaurant meals, room service, the room itself—it's always smart to check with your host to make sure everything is in order. This spares any embarrassment or anger during checkout when something you expected to be taken care of is not.

You can also use hosts to scout out the comping possibilities before your trip. Call the casinos you're interested in and speak to a host. They'll check the computer to see if you've played at the casino before. If you haven't, explain your level of play. The host should be able to tell you that if you play for a certain amount of hours at a certain rate, you can get a reduced room rate and buffet and dinner or whatever. Get as much info as possible. Then comparison shop.

Once you've played at a casino, you can use casino hosts for your return trip. Make your reservations by calling the host department and asking for your chosen host. You might get more than you "deserve" if the host is trying to "develop" you as a player. Hosts make their careers by finding and keeping good players— and by turning casual visitors into regular guests.

COMP STRATEGY AND SMARTS

Comps really are like money there for the asking, but that is the whole key. You need to ask, ASK, ASK! You need to ask to get comps! Talk to someone in the pit or talk to a casino host. Sometimes you get pleasantly surprised. You ask for the buffet and you get the restaurant. You ask if good seats for a show are available and you get the tickets for free. Sometimes you're rebuffed. At a table game, your play may not rate much or even be rated at all. But you might still get a meal out of it if you make a polite inquiry. A good opener is asking, "What are the chances of you comping me a dinner?"

Don't feel guilty or embarrassed or inhibited. You receive a comp because a casino wants you to continue to play in their house. They want you to play because they know you will provide them revenue. To the casino, a comp is a rebate on your play in anticipation of your future play. Don't think of comps as a gift or bonus. Also, everyone goes for the comps; it's part of the casino experience. You're not a pest

by doing so. After you have played at a few casinos you will learn the worth of your action and be able to gauge the value of the comps you deserve.

Once you're comfortable with what to expect and how much you'll get back, you can figure comps into your budget. Jean Scott's *The Frugal Gambler* and other books listed in Appendix D will help you refine the fine art of comps and fully understand the comp culture. In the meantime, here are some basic rules for getting your money's worth with casino comps:

- Be a card shark. Join the slot club or player's club wherever you play. You'll get started on your way toward free food for this trip and you'll be getting offers in the mail for your next trip.

- Make sure all your play is rated by the casino. Never start playing until the pit person has taken your player's card and started your rating. Never put a nickel in a machine before you put your card in.

- Make your presence known. Always make sure someone has your name, preferably a casino host. If a casino floorperson or host comes by to introduce himself and asks you if there is anything you want, ask him, right then and there, for a lunch or dinner comp or a reduced rate for your room. Any time pit bosses or casino hosts offer you anything, they're not going out of their way to be overly friendly—it means your level of action probably warrants some casino perks.

- Never turn down a comp that is offered.

- Be pleasant and friendly with the personnel unless they don't deserve it. Be nice to the casino floorperson. She is the one rating you and she has the leeway to be generous or stingy in her evaluation.

- Don't be afraid to order anything on the menu that you want when you get a coffee shop comp, including appetizers and dessert. It's okay. It really is!

- A comp never includes the tip, so don't forget to leave one.

- Never, ever play just to get a comp. Don't increase the size of your bets or play longer in order to get better comps. This is foolish. A comp is a return on your losses. But you don't want to create exorbitant losses just to receive a portion of them back. Yes, you might win, but you still shouldn't play above your means.

- Don't be awed by another person's comps. Most likely they're paying through the nose for their special treatment. There's no such thing as a free comp.
- The casino does *not* care if you win. There is no need to hide your winnings. Players who win giant jackpots are treated like dignitaries at the casino, not run off the property. Happy winners return to the casino and lose their winnings. Happy winners also tell their friends to come and play.
- Shop around (over the phone or in person) for the kind of comps that appeal to you. Strip resorts in Las Vegas will probably require higher stakes for each level of comp they give out compared to what a downtown Vegas casino offers. For example, playing $25 a hand at blackjack or several hours at the dollar slot machines will likely get you free room and food at a casino off the Strip while the same level of play might get you only a trip to the buffet at one of the ritzier places in town. Go where they treat you well, as long as you're aware of what you're sacrificing (if anything) in playing conditions.

OTHER OFFERINGS AND PERKS

Comps are just the beginning. In their desire to have you play with them, casinos offer a whole host of incentives.

CASINO PROMOTIONS

If you look about you, there's always some sort of promotion going on at a casino. You might as well participate in the ones that cost nothing except your time in filling out a raffle ticket. Chances are slim that you'll win the car or cash being offered, but if it's free, it's a chance worth taking if you're in the casino already. (You often have to be present for drawings).

Also, you may as well take advantage of promotions that don't make you do anything you aren't already doing. If a casino offers scratch-off tickets for four of a kind in video poker and you're a video poker player, you should get your ticket when quads hit. However, never play longer or risk more money than you intended just because of some promotion.

FUN BOOKS

When you head to a casino destination, always scout around for coupons and special offers. Check out the local newsstand, casino magazine rack, promotions booth, tourist bureau, and hotel room magazines. "Fun books" are popular packets of coupons put out by casinos, particularly in Las Vegas. Some are cheesy and include little of value. But others have good food offers and valuable coupons such as the matchplay coupons described below.

MATCHPLAY CHIPS AND COUPONS

Be on the lookout for offers involving match-play chips or coupons. A *matchplay* chip is a nonnegotiable chip, usually given by the casino to induce play at its tables. The chips are typically allowed only on even-money bets, meaning the payout is 1 to 1. For instance, you can bet them on red or black in roulette but not on a single number.

When you play a matchplay chip you must match it with a chip of your own (hence the name). The matchplay chip is sacrificed whether you win or lose. Thus, if you bet $5 on black in roulette along with a $5 matchplay chip, you would win $10 if black comes up. If red comes up, you lose $5. In either case, you don't get the matchplay chip back. Matchplay coupons are like matchplay chips, except they—no shock—are printed on paper and look like coupons.

Some casinos have promotions where you can get "action" chips (or something similarly named). These offers generally let you get more chips than the amount you pay; for instance, you may get $125 in action chips for $100. These chips cannot be redeemed for cash, but can be used as regular chips at the tables. If you win on an "action" chip bet, you win a normal chip in return. Yes, the only way to get rid of an action chip is to lose it, but if you play for any length of time, you cycle through your chips with wins and losses anyway. Therefore, you get at least $125 worth of action for your $100. Just remember to always bet the action chip before a real chip.

Promotions are great except when the casino staff doesn't know about them or sneers at them. Getting more play for free, however, can be worth any funny or blank looks you may get.

CREDIT AND MARKERS

You can set up a line of credit at a casino. Your credit history will be checked by Central Credit, which is basically TRW for the casino world. After you establish credit at a casino, you can sign *markers*. Markers are counter checks against your bank account. You usually have a certain period of time—two weeks to a month—to pay back your marker before money is taken out of your account. It may make you feel like a big shot and get you added attention, but freewheeling access to your bank funds and gambling doesn't sound like a good combo to me. Too often "high rollers" sign their names and treat the money as if it weren't real (especially when drunk). It's another step removed from reality. Be careful.

One way to use this service wisely is to refuse any additional credit above the amount you intend to gamble with. Then, if you use only markers, you will be forced to stop when you reach your predetermined loss limit. Judicious use of casino credit can also help you earn comps. Some casinos will provide you with a VIP club card to use when you cash a marker at a table.

TRIP PLANNING

As with any trip you take, a casino vacation or weekend should be planned out. Here are some tips for making your trip more enjoyable and saving money even before you enter the gambling halls:

- Shop around on the Internet, in guidebooks, or through the travel section of newspapers. The casinos want you to stay in their hotels so they can have first crack at your gambling money. They will likely compete for your business.
- Many Las Vegas hotels advertise in the travel section of the *Los Angeles Times*. Use the Internet or your local library to check it out if you don't have access to the paper directly. This will help you get a feel for good rates before you make phone calls to specific casinos.
- Californians are often wooed by casinos because they are in the position of making a weekend trip while most of the rest of the country can't be so impulsive. When you call to find out rates, it wouldn't hurt to ask if they have special deals for people coming in from Los Angeles—even if you're not.
- While you comparison shop, ask for unadvertised specials. If you find what seems like a good deal, clarify the cancellation policy and then make your reservation. You can always cancel if you happen on something better.
- In Vegas and other gambling meccas, the best hotel rates at casinos are generally obtained on weekdays (Sunday through Thursday nights), during the summer, or in mid-December. The only exception to this rule is when there is a convention scheduled—prices tend to soar and availability can be limited.

TAXES

All the winnings in a casino are subject to taxation. The good news is that you can deduct your losses against your winnings. You can substantiate your losses through a gambling diary (another handy use for the diary that was mentioned in the money management section). This is especially useful for table games, where it is hard to substantiate what actually occurs. You also need to keep all canceled checks, bank withdrawal statements, and credit receipts. It's easier to substantiate your losses on the slots if you're a member of a slot club. The casino should be able to give you a printout of your play for the year, specifying your wins and losses.

Any slot machine (including all video games) jackpot of $1,200 or more immediately gets you a W2-G form from the IRS. This must be filled out at the casino, which is why you should carry proper ID with you at all times.

Canadian citizens have the good luck to not have to pay taxes on their winnings.

THE ESSENTIALS FOR PLAYING LIKE A GENIUS IN ANY CASINO

- Use this book to decide what games interest you and get the rules down before you play. Don't play any game or make any bet you know little about. Learn it first.
- Comparison shop for the best buys on meals and accommodations and for the best rules for the particular games you're going to play.
- Plan other activities like shows, shopping, sightseeing, workouts, or golf. Diversify your entertainment; it doesn't have to be all about gambling.
- Set a limit before you leave home on the total amount you are willing to spend gambling. No matter what, don't exceed this limit.
- Don't consider using your checkbook, ATM card, or credit card once you've reached your loss limit. Perhaps it's best to bring only one credit card on your trip just to meet the basic necessities—room, food, massage.
- Only bet what you can afford to lose. Don't play with scared money.
- Get your equilibrium in the casino and stay with your plan. Many people lose in the first few hours or minutes. If you feel out of control, step back and relax. If you decide you've had enough gambling, get away from the casino. It's hard to resist when you're in the thick of it.
- Monitor the status of your bankroll. You should know at all times where you are financially.
- Try to preserve your wins. Slow down your play. Put some profit aside and make it untouchable. How quickly and how severely you do this depends on your desire to play versus your desire to win.
- Never increase your bets to win back what you've lost.
- Systems don't work. At best, they're entertaining; at worst, they're destructive.
- Don't gamble when you are tired, depressed, or sick. Don't play with desperation.
- Use time as a limit.
- Don't be superstitious. Knowledge is the key, not luck.
- Don't be afraid to ask questions.
- Don't drink excessively and gamble at the same time. Sip for pleasure, don't gulp for effect.
- Separate your ego from your winnings or losses and be pleased with a small win. Don't expect to break the bank.
- Get the most out of your money by getting all the comps you can.
- Casinos are up and running 24 hours a day. You don't have to be. Get some rest.
- Don't let things get out of your control. Check out the Gamblers Anonymous "Twenty Questions" on page 268 if you think you have a problem.

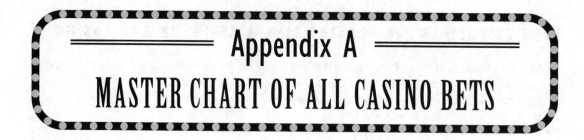

Appendix A
MASTER CHART OF ALL CASINO BETS

This chart covers a broad variety of bets you'll find in the casino. The bets are ranked from best to worst in terms of expectation. As covered in Chapter 2, expectation is the percentage of each bet you can expect to lose or win on average. This chart will also tell you the house edge; expectation is exactly the same as house edge but with the plus or minus symbol reversed. A bet with a −5% expectation has a house edge of 5%. I go with expectation because it works from the player's perspective. Expectation per $100 bet simply gives you a dollars-and-cents notion of how much each bet will leave you with in the long run.

Unless otherwise noted, the expectation for each bet is based on a player using the optimal (or near-optimal) strategy. For example, on video poker machines, the expectation is based on perfect strategy and maximum coins in. Playing less than expertly and/or with less than maximum coin will decrease your video poker expectation by about 1–5%. Some expectations for games with varying or unknown payouts, such as keno and slots, are approximations. Progressive jackpots weren't included because of their wide variance. When there is no other way to describe a bet, I use the term "base bet."

If you don't understand the bet referenced, check the chapter of the appropriate game to get a full explanation.

Game	Bet	Expectation	Per $100 Bet
Blackjack	Card-counting	+1.00%	$101.00
Video poker	Deuces Wild: full pay	+0.76%	$100.76
Video poker	10/7 Double Bonus	+0.17%	$100.17
Craps	Don't pass/don't come with 100× odds	−0.01%	$99.99
Craps	Pass/come with 100× odds	−0.02%	$99.98
Craps	Don't pass/don't come with 20× odds	−0.07%	$99.93
Craps	Pass/come with 20× odds	−0.10%	$99.90
Video poker	9/6 Jacks or Better (with 4,700 coin jackpot)	−0.10%	$99.90
Craps	Don't pass/don't come with 10× odds	−0.12%	$99.88
Craps	Pass/come with 10× odds	−0.18%	$99.82
Craps	Don't pass/don't come with 5× odds	−0.23%	$99.77
Craps	Pass/come with 5× odds	−0.33%	$99.67
Craps	Don't pass/don't come with 3× odds	−0.34%	$99.66
Craps	Don't pass/don't come with 2× odds	−0.46%	$99.54
Video poker	9/6 Jacks or Better	−0.46%	$99.54
Craps	Pass/come with 3× odds	−0.47%	$99.53
Blackjack	Basic strategy player	−0.50%	$99.50
Baccarat/mini-bac	Banker (4% commission)	−0.60%	$99.40
Craps	Pass/come with 2× odds	−0.61%	$99.39

Game	Bet	Expectation	Per $100 Bet
Craps	Don't pass/don't come with 1× odds	−0.69%	$99.31
D'ble Exposure BJ	Basic strategy player	−0.75%	$99.25
Spanish 21	Basic strategy player	−0.80%	$99.20
Craps	Pass/come with 1× odds	−0.85%	$99.15
Video poker	9/7 Double Bonus	−0.89%	$99.11
Baccarat/mini-bac	Banker (5% commission)	−1.06%	$98.94
Baccarat/mini-bac	Player	−1.24%	$98.76
Pai gow poker	Banking every other hand	−1.27%	$98.73
Roulette	Single-zero wheel: en prison	−1.35%	$98.65
Craps	Don't pass/don't come	−1.36%	$98.64
Craps	Pass/come	−1.41%	$98.59
Blackjack	Average player	−1.50%	$98.50
Craps	Place 6 or 8	−1.52%	$98.48
Craps	Lay 4 or 10 (vig on win only)	−1.67%	$98.33
Craps	Buy 4 or 10 (vig on win only)	−1.67%	$98.33
Craps	Don't place 6 or 8	−1.82%	$98.18
Craps	Lay 5 or 9 (vig on win only)	−2.00%	$98.00
Craps	Buy 5 or 9 (vig on win only)	−2.00%	$98.00
Video poker	9/6 Double Bonus	−2.19%	$97.81
Craps	Buy 6 or 8 (vig on win only)	−2.27%	$97.73
Craps	Lay 6 or 8 (vig on win only)	−2.27%	$97.73
Three Card Poker	Pair Plus	−2.32%	$97.68
Craps	Lay 4 or 10	−2.44%	$97.56
Craps	Don't place 5 or 9	−2.50%	$97.50
Pai gow poker	No banking	−2.54%	$97.46
Roulette	Double-zero wheel: surrender	−2.63%	$97.37
Roulette	Single-zero wheel	−2.70%	$97.30
Video poker	8/5 Jacks or Better	−2.70%	$97.30
Craps	Field (2 or 12 pays triple)	−2.78%	$97.22
Sic bo	Big/small	−2.78%	$97.22
Casino War	Base bet	−2.88%	$97.12
Blackjack	Weak player	−3.00%	$97.00
Slots	Dollar slots (best conditions)	−3.00%	$97.00
Video blackjack	Basic strategy (blackjack pays 1–1)	−3.00%	$97.00
Craps	Don't place 4 or 10	−3.03%	$96.97
Craps	Lay 5 or 9	−3.23%	$96.77
Three Card Poker	Ante	−3.37%	$96.63
Red dog	Base bet (eight decks)	−3.49%	$96.51
D'ble Exposure BJ	Weak player	−3.50%	$96.50
Let It Ride	Base bet	−3.50%	$96.50
Spanish 21	Weak player	−3.50%	$96.50
Video poker	7/5 Jacks or Better	−3.85%	$96.15
Red dog	Base bet (one deck)	−3.95%	$96.05
Craps	Lay 6 or 8	−4.00%	$96.00
Craps	Place 5 or 9	−4.00%	$96.00
Slots	Quarter slots (best conditions)	−4.00%	$96.00
Sports betting	Bet $11, win $10	−4.50%	$95.50
Craps	Buy 4, 5, 6, 8, 9, or 10	−4.76%	$95.23
Baccarat/mini-bac	Tie (pays 9 to 1)	−4.84%	$95.16

Game	Bet	Expectation	Per $100 Bet
Video poker	6/5 Jacks or Better	−5.00%	$95.00
Caribbean Stud	Ante	−5.22%	$94.78
Roulette	Double-zero wheel: all bets (except five-number)	−5.26%	$94.74
Crapless craps	Pass/come	−5.40%	$94.60
Craps	Field (2 and 12 pay double)	−5.56%	$94.44
Video poker	Deuces Wild: short pay	−5.66%	$94.34
Slots	Dollar slots (average conditions)	−6.00%	$94.00
Craps	Place 4 or 10	−6.67%	$93.33
Sic bo	One of a kind	−7.87%	$92.13
Roulette	Double-zero wheel: five-number bet	−7.89%	$92.11
Slots	Quarter slots (average conditions)	−8.00%	$92.00
Video keno	Typical machine	−9.00%	$91.00
Craps	Big 6 or 8	−9.09%	$90.91
Craps	Hard Six or Hard Eight	−9.09%	$90.91
Sic Bo	7, 14	−9.72%	$90.28
Slots	Nickel	−10.00%	$90.00
Big six wheel	$1	−11.11%	$88.89
Craps	Any craps	−11.11%	$88.89
Craps	Hard Four or Hard Ten	−11.11%	$88.89
Craps	One-roll bet: 3 or 11 (pays 15 to 1)	−11.11%	$88.89
Craps	Hop bet (two ways to make)	−11.11%	$88.89
Craps	One-roll bet: horn bet	−12.50%	$87.50
Sic bo	10, 11	−12.50%	$87.50
Sic bo	8, 13	−12.50%	$87.50
Craps	One-roll bet: 2 or 12 (pays 30 to 1)	−13.89%	$86.11
Craps	Hop bet (one way to make)	−13.89%	$86.11
Sic bo	Any three of a kind (pays 30–1)	−13.89%	$86.11
Sic bo	5, 16 (pays 30–1)	−13.89%	$86.11
Baccarat/mini-bac	Tie (pays 8 to 1)	−14.36%	$85.64
Sic bo	4, 17 (pays 60–1)	−15.28%	$84.72
Sic bo	Three of a kind (pays 180–1)	−16.20%	$83.80
Craps	Any seven	−16.67%	$83.33
Craps	One-roll bet: 2 or 12 (pays 30 for 1)	−16.67%	$83.33
Craps	One-roll bet: 3 or 11 (pays 15 for 1)	−16.67%	$83.33
Sic bo	Two-dice combination	−16.67%	$83.33
Sic bo	6, 15 (pays 17–1)	−16.67%	$83.33
Big six wheel	$2	−16.67%	$83.33
Big six wheel	$10	−18.50%	$81.50
Sic bo	Two of a kind (pays 10–1)	−18.52%	$81.48
Casino War	Tie	−18.65%	$81.35
Sic bo	9, 12	−18.98%	$81.02
Big six wheel	$5	−22.22%	$77.78
Big six wheel	$20	−22.22%	$77.78
Big six wheel	Joker/casino logo	−24.07%	$75.93
Keno	Typical game	−30.00%	$70.00

Appendix B
COST PER HOUR CHART

The purpose of this chart is to let you compare your gambling options and to put a realistic "cost" on the games and bets the casinos offer. The cost per hour is calculated as follows:

Cost per hour of play = house edge ×
bets per hour × common bet amount

Keep in mind that this is a theoretical value; it tells you what you're "expected" to lose (or win) on average. Your actual results in any given hour will be quite different. When assessing your own cost per hour on a given bet, make sure you adjust for the size of your wager, the speed of play, your skill (in games with strategy), and/or a particular machine (for video poker). Obviously, a change in any of these components will alter your cost per hour—for better or worse. That's for you to determine!

Bet	House Edge	Bets per Hour	Common Bet Amount	Cost per Hour of Play
Baccarat				
Bank	1.06%	60	$50	$31.80
Player	1.24%	60	$50	$37.20
Tie	14.36%	60	$5	$43.08
Mini-baccarat				
Bank	1.06%	110	$5	$5.83
Player	1.24%	110	$5	$6.82
Tie	14.36%	110	$1	$15.80
Blackjack				
Basic strategy player	0.50%	80	$5	$2.00
Average player	1.50%	80	$5	$6.00
Weak player	3.00%	80	$5	$12.00
Card-counter	−1.00%	80	$25	(+$20.00)*
Craps				
Pass	1.41%	40	$10	$5.64
Pass with single odds	0.85%	40	$10	$3.40
Don't pass	1.36%	40	$10	$5.44
Don't pass with single odds	0.69%	40	$10	$2.76
Place 6 or 8	1.52%	40	$6	$3.65
Hard Six or Hard Eight	9.09%	40	$1	$3.64
Any 7	16.67%	140	$1	$23.34
Caribbean Stud Poker				
Ante	5.32%	45	$5	$11.97

Bet	House Edge	Bets per Hour	Common Bet Amount	Cost per Hour of Play
Keno				
Typical game	30.00%	10	$1	$3.00
Video keno	8.00%	400	$1	$32.00
Let It Ride				
Base bet	3.50%	45	$5	$7.88
Pai gow poker				
No banking	2.54%	40	$25	$25.40
Banking every other hand	1.27%	40	$25	$12.70
Roulette				
Double-zero	5.26%	40	$5	$10.52
Single-zero	2.70%	40	$5	$5.40
Double-zero with surrender	2.63%	40	$5	$5.26
Slot machines				
Nickel slots	10.00%	500	$0.15	$7.50
Quarter slots	7.50%	500	$0.75	$28.13
Dollar slots	5.00%	500	$3.00	$75.00
Sports betting				
Point spreads/totals	4.50%	0.5	$11	$0.25
Video poker machines				
9/6 Jacks or Better (25¢)	0.46%	500	$1.25	$2.88
8/5 Jacks or Better (25¢)	2.70%	500	$1.25	$16.88
10/7 Double Bonus ($1)	−0.17%	500	$5.00	(+$4.25)*
9/6 Double Bonus ($1)	2.19%	500	$5.00	$54.75
Full-pay Deuces Wild (25¢)	−0.76%	500	$1.25	(+$4.75)*
Three Card Poker				
Pair Plus	2.32%	70	$5.00	$8.12
Ante	3.37%	70	$5.00	$11.80
Casino War				
Base Bet	2.88%	120	$5	$17.28
Tie	18.65%	120	$1	$22.38

*Profit per hour of play

Appendix C
GAMBLING GLOSSARY

Action: The total amount of money bet over a period of time.

Aggregate limit: *(Keno)* Maximum total amount paid to all players for a single game.

All-in: *(Poker)* To put your last remaining chips into the pot.

American wheel: *(Roulette)* A wheel with 0 and 00.

Anchor: *(Blackjack)* The seat to the dealer's immediate right; the last player to be dealt cards. Also called "third base."

Ante: *(Poker)* Contribution to the pot required of each player at the beginning of a hand.

Ante: *(Three Card Poker, Caribbean Stud)* Player's initial bet.

Any craps: *(Craps)* A bet that the next roll will come up 2, 3, or 12.

Any seven: *(Craps)* A bet that the next roll will come up 7.

Arm: *(Slots)* Lever attached to the right side of a machine that activates the reels.

Automatic shuffler: Machines on certain tables that shuffle cards, and sometimes deal cards out.

Backdoor: *(Poker)* A hand in Texas hold'em that makes use of both of the final two community cards.

Back hand: *(Pai gow poker)* The five-card, high hand placed closer to the player.

Back line: *(Craps)* The don't pass line.

Back the bet: *(Craps)* Make the free odds bet. Also known as a "behind the line" bet.

Bad beat: *(Poker)* Losing with a strong hand that, based on probability, should have won.

Bank: *(Slots)* A row of machines.

Bank: Person covering all bets, usually the casino itself.

Banker hand: *(Baccarat)* Second of two hands dealt; has a lower house edge than player hand.

Bankroll: All the money a player uses for betting. Also called "gambling stake."

Bar: To refuse service to a player.

Bar: *(Craps)* Indication of which number is a push for don't bettors.

Basic strategy: *(Blackjack)* A playing strategy, based on expected value, that minimizes the house edge.

Bet against the dice: *(Craps)* A bet that the shooter will lose. Also known as a "back line" bet.

Bet blind: *(Poker)* To bet without seeing the cards.

Bet with the dice: *(Craps)* A bet that the shooter will win. Also called a "pass line bet."

Biased wheel: *(Roulette)* A wheel that favors particular sections of numbers out of proportion to probability, because of flaws in manufacture or placement.

Big 6 or Big 8: *(Craps)* A bet that a 6 or 8 will be rolled before a 7.

Blackjack: *(Blackjack)* A hand that totals 21 on the first two cards—an ace and a 10-value card. Also called a "natural."

Blank: *(Keno)* The ticket with the numbers 1–80, used to mark the numbers to be played.

Blind: *(Poker)* A required bet, made before any cards are dealt.

Bluff: *(Poker)* To raise with an inferior hand in the hope that other players will be fooled into folding superior hands.

Board: *(Keno)* The electronic sign displaying the keno game in action.

Board: *(Poker)* The community cards (flop, turn, river) in a hold'em game.

Bonus Poker: *(Video poker)* Jacks or Better variation.

Bookie: *(Sports betting)* A person who accepts and pays off bets, often illegally.

Boxcars: *(Craps)* A roll of 12. Also called a "hobo bet."

Boxman: *(Craps)* The game supervisor who sits at center of table, in front of the chips and between two standing dealers.

Bring-in: *(Poker)* Forced bet in stud games.

Brush: Poker room host.

Burn card(s): Card(s) that are discarded without being put into play.

Bust: *(Blackjack)* To have a hand that totals more than 21. Also called "break."

Button: *(Poker)* A white disk placed near the person who is considered the dealer for purposes of order of play.

Buy bet: *(Craps)* Bet on a point number that's paid at true odds.

Buy in: The process of exchanging cash for chips prior to play.

C & E: *(Craps)* A one-roll bet that the next throw will be any craps (2, 3, or 12) or 11.

Cage: The casino cashier window. The place to exchange chips or coins for cash.

Call: *(Poker)* To "see," or match a bet made by another player.

Caller: *(Baccarat)* The dealer who runs the game and makes sure the correct procedures are followed. Also called a "croupier."

Cap: *(Poker)* To make the last raise allowed on a betting round.

Cap: To surreptitiously add chips to a winning bet.

Card-counting: *(Blackjack)* An advanced method of play intended to increase the player's advantage. Generally executed by keeping track of cards already dealt to determine the composition of the cards remaining to be dealt.

Carousel: *(Slots)* A bank of machines of the same type, often linked to a progressive jackpot.

Cashback: Part of the comp system, a rebate on money played at the casino.

Casino advantage: See "house edge."

Casino host: A casino employee who assists players, primarily high rollers.

Casino manager: The main executive in charge of the casino during a shift.

Catch: *(Keno)* To have the numbers selected by a player match those drawn during the game.

Center bets: *(Craps)* The proposition bets in the center of the table that hold a large negative expectation for the player.

Certified: *(Slots)* A clearly marked machine that guarantees a certain percentage payback over the long run.

Change color: Trade in one denomination of chips for chips representing smaller or larger amounts. Also known as "color up."

Change person: *(Slots)* A casino employee who changes cash for coins or tokens.

Chasing: Increasing bets in an effort to regain earlier losses.

Check: *(Poker)* Choosing not to bet, with the option to call or raise later in the betting round.

Check-raise: *(Poker)* To check and then raise on the same round of betting. Also called "sandbagging."

Checks: Casino chips. Sometimes spelled "cheques."

Chemin de fer: The European form of baccarat.

Chung: *(Pai gow poker)* A plastic marker indicating the banker's hand.

Churn: Constant rebetting of your stake, which leads to greater losses.

Closing line: *(Sports betting)* The final point spread.

Cocked dice: *(Craps)* Dice that are leaning against the table edge or some object and are not flat on the table.

Coin-in: *(Slots, video poker)* Amount of money played through a machine. Used in figuring comps.

Cold: A table, machine, deck of cards, or dice that players associate with losing.

Column bet: *(Roulette)* A bet that any number in one of the three columns of 12 numbers will come up.

Combination ticket: *(Keno)* A single ticket on which the player has marked at least two groups of numbers that form several combinations to allow more "ways" to play.

Come bet: *(Craps)* A bet similar to the pass line bet, but made after the come-out roll.

Come-out roll: *(Craps)* The initial roll that determines the point for pass and don't pass bettors.

Commission: A percentage of winning bets taken by the house. Used in baccarat, pai gow poker, and buy bets in craps. Also called "vig."

Community cards: *(Poker)* The cards placed face-up in front of the dealer that are part of all players' hands.

Comps: Free rewards for gambling a certain amount at a casino. Could include buffets, discounted or free rooms, gourmet dinners, shows, transportation.

Copy: *(Pai gow poker)* Term for the player and the banker having hands of the same value.

Corner bet: *(Roulette)* A wager made on four numbers at a time by placing a bet on the point where the boxes of four numbers meet.

Countdown: *(Slots, video poker)* A number on a card reader indicating the number of coins necessary to earn one club point.

Covering the spread: *(Sports betting)* A winning bet if, after subtracting the point spread from the favorite's score, the team bet on has the higher score.

Crap out: *(Craps)* To throw a 2, 3, or 12 on the come-out roll.

Craps: *(Craps)* 2, 3, and 12.

Crew: Casino employees who work at a craps or baccarat table.

Croupier: *(Baccarat, roulette)* European term for dealer.

Cut card: *(Blackjack)* Colored plastic card used to cut the deck as well as to indicate the point at which the dealer needs to reshuffle.

Cut the deck: To divide the deck in two, placing the front cards in the back.

Deuce: A 2 in a deck of cards or two spots on a die.

Die: A six-sided cube with dots on each side representing the numbers 1 through 6.

Dog: Shortened form of "underdog," the player or team that is not favored to win.

Dollar: A chip worth $100.

Don't come bet: *(Craps)* A bet similar to the don't pass bet, but made after the come-out roll.

Don't pass bet: *(Craps)* A bet that the shooter will roll craps on the come-out roll or not make the point before a 7 is rolled.

Double down: *(Blackjack)* To double the original wager and receive only one more card.

Double Exposure: *(Blackjack)* Variation where both of dealer's cards are face-up. Also known as See Thru Blackjack.

Double odds: *(Craps)* An odds bet equal to twice the original pass/don't pass or come/don't come bet.

Draw: To have an additional card or cards dealt to your hand.

Drawing hand: *(Poker)* A viable hand that needs cards to improve.

Drop: The total amount of money bet at a table.

Drop box: A locked box below a slot in each table where cash (from players buying in) and receipts are dropped.

Duplicate ticket: *(Keno)* A casino-produced copy of a player's ticket, returned to the player after bets are made; can be used as an original ticket in a new game.

Early surrender: *(Blackjack)* An extremely favorable form of surrender allowing the player to forfeit half the bet whether or not the dealer has blackjack.

Easy way: *(Craps)* A roll of 4, 6, 8, or 10 made without doubles.

Edge: A mathematical advantage usually held by the casino, occasionally by the player.

En prison: *(Roulette)* Option only available on a European wheel when a 0 comes up— even-money bets are held over to the next roll instead of being lost.

European wheel: *(Roulette)* Wheel with 37 pockets; does not have the 00 pocket found on American wheels. Also called "French wheel."

Even money: *(Blackjack)* Offered to players with blackjack when the dealer's upcard is an ace.

Even money: A bet that pays off at 1 to 1.

Expectation: The percentage of money a player can expect to gain or lose on average by making a certain play. Also known as "expected outcome," "expected value," "expected return," and "expected winnings."

Expert play: *(Video poker)* Playing each hand exactly as indicated by computer-derived strategies.

Eye in the sky: Surveillance system mounted in the ceilings throughout the casino.

Face card: King, queen, or jack. Also known as a "picture card."

Favorite: *(Sports betting)* The player, team, or horse favored to win.

Field bet: *(Craps)* A bet that the next roll will be 2, 3, 4, 9, 10, 11, or 12.

Fifth street: *(Poker)* The round of betting after the fifth card has been dealt.

First base: *(Blackjack)* The seat to the dealer's immediate left; the first player to be dealt cards.

Fixed limit: *(Poker)* A betting structure where bets can be made only in specified increments during each round.

Flat top: *(Slots)* A machine that has a fixed, non-progressive amount as its top payoff.

Floorperson: A pit supervisor, who reports to the pit boss.

Flop: *(Poker)* The first three community cards, placed face-up in front of the dealer.

Flush: *(Poker)* Five cards of the same suit.

Fold: *(Poker)* To drop out of play.

Form: *(Sports betting)* A horse's past performance, analyzed by handicappers.

Foul: A hand that is disqualified.

Four-flush: *(Poker)* Four cards of the same suit, needing just one more to make a flush.

Fourth street: *(Poker)* The round of betting after the fourth card has been dealt.

Free odds: *(Craps)* After a point has been established, players can back their pass, don't pass, come, and don't come wagers with this bet, paid at true odds.

French wheel: *(Roulette)* See "European wheel."

Front hand: *(Pai gow poker)* The two-card, second-highest hand, placed closer to the dealer.

Full house: *(Poker)* A hand consisting of three cards of the same rank and a pair.

Full odds: *(Craps)* The maximum amount of free odds allowed.

Full-pay: *(Video poker)* The highest-paying available form of a given type of video poker. For Jacks or Better, full-pay machines are also called 9/6 machines.

Futures bet: *(Sports betting)* A bet on a sports event taking place some time in the future, usually a championship game; for example, the Super Bowl.

Gambler's fallacy: An erroneous assumption that events in the short term will behave in a way to mimic long-term expectations.

Gambler's ruin: The likelihood of going broke in a casino. The longer a player exposes his stake to a negative expectation, the more likely it is he will lose all his money.

Ghost: *(Slots)* A blank stop on a reel.

Greens: Chips worth $25. Also known as "quarters."

Grifter: A scam artist or con man.

Grind: The loss of money through constant betting and rebetting of your initial stake in a negative expectation game.

Hand-held games: *(Blackjack)* Games dealt out of the dealer's hand; usually single- or double-deck games dealt face-down to players who can touch the cards.

Handicapper: *(Sports betting)* A bettor who studies data in order to accurately predict results.

Handle: See "action."

Hard hand: *(Blackjack)* Any hand that does not contain an ace valued as 11.

Hardway: *(Craps)* A roll of 4, 6, 8, or 10 made with doubles.

Heads up: *(Poker)* A pot contested by only two players.

Head-to-head: Playing one-on-one with the dealer.

High hand: See "back hand."

High-low split: *(Poker)* Game where the pot is split between a player with the winning high hand and a player with the winning low hand.

High roller: Big bettor.

Hi-lo system: *(Blackjack)* A basic system for card-counting.

Hit: *(Blackjack)* Drawing a card.

Hit frequency: *(Slots)* The percentage of time that a machine will give any payout.

Hold: *(Slots)* The percentage of money a slot machine is programmed to earn for the casino. Also, the net win a casino realizes.

Hole card: A dealer or player card that is dealt face-down.

Hop bet: *(Craps)* A bet that the next roll will result in one particular combination of the dice, such as 2-2 or 3-5.

Hopper: *(Slots)* The receptacle under the slot machine that holds coins.

Horn bet: *(Craps)* A bet that the next roll will be 2, 3, 11, or 12. The bet is made in multiples of four, with one unit on each of the numbers.

Horn high bet: *(Craps)* A bet made in multiples of five with one unit on three of the horn numbers, and two units on the "high" number of the player's choosing.

House: The casino.

House edge: The mathematical advantage the casino has on almost every wager. It is the house's expectation expressed as a percentage.

House odds: Proportion signifying relationship between amount won for a successful bet and amount wagered.

House Ways: *(Pai gow poker)* The casino's rules for the setting of the banker's hand.

Inside: *(Roulette)* Bets made on the 38 individual numbers or combinations of these numbers on the layout.

Inside straight: *(Poker)* A straight that is completed by a card in the middle of the sequence.

Insurance: *(Blackjack)* A side bet that the dealer has blackjack when showing an ace.

Joker Poker (Jokers Wild): *(Video poker)* Variation on Jacks or Better where there is one joker wild card in the deck.

Juice: *(Sports betting)* The sports book's commission. Also called "vig."

Junket: A trip arranged and paid for by a casino for a special group of players.

Keno runner: *(Keno)* A casino employee who walks throughout the casino providing keno tickets and then placing bets for players.

Keno writer: *(Keno)* A casino employee who registers players' tickets and takes wagers.

Kicker: *(Poker)* An unpaired card held in conjunction with one or more pairs; it can be used to determine the winner between two almost equal hands.

King: *(Keno)* A single number marked and circled on a ticket, played in conjunction with other groups of numbers on the same ticket and providing more "ways" to play.

Ladder man: *(Baccarat)* The casino supervisor who watches the game from a high chair.

Lammers: Plastic markers signifying the value of the roulette chips in use by a player. Also used to keep track of the amount of commission owed by baccarat players.

Late surrender: *(Blackjack)* A form of surrender allowing the player to forfeit half the bet after the dealer has checked for blackjack.

Law of large numbers (law of averages): Probability theory stating that over time the observed outcome of an event will conform to the expected outcome for that event.

Lay bet: *(Craps)* A bet that the shooter's point number will not be rolled before a 7.

Le grand naturel: *(Baccarat)* Two-card total of 9; the best possible hand.

Le petit naturel: *(Baccarat)* Two-card total of 8; the second-best possible hand.

Line: *(Sports betting)* The point spread.

Line bet: *(Craps)* A bet on either the pass or don't pass line; required in order to shoot the dice.

Line bet: *(Roulette)* A six-number bet covering two adjacent rows of numbers, placed on one of the outside lines at the intersection of two rows.

Linemaker: *(Sports betting)* Person who sets odds and point spreads. Also called "odds-maker."

Long shot: *(Sports betting)* A player, team, or horse unlikely to win.

Loose machine: *(Slots)* A machine that has been programmed with a high hit frequency; often loose is a perception of players rather than fact.

Low hand: *(Pai gow poker)* See "front hand."

Low poker: *(Poker)* Game in which the lowest hand is the best hand. Also know as "Lowball."

Make the point: *(Craps)* To roll the point number that was determined by the come-out roll.

Marker: An indicator of credit established at a casino.

Matchplay: Special promotional chips to be bet along with player's regular chips. Winning wagers are paid with regular chips.

Middle: *(Sports betting)* A pair of bets on opposing teams using two lines that differ by at least 1½ points; if the final score is in between the different lines bet, both bets are won.

Money line: *(Sports betting)* A bet on which team will win outright without factoring in a point spread. Standard for baseball, hockey, and boxing; also offered for football and basketball.

Muck: *(Poker)* Pile of burn cards and folded hands in front of the dealer.

Natural: A perfect hand. In blackjack, 21 on first two cards; in craps, a 7 or 11 on the come-out roll; in baccarat, a total of 8 or 9 in the first two cards.

Negative progression: Any betting system where the player increases bets after a loss.

Nickels: Chips worth $5. Also called "reds."

No-limit: *(Poker)* Variation where each player may bet up to the amount of chips he currently has on the table.

Number: *(Sports betting)* Point spread.

Nuts: *(Poker)* The best possible hand given the board.

Oddsmaker: *(Sports betting)* See "linemaker."

Odds off: *(Craps)* Odds bets that are not currently in play.

One-armed bandits: *(Slots)* Slot machines.

On tilt: Playing recklessly in order to make up for previous losses.

Open: *(Poker)* To make the first bet.

Opening line: *(Sports betting)* The first point spreads released for a group of games.

Outside: *(Roulette)* Bets made on the outer portion of the layout, furthest from the dealer, including even-money bets, column bets, and dozens bets.

Over-under: *(Sports betting)* A bet on whether the combined points scored by both teams will be more or less than the posted number.

Pack: *(Blackjack)* The full amount of cards (all the decks) in play at a table.

Paint: A face card.

Pair Plus: *(Three Card Poker)* A separate, non-competitive bet, paying bonuses for a pair or better.

Pari-mutuel: *(Sports betting)* A betting structure in which each bet made affects the odds; also, the house takes a fixed percentage of the betting action before winners are paid.

Parlay: To increase a bet after a win.

Parlay card: *(Sports betting)* A bet on a group of games and propositions that wins only if all events picked win.

Pass bet: *(Craps)* A bet that the shooter will roll 7 or 11 on the come-out roll, or make the point before rolling 7 after the come-out roll.

Pat hand: A hand of cards that requires no additional cards dealt to it.

Payline: *(Slots)* The line on which symbols must line up in order to be considered a winning spin.

Payoff or **payback:** *(Slots, video poker)* Player's expectation expressed as a percentage for a given machine.

Pay table: *(Video poker)* The schedule of payouts for each winning hand, listed on the screen or top glass of the machine.

Penalty card: *(Video poker)* A discard that can affect the expected value of the cards held.

Penetration: *(Blackjack)* A measure of how far into a pack the dealer will go before reshuffling.

Penny ante: *(Poker)* A small-stakes game.

Pick or **pick 'em:** *(Sports betting)* A bet where neither team is a favorite; the team picked must win outright.

Pinch: To surreptitiously remove chips from a losing bet.

Pip: A spot on a die.

Pit: A group of gaming tables.

Pit boss: A casino employee in charge of a pit.

Place bet (to lose): *(Craps)* A bet that a 7 will be rolled before a particular number placed comes up.

Place bet (to win): *(Craps)* A bet that a particular number placed will be rolled before a 7 comes up.

Play: *(Three Card Poker)* The second required bet in order to play out the hand.

Player hand: *(Baccarat)* First of two hands dealt.

Player's edge: The advantage enjoyed by the player in a positive expectation game.

Play the board: *(Poker)* To use only the community cards to make a hand.

Pocket: *(Poker)* Player's individual cards. Also called "hole."

Pocket: *(Roulette)* Slot where the ball lands, marked by numbers 00, 0–36.

Point: *(Craps)* A number (4, 5, 6, 8, 9, or 10) rolled on the come-out roll. In order to win, the shooter must make the point again before rolling a 7.

Point box: *(Craps)* One of the six numbered boxes above the come line on a craps table.

Point spread: *(Sports betting)* The number of points that must be added to the underdog's score or subtracted from the favorite's score before the bets on the game are resolved.

Pot: *(Poker)* Total amount of money at stake on a particular hand.

Pot limit: *(Poker)* Variation where each player may bet up to the amount of money in the pot.

Pot odds: *(Poker)* Proportion of the amount of money in the pot to the amount that must be put in the pot to continue playing.

Preferential shuffling: *(Blackjack)* Technique used to foil card-counters involving shuffling at times when the deck is favorable to players, and continuing to deal when the deck is unfavorable to players.

Press: To include winnings in the next bet.

Progressive jackpot: *(Slots, video poker)* The constantly growing sum of money offered on linked or individual machines.

Proposition bet: *(Craps)* Any of the sucker bets in the center of the craps layout.

Proposition player: Self-funded player who is employed by the casino.

Props: *(Sports betting)* Unique proposition bets developed around specific events.

Puck: *(Craps)* Plastic button with black (OFF) side and white (ON) side used to indicate the current point.

Push: A tie.

Put bet: *(Craps)* A bet made on the pass line after the come-out roll.

Quads: Four of a kind.

Qualify: Requirement that the dealer's hand must meet a preset minimum rank in order for the round to continue.

Raise: *(Poker)* To increase the amount of the previous bet.

Rake: *(Poker)* The commission charged by a poker room on each pot.

Rank: A card's numerical value.

Rating: A casino's evaluation of a player's gambling activity.

Reds: $5 chips.

Reels: *(Slots)* The metal hoops inside the machine that spin when the arm is pulled or the button is pressed.

Represent: *(Poker)* Play as if holding a certain hand.

Reraise: *(Poker)* To make an additional raise in the same round of betting.

RFB: Abbreviation for room, food, and beverage.

Rich deck: *(Blackjack)* A deck whose remaining cards are favorable to the players.

Ring game: *(Poker)* A regular game, not a tournament.

River: *(Poker)* Fifth and final community card in hold'em or final card in stud.

RNG: *(Slots, video poker)* Random number generator. Computer chip that randomly generates results seen on machine.

Royal flush: *(Poker)* An ace-high straight flush.

Sandbagging: *(Poker)* See "check-raise."

Scared money: Money a player cannot afford to lose.

Seven out: *(Craps)* Shooter's loss caused by rolling a 7 before making the point.

Shill: A casino employee playing with house money and posing as a player to draw real players to a table.

Shoe: A rectangular, wedge-shaped plastic box used to hold four to eight decks of shuffled cards.

Shoe games: *(Blackjack)* Games dealt face-up from a shoe, usually with four, six, or eight decks.

Shooter: *(Craps)* The player who is throwing the dice.

Short odds: Less than true odds.

Short-pay: *(Video poker)* Type of machine paying less than the best machines of the same variation.

Showdown: *(Poker)* The completion of the hand where a winner is declared.

Shuffle up: *(Blackjack)* An increased frequency of shuffling to foil card-counters.

Side bet: A separate, secondary bet placed in addition to a primary bet.

Side pot: *(Poker)* A second pot created when one player has gone all-in. The all-in player has no interest in the side pot.

Single odds: *(Craps)* Odds bets allowed only up to the value of the original pass/don't pass or come/don't come bet.

Slot club: Program in place at most casinos that provides comps and cashback to slot and video poker players.

Snake eyes: *(Craps)* A roll totaling 2.

Snapper: *(Blackjack)* Slang term for blackjack.

Soft hand: *(Blackjack)* Any hand that has an ace that can be valued as 11.

Split: *(Blackjack)* To divide a pair into two hands by putting down an additional bet.

Split pot: *(Poker)* A pot that is shared by two or more players with equivalent hands.

Sports book: *(Sports betting)* An area within the casino for sports and race betting.

Spot: *(Keno)* A number marked on a ticket that the player is trying to catch.

Spread limit: *(Poker)* A betting structure in which players may bet any amount within a certain range.

Stand: *(Blackjack)* To refuse any additional cards.

Standardbred: *(Sports betting)* A horse bred for strength and gait and trained for harness racing.

Standard deviation: Probability term describing the amount of variation in a prediction.

Steaming: See "on tilt."

Stick: *(Craps)* A device used to move the dice around the table.

Stickman: *(Craps)* Dealer who announces the number rolled and returns the dice to the shooter.

Stiff: *(Blackjack)* A hard hand (totaling 12 to 16) that is unlikely to win regardless of the decision made by the player.

Stops: *(Slots)* The reel's symbols and blank spaces that can line up on a payline.

Straight: *(Poker)* Five cards in sequence.

Straight flush: *(Poker)* Five cards of the same suit in sequence.

Straight ticket: *(Keno)* The simplest ticket; one group of numbers is played.

Street: *(Roulette)* Bet placed on a set of three numbers.

String raise: *(Poker)* An improper raise made by placing chips in the pot in two waves.

Sulky: *(Sports betting)* A light, two-wheeled cart used in harness racing.

Surrender: *(Blackjack)* A rare option allowing the player to give up half the bet before drawing any cards.

Table stakes: *(Poker)* A rule preventing a player from going to his pocket for money during a hand.

Take down: *(Craps)* To remove a bet from the table before the next roll of the dice.

Taking time: See "time."

Teaser: *(Sports betting)* Parlays in which the player is allowed to adjust the line by adding or subtracting a certain number of points from a point spread or total.

Tell: An unintentional signal from a dealer or a player communicating information about the value of a hole card or hand.

Third base: *(Blackjack)* See "anchor."

Thoroughbred: *(Sports betting)* A horse bred for speed and endurance.

Throwing numbers: *(Craps)* Making points without sevening out.

Tight machine: *(Slots)* A machine that has been programmed with a low hit frequency or one that is perceived by players as paying out infrequently.

Time: *(Poker)* A player request to hold play while deciding on a course of action. Also called "taking time."

Toke: A tip or gratuity.

Total: *(Sports betting)* See "Over-under."

Total return: *(Video poker)* Expected return for the whole game when played perfectly over the long run. Also called "payback percentage."

Tote board: An electronic display providing information about previous winning numbers at roulette or the amount bet on different horses at a track or sports book.

Tout: *(Sports betting)* A person who sells tips and information on upcoming games or races.

Triple play: *(Video poker)* Variation where original hand becomes three separate hands.

Trips: *(Poker)* Three of a kind.

True odds: The statistical likelihood of any given event actually happening; as compared to casino odds.

Turn: *(Poker)* The fourth community card.

21: *(Blackjack)* Another name for the game of blackjack.

Underdog: *(Sports betting)* The player, team, or horse not favored to win.

Upcard: A card that is dealt face-up.

Variability: Short-term deviations from the expected outcome for a given event.

Variance: A measure of the highs and lows of a bankroll.

Vigorish or vig: Term used to describe commission taken by the house (as in sports betting). Can also mean house edge.

Volatility: The short-term fluctuations in payback.

Wash: One bet canceling out another.

Way: *(Keno)* A set of numbers played on a ticket.

Whale: Super high roller.

Wheel: *(Roulette)* The casino's term for roulette.

Working: *(Craps)* Any bet currently in action but not yet completed.

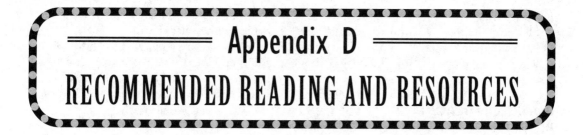

Appendix D
RECOMMENDED READING AND RESOURCES

Readers who wish to further explore the world of gambling will find much of interest below. In particular, for those who want to tackle sophisticated games like video poker, live poker, and blackjack, there's plenty of good reading to be done that goes beyond the scope of this introductory guide.

Something to keep in mind: Much of the best reading on gambling comes from small presses. This has several consequences. Book prices are sometimes higher than you might expect, due to small print runs. In general, the printing quality is good, but some books do have a basement printing press feel. The books don't always get wide distribution so you may have a difficult time finding some of these items at your local bookstore. You can use the "Resources" information to get ahold of elusive items that pique your interest. You can also check out on-line bookstores such as Amazon.com (www.amazon.com) and Barnes & Noble (www.barnesandnoble.com).

Another consequence of the mom-and-pop approach to gambling publishing is that you may find a lot of advertising and "plugs" within the books. You'll see the same authors and titles mentioned all over the place. This may make the gambling publishing industry seem somewhat in-bred, self-referential, and self-promoting. That may be true, but that doesn't make all the offerings schlock. Use your own judgment and, as always, beware of anything that guarantees winnings.

GENERAL INTEREST BOOKS

American Casino Guide 2004 by Steve Bourie, 2003, Casino Vacations. Bourie's annual publication gives the lowdown on every legal U.S. gambling venue. Plus it has informative gambling chapters. Filled with advertisements and coupons.

Smart Casino Gambling by Olaf Vancura, 1996, Index Publishing Group. If you liked the more mathematical parts of this book, you'll enjoy Vancura's in-depth analysis and varied anecdotes.

Can You Win? by Michael Orkin, 1991, W.H. Freeman. Rich analysis for math lovers.

Casino Operations Management by Jim Kilby and Jim Fox, 1998, John Wiley & Sons. Geared toward casino managers, this book lets you know what the other side is up to.

BOOKS ON COMPS AND BARGAINS

Huntington Press seems to have cornered the market on quality books that teach you how to get good deals at the casinos. One or two of these selections should make you just as wily as any veteran bargain hunter.

The Frugal Gambler by Jean Scott, 1998, Huntington Press. The author has been dubbed the "Queen of Comps" and here she reveals the tricks of her trade. Likable and well-organized.

Comp City by Max Rubin, 2001, Huntington Press. An exhaustive and witty guide to all the moves needed to get every comp and freebie possible in Las Vegas. Best for the player with a bankroll of $1,000 or more.

The Las Vegas Advisor Guide to Slot Clubs by Jeffrey Compton, 1995, Huntington Press. Introduces the reader to the world of slot clubs and explains how best to take advantage of them. Desperately needs a new edition.

Bargain City by Anthony Curtis, 1995, Huntington Press. A little dated, but still has enough information to make it worthwhile to the cost-conscious Las Vegas visitor.

BOOKS ON BLACKJACK

Blackjack books are abundant because it's a game you can win if you count cards. All these books address card-counting.

Knock-Out Blackjack by Olaf Vancura and Ken Fuchs, 1998, Huntington Press. A smartly written and entertaining book for beginners who want to learn card-counting. Introduces a very simple and very powerful system.

Blackbelt in Blackjack by Arnold Snyder, 1999, RGE Publishing. General primer on card-counting; includes a relatively simple count system.

Professional Blackjack by Stanford Wong, 1994, Pi Yee Press. Wong is one the most respected blackjack experts around. This reference work, full of charts and tables, is a must for those who use the Hi-Lo counting system, but it throws you in the deep end rather quickly.

Blackjack Attack by Don Schlesinger, 2000, RGE Publishing. A cornucopia of fascinating articles for card-counters. While indispensable to blackjack buffs, this is not a recommended starting point for neophytes.

The Theory of Blackjack by Peter Griffin, 1996, Huntington Press. Griffin is considered the Einstein of blackjack and this book, both witty and complex, is the best book ever written on the mathematics of blackjack.

Las Vegas Blackjack Diary by Stuart Perry, 1997, ConJelCo. If you're curious about the life of a card-counter, this day-by-day chronicle will fascinate. If you're not sure you're curious, don't make this vicarious excursion into the counter's world your first stop.

Basic Blackjack by Stanford Wong, 1992, Pi Yee Press. Contains basic strategy information for every variation you ever heard of—and plenty that you haven't.

The World's Greatest Blackjack Book by Lance Humble and Carl Cooper, 1987, Doubleday. A crash-course on the game that's somewhat outdated, but still highly informative.

Warning: The authors are much too preoccupied with dealer cheating.

Beat the Dealer by Edward O. Thorp, 1966, Random House. The classic that established blackjack as a beatable game. Thorp's counting system may be antiquated, but he paved the way for everyone else.

BOOKS ON VIDEO POKER

Video Poker: Optimum Play by Dan Paymar, 1998, ConJelCo. An accurate and informative guide to the game's mechanics and concepts. Paymar emphasizes written rules rather than hand rank charts for the most popular games. The best single volume on video poker available.

Bob Dancer Video Poker Reports. When you want the final word in any video poker matter, you look to Bob Dancer. You can rely on the widely published columnist for incisive analysis and (sometimes fanatical) mathematical accuracy. These three reports cover strategy for Deuces Wild, 9/6 Jacks or Better, and 10/7 Double Bonus. The strategies are great to have, but the clarity of the writing isn't up to Dancer's usual standard and the production quality of the three booklets is poor. Still, the information is well worth $10 each for the serious player. Be warned: Dancer is not shy about complexity when it leads to accuracy. The reports can be ordered through Huntington Press (see Resources below).

Winning Strategies for Video Poker by Lenny Frome, 1997, Compu-Flyers. Frome was one of the founding fathers of video poker analysis. This handy-but-slightly-dated volume contains strategies for 60 games.

BOOKS ON POKER

Thursday-Night Poker: How to Understand, Enjoy—And Win by Peter O. Steiner, 1996, Random House. Must reading for the semiserious, recreational player. Covers essential concepts that guide smart play. Use this book to master the kitchen table game and then decide if you want to head out to the casino.

Positively Fifth Street: Murderers, Cheetahs, and Binion's World Series of Poker by James McManus, 2003, Farrar, Straus & Giroux.

In this brilliant poker chronicle, novelist and poet McManus crosscuts his unlikely trip to the final table at the World Series of Poker with the lurid details of the Ted Binion murder trial.

Winning Low Limit Hold'em by Lee Jones, 2000, ConJelCo. An excellent introduction to this complex game. This survival guide for beginning and intermediate players is intelligent and fun to read.

The Theory of Poker by David Sklansky, 1999, Two Plus Two Publishing. Serious players consider this the bible of poker. Not a "how-to" in terms of specific tips and guidelines, but a fascinating and difficult look at the concepts and logic behind successful poker play.

Doyle Brunson's Super System: A Course in Power Poker by Doyle Brunson, 1979, Cardoza Publishing. If you hope to be a high-stakes player, you must have this book. If you don't, it may seem like overkill.

BOOKS ON OTHER GAMES

Armada Strategies for Spanish 21 by Frank Scoblete, 1998, Bonus Books. Serves up the best advice and basic strategy for this wild blackjack spin-off.

Optimal Strategy for Pai Gow Poker by Stanford Wong, 1993, Pi Yee Press. The only in-depth examination of the game available.

Beating the Wheel by Russell T. Barnhart, 1992, Lyle Stuart. An account of a team that supposedly won millions on biased wheels. Exaggerated or not, it's a riveting look at the possibilities when a random event becomes less than random.

Mastering the Game of Let It Ride by Stanley Ko, 1995, Gambology. Essential analysis, but only die-hard players need apply.

The Complete Idiot's Guide to Betting on Horses by Sharon B. Smith, 1998, Alpha Books. Answers all the basic questions for horseplayers. A good place for beginners to begin.

PERIODICALS

Las Vegas Advisor, 3687 S. Procyon Ave., Las Vegas, NV 89103, (800) 244-2224. Publisher Anthony Curtis (who also heads Huntington Press) has established his monthly newsletter as the premier insider's guide to the best values Vegas has to offer. Covers entertainment, dining, and gambling. You get coupons with a subscription.

Casino Player, 2424 Arctic Ave., Atlantic City, NJ 08401, (800) 969-0711. Well-produced monthly magazine containing articles on game strategies, getting comped, and the casino industry. Renowned for its monthly listing of slot payouts. Some of the top gambling experts contribute.

Strictly Slots, 2424 Arctic Ave., Atlantic City, NJ 08401, (800) 969-0711. Consumer-advocate-style ratings of the latest slot and video poker games, along with in-depth features on some of the most popular games in casinos across the country.

Card Player, 3140 South Polaris Avenue #8, Las Vegas, NV 89102, (702) 871-1720. Devoted to the dedicated casino poker player. Plenty of information on strategy and tournaments.

Current Blackjack News, Pi Yee Press, 4855 W. Nevso Dr., Las Vegas, NV 89103, (702) 579-7711. The fastest way for players to get reports of rule changes and conditions at virtually every U.S. casino.

Blackjack Forum, Huntington Press, 3687 S. Procyon Ave., Las Vegas, NV 89103, (800) 244-2224. For die-hard blackjack players. Offers articles from the game's top experts. Get it when you're getting serious.

Video Poker Times, Dan Paymar, PMB 141, 2540 S. Maryland Pkwy., Las Vegas, NV 89109. For both beginning and advanced video players this bimonthly, four-page newsletter is a must. Each issue includes an in-depth analysis of a video poker game, news about new machines, and a comparison of what the various casinos are offering. Can be ordered from ConJelCo.

SOFTWARE

Blackjack Trainer (ConJelCo). An excellent tool for serious blackjack players. Allows you to practice strategy, learn different counting systems, and simulate real casino environments. Order from ConJelCo.

Super Blackjack. Drill yourself on basic strategy and start to learn some card-counting with this colorful software. Best of all, you can examine it for free for 15 days. Download on the Web at www.superblackjack21.com.

Bob Dancer Presents WinPoker (Zamzow Software Solutions). Play and analyze almost any video poker game. You can change the pay tables to your specifications and then run a simulation that will give you the theoretical long-term return. It will correct your mistakes and tell you the best play. Indispensable for anyone who takes video poker even slightly seriously. Call Zamzow at (480) 816-8995 or download the limited shareware version at the Web site (zamzone.com).

Video Poker Strategy Master by TomSki (Zamzow Software Solutions). Put in the pay table for almost any video poker machine and this program will generate a strategy table specific to the game. You can then print out the strategy and practice on the video poker simulations mentioned above. (See Bob Dancer, above.)

WinCraps (Cloud City Software). A comprehensive simulation that lets you learn craps without any intimidation. The help file is a gold mine of information that will benefit you at the real tables. A shareware version can be downloaded on the Web at www. cloudcitysoftware.com.

Turbo Poker Series (Wilson Software). Wilson creates the ultimate poker programs for all the popular casino games (Texas hold'em, seven-card stud, Omaha). Each program delivers analysis, advice, statistics, and opponents that are as tough and unpredictable as the flesh-and-blood variety. Believe it or not, at $90 a pop these tools are a bargain for the serious poker player. Download the demo versions at the Web site (wilsonsoftware.com).

RESOURCES

ConJelCo: Publisher of books and software (some listed above) that also sells books, software, and videos from other publishers. Periodically publishes a stimulating newsletter, *The Intelligent Gambler*, that is sent free to customers. To place an order, get a free catalog, or be put on the mailing list for *The Intelligent Gambler*, contact:

> ConJelCo
> 1460 Bennington Ave.
> Pittsburgh, PA 15217
> Phone: (800) 492-9210
> Web: www.conjelco.com

Gambler's Book Club: This is the number-one gambling bookstore. Stop by the store when visiting Vegas. Call for their huge, free catalog or check out the Web site.

> Gambler's Book Club
> 630 South 11th Street
> Las Vegas, NV 89101
> Phone: (800) 634-6243
> Web: www.gamblersbook.com

Huntington Press: Sells (and publishes) many of the items recommended above. To get their free Great Stuff for Gamblers catalog or order items, contact:

> Huntington Press
> 3687 S. Procyon Ave.
> Las Vegas, NV 89103
> Phone: (800) 244-2224
> Web: www.huntingtonpress.com

THE INTERNET

I have two rules about the Internet. First, don't believe anything you read on it. Second, use it for its endless information as often as possible. Glibness aside, I'm saying this: Use the Internet to discover more about your favorite games and gambling destinations, but approach everything you see with some caution. I'm sure readers will fine-tune their "crap detection meter" after assimilating the material in this book.

Internet newsgroups in particular are full of opinions, tirades, half-truths, and more spam than a Hormel factory. Use your common sense to separate the wheat from the chaff. Below are some newsgroups and Web sites I find useful, but that hardly means I endorse every link, advertisement, or opinion on them. Generally, they contain either good editorial content or a useful way to connect with (hopefully) intelligent gamblers.

Newsgroups

rec.gambling.blackjack
rec.gambling.poker
rec.gambling.craps
rec.gambling.racing
rec.gambling.sports
rec.gambling.other-games (includes video
  poker, Caribbean Stud, Let It Ride, etc.)
alt.vacation.las-vegas (trip and bargain info)

Web Sites

About.com's Casino Gambling (casinogambling. miningco. com): A smart selection of links to a wide variety of topics. An excellent starting point for your Web wanderings.

Casino Center (www.casinocenter.com): Home page of the Casino Publishing Group, publisher of *Casino Player*, *Strictly Slots*, and more. Links to the various publications and their articles.

Casino City (www.casinocity.com): Features a massive directory of casinos across the globe. Has a good search engine and many links.

The GameMaster (www.GameMasterOnline. com): Excellent articles on blackjack, video poker, and the gambling life.

The Wizard of Odds (www.wizardofodds.com): Actuary Michael Shackleford earns his moniker by breaking down the numbers for nearly every casino game.

Henry Tamburin on Casino Gambling (www.smartgaming.com): Generally sound advice from a knowledgeable and prolific gambling writer.

Rolling Good Times Online (www.rgtonline. com): Overstuffed with ads, this site is also chock-full of strategy articles, news items, audio segments, and links.

Card Player (www.cardplayer.com): Online home to the magazine. Filled with fascinating—and free—articles by top poker experts.

Skip Hughes on Video Poker (www.vid-poker. com): Paysite that features locations of full-pay machines around the country and good strategy articles.

Jazbo's Home Page (www.jazbo.com): Sure, Jazbo wants to sell his strategy cards (which are good), but he also provides plenty of free information on video poker and Atlantic City poker rooms.

BlackjackInfo.com (www.blackjackinfo.com): Home of the "basic strategy engine." Generates accurate charts for almost any set of playing conditions.

Advantage Player (www.advantageplayer.com): Blackjack and video poker site run by Viktor Nacht of RGE Publishing. Some free bulletin boards and articles, but you have to pay to get the "insider" information from the pros. RGE also has a good catalog of gambling items for sale.

The Blackjack Page (www.bj21.com): Serious blackjack site run by author Stanford Wong. Includes some free material along with forums that require paid membership.

BJ Math (www.bjmath.com): This site has intriguing but complex articles on the mathematics of blackjack. But even a novice can appreciate the fact that Edward Thorp's book *The Mathematics of Gambling* is available for free download in the "articles" section.

Keno Odds (www.conjelco.com/faq/keno-odds. html): A quick reference for keno fans who like number-crunching.

DO YOU HAVE A PROBLEM?

Gamblers Anonymous offers the following questions to anyone who may have a gambling problem. These questions are provided to help the individual decide if he or she is a compulsive gambler and wants to stop gambling. Most compulsive gamblers will answer yes to at least seven of these questions.

If you need help, you can contact them at:
Gamblers Anonymous
International Service Office
P.O. Box 17173
Los Angeles, CA 90017
(213) 386-8789
www.gamblersanonymous.org

THE TWENTY QUESTIONS

1. Did you ever lose time from work or school due to gambling?
2. Has gambling ever made your home life unhappy?
3. Did gambling affect your reputation?
4. Have you ever felt remorse after gambling?
5. Did you ever gamble to get money with which to pay debts or otherwise solve financial difficulties?
6. Did gambling cause a decrease in your ambition or efficiency?
7. After losing did you feel you must return as soon as possible and win back your losses?
8. After a win did you have a strong urge to return and win more?
9. Did you often gamble until your last dollar was gone?
10. Did you ever borrow to finance your gambling?
11. Have you ever sold anything to finance gambling?
12. Were you reluctant to use "gambling money" for normal expenditures?
13. Did gambling make you careless of the welfare of yourself or your family?
14. Did you ever gamble longer than you had planned?
15. Have you ever gambled to escape worry or trouble?
16. Have you ever committed, or considered committing, an illegal act to finance gambling?
17. Did gambling cause you to have difficulty in sleeping?
18. Do arguments, disappointments, or frustrations create within you an urge to gamble?
19. Did you ever have an urge to celebrate any good fortune by a few hours of gambling?
20. Have you ever considered self-destruction or suicide as a result of your gambling?

WHAT IS MENSA?

Mensa
The High IQ Society

Mensa is the international society for people with a high IQ. We have more than 100,000 members in over 40 countries worldwide.

Anyone with an IQ score in the top two percent of the population is eligible to become a member of Mensa—are you the "one in 50" we've been looking for?

Mensa membership offers an excellent range of benefits:
- Networking and social activities nationally and around the world;
- Special Interest Groups (hundreds of chances to pursue your hobbies and interests—from art to zoology!);
- Monthly International Journal, national magazines, and regional newsletters;
- Local meetings—from game challenges to food and drink;
- National and international weekend gatherings and conferences;
- Intellectually stimulating lectures and seminars;
- Access to the worldwide SIGHT network for travelers and hosts.

For more information about Mensa International:

www.mensa.org
Mensa International
15 The Ivories
6–8 Northampton Street
Islington, London N1 2HY
United Kingdom

For more information about American Mensa:
www.us.mensa.org
Telephone: (800) 66-MENSA
American Mensa Ltd.
1229 Corporate Drive West
Arlington, TX 76006-6103 USA

For more information about British Mensa (UK and Ireland):
www.mensa.org.uk
Telephone: +44 (0) 1902 772771
E-mail: enquiries@mensa.org.uk
British Mensa Ltd.
St. John's House
St. John's Square
Wolverhampton WV2 4AH
United Kingdom

INDEX

ABOUT THE AUTHOR

ANDREW BRISMAN is a writer and editor who has been an avid casino player for years. A former editor at *Games* magazine, he is a nationally recognized authority on games and puzzles. In addition to writing on a variety of topics, he also creates games and puzzles for adults and children. A member of Mensa and a voracious researcher, he enjoys figuring out the puzzle of getting the most from the gambling experience. He lives in New York City, a quick three-hour drive from Atlantic City.